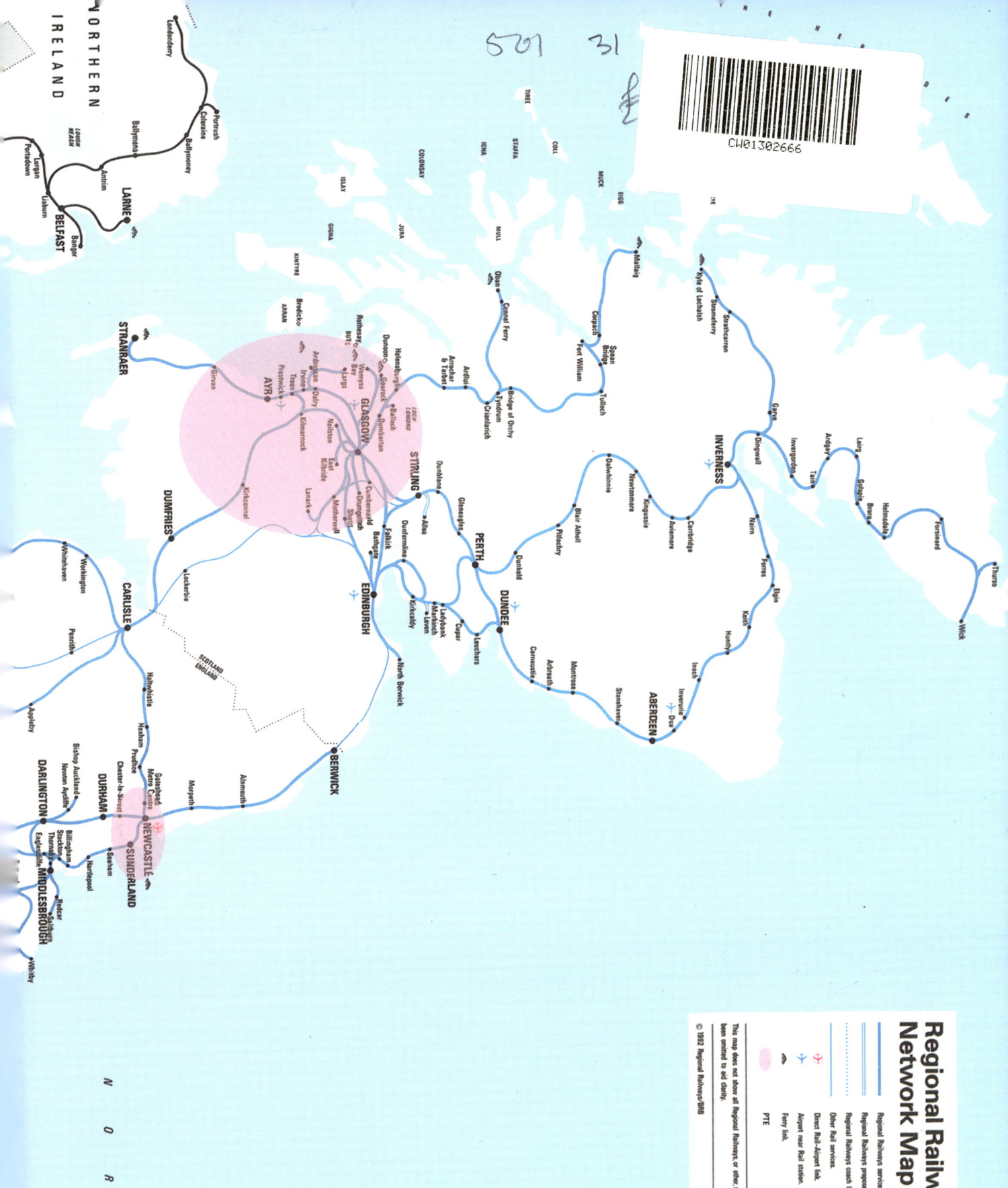

# THE REGIONAL RAILWAYS STORY

Sectorisation to Privatisation: Three Decades of Revival

# THE REGIONAL RAILWAYS STORY

Sectorisation to Privatisation: Three Decades of Revival

GORDON PETTITT & NICHOLAS COMFORT

An imprint of
Ian Allan Publishing

**ABOVE** A two-car Class 175 threads its way past Conwy Castle heading for Bangor on 27 March 2011. *Antony Christie*

First published 2015

ISBN 978 0 86093 663 3

All rights reserved. No part of this book may be reproduced or transmitted in any form or by any means, electronic or mechanical, including photocopying, recording, scanning or by any information storage and retrieval system, on the internet or elsewhere, without permission from the Publisher in writing.

© Gordon Pettitt and Nicholas Comfort 2015

Published by Oxford Publishing Co

an imprint of Ian Allan Publishing Ltd, Addlestone, Surrey KT12 2SF

Printed in Bulgaria

Visit the Ian Allan Publishing website at **www.ianallanpublishing.com**

### Copyright

Illegal copying and selling of publications deprives authors, publishers and booksellers of income, without which there would be no investment in new publications. Unauthorised versions of publications are also likely to be inferior in quality and contain incorrect information. You can help by reporting copyright infringements and acts of piracy to the Publisher or the UK Copyright Service.

### Picture credits

Every effort has been made to identify and correctly attribute photographic credits. Should any error have occurred this is entirely unintentional. All uncredited photographs are from the author's collection.

**FRONT COVER** Brunel's majestic Royal Albert Bridge dominates the scene as 158714 begins the descent into Plymouth on a Regional Railways South Wales & West service from Cornwall. *Author's collection*

**FACING FRONTISPIECE** West Cumbrian spectacle: a 'Sprinter' formation edges its way northward toward Carlisle through one of the most spectacular - and costly to maintain - seascapes in the Regional system. *Northern Rail*

**BACK COVER** Showing the remarkable and sustained improvements to regional interurban services, from the 1980s' Class 31 haulage of Mk II coaching stock, through the present magnificent Siemens Class 350/4 with TransPennine Express, to the future of Hitachi AT200s shortly to be built for ScotRail and no doubt other interurban networks.
(**Top:** *Martin Loader*, **Centre left:** *Dr Phil Brown of www.docbrown.info/docspics*, **Centre right:** *Hitachi*)

# CONTENTS

**FOREWORD** — 6
**ACKNOWLEDGMENTS** — 7

| | | |
|---|---|---|
| *Chapter 1* | **INTRODUCTION: BY THE SKIN OF THEIR TEETH** | 8 |
| *Chapter 2* | **THE PROVINCIAL SECTOR: TURNING THE TIDE, 1982-86** | 16 |
| *Chapter 3* | **THE PROVINCIAL SECTOR: GATHERING SPEED, 1986-90** | 26 |
| *Chapter 4* | **REGIONAL RAILWAYS, 1990-97** | 38 |
| *Chapter 5* | **THE TRANSITION TO A PRIVATISED RAILWAY** | 56 |
| *Chapter 6* | **UNDER PRIVATISATION, 1996 TO DATE** | 68 |
| *Chapter 7* | **THE URBAN CHALLENGE** | 86 |
| *Chapter 8* | **THE MAGNIFICENT SEVEN: PTEs** | 102 |
| *Chapter 9* | **INTERURBAN SUCCESS STORY** | 118 |
| *Chapter 10* | **RURAL LINES** | 134 |
| *Chapter 11* | **ENGAGING WITH COMMUNITIES AND STAKEHOLDERS** | 146 |
| *Chapter 12* | **CHOOSING THE TRAINS** | 158 |
| *Chapter 13* | **THE WAY AHEAD** | 174 |
| *Postscript* | **THE SETTLE & CARLISLE LINE** | 186 |

**FACTFILES**

| | | |
|---|---|---|
| *Factfile A* | Chronology | 192 |
| *Factfile B* | Financial facts, 1982-94 | 195 |
| *Factfile C* | The train/passenger interface | 196 |
| *Factfile D* | Train services | 198 |
| *Factfile E* | Train fleets, 1981-2014 | 201 |
| *Factfile F* | Infrastructure | 203 |
| *Factfile G* | Stations | 211 |
| *Factfile H* | People | 228 |
| *Factfile J* | Train franchises and operators | 232 |
| *Factfile K* | McNulty Report Recommendations, 2011 | 233 |

**BIBLIOGRAPHY** — 234
**INDEX** — 235

# FOREWORD

This book is not about trains; it is about the development of a business, enterprising and highly responsive to the needs of its customers, which has – through a series of upheavals – sought over the past three decades to deliver a steadily better service in the safest and most professional way. It tells the story of how British Rail's Provincial sector and its successor Regional Railways turned a ramshackle and threatened inheritance into an efficient and generally attractive network of urban, interurban and rural railway services in surprisingly short order – and how this work was taken forward by the franchises who inherited the Regional Railways network under privatisation.

Our story covers the period from 1982 to 2015. For the first 12 years our railways, as British Rail, were under public ownership. Three years of transition followed, during which they were floated off into the private sector in more than 100 separate pieces, including eight regional passenger train operators. Since 1997 the structure of the privatised railway has changed enormously, with frequent upheavals and a far greater degree of direct state control than its architects could have foreseen.

We aim to take the reader first chronologically through the period covered by Provincial and Regional Railways and their successors under privatisation, then to outline the differing challenges faced by urban and interurban railways away from London and Britain's rural lines, and next to deal with issues of community and stakeholder involvement and with how the trains have been chosen to do the job. Finally we take stock of where we have got to in 2015, and look ahead to how the challenges and opportunities facing the regional railway today can and should be addressed.

GORDON PETTITT
NICHOLAS COMFORT

Gordon Pettitt on the final day of his career with British Railways, with (from left), his wife Ursula, and his daughters Annette Weatherell, Katrina McCrory (sitting) and Denise Pettitt.

GORDON PETTITT joined British Railways as a junior clerk in its Knebworth control centre in 1950, and retired as managing director of Regional Railways in 1992. Appointed director of BR's Provincial Sector in 1990, he built on its success by transforming it into the vertically-integrated Regional Railways, which showed BR at its customer-orientated and cost-conscious best.

Previously he was general manager of the Southern Region, working with Chris Green, director of Network SouthEast, to extend the reach of electrification. Other posts in a distinguished railway career included chief passenger manager on the Western Region as the HST fleet was introduced, divisional manager at Liverpool Street – paving the way for the creation of the present-day station – and deputy director London & South East/deputy general manager Southern Region.

After retiring Gordon Pettitt worked with John Swift QC, the first railway regulator, and contributed as an independent consultant to the development of High Speed 1 and the Heathrow Terminal 5 rail link.

NICHOLAS COMFORT (*Right*) has spent most of his career reporting politics for the *Daily Telegraph* and other papers. He has worked in Whitehall, and been a consultant to the Association of Train Operating Companies, London & Continental Railways and Virgin. He contributes to *Today's Railways*, and has written *The Slow Death of British Industry* (2013), *The Channel Tunnel and its High-Speed Links* (2006) and *The Mid-Suffolk Light Railway* (1997). He is a volunteer on the Bluebell Railway.

# Acknowledgments

The long list of acknowledgments below reflects the enthusiastic help that the Authors have received from the many friends and colleagues who have been so generous with their time and in many cases providing records from own archives. They provided important material, and also gave an insight into the times and the people who saved Britain's regional railways from relentless decline and then built them into the vibrant and expanding network we have today.

My special thanks are due to Nicholas Comfort, my co-author, who took on an increasing role in writing this book due to illness in my family, and to Theo Steel for his support throughout and in particular for his research and then tracking down all the people we interviewed. I am also grateful to Chris Green for his support and encouragement to me, and to Alex Green who took on the job of finding the photographs.

Finally, the book could not have been completed without the support and encouragement of my wife Ursula, a constant tower of strength throughout my railway career. Nicholas' wife Jeanette also did much to ease our task.

*Gordon Pettitt*
Woking April 2015

Chris Austin; Stuart Baker; Vernon Barker; Charles Belcher; Richard Bonham Carter; Cyril Bleasdale; Colin Boocock; Dominic Booth; Pete Brown; Tom Brown; Neil Buxton; Mark Causebrook; David Cobbett; Jim Cornell; Simon Coventry; Tony Crabtree; John Curley; John Davies; Steve Dentith; Charles Devereux; Jim Dorward; John Edmonds; Dick Fearn; David Fry; Chris Gibb; Richard Goldson; John Gough; Bob Goundry; Gill Greatorex; Alex Green; Chris Green; Chris Heaps; Don Heath; Mike Hodson; Maurice Holmes; Mark Hopwood; David Horne; Alex Hynes; Mike Keen; Paul King; Terence Jenner; Roger Jones; Glen Kennedy; Clive Kessell; Chris Leah; Paul le Blond; Mark Livock; Jeremy Long; Dennis Lovett; David Mather; Roger McDonald; Alec McTavish; Heidi Mottram; Sydney Newey; John Palmer; John Pearse; Richard Peck; Andy Pitt; David Prescott; Dr Malcolm Reed; John Reid; John Rhodes; Alec Ritchie; Mervyn Rodgers; Paul Salveson; Andy Savage; Ken Shingleton; Adrian Shooter; Larry Shore; Martin Shrubsole; Helen Stewart; Theo Steel; Chris Stokes; Jim Summers; Alan Taylor; Wendy Tobitt; Ian Walmsley; Ivor Warburton; David Ward; John Welsby; David Wharton-Street; Alan Williams; John Yellowlees

# Chapter 1
# INTRODUCTION: BY THE SKIN OF THEIR TEETH

*'There was no lobby inside the Department pushing for a smaller railway; I didn't think that that was a sensible course of policy. But papers were regularly put to Ministers, to see what they wanted.'*
**JOHN PALMER**, HEAD OF THE RAILWAYS DIRECTORATE, DEPARTMENT OF TRANSPORT, 1976-89

**ABOVE** Lowestoft station in the 1980s, looking forlorn with signing from the 1950s (now listed!) but little to attract customers. *Dennis Lovett*

## Chapter 1: INTRODUCTION: BY THE SKIN OF THEIR TEETH

Our starting point – 1982 – coincides with the most fundamental reorganisation of British Railways since nationalisation in 1948, although it did not necessarily appear so at the time. The railway had hitherto been managed on functional lines, with a large central headquarters in London, operating through five regions (Eastern, London Midland, Southern, Western and Scottish). This functional structure had two major disadvantages: costs and income only came together at Board level, and there was no focus on individual businesses. Both resulted in a lack of accountability for managers at all levels in the organisation, and a failure to focus on the needs of the customers.

By 1982 the full extent of these problems had come to a head. Costs had been increasing and income falling for some years. Passenger numbers had been in steady decline since 1957 (only 1978-80 had seen consecutive years of growth). At 1982 prices, revenues had decreased steadily from £2.3 billion in 1970 to £1.8 billion, but costs had risen from £2.5 billion in 1970 to £2.7 billion. So BR's deficit had increased by a factor of 4.5.

A series of industrial disputes culminating in the flexible rostering strikes of 1982 (dealt with later in this Introduction) added to the problems, and gave little confidence to Government or customers that the decline in the use of the railways could be reversed. Yet 1982 would be the start of a renaissance organised from within by Bob (later Sir Robert) Reid, who at the time was BR's Vice-Chairman. The appointment of five Sector Directors, one for each of five businesses – Inter-City, London & South East, Freight, Parcels and 'Other Provincial services' that January – would be the start of a process of change that would, over the next eight years, affect every corner of the business at every level. (How the Provincial sector was established is set out in the next chapter.)

But it was the direction of travel that was crucial in this business-led reorganisation. The Sector Directors set the strategy, approved budgets and authorised expenditure, and gained a steadily greater grasp over how the railway operated and what its priorities were to be. Any jobs not required to support business objectives at whatever level were to become redundant. And while the railways' industrial problems persisted throughout the 1980s, not a day was lost in industrial action as a result of these upheavals.

To tell the story of our regional railways, it will be necessary throughout to explain changes in the political, economic and regulatory climate affecting the entire railway network. However, we focus on what started life as 'Other Provincial Services'. We track how a succession of decisive senior managers working under successive

**BELOW** An unidentified Class 31 with a rake of ex-InterCity Mk II coaches at March in 1987, as the Provincial sector was planning a new fleet of bespoke interurban units to reduce its costs.
*Dennis Lovett*

brands transformed both the level and quality of services across the nation. That original title certainly understated the shape, the size and above all of the potential of this business, which was to be responsible for 45% of BR's route miles and 59% of its stations.

That Provincial sector was born, in January 1982, into a troubled world. Many of the secondary railways that had survived the Beeching era had only made it through by the skin of their teeth. They had lost out financially to BR's intercity, London commuter and trainload freight offerings – and almost every route was suffering from historic non-investment and offering a substandard service for passengers and staff alike. Nor was the shape and size of the sector planned, but, rather, it emerged – it comprised the passenger lines and services left over after extracting the InterCity services that were profitable and the commuter networks around London that would be reborn in 1986 as Network SouthEast. Not surprisingly, the extensive network of the Provincial sector required from the outset a major share of the financial support given by the Government to BR (the PSO: Public Service Obligation), and would be under the greatest pressure to reduce costs.

The task was made doubly difficult as most of the rolling stock was life-expired and needed renewal. Many observers both inside and outside the railway expected closures, as replacements procured in a conventional fashion could not be financially viable. The achievement of this without closures set the scene for the sector's managers to exploit the improved performance of its new trains to launch new services and fill more seats.

The creation of the Provincial sector, its decentralisation into sub-sectors in 1986, and further devolution to and by Regional Railways from 1991, released the energies of talented young managers who had for the first time the freedom to challenge how things were to be done and the encouragement to experiment. The success of this was reflected not only in a steady improvement in passenger numbers and financial performance, but the way so many of the managers responsible went on to greater things.

A great 'explosion of talent and freedom' is how Mark Causebrook, later head of Central Trains and Thameslink, recalls it. 'We hadn't got the wisdom yet, but we knew enough to challenge. We challenged the regions and the functions on crewing, depot manning, the proposed singling of double track. Some regional general managers and the barons who ran the functions couldn't handle being challenged by these young whippersnappers.'

Gerard Fiennes, an innovative senior railway manager of the 1960s forced out after giving vent to his frustrations in print, asserted that 'when you reorganise, you bleed'. These reorganisations of the 1980s proved the exception, as the monolithic regional structures and the empires of the functions (controlling infrastructure, motive power, signalling and the like) came under challenge from Young Turks who often proved that there was a better way. When the regional railway was reorganised, it blossomed. And the proof lay in what happened after privatisation; successful bidders for regional franchises who had banked on rooting out inefficiency discovered that they had been very imaginatively, and very tightly, run.

John Welsby and John Edmonds, the first two directors of the Provincial sector, went on to be Chairman of BR and Chief Executive of Railtrack respectively. Gordon Pettitt retired to an influential role in consultancy, Jim Cornell played a critical role in stabilising Railtrack and recreating Network Rail's engineering function, and Paul King ended his railway career running all the InterCity businesses and floating off all the regional franchises in such a watertight way that not a single lawsuit resulted. Wave after wave of middle managers cut their teeth creating new opportunities for the sector and delivering improvements. Mark Causebrook, Dick Fearn, Chris Leah and Aidan Nelson from the early years went on to run their own railways (Fearn in Ireland), and from Regional Railways days Tim Bell, Chris Gibb, Mike Hodson, David Horne and Andy Pitt graduated to head privatised train operating companies.

There were reasons for this. The infant Provincial sector attracted younger managers because more established figures mainly preferred to go to InterCity. 'Controlled delegation' of spending, with the component parts of Regional Railways at liberty to decide on investment projects up to £1 million provided they had been given budgetary approval as a viable project, encouraged responsible enterprise. 'You could do things without actually asking anybody if it was budgeted,' Theo Steel, then heading South Wales & West, recalls. And Gordon Pettitt took things further in his desire to 'run Regional Railways like a company', bringing in a finance director from industry in the shape of David Rutherford.

## The role of government

Britain's railways can never operate beyond the reach of government. With most of the network bound to require support from the taxpayer no matter how well it performs, ministers and civil servants will always expect to call the

**ABOVE** Glasgow Central before the magic sparkle of the 'Chris Green era'. *Dennis Lovett*

Table 1.1: Governments in power, 1982-2014

| Government | Prime Minister | Years | Secretaries of State |
|---|---|---|---|
| Conservative | Margaret Thatcher | May 1979-Nov 1990 | 7 |
| Conservative | John Major | Nov 1990-May 1997 | 4 |
| Labour | Tony Blair | May 1997-June 2007 | 4 |
| Labour | Gordon Brown | June 2007-May 2010 | 3 |
| Coalition | David Cameron | May 2010-May 2015 | 3 |
| Conservative | David Cameron | May 2015- | 1 |

shots. None of the regional services are profitable, though those operated by TransPennine Express do better than cover their immediate costs, and also deliver a satisfying profit for the franchise holders. But there is now a maturity of understanding at Westminster and in most of Whitehall that the railway adds social and economic value to the community, provided it is efficiently, reliably and safely operated. It should come as no surprise that Government policy features throughout this book, from the commissioning and rejection of the Serpell Report of 1982 to the McNulty Report of 2011, which, significantly, reiterated a number of the points made by Serpell about the cost of the regional railway. While drawing very different and much more positive conclusions, McNulty felt obliged to point out that the net annual cost to the taxpayer of the regional franchises was £1.8 billion, 61% of total costs, equating to 31.1p per passenger mile. It should be stressed, though, that the need to reduce costs and increase efficiency continues to be at the centre of the business; yet the purpose is always to give good value for money to customers and the taxpayer alike, whether at national or local level.

### Table 1.2: Car ownership

Numbers of cars licensed each year (millions)

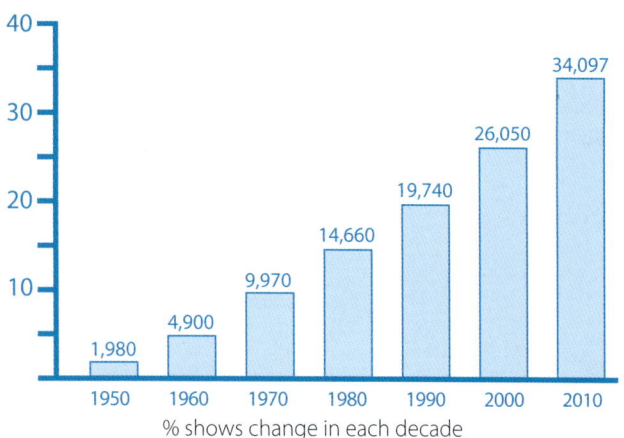

% shows change in each decade
Source: DfT statistics

While through the years we are concerned with there has been a profusion of Secretaries of State for Transport (see Table 1.1), there has been an at times depressing continuity of view within their Department, as is explained later. There had also been – up to the General Election of 2015 – just two changes of political control: from Conservative to Labour in 1997, and from Labour to the Conservative/Lib Dem Coalition in 2010. In practice, neither of these proved as important to the railways as the replacement in November 1990 of Margaret Thatcher – who had baulked at privatising the railways – by John Major, who was eager to take on the challenge.

Up to 1982 the continuity of outlook in Whitehall appeared to be strongly against the railways – which was not surprising, given the ongoing inability of the industry to cover its costs despite widespread closures, particularly in the mid to late 1960s in the wake of the Beeching Report. Britain's regional railways had by then undergone 20 'wasted years' resulting from successive Governments being unable to decide on the future of those lines, left unloved in the age of the private car, that had survived Beeching. The steady rise in car ownership (see Table 1.2) and – just as important – in car use during the post-war decades was crucial in eroding demand for many marginal rail services, as well as sapping the morale of many in railway management. Just as important, it encouraged Whitehall – and the Treasury in particular – to conclude that except for certain niche markets the passenger railway was on the way out.

The rise in car ownership set out in Table 1.2 had a major effect on the modal split between all transport modes from 1952 to the present day and is shown in table 1.3 below. The greatest effect on public transport has been on the demand for buses and coaches, which has continued to decline for over 60 years. In the case of rail, the decline was abrupt at first, then more gentle before remaining stable for two decades. It is these trends that dominated the thinking of politicians and planners of the period. But then, remarkably, rail began to regain ground lost to public transport, and did so with a vigour that could not have been anticipated, owing in the most part to changes in management of the industry and investment which followed. Both are central to the core of this book.

Initially, demand from passengers dwindled, subsidies soared (see Factfile B1) and quality collapsed. Whitehall archives suggest that civil servants saw the future of most rural services lying in replacement bus services, and exuded a general desire to shrink the system.

### Recognition of a 'social' railway

It is, however, important to recognise that some of the foundation stones for the subsequent success of both Provincial and Regional Railways were laid in this difficult preceding era when every achievement that left a welcome dowry for the new sector was gained through struggle. The first was the final winning of

### Table 1.3: The changing modal split between road and rail

| Year | Buses and coaches (%) | Cars, vans and taxis (%) | Total road including motor and pedal cycles (%) | Rail (%) |
|---|---|---|---|---|
| 1952 | 42 | 27 | 82 | 17 |
| 1962 | 24 | 57 | 87 | 12 |
| 1972 | 14 | 76 | 91 | 8 |
| 1982 | 10 | 81 | 93 | 6 |
| 1992 | 6 | 86 | 94 | 6 |
| 2002 | 5 | 86 | 93 | 6 |
| 2013 | 5 | 83 | 90 | 9 |

Source: Transport Statistics Great Britain, DfT
Percentages are of all forms of transport including air (between 0.1% and 1.3% over this period)

Chapter 1: **INTRODUCTION: BY THE SKIN OF THEIR TEETH** 13

## Making closures harder and openings easier

The sterile running battle over bus substitution on rural lines would continue throughout the 1980s. Civil servants had seen bus substitution – abbreviated by its critics to 'bustitution' – as a cheaper way in principle of providing rural transport. However, most of the studies showed that the likely net savings were actually very small – and the political flak for elected politicians was out of all proportion to the benefits.

A list of 41 lines (see Factfile F7) drawn up by the British Railways Board and involving 900 route miles was leaked to the press in September 1979. This led to a very clear statement from the Conservative Secretary of State Norman Fowler, which has implicity remained the policy to this day: 'I see no case for another round of massive cuts in the railways.' Of those 41 lines, all but eight would be inherited by Regional Railways, and 21 are now supported by Community Rail Partnerships.

Provincial was also to make good use of timely legislation that allowed it to open new stations and lines on an experimental basis. The Speller Act of 1980 – named after the Tory backbencher Tony Speller, who promoted it – allowed BR to take more risk in supporting the reopening of lines to passenger traffic. It could close them again with as little as six weeks' warning if they proved to be financially disastrous, without having to go through the complicated and expensive statutory closure procedures. While Speller ironically did not secure the reopening of his own local line in north Devon, the Act would in time bring about revived passenger services on lines including Blackburn-Clitheroe, Coventry-Nuneaton and Walsall-Hednesford, and the reopening of some 80 stations.

**ABOVE** Rt Hon Barbara Castle MP introduced her 1968 Transport Act, which revived the concept of the social railway and road-rail integration. *British Railways Board*

political recognition that parts of the network had a strong social and economic value that justified their subsidy. This was largely secured through Barbara Castle's landmark 1968 Transport Act, which finally recognised a distinction between the 'viable' railway, which was expected to break even, and the 'social' railway, where losses would be met by the state. The Act also created the Passenger Transport Executives (PTEs), which were to become so important in the revival and funding of Provincial's urban services. Surplus Capacity Grants were created to fund the singling of lines and the rationalisation of track layouts and stations. Both saved money, but reduced the capacity of the system.

Next came the 1974 Transport Act, a Conservative measure under which subsidies for individual lines arising from the 1968 Act were ended and a single annual payment made to BR, which became known as the PSO (Public Service Obligation). This was not a perfect mechanism – the Government could still squeeze BR's External Funding Limit (EFL) in difficult years – but it gave the future Provincial sector more freedom to manage costs overall and get the best business results.

**BELOW** A youthful David Steel MP supports the protests over the closure of the Borders railway in August 1966. The line is now being rebuilt from Tweedbank to Edinburgh and is due to open in 2015 at a cost of £300 million. *Author's collection*

**14** *Chapter 1:* **INTRODUCTION: BY THE SKIN OF THEIR TEETH**

### Making trains more productive

Provincial was fortunate to have been established after BR had fought and won some damaging battles to improve the productivity of its train manning. This had become a 'last frontier' because it involved renegotiating hallowed national agreements after all the easier economies had been made.

A start was made in 1978 with extra payments to paytrain guards, which allowed more stations on rural routes to be unmanned. The initiative moved up a notch in 1981 when the unions agreed to talks on three key issues: flexible rostering, open stations with tickets checked on the trains, and single manning. The ensuing dispute over flexible rostering pursued during the first half of 1982 by the drivers' union ASLEF was immensely damaging in the short term – but the agreement secured by BR management digging in its heels helped save much of the regional network in the long term.

Flexible rostering cut out some of the worst excesses in operating costs, and as sectorisation developed drivers finally started to work across regional boundaries and crews were booked for periods relevant to their duties at locations optimised for productivity – rather than for fixed shifts that were too short or too long for them to be deployed efficiently. The settlement not only changed the economics of the network, but gave Government confidence in the nick of time that additional funding for the railway did not mean a wasted investment.

**ABOVE AND RIGHT** A Speller reopening: Hednesford station in 2015. *Alex Green*

These disputes did mean, though, that 1982 was the low point for BR – its worst year for receipts since 1968, and the fewest passenger journeys in the second half of the 20th century. Resolution of the flexible rostering dispute and the start of the fundamental reorganisation were indeed timely, as the Government had become totally frustrated with both the financial and operational performance of the railways, and set up a Review of Railway Finance in 1982 under the chairmanship of Sir David Serpell, former permanent secretary at the Department of Transport. In the event BR's response to the challenges it faced became the strongest defence yet against a further attempt at a round of Beeching-type closures, but it was far from evident at the time that 1982 would turn out to be the point from which the railways recovered.

### Serpell backfires

Serpell began as a review of the potential for further productivity, but turned into a listing of options – reminiscent of Beeching – for greatly reducing the size of the network.

Gordon Pettitt subsequently discussed this paradox with John Palmer, then head of the Department's

Railways Directorate. Palmer said that the committee had been set up following representations from the Board – including Serpell himself – that ongoing Government financial support was insufficient to maintain the railway at its current level. But 'the report was swamped by one member – Alfred Goldstein of Travers Morgan – who insisted that the Board had to know what their long-term aim should be, and that this was to be expressed in terms of the size of the network. This was not what the committee had been asked to do and was a matter of continual conflict within the committee.'

Serpell's conclusion on BR's finances, said Palmer, was that 'the statement that the Board could not maintain the business at the present level of resources was not substantiated. But on the other hand it put forward all these network options. It was a disaster from everybody's point of view. It was simply not the case that Ministers in the Conservative Government wanted to pursue a smaller railway; they made it absolutely clear that they were not interested in that. There was no lobby inside the Department pushing for a smaller railway; I didn't think that that was a sensible course of policy.'

The Serpell Report was published in December 1982. With an election expected in months, the outcry (not least from Conservative MPs) ensured that it was stillborn, but the fact that its conclusions were pigeonholed so quickly also demonstrated that ministers were setting their minds against wholesale closure of railways. However, according to John Palmer papers covering the issue 'were regularly put to ministers to see what they wanted'.

The first consequence of Serpell for the emerging Provincial sector was to render any further significant closures politically unthinkable. A second was that Government finally accepted the need to set medium-term targets for financial support for the railways to allow the new sectors to develop clearer objectives. A third was that BR realised it had to come up with more robust business cases to justify its investment plans. It was this need for more professional management that had led the Board to reorganise into business sectors.

### Foundations laid for a new railway age

The Provincial sector emerged strengthened from this period of turmoil, and was to owe much to those who fought to lay the foundation stones for a more efficient railway following the 20 thankless years since the Beeching Report had written off much of the regional network.

Yet this was only the beginning: from what was initially still a largely hostile and unforgiving climate for a railway that had spent decades on the back foot, a journey had begun which would lead to what in those days would have been viewed as a new railway age. Many obstacles and upheavals lay ahead, but in the Board's victory over flexible rostering and the rejection of Serpell – and even more in the creation of BR's Provincial sector – the seeds were sown for the confident, well-financed, larger and far busier regional passenger railway that we enjoy today. This turn of the tide in the early 1980s would be followed by a surge of creativity that would deliver new generations of affordable trains, new stations and new and appealing services and routes. The public's response to its reborn regional railway would be dramatic: a surge in demand, bringing – as shown in Table 1.4 – a 145% increase in passenger miles travelled, from 2.9 billion in 1982 to 7.1 billion by 2013-14.

**Table 1.4: Growth of regional railways, 1982-2014**

|  | 1982 | 1997 | 2014 |
|---|---|---|---|
| Network size (route miles) | 5,124 | 5,218 | 5,295 |
| Number of stations | 1,364 | 1,504 | 1,540 |
| Number of coaches | 4,537 | 2,286 | 2,849 |
| Number of passenger miles (billions) | 2.9 | 3.9 | 7.1 |

Source: Theo Steel

# Chapter 2
# THE PROVINCIAL SECTOR: TURNING THE TIDE, 1982-86

*'Before the formation of Provincial in 1982, management of these resources was a marginal activity of the Board's regional organisation. Fares on this residual railway covered only 25% of its operating costs. It would have been hard to imagine a less promising business.'*
**MONOPOLIES & MERGERS COMMISSION REPORT**, 1989

**ABOVE** A refurbished Class 101 at Durham in the short-lived 1970s BR pre-sector livery. *Dennis Lovett*

## Chapter 2: THE PROVINCIAL SECTOR: TURNING THE TIDE, 1982-86

### Birth of the sector

On 1 January 1982 British Rail's business was divided into seven commercial sectors. Initially these coexisted with the regions, but over time the reorganisation would prove fundamental, enabling a more confident, business-focused railway to gain the initiative. And crucially, one of the sectors was 'Other Provincial Services' (OPS).

To Sidney Newey, later its Director, 'Other Provincial Services was a "double diminutive" lacking any coherence, and apparently forming, except in the PTEs, something of a no-hope railway. The services it comprised were at the tail-end of everyone's priorities. Some merely existed to connect with main-line trains; others appeared to be the last remnant of a route closure; some ran just as the route had always run. Some 20 Divisional Passenger Managers "did their own thing". This was a recipe for disaster.' Indeed, in 1979 the Board had adopted a downbeat strategy for OPS: those managers were to measure lines against four options: closure, bus substitution, retention, and quality improvement.

Yet from being what BR's official historian Terry Gourvish termed 'a ragbag of services expected to be axed at any moment', the sector would recover. Provincial's enormous stake in the PSO made its effective operation essential to BR; but its creation would also lead to imaginative planning, marketing and delivery of existing and new services that would transform the image and fortunes of previously threatened lines as a prelude to a surge in demand.

### The vision within BR

'The vision behind the sectorisation of BR was Peter Parker's,' says Cyril Bleasdale, whose brain the Chairman had picked about how to ascertain the profitability of individual trains. 'But Bob Reid made it happen.'

Pressure for it also came from BR's strategy unit – Geoffrey Myers, Bill (now Lord) Bradshaw, Arnold Kentridge, John Prideaux and John Welsby – with crucial backing from Bob Reid, then Board member for marketing. Some regional General Managers (GMs) resisted, arguing that practical issues like through working made a division of services between business units unfeasible. When Reid, becoming chief executive, complained that 'my desk is the only place where costs and revenues come together and I can't get either', Welsby – an economist on secondment from the Department with a reputation for keeping costs tight – pointed out that BR was not structured on business lines but run by 'barons' (GMs) and 'bishops' (functional chiefs). Bob Reid would have liked to eliminate the regions and functions at this stage, but recognised that these power bases controlled all BR's resources – and all its information.

BR's accounts for 1977 for the first time divided the costs and revenues of its passenger businesses into InterCity, London & South East (L&SE), PTE services, and OPS. The last two accounted for just 13% of the market, against 48% for InterCity and 39% for L&SE. This was a response to the Government adopting different subsidy policies toward InterCity (none), L&SE (objectives to be set), and the rest (the PSO, minus any subsidy paid to L&SE). A 'product-centred' reorganisation was worked up by Bob Reid and Philip Sellers, BR's Director of Finance, the critical questions being how many sectors there should be and what each should cover; a separate

**RIGHT** Sir Bob Reid I, Chairman of British Rail and 'champion' of the sectorisation of the railways into businesses, with Jim Cornell, General Manager, ScotRail, in the background.
*British Railways Board*

## Chapter 2: THE PROVINCIAL SECTOR: TURNING THE TIDE, 1982-86

**ABOVE** John Welsby, from 1982 Provincial's first director and later last chairman of a fully functioning BR, speaking in 2015. *Mike Tyrell*

sector for the PTEs was rejected. Early in the 1970s an accounting exercise had managed to attribute just 54% of costs to specific parts of the business; a fresh study got the proportion up to 78%.

In August 1981 the Board approved the new structure. The sectors were to be InterCity, L&SE, OPS, Freight, Parcels and Freightliners, with Travellers Fare a separate company. Remarkably, BR persuaded the Department that this fundamental change was merely a modification of top management, so did not require the Secretary of State's consent.

Bob Reid knew that the railway needed shaking up, and he knew who could do it, reckoning that change at the top would cascade down. For his Sector Directors, he selected tested managers who could cut costs and increase revenue while keeping the bishops and barons at bay. They had to remain absolutely loyal to Board policies; 'It was very easy to forget this,' says Terence Jenner, solicitor to the Board and eventually its Chairman, 'and every so often people found themselves out in the cold.' Reid chose Cyril Bleasdale from Freightliner for InterCity, and David Kirby, General Manager of BR Shipping, for L&SE. But for Provincial, with its heavy reliance on the PSO and broad interface with Government, he wanted a manager who understood the industry/government interface – so settled on John Welsby.

### John Welsby starts the ball rolling

The Provincial sector began with an office in London housing only John Welsby, a secretary and three staff from HQ passenger department – 'Good and keen to make the new system work.' he recalls. His inheritance was not promising. OPS operated one-sixth of BR's passenger miles, but incurred most of its losses; revenue was just 24.5% of costs, outweighed on some services by 13:1.

Welsby needed to show that the sector would make significant savings, so he looked first at where those costs lay: track, signalling, rolling stock, over-provision of services. 'I decided to leave service provision largely alone in the initial stage; it would have involved major rows with general managers who would have gone out of their way to make sure I screwed up. The last thing I wanted was to get off to a bad start with them and the functions. Acceptance was more difficult for me because I did not have a railway background; worse still, I was a Department man.'

Instead he started with Provincial rolling stock, mostly nearing the end of its economic life and increasingly unreliable. Beyond the 'Pacer' prototypes, no plans existed for new stock; moreover, a refurbishment of ageing diesel multiple units (DMUs) had petered out when serious problems with asbestos, very expensive to solve, became evident. Nor was there any prospect of like-for-like replacements meeting the Department's investment criteria. Yet without more appealing and reliable stock, services would grind to a halt.

**BELOW** A cluster of Class 117s at Birmingham Moor Street terminus in 1987. The former GWR through lines to Snow Hill, reopened that year, can be seen in the background. *Dennis Lovett*

ABOVE An early 'Pacer' unit, No 141014, at York on a service to Harrogate on 4 August 1984. These units were subsequently re-engineered in 1989 and renumbered, the leading coach of this unit becoming part of No 14115. *Graeme Phillips*

## Saving on rolling stock

Welsby concluded that Provincial could achieve major savings by cutting back from around 4,000 vehicles to 2,500 within ten years, including the withdrawal of 1,000 loco-hauled carriages (see Factfile E). Previous policy had been to cascade older locomotives from InterCity, but to him these were unsuitable, expensive to operate, unreliable and enjoyed poor availability. If a Class 50 loco had a serious breakdown in the West Country, it would be hauled to Doncaster and stay there for months.

'What was needed was modern, reliable equipment that could be fully maintained in local depots. I was also a fan of "distributed power trains". I had regularly to go to Leeds when HSTs were at their most unreliable. With dual power cars they managed to get there, if somewhat late; with single power cars they would have stopped. So I wanted DMUs with power units under each carriage.' Meanwhile, thanks to David Kirby at L&SE agreeing to postpone receipt of a batch of EMUs, a way was found of fitting into the limitations of BR's External Funding Limit what became the first production batch of 'Pacers'.

John Welsby saw that minimising vehicle, and hence axle, weights could lower track maintenance costs. He found BR's engineers reluctant to discuss this, being rebuked by a divisional engineer for talking with a 'junior' – with 20 years' experience – who saw merit in the proposition. Over time, though, he gained supporters – among them, crucially, Jim Cornell – 'and although the start was slow, the introduction of the new fleet did allow gradual savings on track maintenance.'

## Creating a culture and a structure

Initially directly responsible only for planning, the Sector Directors soon took on financial performance despite there being no easily quantifiable 'bottom line'. No template existed for managing the sectors, and until 1986 the directors managed through the regional machinery. It took the strength of the personalities chosen by Bob Reid to begin a transfer of the 'controlling mind' to the sectors. 'Bob knew that the system he had set up was merely a step towards the ultimate solution,' says John Welsby, and over time there was a shift in responsibilities from the General Managers to the Sector Directors. Welsby himself began to create a culture and a structure. He dispensed with unrealistic five-year plans, expected individual managers to achieve their forecast results, and appointed a Passenger Business Manager to each region or division.

# Chapter 2: THE PROVINCIAL SECTOR: TURNING THE TIDE, 1982-86

**ABOVE** BR Scottish Region's Perth station before the bow-wave of ScotRail's rapid modernisation. *Dennis Lovett*

Outdated stations and unreliable trains were not the only challenge. The singling of some secondary main lines had reduced capacity and increased the disruptive effect of late running. Planning for maintenance and renewals by the regions' engineers and S&T (Signal & Telegraph) teams seldom had Provincial services as a priority. Timetable planning – in the hands of regional staff, who at Crewe did not cooperate until ordered to – did Provincial services few favours. Train crews were embedded in steam-age depots rather than booking on where needed. DMUs were often maintained far from the points between which they had to operate. Moreover, secondary routes were managed at divisional level, and – in Chris Stokes's experience of the LMR – 'not with any verve'.

## Flexible rostering and Serpell

Provincial was just six months old when ASLEF struck over flexible rostering. While the handling of the dispute lay with the Board and maintaining services with the regions, the disruption torpedoed Provincial's bottom line; Chris Green told staff in Scotland that it 'cost us over 10% of our passenger business'.

Then came Serpell. While fighting it was again a matter for the Board, John Welsby contributed to BR's defence, as the implications for Provincial were potentially catastrophic. Developing the sector, and strengthening its management while almost every service it offered was under threat, posed a severe challenge. Yet he overcame it, and when Serpell's publication generated such hostility as to rule out further significant closures, he was not only able to get on with building Provincial but could press for investment – though at first purely to reduce costs. Against this background the long-running battle over the attempted closure of the Settle & Carlisle line (see the Postscript) comes across as an aberration from the Board's general policy.

John Welsby cut through the investment knot by developing a business case for new trains based on replacing every two carriages with one. At a stroke, he began the process of cutting costs while improving quality which would get Provincial off the ropes; the 'Sprinter' programme was born, in the nick of time. Critical also to the Department approving new trains for Provincial was an improved investment appraisal process, prompted by Bob Reid, which removed doubts in Whitehall over BR's perceived lack of rigour.

## Rail in Scotland reinvents itself

Some things were already moving as the Provincial sector was created. Arriving from Headquarters as Scottish Region operating manager, Chris Green with his train planning officer Jim Summers in May 1982 replaced a 'ragged web' of uncompetitive services with a basic-interval timetable modelled on Switzerland's Taktfahrplan. Chris Green says, 'The arrival of the London HST at Edinburgh triggered a wave of connecting services, making connections to Wick,

## Chapter 2: THE PROVINCIAL SECTOR: TURNING THE TIDE, 1982-86

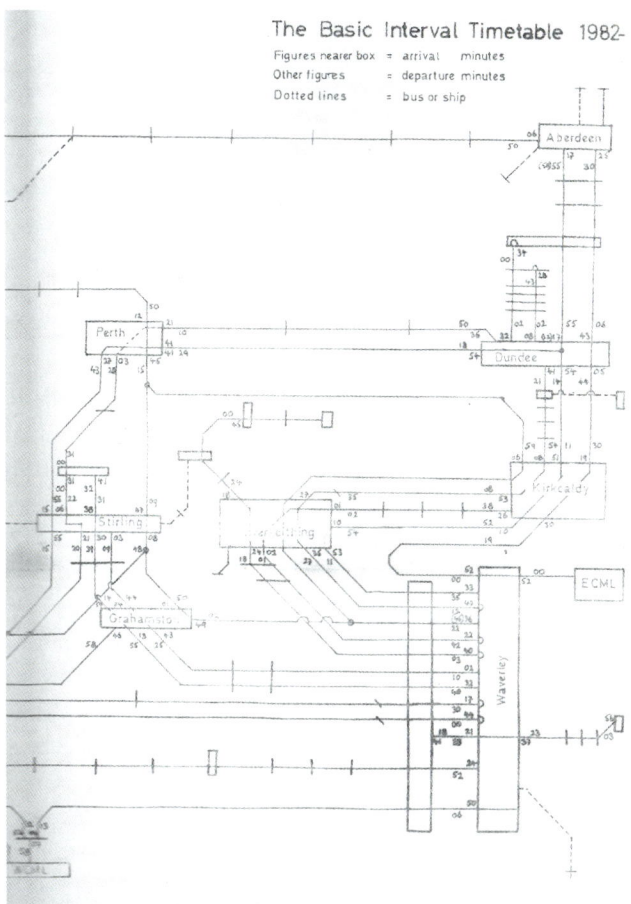

**ABOVE** ScotRail's original basic interval timetable, as constructed by Jim Summers when Train Planning Manager in 1982. *Chris Green*

Kyle, Fort William and Stranraer, with easy-to-remember interval services to every route – from every 10 minutes in Strathclyde to every 4 hours in the Far North. The Mk III Edinburgh-Glasgow push-pull fleet was "sweated" to work some Glasgow-Aberdeen services. An East Coast HST worked a commuter service from Edinburgh to Glasgow Queen Street before offering a new direct service to Newcastle and London. Others supplemented Scottish Express services, and InterCity's "Clansman" and "Highland Chieftain" services revolutionised rail's competitive position from Inverness and Perth. [Trains between Euston, Birmingham, Perth and Inverness would sadly not survive into privatisation.]

'We upgraded secondary routes where coach competition was biting; the "Royal Scot" even started back from Ayr as a quality commuter service. Old DMUs on the Inverness-Aberdeen and Glasgow-Stranraer routes were replaced with air-braked Mark I or II sets. On rural lines, Class 37s brought accelerated services – and finally electric train heating. The new timetable above all accelerated timings, with 15-minute reductions on Aberdeen-Edinburgh and 26 minutes from the West Highland and Far North schedules.'

But the iconic initiative was yet to come. 'I became Deputy General Manager in 1983,' Green recalls, 'and my mission with the quality improving was to transform the public image of rail in Scotland. A small group of us met in Buchanan House and – without the help of any agencies – reached unanimous agreement on the new name "ScotRail". [Equally, no agency would be involved in choosing the Regional Railways brand name].

'At one stroke we were free of the cumbersome "British Rail, Scottish Region" – and its pejorative overtones. The Board and Provincial sector were totally supportive; the only BR stipulations were that the double-arrow BR symbol should always be used before the word ScotRail, and that all graphics should be in the corporate alphabet.'

The rebranding of BR in Scotland (except InterCity services and freight) was launched in Glasgow on 22 September 1983 by the region's General Manager, George Mackie – overshadowed by comments Chris Green had made about launching a 'charm school' for train conductors. Chris Green continues: 'The new name was an immediate success. Suddenly ScotRail was top of the headlines as a patriotic name that made Scots feel they had acquired their own railway. The staff loved the sense of belonging – and the name entered the language almost overnight.

'The marketing team backed the new-look services with aggressive pricing, down to £1 Inverness-Glasgow to match the predatory coaches. A "Jacobite" named train on Fridays provided a limited-stop service from Glasgow to Inverness and back, and Jim Summers created the overnight "Nightrider" to London offering coach fares.

'Stations were re-signed. The entire fleet was re-branded, with the flagship Edinburgh-Glasgow trains in an eye-catching livery complete with Provincial Sector blue line. A ScotRail map appeared throughout the network. The staff were soon wearing an attractive uniform. John Boyle, ScotRail's Director of Public Affairs, created real interest and support amongst a Scottish media that had been in danger of writing rail off. ScotRail pushed back coach competition – increasing travel by 25% in 1986 – and is one of the few BR brands to have survived privatisation, still flourishing and respected.'

That respect was heightened by ScotRail declining to bid for any 'Pacers'. Chris Green says that the Scottish Region, Strathclyde PTE, the Scottish Office, the regional councils and MPs from all parties were all 'adamant that "Pacers" were totally unacceptable for the Scottish environment.' On long rural lines passengers could be on a train for 2 to 4 hours, and trains were needed that 'offered high levels of reliability on lines where rescue could take a long time and with good ride qualities and insulation against the climate.' Moreover, the region's signalling engineers had concerns about the compatibility of 'Pacers' with their infrastructure.

## John Edmonds drives things forward

After the 1983 election Tom King replaced David Howell as Transport Secretary. Sir Peter Parker was also due to retire. The minister and the Department wanted another businessman to chair BR, but Margaret Thatcher got on well with Bob Reid; he was also friends with Denis Thatcher, and shot and fished with the Tory inner circle. So Reid was appointed that September – one of the best decisions concerning the railway that any Government has taken. Weeks later Nicholas Ridley, whom Reid liked and who crucially enjoyed the Prime Minister's confidence, succeeded Tom King.

Installing a railwayman to chair BR did not diminish the Government's pressure for financial rigour. John Palmer recollects: 'Before Bob Reid was appointed, Tom King asked him, "Do you go along with the Serpell Report?", meaning the efficiency parts of it, and Reid said "Yes". So we could at last write a letter for the Secretary of State to send to the Chairman, setting out clear three-year objectives – and ones that were agreed with the Chairman before the letter was sent.' Nicholas Ridley's letter instructed BR to cut its losses faster without major closures. Provincial barely had time to react before, in January 1984, Bob Reid moved John Welsby on to sort out BR's workshops as Director, Manufacturing & Maintenance Policy.

John Edmonds, Chief Freight Manager, London Midland Region, took over, becoming the sector's chief architect. His objectives, says Alec McTavish, Provincial's planning and investment manager, were 'to transform the business, and get Provincial from something that was largely ignored to something that had a vision and a reason for being there.' He set out to control production costs incurred by the regions; improve customer service (and, hence, revenue); control the urges of the PTEs; and develop and implement strategies to reinvigorate Provincial services and achieve a cost-effective railway. Mark Causebrook says, 'John was about challenging the engineers and operators, driving costs down and supporting creative service opportunities that cut costs. Such were the economics on many routes that you could double income and it would make no difference; you had to get costs under control.' Moreover, while no closures were on the table, fear of them remained intense; as Alec McTavish puts it, 'Everything we did had to be proofed against closure.'

## Dividing up the costs

The Board, after some pain, settled the accounting conventions essential for the sectors to move forward. The change from Prime User to Sole User, stemming from David Allen's appointment in 1982 as BR's Director, Sector Evaluation, proved critical: Provincial could now decide on the infrastructure (and standards) needed for its services and make other users pay for anything different; this enabled John Edmonds – working in lock-step with John Welsby – to mandate low axle weights for new rolling stock.

**LEFT** ScotRail's enthusiasm and urgency for change are still breathtaking – even after 30 years! *British Railways Board*

**RIGHT** Edinburgh's Calton Tunnels after the controversial singling through each bore, during the early years of sectorisation.
*Kim Traynor*

Sole User was intended to identify incremental costs to sectors and eliminate surplus capacity, but in the short term it led to arguments. At one point Alec McTavish sat down and wrote what Terry Gourvish reckons to be one of the rudest letters to the Chairman he has ever seen.

Provincial was still having problems with the regions, and was engaged in what Mark Causebrook remembers as 'trench warfare' with the PTEs. Relations with InterCity could also be fraught. On sectorisation, BR had suggested splitting services with Provincial at the point where InterCity would break even. With its finances deteriorating, InterCity in 1984 proposed offloading some marginal North-East/South-West services, and in 1985/86 the WCML north of Preston, concentrating all its Scottish services on the ECML. But John Edmonds had, as we shall see in Chapter 9, a more ambitious view of Provincial's interurban potential.

John Edmonds locked horns with InterCity's Cyril Bleasdale over a decision to electrify only two of the four tracks north from Peterborough on the ECML because that was all InterCity would pay for, the scope of resignalling at Leicester, and a partial resignalling at Newcastle that would hamper Provincial's train movements. InterCity agreed to contribute toward Provincial's share of revised projects with greater capacity. There were arguments over rationalising Holgate Junction, York, and InterCity's proposal to single the track through Edinburgh's Calton Tunnels. There were clashes also over timetable planning. In an early Christmas card, Provincial depicted itself as a band of pirates; yet, just as after the early nonsenses of privatisation, practices and relationships matured.

Cyril Bleasdale recalls, 'John Welsby and I had an excellent working relationship. We'd just meet informally if there were issues, like one sector holding connections for trains from the other. John Edmonds came and I can't say we had any disputes. But he was perhaps as hard-nosed about what he would pay for as I was.'

In 1984 the regions' traffic divisions lost their responsibilities to a reduced number of Area Managers, who reported directly to the regions. This disadvantaged Provincial, as Area Managers had no scope for achieving economies of scale and found it hard to share services; some were mainly concerned with freight, and all had a first loyalty to the region. The change did reveal some problems; Manchester divisional control argued against its abolition on the ground that no one else could cover for ongoing DMU shortages at Newton Heath. This was the first senior management had heard of the issue, and changes ensued at the depot. In 1986 Provincial crucially took charge of medium- to long-distance loco-hauled services, which could not be managed at area level.

## The impact of strikes

While Provincial's finances were improving (see Factfile B), BR overall was suffering through a decline in freight. When the sectors were created, Freight's revenue was close to total passenger income. But a wave of steelworks closures led to its falling behind ... then the miners' strike of 1984-85 brought a sharp drop in traffic as bulk production halted at the majority of pits. Pit closures once the strike was over left carryings of coal greatly reduced, and lines unused; as will be seen later, even some secondary main lines were reduced to a few two- or four-car Provincial services. And the impact on BR's finances heightened pressure on its loss-making sectors.

Strikes in the industry – culminating in six one-day stoppages by the NUR over pay in 1989 – further risked the gains won through sectorisation. Taking over as General Manager, Scottish Region, at the start of 1984, Chris Green told staff: 'Even those little 24-hour strikes have their price. This year's bill for ScotRail alone is: GCHQ one-day strike [sympathy strike with civil service unions over Margaret Thatcher's withdrawal of union recognition], £250,000; Strathclyde one-day strike, £85,000; miners' one-day strike, £200,000; threat of national strike (i.e. loss of advance bookings), £400,000; impact of other regions' strikes, £265,000: Total £1,200,000. That is just about as much as we have lost through coach competition in the year! We really have to stop involving our customers in our disagreements if we are to be serious about survival.' The industrial climate within BR remained an obstacle to better performance, and to trust from customer and Government alike.

Train service development, unit replacement, streamlined train maintenance and depot rationalisation were all now improving the bottom line. But despite flexible rostering and a reduction in BR staff from 121,084 to 98,441 between 1983 and 1988, productivity improved little because the staff were still employed on outdated terms and conditions. There had also been a failure to tackle restrictive practices. Several of the 400 action points in BR's 1988 Rail Plan – such as driver-only operation (DOO), tighter manning of stations, and level crossing modernisation – had been mooted years before and only patchily adopted. Provincial was keen on the 'Traincrew Concept' with the second staff member on a train, hitherto the guard, providing customer service including selling tickets, instead of sitting in the rear cab and emerging to operate the doors. This arrangement was considered more economic than staffing quiet stations.

### John Edmonds's management style

The sector gained influence and managerial depth as John Edmonds developed the concept of Group Service Management, of forming a team and 'keeping it tight'. A creative, if hard, taskmaster, he set his managers clear objectives for reducing the PSO. Yet he gave them freedom to act, subject to quarterly reviews still vividly remembered – to his surprise – by their 'victims'. Bob Goundry, who had worked under him in freight, recalls: 'Every three months the team from Headquarters would spend a day in a profit centre and invigilate its performance in finance, resource utilisation and strategic planning as well as looking at its overall results. These could be rather painful. Yet despite their aggressive nature and the sheer terror they induced, morale was generally high; we could see we were changing the face of the railway and making great strides in understanding the concept of value for money. A falling subsidy and rising revenue spoke volumes.' And quietly, the foundations were being laid for growth.

Price Waterhouse had proposed a five-year programme for the formation of sub-sectors, and John Edmonds used this to bring on young talent: Mark Causebrook, Tom Clift, John Curley, Charles Devereux, Chris Gibb, Don Jary, Andy Pitt and more. In June 1984 Provincial set up a Western sub-sector at Swindon (with an outbase at Cardiff) under John Pearse, covering non-InterCity and non-London commuter trains on the Western Region, plus Newport to Crewe and through services to the South Coast. An Eastern sub-sector was founded in York under David Wharton-Street, including trans-Pennine services, and a Midland unit under Chris Stokes. Chris Leah later became Provincial Sector Manager in Scotland when Chris Green – by then General Manager – moved south; Jim Cornell, previously Green's deputy, took over as GM, Scotland. (Details of the Provincial sub-sectors are given in Factfile H.)

Bob Goundry was tannoyed on the concourse at Euston to take a call from John Edmonds: 'I want you to be my sub-sector manager for the LMR: yes or no?' Chris Stokes had set up a tiny staff in Birmingham and four profit centres – Birmingham for the West Midlands and mid-Wales (Brian Johnson); Manchester (Mike Anderson) for the North West and North Wales; Liverpool (Bob Bates) for Merseyside; and Derby (Roger Jones) for cross-country services south of the Pennines. 'Chris Stokes was moving on, and I was to flesh out the structure and help the profit centres achieve the organisation's objectives.

'In each sub-sector a Resources Manager, a Commercial Manager and a Finance Manager reported to the sub-sector manager,' says Bob Goundry. 'The Resources Manager had managers to deal with the planning, allocation and specification of rolling stock, terminals and infrastructure; the Commercial Manager was responsible for marketing and sales, pricing and timetable specification; and the Finance Manager wrestled with the Region's intractable finance systems in pursuit of a credible bottom line. Our freedom was circumscribed by using resources provided by the regions – trains, crews and station staff; the enormous power of the PTEs; and the lack of clear financial accounting to support sectorisation. And Headquarters played a key part in replacement of the rag-bag of trains we had inherited.'

Some Provincial managers found themselves 'piggy in the middle' between John Edmonds and their General Managers. Chris Stokes recalls having 'a solid line to the GM, and a dotted one to John.' But Bob Goundry found his relations with the LMR 'workmanlike and effective, with strong support from the general management. There were individuals who did not at first understand, but I don't remember hostility or obstruction from anyone. Nearly everyone welcomed change that advanced the cause of the railway, even when it created work. More difficulty was experienced with the mechanical engineers at Derby –

**ABOVE** No 31142 passes Frisby on the Wreake with the 12.10 Provincial service from Cambridge to Birmingham on 8 December 1984. *Martin Loader*

though they welcomed the new stock we were able to procure – and some Area Civil Engineers and specialist departments (e.g. bridge engineers) took time to recognise that the world was changing.'

The new sub-sectors worked across regional boundaries: Eastern ran trans-Pennine services to Holyhead in the LMR, Midland to Norwich in the Eastern Region, and Western to Portsmouth in the Southern. The boundaries were further challenged when Eastern took over the Settle & Carlisle line.

### New trains start to transform the economics

Up to 1984 the PSO was reduced through economies, from then until the early 1990s rising revenues helped trim it further. It may be no coincidence that the first production 'Pacers' – for West Yorkshire services – arrived late in 1984. They were to Mark Causebrook a 'political necessity – without them lines wouldn't have survived,' and John Edmonds would order a final tranche, with the Department declining to fund anything better.

John Edmonds concluded that the game-changer for Provincial lay in eliminating the expensive 1950s DMUs and loco-hauled trains even faster than John Welsby had proposed. Arrival of the 'Pacers' facilitated a swathe of depot closures – Bradford Hammerton Street, Darlington, Hull Botanic Gardens, Lincoln, Thornaby, York Clifton (a brand new depot) – while discarding redundant carriages reduced the sector's reliance on BR's workshops. John Edmonds prioritised maximum availability, but problems remained in delivering a reliable service when units at the same depot lacked common couplings or had different maximum speeds. Moreover, some managers in the regions saw Provincial's quest for 90% availability and the maintenance of all units outside diagrammed hours as simply not practicable.

### An end to cuts in capacity

The steady decline in traffic up to 1982 had been matched by steps to take out surplus capacity, and these continued as a means of securing economies. One involved replacing life-expired double junctions with far cheaper single-lead junctions. The media blamed subsequent accidents – including fatal ones on ScotRail at Bellgrove in 1989 and Newton in 1991 – on such junctions' inherent lack of safety, but the cause (mitigated by shortcomings in the design of the lead at Newton) was drivers passing red signals. However, single leads installed at busy points like Haughley Junction, where the London-Norwich and Felixstowe-Peterborough lines diverge, limited capacity, and many have since been removed; redoubling Newton brought a major improvement in performance.

Meanwhile the Eastern Region reduced several secondary routes from double to single track, and the Western some sections of main line, most now reinstated (see Factfile F). Among the last stretches tackled were over Ribblehead Viaduct (to reduce the strains on it) and the East Suffolk line. The most extreme singlings – between York and Scarborough, Bradford and Halifax, Leeds and Harrogate, and Newport and Shrewsbury – were called off as Provincial's influence grew. Singling fell out of vogue because the outlay was only justified if signalling was also renewed; reduced flexibility imposed rigid service patterns; and pinch points were created. As Mark Causebrook puts it, 'These schemes had no business case and would have constrained business development. What we did promote was line speed improvements, as reduced journey time created not only passenger benefits but resource savings (unit and train crew).'

# Chapter 3
# THE PROVINCIAL SECTOR: GATHERING SPEED, 1986-90

*'Over the last six years the Provincial sector has been able to reduce costs, increase traffic, improve quality and charge more for it.'*

**CECIL PARKINSON**, 1989

**ABOVE** 'Sprinter' No 150129 with two other classmates in Provincial livery depart from Kidderminster on 4 July 1987 forming the 09.29 Hereford to Birmingham service. *Martin Loader*

## Chapter 3: THE PROVINCIAL SECTOR: GATHERING SPEED, 1986-90

### The 'Sprinter revolution'

On 20 January 1986, amid a blaze of publicity, the first Class 150 'Sprinters' took civic dignitaries, press and athletes from towns across the Midlands to Nottingham for a series of 100-metre races along the platform, the Lord Mayor presenting 'Sprinter' trophies. That May just 50 units replaced elderly DMUs or loco-hauled trains on all of the following routes: Birmingham-Nottingham-Lincoln, Birmingham-Leicester-Cambridge, Chester-Crewe, Crewe-Derby-Nottingham-Grantham, Derby-Matlock, Manchester-Llandudno/Holyhead, Nottingham-Sheffield-Leeds, Shrewsbury-Aberystwyth/Pwllheli, Shrewsbury-Crewe, and Shrewsbury-Chester. They even appeared on trans-Pennine services, the 150s being so scarce that four cars ran only between York and Manchester Victoria, and two cars on the Liverpool and Scarborough extremities. Not only were the 'Sprinters' modern and more reliable, they were also faster, knocking 20 minutes off some Pwllheli timings. John Welsby even speculated that they could operate some of InterCity's North East/South West services.

Provincial's new trains made a huge difference. Bob Goundry recalls: 'The first "Pacers" showed it was possible to replace the DMU fleet with fewer vehicles that were cheaper to maintain and could run on less expensive track. As the technology advanced from Class 142 "Pacers" through Class 150 "Sprinters" and Class 156 "Super Sprinters" to the Class 158 "Provincial Express" it became possible to develop new patterns of service, particularly on cross-country routes, which revolutionised this neglected area of travel, producing very significant revenue increases while making major cost reductions.' These reductions took longer to achieve on ScotRail, where the public preference for loco haulage and the nature of the routes operated meant that (save for just six 150s on Edinburgh local services) the 156s were the first 'Sprinter' class deployed. Even the 158s were only taken grudgingly and at the insistence of Provincial HQ, which, says Chris Green, was 'rightly concerned about the sheer cost of running loco-hauled and HSTs'. (Thirty years on, shortened HSTs are to replace ScotRail's even newer three-car Class 170s.)

The new trains brought a fall of 57% in Provincial's maintenance and overhaul costs between 1982 and 1988 – contributing heavily to a 19% reduction in this activity for BR as a whole. Yet these still came to £339.9 million, or 46.2% of total operating costs. Maintenance costs varied from £17.66 per hour at

**BELOW** No 156442 on heavy lifting jacks at Corkerhill Depot, Glasgow. *Dennis Lovett*

# Chapter 3: THE PROVINCIAL SECTOR: GATHERING SPEED, 1986-90

**ABOVE** Track maintenance – the old way! *Colas Rail*

Newton Heath, Manchester, to £27.49 at Heaton, Newcastle. Casualty rates also differed. Costs remained high in part through a lack of dedicated depots handling particular classes of stock. BR had judged Leeds Neville Hill solely on its handling of HSTs, with West Yorkshire PTE frustrated by poor availability among the 11 DMU types the depot hosted. Provincial concentrated heavy maintenance on a few large depots – Birmingham Tyseley, Cardiff Canton, Edinburgh Haymarket, Neville Hill, Norwich Crown Point, Heaton and Newton Heath – with exclusive use of all but Crown Point and Neville Hill. They were based around component exchange and heavy lifting gear, enabling 90% availability targets to be set across the fleet and 75% for the 1950s DMUs. With the 'Sprinters', Crown Point handled the entire Midland Class 156 fleet and Canton the Western 155s, with sharp improvements in availability. But tight finances resulted in slow progress towards specialised depots – Haymarket in 1988 was among the first.

## Getting to grips with the infrastructure

As the new trains arrived, signalling was being simplified and level crossings automated. Provincial services benefited from resignallings at Cambridge, Exeter and Westbury, but – the introduction of RETB radio control on the Far North line and the Cambrian apart – the only major schemes it (co)sponsored were the Ayrshire Coast (1983, costing £23 million), Leicester (1983, £22 million after heavy de-scoping), and North Clyde (1987, £23 million). This last, completed over six years, involved a ground-breaking IECC at Yoker, controlling 49 route miles.

A key thread in Provincial's developing philosophy, recalls Sidney Newey, was 'the need to consider the passenger ahead of the engineers' quest for perfection. When Crewe was resignalled, they wanted 80 weekend possessions. We pushed, and they agreed to do it in one go in five weeks – we overran by about five days. The idea that the engineers didn't dictate to the railway was something that was coming. The huge change Provincial brought about was a revamping of lines suffering from speed restrictions and having them relaid with continuous welded rail and concrete sleepers. Not doing more than you needed to had to be learned – and it was a radical change.'

For John Edmonds's managers, says David Wharton-Street, 'the challenge was to stop investment in pet schemes that bore no relationship to where the businesses were aiming. I informed the M&EE [Mechanical & Electrical Engineer] not to include trackwork into maintenance depots at York or Darlington in the East Coast improvements, as they would no longer be needed for Provincial. The functions were stunned.' Jim Cornell found different standards region by region; when he was Divisional Engineer in Newcastle 'we were ordering second-hand rail which on the Western they were chopping up; Western relaid every siding with brand new rail.'

Much of the continuous welded rail (CWR) laid on Provincial routes was recycled from main or recently closed lines such as the bypassed ECML between Selby and York; for York-Scarborough the rails had done 17 years on the ECML, and with fewer trains and lower axle weights was good for 14 more ... or 50 with concrete sleepers. The cost was £130,000 a mile, against £335,000 for new track. David Wharton-Street explains: 'What we tried to do was manage down the need for maintenance and renewal. Without loco haulage it was possible to get down to 12 tons axle weight with the new DMUs.' Line speeds could also be raised from 70 to 90mph. In Scotland, Jim Cornell secured decades of further track use by postponing relaying until wear had gone further into the rail depth; this was perfectly safe where lighter trains were run, and became applied more widely.

Until 1987/88 the engineers allocated resources for maintenance and renewals according to a matrix of 16 track categories: four bands for speed and four for annual tonnage. With the spread of the 'Sprinters' a 36-category matrix was developed, focusing on the different sectors' infrastructure needs – and lowering costs. One initiative was inspecting track, structures and fencing with a two-man crew on a 15mph permanent way (PW) trolley, instead of walking the line at 2mph. Nationally, Jim Cornell says, 'The infrastructure cost review from 1987 onwards covered

## Chapter 3: THE PROVINCIAL SECTOR: GATHERING SPEED, 1986-90

**RIGHT** Bathgate station as reopened in 1986. *Dennis Lovett*

our core activities in civils, S&T and mechanical engineering. We looked at a whole series of long welded rail depots and precast concrete works. Their productivity, compared with what you could buy in the market place, was no contest.' They closed.

### Whitehall takes time to catch on

The upturn in Provincial's fortunes took time to register in the Department, and pressure continued not just for 'bustitution' but for converting railways into roads. In 1984 BR defensively commissioned Coopers & Lybrand to review the practicability of this; the company concluded that 'none of the routes examined could be converted to roads conforming to the minimum standards laid down by the Department except by the expenditure of substantial capital sums.' The highway planners coveted sections of the Nottingham-Lincoln line at Bottesford and the Newcastle-Carlisle line at Haltwhistle for bypasses to the A46 and the A69 respectively. No alternative rail alignment was proposed, a DoT official in the latter case telling Eastern Region General Manager David Rayner that the railway was redundant. The Bottesford proposal was killed by Nottinghamshire and Lincolnshire county councils; the Haltwhistle scheme by Rayner's blunt warning of the outcry that severing an important passenger and freight connection would provoke.

In 1986 the Board gave the sectors the lead on product specification, funding and – crucially – investment priorities. The sectors also took over strategic resource management and marketing from the regions, with their staffs becoming more than a nucleus. 'We switched the money from civil to mechanical engineering once we could see the figures,' says Alec McTavish. That meant less for the regional engineers – and more for new trains. Investment in Provincial ramped up, between 1985/86 and 1987/88 receiving £117.5 million out of £440.7 million for BR as a whole. Most was for rolling stock; indeed, in 1989 Provincial told the Monopolies & Mergers Commission (MMC) that the main constraint on investment had become the sector's ability to absorb change.

For a Provincial sub-sector to win new trains, it had to compete with others desperate for stock and show how it would impact on a route's operating costs and revenue; a key figure was how many old vehicles each could replace. David Wharton-Street remembers: 'TransPennine were desperate to get rid of loco haulage, but we were competing with ScotRail and North Wales. However, once a bid had been successful, you could cascade what you had.' Crucially, John

**ABOVE** From little acorns grow big stations: Bathgate as expanded in 2010. *Dennis Lovett*

Edmonds specified what became the Class 158 to deliver a further step change in quality and service, just as John Welsby – though rated a 'Pacer' man by his staff – had specified the 'Sprinters'.

### The reopenings begin

In 1986 ScotRail reopened the Edinburgh-Bathgate line for passengers, attracting more than twice the traffic forecast. Chris Green says, 'This first big restoration of a Beeching closure proved an outstanding success, to the point where overcrowding became a problem – a living message to the Scottish Office and others that passengers wanted to keep their railways.' The trains now continue to Glasgow via an electrified, double-track railway.

## Table 3.1: Summary of stations opened, 1981-2014

(See Factfile G for individual stations)

|  | Urban | | Interurban | Rural | Total stations | |
|---|---|---|---|---|---|---|
|  | PTE | Other |  |  |  |  |
| England | 62 | 49 | 3 | 14 | 128 | 52% |
| Scotland | 36 | 22 | 2 | 9 | 69 | 28% |
| Wales | - | 41 | 3 | 4 | 48 | 20% |
| **Total** | **98** | **112** | **8** | **27** | **245** | **100%** |
|  | 40% | 46% | 3% | 11% | 100% |  |

Source: Alex Green

The period from 1985 to 1994 was the golden age of station openings and reopenings, with 157. Of the openings during this time, 203 were for urban services – 95 for the PTEs (36 in Strathclyde) and 108 in other urban areas, mainly South Wales (41), Derbyshire, Lancashire and Nottinghamshire. 1987 alone saw 26 stations and seven lines totalling 32.7 miles reopen, including Coventry-Nuneaton, Coatbridge-Motherwell and the Cardiff City line; none, however, matched Bathgate's commercial success.

Government funding for mining communities as pits closed helped reopen the line to Aberdare in 1988, and subsequently the Nottingham-Worksop 'Robin Hood Line'; the 'Ivanhoe Line' between Leicester and Burton-on-Trent proved too difficult. But as coal carryings declined, other traffics that had sustained a 24-hour railway were lost. Newspapers went in 1988

**BELOW** The beautifully restored Great Malvern station complete with its unique decorations on the columns. *Steve Glennie-Smith*

after printing of the nationals was decentralised, ending such overnight passenger workings as Manchester-Cleethorpes. Sleepers were cut back to the core Anglo-Scottish and Cornish routes. Royal Mail traffic was concentrated on the heaviest flows. So Provincial had to bear an ever larger share of its infrastructure costs. Secondary main lines became, in effect, rural railways.

Improving the railway's image, Provincial undertook major station renovations at Beverley, Skegness and Ulverston, and rebuilt with local authority help Chester-le-Street, Maryport, Rotherham Central and others. (One refurbishment hurriedly pushed through was of the fine structure at Great Malvern, burned down in 1987 the day before Bob Reid arrived to distribute the prizes at his old school.)

ScotRail, Chris Green recalls, 'was blessed with an inspired team of architects led by Ronnie McIntyre. Glasgow Central [refurbished in 1985 with new entrances, a terrazzo, travel centre and 66-foot electronic train indicator], Queen Street and Aberdeen were lovingly restored – and they created striking modern buildings at Dundee, Falkirk High and Larbert.'

## The challenge of deregulated buses

In October 1986, with the economy on the up, John Moore, who had succeeded Nicholas Ridley, set BR the objective of cutting the PSO from £736 million to £555 million over three years. (Moore would in turn give way in June 1987 to the patrician Paul Channon. While Channon's two-year tenure at the DoT is best remembered for the aftermath of the Clapham train crash, the King's Cross fire and the Lockerbie air disaster, he worked well with Bob Reid and was supportive of the railway; on his watch the Settle & Carlisle would finally be reprieved.)

The financial challenge set by Moore was made tougher by the deregulation of bus services outside London, pushed through by his predecessor. This had a host of unintended consequences, notably the near-collapse of the UK bus manufacturing industry (Leyland's factory at Workington only having been kept going by orders from BR). Forcing the PTEs out of operating buses led them to take a greater interest in rail. Deregulation also led to the break-up of the National Bus Company into 70 businesses, and to management buyouts of these and their municipal counterparts. This in turn gave rise to the bus operators that from 1996 would operate rail franchises: Arriva, First Group, Go Ahead, National Express, Prism and Stagecoach.

Deregulation brought a direct challenge to interurban trains from National Express and Stagecoach, some of whose services were timetabled to exceed the speed limit. Provincial feared, though, that it might drive urban railways to the wall, with 25 lines reckoned under threat. But after an initial flurry of competition, mainly on routes where the bus was unchallenged, overall levels of service fell back and the Provincial railway, its quality at last starting to improve, became in many areas the reliable option.

## New techniques help grow the business

To grow the business, Provincial brought in consultants on product development. Joint timetabling work with InterCity produced a new, more integrated approach. Improved data on ticketing provided by the APTIS and PORTIS sales systems, the management accounting capability of CAPRI, and the forecasting capability of MOIRA helped identify what mattered in the business, and what did not. This information allowed informed decision-making on the train plan and calling patterns, and was instrumental in closing a few low-use stations in the Eastern sub-sector. Bob Reid also championed the ORCATS (Operational Research Computer Allocation Of Tickets to Services) revenue allocation system; on a route such as Doncaster-Hull, shared with InterCity, 'our share of ORCATS became the difference between winning and losing,' says Dick Fearn, then resources manager at Provincial North Eastern.

New trains and services were backed up by sophisticated marketing. David Prescott, then Marketing Manager in York, recalls, 'We were seen as a poor relation compared with InterCity, with much lower budgets, but it was a step change from the past. Strong branding was introduced, and a national local press campaign combining the benefits of bulk buying with the responsiveness of local management. Scenic lines promotion was expanded, building links with local authorities, National Parks and other stakeholders. A standardised format was developed, forming a base on which in time Community Rail blossomed. One campaign, still running today, is "Back a Winner by train", with Northern racecourses providing a free first bet. This generated business to locations and at times where capacity was not an issue – and Provincial sponsored a race of its own at Thirsk.'

Meanwhile cheap peak summer fares, which generated expensive-to-handle passenger volumes when some lines – notably to Skegness – were struggling to cope, were phased out. By 1989 higher fares were charged from May to September, offset by Railcards, with marketing redirected to filling empty seats.

## 32 Chapter 3: THE PROVINCIAL SECTOR: GATHERING SPEED, 1986-90

**TOP** The short-lived but ground-breaking local marketing exercise 'Wizzy the Lizard' branding for Cornish Railways as devised by Truro Area Manager Rusty Eplett in 1983. *Antony Christie*

### Local brands develop

ScotRail's success was echoed by other initiatives to develop local rail brands. Cornish Railways, launched in 1983 by Truro Area Manager Rusty Eplett, aimed to localise operation, property and engineering. Promotion of the county's railways – with a 'Wizzy the Lizard' emblem – generated some new business prior to the arrival of the Class 142 'Skippers'. Hubristically, extra – untimetabled – trains were run on the Plymouth-Penzance main line. Cornish Railways was absorbed by the Western Region's Plymouth area when divisional traffic managements were abolished. The experiment hastened the creation of a nationwide chain of profit centre managers – but firmly embedded within Provincial's disciplinary matrix.

**ABOVE** 'Midline' marketing material heralded the launch of the local Birmingham services in 1986. *British Railways Board*

'Midline' was a unified branding for the web of Birmingham-centred services stretching beyond the boundaries of West Midlands PTE. The Midland subsector created it to counter bus competition expected after deregulation; a logo was devised including the emblems and house colours of BR and the PTE, and in 1986 a DMU emerged from Tyseley depot in experimental 'Midline' livery. The reopened Snow Hill carried station signage involving blue Provincial branding stripes and a red lozenge. With the PTE preparing to relaunch itself as Centro, there were disagreements over a further 'Midline' logo. 'Midline' as a concept was eclipsed by Centro's corporate branding, and by the launch of Regional Railways the brand was discarded. (Its time would come under the guise of West Midlands Rail.)

There had never been a Welsh railway network, and the closure of every north-south line within Wales had left three unconnected routes running east to west; the nearest thing to a spinal route ran through the English cities of Shrewsbury and Hereford. Yet there was a political and emotional desire for a unified railway, and the concept had business potential. Hugh

**LEFT** Sidney Newey (left) and John Nelson (centre) both looking the part, with David Wharton-Street at the Provincial-sponsored Thirsk races in 1989. *David Wharton-Street*

Gould was appointed as an 'ear on the ground' in the Principality, then Edmonds gave John Davies responsibility for Wales, though as a manager rather than a full-fledged director. The arrangement did not survive Provincial's 'Organisation Simplification' of 1990, the team seeing 'little coherence in the Welsh railway production activity' despite a need for a 'strong focus for the Welsh identity' across profit centres. Davies stayed, but it would be 2001 before Wales gained a franchise of its own.

The success of Network SouthEast (NSE) was bound to prompt imitations, and in 1989 Network NorthWest (NNW) was launched, comprising Provincial's lines radiating from Manchester and Liverpool, together with Lancashire local services. NNW was a marketing construct, with a route map modelled on NSE's, but in May 1990 it was given flesh with a heavily publicised recast of the timetable.

Sadly, the exercise was a fiasco. More workings were diagrammed than there were crews available. Rolling stock was short, through the unreliability of the 'Pacers', 'Sprinters' being away for modifications and a lack of parts for ageing DMUs. Turnaround times were optimistic. The timetable collapsed, and Peter Leppard, Area Manager at Marylebone, was sent north to sort things out.

By contrast, TransPennine Express would prove an unqualified success and, like ScotRail, eventually become a franchise. Encouraged by John Edmonds, worked up under David Wharton-Street and launched in 1987, the brand gave a marketable identity to Provincial's interurban services, mainly along the Leeds-Manchester axis. Bravely, this was done before the 158s arrived, coinciding with major improvements to a service previously offered by tired locomotives and unappealing stock. Revenue surged, and further improvements followed. (The full story is told in Chapter 9.)

## Sidney Newey takes the reins

Despite the eclipse of the regions, the Board decided that a separate Anglia Region was necessary, and John Edmonds became its General Manager. Sidney Newey, hitherto GM of the Western Region, replaced him at Provincial on 19 October 1987 – and around 6.30 that morning Glanrhyd Bridge on the Central Wales line collapsed after flooding as the first train of the day was crossing it, leaving four people dead. Glanrhyd, the collapse of the Ness Bridge in 1989 in an exceptional tidal surge, and other severe weather incidents obliged Provincial to budget for divers to inspect bridges for scouring.

Under Sidney Newey the focus remained intense, but managers had a longer rein. One challenge for Provincial was two years of 10% growth as the economy peaked; another the continuing unreliability of 'Pacers' and some 'Sprinters', Provincial needing to retain 700 extra older vehicles as cover. These twin pressures of rising demand – 'the Ministry had been extremely sceptical about growth' – and poor availability came to a head for Newey during the 'dreadful' Friday evening peak, exacerbated by weekend travel. 'If you wanted to keep services going, you had to put something on; no matter how unsuitable, you took it.' He focused on maintaining morale until the corner was turned and, crucially, proposed to BR's Investment Committee the splitting of Class 155s to create the single-car 153, a life-saver for the most vulnerable lines by creating at a stroke 'twice the train' – though none have ever been allocated to Scotland.

From December 1987 rolling stock was allocated to the sectors, rather than the regions – the latter had had to find replacements overnight when the Class 155s were withdrawn temporarily because of unreliable doors. Reliability was not something Provincial's depot teams could completely control; Heaton broke the back of problems with the 'Pacers', only for contractors to deliver poor-quality engine overhauls. The depots' role reduced as less maintenance and refuelling were needed, and drivers moved out to major stations; achieving this at Birmingham New Street proved particularly taxing. 'You had to throw away all the old ideas of where train crew depots should be, inherited from steam practice,' recalls Gordon Pettitt. 'You had to organise and pay for new crew accommodation.'

Despite the glitches, the new generation of trains was revolutionising Provincial's offering. With DMUs able to run 1,600 miles before refuelling instead of 400, longer diagrams could be operated; unfortunately the small water tanks specified to keep train weights down did not supply the toilets for as long. New trains went where the business opportunities were greatest; Sidney Newey says, 'One of the great things about Provincial was that it was recognised that, despite there being some very pushy people, there were priorities the sector had to meet.'

## New services and links improve the offering

Well before the 158s, more ambitious diagrams offered new through routes and more intensive services – but the 158's 90mph maximum speed would permit even faster timings. Much was achieved simply by joining existing services end-on, both urban (notably at Birmingham New Street, easing congestion) and interurban (such as West Wales-Cornwall). Canton drivers began working through to Portsmouth, and

**34** *Chapter 3:* **THE PROVINCIAL SECTOR: GATHERING SPEED, 1986-90**

**ABOVE** No 158710 makes its debut at BREL Derby on 30 May 1990. *Colin J. Marsden*

**BELOW** A unique 12-car formation of Class 158s: the staff family day out special from Derby on 13 October 1990. Regional Railways' 90mph flagship train would transform the fortunes of many interurban services. *Steve Dentith*

Fratton men to Cardiff, achieving greater frequencies with the same manpower. From 1989 Inverness drivers could work through to Thurso, and vice versa. However, Sidney Newey recalls that prior to 1988 'the LMR had a policy of not teaching drivers the road over long distances; from Crewe to Cardiff you didn't go much beyond Hereford. The idea of keeping men and units together changed things; if there was any delay the driver simply brought his own train back.'

Some couplings proved over-ambitious, exporting delays from one route to another. Other opportunities depended on unbudgeted signalling upgrades. But between 1987 and 1991 train mileage increased 15% while basic costs per loaded train fell 25%. Heavily loss-making services were trimmed to release stock for the busiest routes, managers bowing to the 'overall good of the business'. With new trains came an incentive to keep them clean: in 1989 Provincial pioneered a training scheme at Neville Hill using interactive video. Within months passengers were rating train exteriors a plus, though interiors and particularly toilets still registered negatives (as they still do).

The first 158s were planned to offer dramatic improvements to timings, frequencies and comfort on selected routes with the May 1990 timetable, but with the programme 29 weeks adrift Sidney Newey started 'planning on the assumption that none will arrive'. It was 17 September 1990 before a 158 ran in service, between Glasgow and Edinburgh, and the next month before an entire route – Edinburgh-Aberdeen – benefited. And it would be Saturday 13 October, with Gordon Pettitt at the helm, before all staff involved with the introduction of the 158s took a family day out in a 12-car formation on a round trip from Derby.

Although the Government had earlier spurned a rolling programme of electrification, the PTEs promoted a steady extension of the wires (and the third rail) on commuter lines. The Department approved a new line to Stansted Airport in 1987, and two years later the connection to Manchester Airport. Provincial, unused to building new lines, had such a tight cash limit that – with backing from the Board – it insisted that the airport (which BR reckoned the main beneficiary) find the money. The rise of out-of-town shopping also created opportunities: Tyneside's MetroCentre gained its station in 1987 and Meadowhall – today South Yorkshire's third busiest station – in 1990.

## The MMC inquiry

In April 1988 Lord Young, Trade & Industry Secretary, referred BR's Provincial sector to the Monopolies & Mergers Commission. National Express had complained of the competition its Leeds-Manchester coaches faced from a TransPennine 'subsidised out of the public purse', but the investigation was part of a wider pattern. The MMC had produced a businesslike report on L&SE before its rebirth as Network SouthEast, and for Provincial the timing, during its most rapid period of growth, could not have been better. Sidney Newey orchestrated Provincial's response, with most spadework done by David Wharton-Street's Eastern team, which the MMC would note was just 32 strong. Mark Causebrook, heading the TransPennine business group, played a major part, with contributions from Dick Fearn on resources, David Prescott on journeys and fares, and Jeff Brown on the bottom line.

The importance of the MMC's report, published in February 1989, in underlining Provincial's credentials for further investment cannot be exaggerated. It presented the sector in a very favourable light, having been 'impressed by the enthusiasm and dedication of Provincial's management team'. That team was still very small, given the range of its activities; Midland was the largest sub-sector, with 54 staff, and Western, with 24 in Swindon, the smallest.

**ABOVE** The Provincial team at the Windermere Conference in 1989. *David Wharton-Street*

The report noted Provincial's bleak outlook on its formation, but showed that, while losses were still heavy, passenger numbers were up and costs had been reduced from four times revenue to 2.5 times.

Subsidy had been trimmed, while £123 million of the PSO was now going to sectors other than Provincial. Of the sector's costs, no less than £200 million was allowed for by the London Midland Region for services provided.

The MMC did have concerns. The costs of individual services were still unquantified. There were mismatches between traffic levels and stock provided on some routes: most East Coast local trains from

**Table 3.2: Monopolies & Mergers Commission Report, 1989**

| Activity | 1982 | 1988/89 |
|---|---|---|
| Income (real terms) | £136m | £195m |
| Operating Loss | £489m | £332m |
| Subsidy | £432m[1] | £384m[1] |
| Subsidy as % income | 49% | 24% |
| Market: Leisure | - | 57% |
| Commuting | - | 37% |
| Business | - | 6% |
| Income (turnover) | - | £736m[2] |
| Costs: Urban | - | £123m |
| Rural | - | £61m |
| Express | - | £60m |
| Overheads | - | £186m |

[1] 1986-1989/90
[2] 1987/88

Source: M&MC Report February 1989

Edinburgh had three cars when two (or even one) would suffice. It saw no need for BR's distinction between capital and revenue investment, or for wide geographical variations in fares; TransPennine's were lower at one end because of the LMR's historic 'low price, high volume' strategy and the cheap urban fares in PTE areas.

In December 1989 Cecil Parkinson, who had succeeded Paul Channon, set Provincial new objectives heavily influenced by the MMC. In a letter to the BR Chairman on 19 December 1989, he wrote:

'Over the last six years the Provincial Sector has been able to reduce costs, increase traffic, improve quality and charge more for it. Revenue has therefore increased in real terms. Subsidy including PTE payments has fallen from 75% of costs in 1983 to 65% in 1988/89. On the Board's own forecasts it should fall further to 57% by 1992/93. It will still be much higher on some service groups and it is clear that very large subsidies will be needed for the foreseeable future.

I expect the Board to increase services to meet growth whenever the incremental investment can be shown to earn the 8% return required. Cost Benefit Analysis should be carried out in conjunction with the DfT to help decide if capital grants can be justified on wider social and economic grounds.'

There was a modest sting in the tail: BR should by 1992/93 reduce the PSO by £20 million further than the £345 million already set.

The good news was that investment schemes could be based on the wider social and economic benefits that a rail service provided – a step change from the previous Holy Grail that all lines must be profitable. However, the problem was that the urban and interurban businesses were expanding fast, but lacked the extra resources to match the overcrowding that this was generating. Local authorities from Aberdeen to Plymouth, together with the PTEs, were pressing for more trains to provide more seats and expand services as the railway reaped the benefits of road congestion, better marketing and the arrival of new trains that were not a disincentive to travel. As these businesses represented 91% of the sector's income, their success was a virtuous financial outcome for regional railways as a whole.

By now, says Sidney Newey, 'the bottom line was under control. We were doing more with less, adding value to routes if the level of business justified opening for longer, for example' – such as Sunday opening once low-cost signalling had been installed. But all the objectives set would be blown away by the recession of 1989-93, total passenger mileage falling 12% and freight by 24%, though by contrast Provincial/ Regional Railways would hold steady (see Factfiles B and C).

By now reorganisation of Provincial into a chain of vertically integrated businesses was in the air as the Board pressed ahead with its Organising for Quality initiative (OfQ) – see the next chapter. Sidney Newey urged Bob Reid not to impose a further reorganisation on Provincial because it was already delivering a 'radical improvement in quality' and had gone through several rounds of change. But with the decision taken for OfQ to cover the whole of BR, he set in train the planning to bring it about. Sub-sector managers suggested to him that the sector be renamed Regional Railways, but the idea was not progressed.

## Gordon Pettitt arrives

In March 1990 Sir Bob Reid retired, having made the railway – and its Provincial sector in particular – far more confident. It was almost a case of 'The King is dead – long live the King', for his successor was … Sir Bob Reid. The former CEO of Shell was chosen by Cecil Parkinson, who had got to know him when Energy Secretary.

There was also change at Provincial: Gordon Pettitt, General Manager of the Southern Region, succeeded Sidney Newey, who moved to Headquarters. John Welsby, by now BR's Chief Executive, sounded him out as they crossed the concourse at Waterloo. Gordon Pettitt says, 'I was delighted. I did want to have done a Sector Director's job as well as having been a General Manager. I had been impressed by the changes made by my predecessors since sectorisation, and admired how the decline in regional services had been arrested by investment in new "Pacer" and "Sprinter" fleets and the introduction of the longer-distance interurban services.

'I took responsibility for Provincial on 8 May 1990, and a month later the Board announced that the regions were to be abolished, with the sectors taking full ownership of infrastructure and safe operation of the railway from April 1992. This reorganisation, Organising for Quality, was the largest and most challenging since nationalisation. For Provincial it meant preparing to take responsibility for 45% of BR's route miles, 59% of the stations and 37,000 staff from Penzance to Wick.

'I made immediate plans to visit substantial parts of all the Provincial profit centres' territories, travelling 15,700 miles by rail by the end of 1990. I had made a

*Chapter 3:* **THE PROVINCIAL SECTOR: GATHERING SPEED, 1986-90** 37

**ABOVE** The North West has always found itself short of rolling stock and has had to improvise with any options available. Here No 101676 has arrived into Manchester Piccadilly from New Mills Central on 1 May 2001 with a Northern Spirit Class 158 in the background. *Antony Christie*

practice of doing this in all my previous jobs, but it was only possible this time through the use of mobile phones, doing most of my office work on trains, and with a highly competent secretary, Dorothy Chiles, in Birmingham.'

Gordon Pettitt recalls, 'One early impression pointed out the enormous scope for development: standing at the platform end at Manchester Piccadilly in the evening peak and seeing a number occupied by a single "Pacer". The emptiness of it all, contrasting with the size of the city, made me realise there was a lot of work to be done.

'When in my first week plans were reported for a second Birmingham-Manchester motorway, I checked out InterCity's timings and frequencies and was alarmed how poor they were. Nor where Provincial was concerned did we seem to have an offer at all.

The "Pacers" and "Sprinters" had brought substantial improvements in productivity of resources, but linking diagrams across different lines of route resulted in a problem on one route being passed to another, particularly in the North West [this was the time of the Network NorthWest timetable collapse]; it was a step too far and was largely abandoned.

'Several of the PTEs (who paid us £100 million per annum) were refusing to pay their bills under Section 20, and £20 million was outstanding,' he says. 'My first meeting with them was very uncomfortable – they expected early improvement, and with good reason. And the major cause was the unreliability of the "Pacers". Their bus technology had not transferred well to the rail environment, with serious problems with brakes and gearboxes reducing availability to 50% on occasions.'

How Gordon Pettitt tackled this problem is described in Chapter 12. So too is the action he took to counter the continued non-arrival of Class 158s after receiving at BREL in his first week a delivery schedule that did not convince him. Meanwhile, he initiated procurement of the Hunslet Class 323 EMUs for the Birmingham Cross-City electrification and to replace elderly trains in Manchester. Provincial had been expected to place a follow-up order to NSE's 'Networkers', but when BREL upped the price he called their bluff.

In July 1990 Gordon Pettitt announced that the sector would be renamed 'Regional Railways' as it took up new responsibilities. And that November Margaret Thatcher was replaced by John Major, who had his own ideas about the future of the railway.

# Chapter 4
# REGIONAL RAILWAYS, 1990-97

*'Regional Railways has a firm, business-like sound to it. It is a better description [than Provincial], in two words, of the wide range of markets that the business serves.'*

**SIR BOB REID II**

**ABOVE** The first Class 158, No 158701, recently delivered to Derby in the new 'Express' livery in 1990. *David Wharton-Street*

## Creating Regional Railways

The transformation of BR into devolved and vertically integrated businesses, including Regional Railways, was worked up with enthusiastic support from Bob Reid I and II and driven from the Board by John Edmonds. But Regional Railways was Gordon Pettitt's baby, the brand taking effect from 3 December 1990 with the business taking on most of its responsibilities the following April.

'Between accepting the post and starting the job there were two things that I decided had to change, to reflect the fact that the Provincial sector was introducing new trains and new and faster services and opening new lines and stations,' says Gordon Pettitt. 'My first target was the name: "Provincial" seemed a totally misleading name for just under half of the national network, and dismissive towards Scotland, Wales and much of England, which the sector served. It just seemed utterly wrong. My preference was for Regional Railways and this was supported by the rest of my team. I didn't ask the BR Board; I just slipped a slide on the renaming of Provincial into a presentation I did for them on Organising for Quality.

'The second was the headquarters. While all the sectors had been located in London, it seemed totally inappropriate for Provincial. Furthermore I saw no case to justify a London office with its higher staff costs, bearing in mind the severe cuts in PSO. Birmingham, the UK's second city, was my first choice and the search for office space at the right cost became a top priority.'

Bob Goundry, appointed strategy manager, opened a 'bridgehead' office there in October 1990. 'I started with a fairly clean sheet,' says Gordon Pettitt. 'The big job was to create a vertically integrated railway concentrating on provincial matters for the first time ever, running trains over most of England, the whole of Wales and the whole of Scotland. And the difference from simply being a profit centre was huge. This was one of the most difficult jobs I ever had.'

Very early on he recruited a few hand-picked BR engineers to secure his infrastructure and S&T priorities. Old Provincial hands like Alec McTavish believe the sector would have had less of a 'hearts and minds' problem had it been able to do this earlier.

'Running the Provincial organisation meant responsibility for planning and finance, and I had to transfer that into a vertically integrated railway and set up a headquarters team.' Within weeks Gordon Pettitt identified most of the managers he wanted to head the sub-sectors, bringing them together at the Charing Cross Hotel in mid-July 1990, with some in post soon after. 'Everyone else was scrabbling for the best people, of course,' he recalls.

His team (see Table 4.1 overleaf) for delivering an 'utterly reliable railway' was a strong one, a blend of experience and youth – Mark Causebrook was just 36 – and experience. David Rutherford was recruited from Plessey Naval Systems as Finance Director 'to change all the financial systems so we could actually operate a vertically integrated railway'. And, crucially, Dr Paul King joined from the British Shoe Corporation in January 1991 as Planning and Marketing Director. A company doctor and former academic, he took 'a lot of persuasion' to come aboard, but the grasp he showed after just two days astounded Regional Railways' investment panel.

'We ended up with an organisation of 30,000 people,' says Gordon Pettitt. 'It was a huge managerial challenge because we were changing the railway from top to bottom. I appointed all the Headquarters team, and all the sub-sector managers, and approved their direct report appointments. The managers in profit centres were given full responsibility for costs and income; in many cases this meant appointing new financial managers.'

**RIGHT** Gordon Pettitt, Managing Director, Regional Railways. *British Railways Board*

**ABOVE** The Regional Railways Corporate Identity Manual was the creation of Gill Greatorex and was launched on 10 July 1992. This was the first time that local services had had their own corporate identity. *Author's collection/British Railways Board*

# Chapter 4: REGIONAL RAILWAYS, 1990-97

### Table 4.1: Regional Railways team, 1991-94

| Regional HQ | Director |
|---|---|
| **Managing Director** | |
| To August 1992 | Gordon Pettitt |
| Aug 1992-July 1993 | Jim Cornell |
| July 1993- April 1997 | Paul King |
| **HQ, 1991-94** | |
| Planning & Marketing | Paul King |
| Operations | John Mummery |
| Fleet | Tom Monkhouse |
| Infrastructure | Richard Bonham Carter |
| Finance | David Rutherford |
| Personnel | Bernard Westbrook |
| Total Quality | Martin Shrubsole |
| **Profit centres, 1991-94** | |
| Central | Mark Causebrook |
| North West | Chris Leah |
| ScotRail | Cyril Bleasdale |
| North East | David Wharton-Street (Aidan Nelson from April 1991) |
| South Wales & West | Theo Steel |

Chris Gibb, a less senior arrival, recalls: 'I decided to move [from Scotland] to what was being rebranded from "Provincial", and joined Theo Steel and John Pearse at Swindon. It was a very innovative organisation; that little team produced four managing directors, and had a big say in how the railway has developed. I was responsible for the Cardiff-Portsmouth and Cardiff-Manchester routes; I designed the timetable, planned how they were going to operate, drove the performance and drove the revenue. It was a great experience.

Gordon Pettitt had been given a lot of railways that didn't make financial sense, and he turned them into something we could be proud of. And what I as a middle manager was responsible for – infrastructure, stock allocations, timetabling and much more – would today be handled by four or five different companies.'

## Devolving the railway

Organising for Quality (OfQ), says John Welsby, was designed 'to get people down the line to "own" their businesses – something impossible when things were run from Euston. The success of the system was demonstrated fully to me when on one of my visits to a profit centre I started to quiz the director about details of the business. His response was fascinating: "This is my business and the detail has got nothing to do with you. I'm meeting my financial and quality targets and that's all you need to know." While not necessarily agreeing with him, it demonstrated clearly that profit centre directors were now seeing the business as theirs – one of the cultural changes we had sought.'

## Organising for Quality (OfQ)

Final BR organisation introduced January 1992:
- A vertically integrated national railway run on business lines
- A restructuring project, built on the earlier Sector Management model
- All BR infrastructure, rolling stock and staff transferred to the business sectors
- Sectors became responsible for running safe, efficient and reliable services
- BR Regions and HQ functional organisations (e.g. Operations) ceased to exist
- Trading rules allowed businesses to charge each other for services, e.g. trains, tracks, stations

For Gordon Pettitt, the essentials of OfQ were clear accountability, true devolution, the commitment of middle and junior management, practicality, and minimum disturbance to people. 'I tried to devolve the maximum I could. In the end we even split up the PSO – though we couldn't be accurate to the last penny.' In December 1990 he issued a 'Prospectus for Quality' committing Regional Railways to 'better reliability, punctuality and cleanliness' and smarter performance, setting 'demanding but realistic objectives to meet our

**LEFT** Nos 155303 and 15533 make an historic sight in Regional Railways livery approaching the Severn Tunnel at Pilning on 22 July 1990 working the 14.10 Portsmouth Harbour to Cardiff service. Shortly afterwards the units were split into single-car Class 153 units. *Martin Loader*

Chapter 4: **REGIONAL RAILWAYS, 1990-97** 41

**ABOVE** Showing the close links that were forged between Regional Railways sub-sectors and their PTE stakeholders, No 150207 passes Ashley with Merseyrail Regional Railways modified livery. *Martin Loader*

**ABOVE** On 28 March 1999 No 142068 passes Edale forming the 11.14 Sheffield to Manchester Piccadilly service in GMPTE livery linking it with Regional Railways. *Martin Loader*

customers' needs and expectations.' Key issues were strategic planning and deployment of rolling stock; reduction of infrastructure costs; definition of Quality Standards; coordination of training; transfer of best practice; clear design standards; updating of Conditions of Service and Employment; rewarding contributions to delivering targets and objectives; development of a people-focused communications strategy; and a changed attitude to safety for customers and staff. He also targeted the 'cost of failure to get things right', especially collision damage to rolling stock. Each profit centre was to have its own Quality Council.

Gordon Pettitt stipulated that 'as much as possible of the day-to-day marketing, planning and operation of the railway' was to be carried out by the profit centres. 'Cross-boundary activities, most notably Express services, will be managed by the profit centre owning the rolling stock used, which will operate from a single maintenance base.'

### Table 4.2: A family of railways

| Service | Location | Route miles | Stations |
|---|---|---|---|
| ScotRail | Glasgow | 1,674 | 311 |
| North East | York | 727 | 241 |
| North West | Manchester | 875 | 368 |
| Central | Birmingham | 1,121 | 297 |
| South Wales & West | Swindon | 728 | 251 |

Source: DTp Franchising Document, October 1992

On 18 May 1990, ten days after Gordon Pettitt's arrival, Provincial's Organisation Simplification team had reported. The need to keep driving down costs was reasserted, but little had been settled beyond what the profit centres would be – with the unwieldy Midland sub-sector split into Central and North West operating units. For Gordon Pettitt this was a prerequisite for OfQ: 'You couldn't manage an organisation the size of Midland in a vertically integrated railway.' The Regional Railways 'family' is shown in Table 4.2.

Splitting the Midland sub-sector created Central and North West, the later taking in two PTEs – Greater Manchester and Merseyside – with a tradition of rail commuting. The split – and especially making sense of Central's 'Barmouth to Yarmouth' reach – was a challenge. Matters were complicated by the LMR, together with S&T, which was in the throes of reorganisation post-Clapham – taking an extra year to join the new structure – and by North West's extensive involvement with the WCML, on which InterCity had primacy. Chris Leah at North West put together a talented management team, and opened BR's first one-stop recruitment centre in Manchester. He also sorted out the guards at Manchester Piccadilly, who had been 'holding the place to ransom'.

Mark Causebrook reckoned Central unmanageable as an operating unit, and found reaching agreements to get it up and running 'a nightmare'. A plus was the 'few key people' who knew their way around; a minus was that 'there wasn't any money for solving the problems'.

## Chapter 4: REGIONAL RAILWAYS, 1990-97

By privatisation, though, his buyout team could claim, 'We have transformed Central from a hotch-potch of left-overs with a heritage in four of the BR Regions into a company with cohesion and direction.'

### Exercising the new freedom

Regional Railways took on its railway functions from BR on 1 April 1991 – and would have just 374 days to focus wholeheartedly on its task before being confronted by the spectre and distraction of privatisation. It also took responsibility for its share of property assets. Provincial's budget had included 14% for 'general overheads' from BR's central services; these could now be reduced.

Gordon Pettitt formed an executive board with David Rutherford as Vice-Chairman, comprising the sub-sector heads and other key managers, which first met on 25 April. He told staff: 'The name Regional Railways reflects what we do in a far more positive way. It describes the new business perfectly – it is a name to be proud of and one that will be publicised nationwide in the coming months.'

A distinct identity, with Provincial's blue stripe predominant, was developed with the design company Lloyd Northover under the guidance of identity manager Gill Greatorex. ScotRail and the PTEs adopted variations in their own colours within the Regional Railways brand identity. Gordon Pettitt explains: 'We wanted the PTEs to have their branding because they were producing so much revenue for us,' and he stressed at the time, 'The corporate identity is a theme with variations, but the variations are preordained so as to create a coherent whole.' Stations were rebranded, and a bold livery featuring two horizontal bands – one of Oxford blue, one Cambridge – against a cream background appeared on rolling stock. Locos too were given the treatment after SW&W abducted a Class 37 from the engineers at Doncaster. For the passenger, the new branding was evident not only on literature (a fresh typeface, Joanna, was used), stations (with new signage and a redesigned standard waiting shelter) and the exteriors of trains, but also – crucially – in the carriage interiors, with a new upholstery moquette called 'Spot'.

Alex Green, Director of Operations North West, recalls the enthusiasm created. 'At last we had a railway to run, with a sense of ownership. To counter overcrowding, the team went hunting and came back with retired Clacton Electrics and Class 31s and 37s with Mark II coaches – all repainted in the smart new Regional Railways livery. We cut out over 100 train crew diagrams, saving £3.5 million a year. Quality standards were tackled, with performance nudged upwards to reach all but one of the reliability and

**BELOW** Regional Railways' executive board. Back row, standing left to right: Bob Goundry, Wendy Tobitt, Aidan Nelson, Paul King, Tom Monkhouse, Martin Shrubsole, Richard Bonham-Carter, Mark Causebrook. Front row sitting: left to right Chris Leah, Bernard Westbrook, Cyril Bleasdale, Gordon Pettitt, David Rutherford, John Mummery, Theo Steel. *British Railways Board*

*Chapter 4:* **REGIONAL RAILWAYS, 1990-97** **43**

**LEFT** A beautifully presented pair of Regional Railways Class 31s – Nos 31439 and 31465 – with a rake of Mark II coaches approach Abergele with the 07.39 Holyhead to Crewe service on 9 August 1995. *Martin Loader*

**BELOW** Regional Railways inherited many magnificent – if expensive – structures, such as ScotRail's iconic Forth Bridge. *Alex Green*

**ABOVE** Showing the importance placed on traffic from Manchester Airport, Regional Railways North West applied a special livery to No 309624 in partnership with the airport authorities. *Alex Green*

**ABOVE** Another technical marvel that has to be maintained from the farebox is the Royal Albert Bridge across the River Tamar near Plymouth. *Alex Geeen*

timekeeping targets. Cleaning targets were achieved, and on-train fare collection reached an all-time high.' One practice Gordon Pettitt himself set out to tackle was the amount of shunting of multiple units in depots, with a heavy toll in damage to stock. 'I had a big purge on this, because it lost units to service and increased our costs.'

Controlling its own finances subject to the PSO, Regional Railways could hire staff specifically to serve the customer. Gordon Pettitt believed travellers would stick to their cars unless offered equal standards of comfort and amenity: adjustable seats, carpets, radio … and better service. OfQ pushed up retail staffing at a time of falling revenue across BR – heightening pressure for further savings, especially in platform staff, which were delivered between 1992 and 1994. Regional Railways also pioneered an incentive scheme for train conductors to collect more fares; this proved very successful, and a handy boost to revenue. The introduction of penalty fares also had a major impact on ticketless travel, and consequently on revenue, on the routes where they were applied.

The end of the regions brought the infrastructure engineers closer to the operating managers – and to the passenger. Regional Railways inherited some of the most challenging parts of the network: its highest summits at Druimachdar, Corrour and Ais Gill; exposed coastal railways in the West Cumbrian, Cambrian Coast and Ardrossan lines; mighty structures, of which the Forth Bridge was the most notable; and huge listed

## Chapter 4: REGIONAL RAILWAYS, 1990-97

ABOVE The North Wales line was still limited to 75mph running because of the cost of moving out-of-date semaphore distant signals, at a time when there were no funds to resite them for 90mph braking. *Adrian Putley*

stations (see Factfile G7). It also inherited vastly different levels of permanent way manning, there having been no incentive to keep it down when regional civil engineers' salaries depended on their payroll. Richard Bonham Carter aimed at 28 staff per 'Equated Track Mile' – a formula based on weight and frequency of traffic – finding actual levels varying line by line from 24 to 84. Meanwhile higher speeds were sought for the new, lighter trains, especially on interurban routes. David Hunt, Welsh Secretary, announced at the North Wales launch of the 158s that Crewe-Chester would be upgraded to 90mph. Chris Gibb got most LMR parts of the North & West line up to 90mph (the Great Western stretches already were) on the basis that 'if we could save a single 158 through line speed improvements – which we did – it was worth it.'

Despite the recession, Regional Railways increased its income in 1991 by 4.2%. Interurban receipts rose 6.9% as the 158s finally showed their mettle. PTE services performed strongly, but rural routes felt the chill. Costs were kept 6.3% below budget; it was a rule of thumb for Pettitt that railway costs inevitably rose by 4% more than inflation, so it was necessary each year to reduce them that much just to stand still. He applied this as much to the cost centres that had achieved major economies as to those yet to deliver them.

### 'Is there a better way?'

In 1991 the Treasury froze new rail investment, BR complaining that it was being 'held accountable for the sudden and recent deterioration in the economy'. Planned investment in Regional Railways totalling £116 million in 1992/93, £55 million in 1993/94 and £129 million in 1994/95 – mainly for new trains – would go undelivered.

This further squeeze led Gordon Pettitt to consider the need for a different type of settlement with Government. 'We were stuck in an existing arrangement under which, every three years, the Secretary of State said to us, "Please run the railway as in 1974, as far as regional services are concerned." I wanted a greater clarity in what Government wanted us to do. Regional Railways was beginning to show major reductions in cost, but also a big increase in business. I felt none of that was being recognised because of the general objective of "get the money down, then take off another £20 million". I wanted us to get over to Government what Regional Railways was achieving and how a general reduction in the PSO – which forced us to do silly things like cutting services to offset closures that could not be achieved – was not the right way ahead.' Moreover, the Board itself was starting to seek a less damaging alternative to short-term cost-cutting.

'We were faced with making cuts as we were starting to generate new revenues; on interurban there were very encouraging signs of growth. On urban services, the PTEs specified what was wanted;

meeting the peak requirements settled how many vehicles we used. I wanted to present the Secretary of State with a picture of Regional Railways as it was, the potential it had and the areas where we needed their decision on whether we continued with the level of support they could give. I wanted them to start directing what that level of support should be. InterCity had a profit motive; Network SouthEast were close to covering their costs. I wanted something which they might want and we could provide. We'd got down to the bare bones on rural lines – one shift and one turn and you made the best of it. We wanted the Government to understand what making further cuts would involve. As it was, we were going to start cutting where growth was possible.

'We weren't asking for more money. We were telling the client they had to make choices and giving them information on which to make them. We weren't trying to define network size; we were telling them facts and figures, and network size should follow from that. This is the big difference with Beeching: we were proposing to help them reach decisions on facts when they had previously been in the philosophical game.'

## Paul King's strategic review

Gordon Pettitt commissioned from Paul King a 'strategic review' of routes, services and products to study cost structures and investment, and recommend strategic options for consideration by the Board. It was overseen by a group comprising Pettitt, King, David Rutherford, Richard Bonham Carter, Chris Leah, Bernard Westbrook and Charles Brown, director of BR's policy unit. Paul King was determined to identify the relative profitability of each service group and how this might be improved through cost savings, revenue enhancement, investment and, if still unprofitable, by including the social benefits not captured in revenue. Management consultants – Mercers – were hired to carry out an in-depth analysis, with Regional Railways personnel seconded to form working groups. Their report met the requirements with great clarity. Initially the Central sector was analysed – staff costs at Etruria and Longport stations being found to exceed their takings – then the analysis was extended to the whole of Regional Railways.

On 19 May 1991 Paul King presented the report to Regional Railways' management conference, and its findings were dramatic: for more than 1,000 route miles out of 5,618, income from fares did not even cover the costs of crewing, fuelling and cleaning the trains, let alone train ownership costs, infrastructure, signalling, station staff, depreciation and overheads.

Paul King established that in a 'resource-led' railway, new trains must be deployed where they would earn the most revenue, not 'trundling round Lincolnshire'. He looked more closely at the highest-cost routes – most of them lengthy rural lines – and undertook, in Gordon Pettitt's words, 'quite a lot of surgery'.

Paul King says: 'Most of my work had been as a company doctor, in loss-making businesses. The first step is to understand what your products are and whether they are profitable or loss-making. It was not possible from any normal set of railway accounts to answer that question. The Strategic Review was to ascertain the profit- and loss-ability of particular services. The fascinating thing is that when we finished, someone said, "Really, you ought to have a look at Beeching." I got Beeching out, and his maps of what ought to be axed almost exactly coincided with our worst loss-makers. [Compare also the conclusions of the McNulty Report 20 years further on.]

'The conclusions were desperately simple: Regional Railways should concentrate on interurban services and those that could contribute to a reduction in urban road congestion. Rural and other heavy loss-makers absorbed a disproportionate and unwarranted share of grant, and it would get worse as car ownership increased. There was a strong argument that the worse congestion became, the value of congestion-busting went up. But with rural, the argument goes the other way. It was all about population density; trains are not a sensible method of transport in lightly populated areas.

**BELOW** Manpower levels are still high on some rural lines, but Network Rail now has a funded programme to eliminate all such unnecessary infrastructure – as at Poppleton in North Yorkshire. But at least the station canopy has been modernised. *Dennis Lovett*

# Chapter 4: REGIONAL RAILWAYS, 1990-97

'Once you could see where we were, what was a realistic level of improvement? What cost can you reduce through efficiency? How much can you reduce costs by investing? When you've finished all this, you've pulled every lever to make it better and you're left with the question for Government: "What do you want to buy, because this is what it costs, and why are you buying it?"'

## The benefits from relieving congestion, the costs of rural and Paul King's formula

The first potential benefit for Government was that rail was relieving congestion, for example by shipping commuters into Birmingham. 'We had a large meeting with the Department where they assembled all their economists to help answer the question, "What's congestion-busting worth?" They didn't have any specific information about the cost of road congestion outside London. We did get some numbers, and my recollection is that it was something like 50p to £1 per journey – but to make economic sense our urban services needed a subsidy of £2-£3 per journey.

'The second benefit was rather more fuzzy. It was to provide a journey on which people have come to rely. People's lives have been built around getting on the train to go wherever, and if you take it away their lives are affected: the hardship argument. We did the numbers on how much the Government would have to pay for each journey to make the rural services cover all their costs. The answer came out somewhere between £17 and £28 in 1992 prices – a thumping, enormous sum of money.'

All this was presented to rail minister Roger Freeman and the Board. But, says Paul King, the Government's mind was by then on privatisation and 'the study went into the long grass'. Yet, he adds, 'it could have articulated the shape and nature of the franchises.

'The analysis of the profitability of the service groups started by looking at the surplus left after vehicle running costs had been deducted from passenger revenue earned per vehicle. In Table 4.3 this is called GM1. For most Regional Railways interurban services this surplus was able to cover the cost of owning/leasing the vehicle, but was almost never enough to pay for track, stations and signalling. For most of the other services the surplus was negative, as shown in the chart.

'As vehicle ownership and operating costs were broadly similar, the focus must be on using the vehicles where they are most productive. The key analytical tool used was to break down revenue per vehicle into the drivers as shown in the formula

Revenue per vehicle = Price (pence per passenger mile) x Load Factor (passengers per vehicle) x Vehicle Utilisation (miles per vehicle)

**Table 4.3: Profitability framework**

Structural characteristics make it difficult for segments to be profitable without grant support

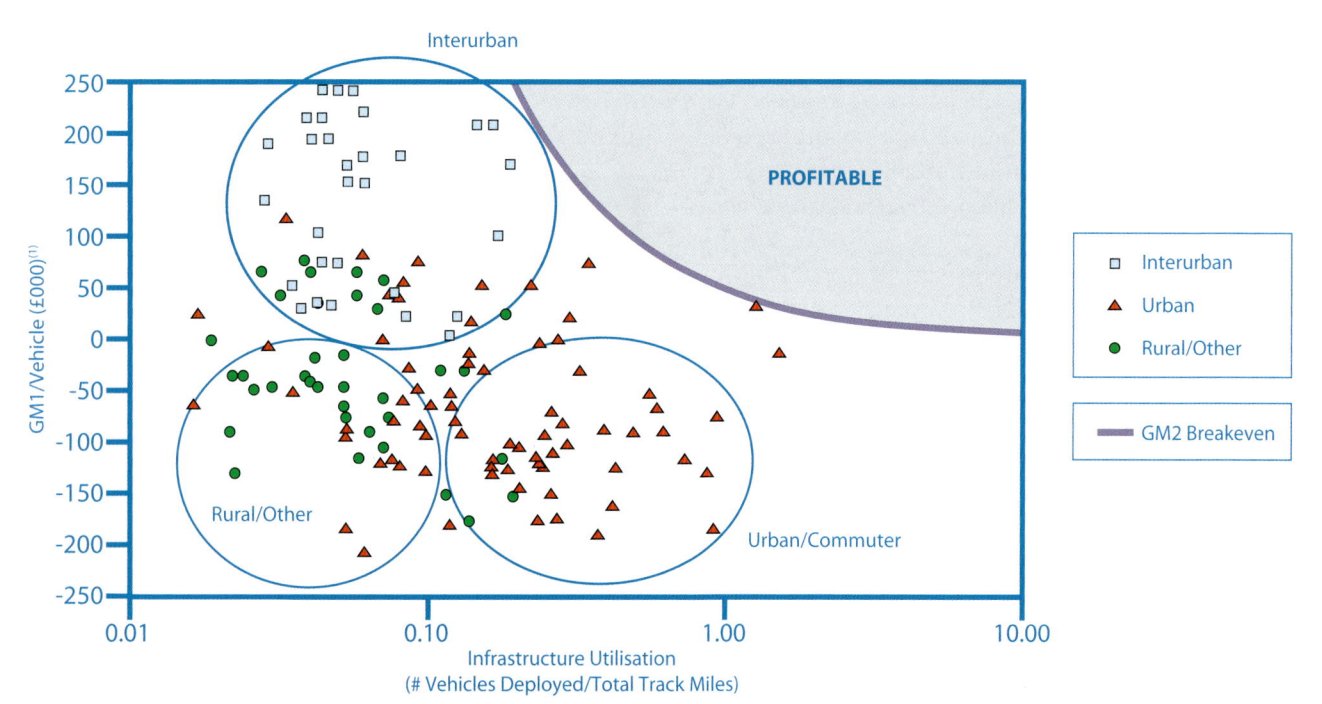

(1) Prediction based on loading, speed and utilisation

'To increase revenues requires a balancing act,' Paul King explains. 'For example, for urban services, run services in the peak yielding higher prices and load factor but poor vehicle utilisation, or run services all day with good vehicle utilisation but low load factors and lower average prices.' The position of Regional Railways by service type is shown in Table 4.4.

This formula captures all the essentials of efficient train operation, and was invaluable in the competition to allocate 12 Class 158s that had been kept as a float while

**ABOVE** No 158870, sporting its 'Western Mail' livery, passes Cockwood Harbour at a time when 'Alphaline' was deploying Class 158s in the West Country. *Antony Christie*

build faults were repaired. Gordon Pettitt set tough criteria – one new vehicle for five old ones, earnings per vehicle and per seat versus costs, and empty stock miles – and managers responded by running every possible stock working as a scheduled service, some surviving to this day.

The big winner was SW&W, with an innovative Cardiff-Bristol-Basingstoke-Waterloo service connecting with Eurostar and a £99 round-trip fare to Paris or Brussels. Peter Field, running what became South West Trains (SWT), did not want an interloper in Waterloo, and based his objection on ORCATS raiding. However, the service had been designed with pick-up/set-down-only calls in sensitive places and not stopping at Salisbury – the only trains not to call there – and SW&W prevailed. The test run doubled as an impromptu 60th birthday party for Pettitt, and on 16 January 1995 the service hosted a 'Gateway to Europe' VIP awayday; guests left Swansea on an 'Alphaline' 158 at 06.48, spent a brief time in Brussels, and were back in Swansea at 23.27. The service built after a slow start, and is now operated by SWT as Bristol-Waterloo.

### Table 4.4: Drivers of GM1 profitability

**Only Interurban makes a profit at GM1, due to its high vehicle loading and utilisation.**

**Drivers of GM1 Profitability**

|  | Average For Regional Railways | | |
| --- | --- | --- | --- |
|  | Interurban | Urban | Other Routes |
| (I) Loading – People per vehicle | 23 | 14 | 14 |
| (II) Utilisation | | | |
| IIa   Speed – Miles/Hour | 51 | 32 | 33 |
| IIb   #Hours Operated/Year | 2,940 | 2,470 | 3,212 |
| (III) Price – Pence/Mile | 9.5 | 9.2 | 9.4 |
| Revenue/Vehicle/Year (£K) | 321 | 103 | 134 |
| GM1 Costs/Vehicle/Year (£K) | (191) | (136) | (190) |
| GM1 Profits/Vehicle/Year (£K) | 130 | (33) | (56) |

## Chapter 4: REGIONAL RAILWAYS, 1990-97

### Driving costs down and innovation forward

Meanwhile, Regional Railways drove down costs. Andy Pitt, Marketing Manager at SW&W and later Managing Director of SWT, saw Regional Railways as 'a very low overheads organisation which would seek to make savings in almost every area before taking the easy approach of reducing the train service. It was perfectly possible to reduce costs while improving product quality and growing the market; cost reduction did not necessarily result in an overall quality loss. And when you thought you had done it all, if you still kept scraping the bottom of the barrel you would find savings. We kept thinking we were never going to pluck the rabbit out of the hat again, but we always did.' Pitt also remembers Pettitt explaining why the final tranche of 158s had been transferred to NSE's Waterloo-Exeter route: 'He didn't like it, but had no choice because we simply did not have the money.'

Under Mark Causebrook, Central rationalised train crew depots, operating more reliable services with fewer drivers as they no longer booked on before travelling to the station where their train was waiting. (An unintended consequence was a vigorous ASLEF branch at Birmingham New Street, which later managements would seek to weaken by encouraging drivers to book on at Coventry, Leamington Spa or Wolverhampton.) Between 1992 and privatisation Central slimmed its fleet from 546 vehicles to 342, closed 17 depots and reduced train crew from 1,541 to 1,133 – while cutting train mileage by just 4%. And across Regional Railways, the concentration of maintenance on a few specialist depots heightened reliability.

Despite the squeeze, devolution of responsibility to cost centres did facilitate small projects; ScotRail's electrification of the North Berwick branch showed what could be done for under £1 million. Pettitt

**LEFT** When Regional Railways ran out of funding for its final batch of 30 Class 158s, NSE converted them into a new Class 159 fleet and maintained them from a new Salisbury Depot. No 159003 is seen at Oborne near Sherborne, Dorset. *Martin Loader*

**BELOW LEFT** 'Heritage' EMU No 305502 is seen at North Berwick in March 1998. It was one of many variants of rolling stock that helped to keep the newly electrified North Berwick line running. Regional Railways electrified it for just £1 million to release DMUs to other routes. The 10-mile Windermere branch is to be electrified in 2016 for £16 million. *Alex Green*

**BELOW RIGHT** Class 90s and DVTs with Mark III coaches were brought in to assist on the North Berwick branch when rolling stock became in very short supply throughout ScotRail in 2004/05. *Jim Dorward*

**ABOVE** Despite chronic unreliability, Class 141s were still being used on Regional Railways North East in 1997. No 141119 runs along the Stainforth & Keadby Canal at Crowle on 31 May 1997 forming the 10.03 Doncaster to Scunthorpe service, just a year before the unit was exported to Iran. *Martin Loader*

explains: 'As the fleet size reduced, the amount of traffic was going up. We had to make carriages out of nothing. Electrifying to North Berwick was as much about releasing DMUs for use elsewhere.' The same logic lay behind the emergence of the Class 153s from mid-1991, reducing costs on the lines they operated, with every single 153 freeing a two-car unit for service elsewhere – or sending a heritage DMU to the scrapyard.

Regional Railways inherited the rolling stock quadruple whammy that had plagued Provincial. Its heritage DMUs were unreliable and required unbudgeted maintenance because they were supposed to have been withdrawn. The 'Pacers' were still far from reliable. Deliveries of Class 158s and 323s were running late, and the new trains frequently had to be sent back for rectification. The heritage units drafted in to cover their diagrams were unreliable… All this at a time of rising demand despite the economic climate, which brought pressure to lengthen trains or augment the timetable. However, the Network NorthWest fiasco had shown the risks of overpromising, and less dramatic problems were encountered with a re-timetabling centred on Birmingham.

### Launching new routes

Regional Railways selectively carried forward Provincial's development of longer routes that the new generation of DMUs could handle. The ideal thing for a modern unit was to travel as far as possible in one crew's turn. 'Trains earn while moving,' Gordon Pettitt told his planners, 'so you string places together.' 'Concatenation' also increased revenue by creating new through journey opportunities. Barmouth to Yarmouth was never a runner, but SW&W did introduce through trains between Milford Haven and Penzance. The concept would outlive Regional Railways in services such as Brighton-Great Malvern.

Routes and workings were also picked up that InterCity found uneconomic. Regional Railways was better placed to run trains from, say, Penzance and Holyhead at times when InterCity could earn more money elsewhere. Business was attracted, costs were kept down by running shorter trains, Regional Railways' profile was raised … and InterCity saved money when forced to look for cuts. 'Crewe to Holyhead was marvellous,' Gordon Pettitt recalls. However, a foray by SW&W into Paddington with a late-evening service from Cardiff caused ructions at Headquarters.

The connection to Stansted, opened in 1991, was hailed by John Major's Transport Secretary Malcolm Rifkind – just before the Treasury's investment freeze – as an 'aperitif' for other new lines. Its major flow was to Liverpool Street, but a north-to-east curve gave Central access to a third, short airport platform. Sluggish demand while the airport caught on led to the original service from, Birmingham being replaced by a weekly 'parliamentary' working from Cambridge. In time an hourly service was restored, and it is now

## Chapter 4: REGIONAL RAILWAYS, 1990-97

**ABOVE** The award-winning Manchester Airport station was financed by the airport and operated by Regional Railways. Opened in May 1994, it immediately became a flagship station with airline standards of customer service. *Austin-Smith:Lord Architects*

**RIGHT** The new team of specially selected staff for the new Manchester Airport station won a Best Kept Station award in 1995. *Alex Green*

proving its value – Cambridge-Stansted has gone half-hourly.

When the £27 million Manchester Airport link opened in 1993, Regional Railways North West (RRNW) went for quality. Alex Green allowed Area Manager Barry Cole – to the horror of the personnel office – to select staff irrespective of seniority or grade, on their ability to offer 'some of the most inspiring customer service I have seen'. The new team set their own dress code, and the conductors were quarantined at the newly created depot to maintain team standards. 'On Opening Day,' says Alex Green, 'everyone proudly wore full uniform; passengers were greeted with a smile and a proffered luggage trolley, and staff waved goodbye from the platform.'

Nor was Regional Railways content to operate just an out-and-back service from Piccadilly. Such trains did run – some working on to Crewe from 1995 – but TransPennine Express services were extended from Piccadilly to the airport, together with trains from Preston and beyond that previously terminated at Victoria. A third platform was added and recently a fourth, and Manchester Airport station now handles more than 3 million passengers a year. Metrolink has arrived, and there will be an interchange there with HS2.

### The 158s start to pay off

Even before the Class 158s had achieved full reliability, they were raising morale among passengers and staff alike. Wendy Tobitt, Regional Railways' Public Affairs Manager, recalls: 'They were unique trains at the time, with external and internal designs integrated so there were seats at every window and the windows were low enough to see out of easily. Colour schemes for the carriage interior, from the carpets to the seat covers, internal paintwork and the illustrations at the carriage ends were all carefully chosen. This attention to detail, along with air-conditioning, high-backed seats and better legroom, at-seat trolley service and more luggage space, combined to make the passengers' experience so much more comfortable than previous trains. The exterior design was streamlined, and the external paintwork designed to complement the interiors. This was "InterCity" quality for Regional Railways passengers.

'The sense of pride (mixed with relief) when they eventually arrived into service was tangible. From maintenance depot engineers to booking office staff, everyone was proud that Regional Railways had rolling stock to deliver an "utterly reliable railway". The Class 158s became "remarkably successful" because people enjoyed travelling on them.'

The public's response to these faster and better trains encouraged Provincial, then Regional Railways, to raise fares when a service was improved instead of simply applying BR's across-the-board increases every January; changes started to be made for individual routes in May and September. Regional Railways introduced a simplified fare structure in September

1992 (ScotRail the following January), tackling anomalies highlighted by the MMC, and others stemming from BR's National Fare Structure of 1985.

Growth in road traffic now began to fall behind that of the economy, a trend that would continue for more than two decades (except in the North East, where demand for rail travel remains soft). The groundwork laid by Provincial and improvements delivered by Regional Railways contributed to that trend by offering more of the public more of a choice. Gordon Pettitt saw an opportunity to win over frustrated motorists; the strategy began with getting the basics of railway operation right, then congestion hotspots – notably the Severn Bridge – were identified, and train service improvements to circumvent them heavily publicised.

In May 1991 InterCity ran a special train from Edinburgh to Glasgow Central via Carstairs to preview the extension of some ECML services. Malcolm Rifkind predicted competition between routes 'not only on service and frequency but on speed and price'. ScotRail the same month staged a record-breaking run between Waverley and Queen Street by a pair of the new 158s in just 32 minutes 9 seconds, at an average 88mph and a maximum 107mph (a log of this journey is included in Factfile D2). The Transport Secretary's comments sparked media speculation about a price war between routes, but the deeper forces of impending privatisation were at play.

## The Passenger's Charter

BR had for some time – with prodding from Government and user groups – been releasing information about punctuality and reliability; as early as 1981 Peter Parker inspired a 'Commuter's Charter' for London services. BR's 1983 Corporate Plan set targets for carriage cleaning and enquiry bureau response times. By 1989 Provincial was publishing standards for punctuality, cancellations, cleaning, booking office queues and answering times. There were no published standards for train loadings, and the MMC encountered many complaints of overcrowding. In addition, train cleaning was short of target, and 23% of calls to enquiry bureaux were not answered in time, or at all.

Gordon Pettitt watched closely Provincial's monthly 'customer perception monitor' carried out with 5,000 passengers by external consultants. In September 1990 two positives were showing – ease of purchasing a ticket, and external cleanliness of vehicles – but there were 11 negatives, the worst being train toilets (-23%), fares (-20%) and information at stations about punctuality (-16%). Pettitt's 'Prospectus for Quality' issued with the launch of Regional Railways raised the bar. It echoed the Board's commitment to Total Quality Management: spending more time on planning to 'get it right first time' to avoid the greater cost of correcting errors, and putting the customer first. The objectives set were: establish the primacy of the customer, value people, and foster a commitment to excellence, enterprise, initiative and innovation. Operations and retail staff were brought together, ironing out problems like poor station work delaying trains, and public address systems were installed on stations and trains, followed by indicators.

The candour with which these messages were driven home is illustrated by this 1992 mission statement from Regional Railways North East: 'RRNE is a company that is only just beginning to understand that its very survival will depend crucially upon its ability to serve its customers better. The realisation has dawned that a quality company is one managed by people who are determined rather than simply enthusiastic, and skilled rather than just competent.'

All this meant that when John Major launched his Passenger's Charter that May, Regional Railways was already getting up to speed. Introduction of the Charter – a spin-off from the Citizen's Charter of the year before – owed much to a perception in Whitehall that the railway was resisting public pressure for better service. This was strange, as the Citizen's Charter drew heavily from what BR was already doing. The Passenger's Charter set targets for enquiry bureaux and ticket offices; carriage cleaning; overcrowding; and punctuality. The ratio of passengers to seats on any

**BELOW** The train crew (on the left) with traction inspector and manager demonstrate a feeling of satisfaction after the Class 158 record-breaking 32-minute run from Glasgow Queen Street to Edinburgh Waverley at an average speed of 88mph. Nos 158708 and 158710 were specially prepared for 6 May 1992. *Don Martin*

train was not to exceed 135% on sliding-door trains and 110% on slam-door; standing time was not to exceed 20 minutes. Regional Railways' punctuality targets were confirmed: 90% of interurban trains to arrive within 10 minutes of the booked time, and urban trains within 5 minutes, and 99% of advertised trains must run. Achieving some of these targets, notably for punctuality on interurban services, would require heroic improvements in performance, but that was what ministers expected. Moreover, while the media gave Major's Charters a patronising reception, they struck a chord with the public. And in January 1993, as the first targets took effect, Passenger's Charter delay compensation payments were introduced, with an entitlement to redress.

The Charter, says Chris Gibb, 'forced the railway to collate and publish performance statistics, which it hadn't before, and obliged us to establish teams to handle customer contacts. Regional Railways embraced all this. The result was that we were very close to customers' needs in respect of timetables, fares, trains and stations. Between 1991 and 1994 we had our hands on most of the levers to improve customer satisfaction, even if we had little funding. On Cardiff-Manchester I sacrificed a clock-face timetable to meet the needs of commuters and schoolchildren along the route – e.g. Hereford and Shrewsbury – who needed services at specific times.' This also optimised the revenue:costs ratio, and has been retained to this day.

The sectorised railway proved its responsiveness early in 1992 when, after floods closed the line from Newport into Gloucester, engineers constructed a temporary station at Over, 2 miles from the city centre, in a week. This enabled commuters and students from Chepstow and Lydney to take their usual trains, then complete their journeys by bus.

## A brief moment of vertical integration

Weeks before the launch of the Passenger's Charter, the OfQ reorganisation was completed with the winding up of the London Midland Region and the transfer of S&T functions. In a short time, Regional Railways had transformed itself from a business planning unit with 150 staff to an integrated railway operator with 36,323. Most were in civil engineering (10,058), then operations (9,186, including 4,372 'front-end train crew'), retail (8,015) and S&T engineering (2,999). Some functions that Regional Railways inherited had ground to make up. There were 614 mechanical signal boxes … and not a single power box in the entire Central sub-sector. First-generation colour-light signals, particularly in the North West, were obsolescent, and several major resignallings had been held up by BR's continuing distinction between capital and revenue investment. Rationalisation at Perth was delayed until 1992/93 despite evidence that it would pay for itself within seven years. There was also a huge maintenance backlog, which David Wilkinson tackled with the sector's first designated S&T teams.

Major investments remained scarce; a remodelling at Ely in 1992 involving a month-long blockade was one of few to impact on Regional Railways. Another was the ground-breaking Sandhills IECC, finished in 1993, controlling Merseyrail's entire third-rail network. 'Sandhills was a quite remarkable beast,' says Chris Leah. 'We had the signallers and the operations guys sitting in the same room, totally integrated. When it opened, reliability went up to 94%.'

Even with vertical integration, strategic breakthroughs involving S&T could prove elusive. At ScotRail, says Jim Summers, 'we and the Derby Research boys tried to make the case for a large signalling centre at Stirling, to be a control centre as well – just as Network Rail is now trying to do. I wanted to move the whole HQ operations staff, and run Scottish operations with about 50 people. Unfortunately that did not sit well with the separation of sector assets, and there was a land deal at Stirling where political pressures played a part. An opportunity was lost to move us cheaply out of Glasgow, and to streamline operations.'

There were downsides to every asset having to be owned by a sub-sector. The Barry-Bridgend line, today due for electrification, was of marginal interest to Freight and could have closed because nobody put up a business case for it; the line through Melksham was nearly lost for a similar reason. Edinburgh Waverley came close to forfeiting some of its through tracks

**LEFT** Semaphore signals at Stirling survived until resignalling in 2013. *Alex Green*

because InterCity did not need them, and if Regional Railways could run a service with a signal box switched out, Freight had to pick up the cost or it would close. Anything not needed by a BR business was effectively redundant: Pettitt even found himself negotiating with BR Solicitors over the amount of their time that Regional Railways needed.

To mark the milestone of vertical integration, a sponsored supplement in the *Daily Telegraph* reviewed Regional Railways' achievements since its emergence from the chrysalis of Provincial, and looked ahead to a decade of progress, particularly in signalling: integrated control centres planned for Birmingham, Cardiff, Edinburgh, Leeds and Manchester to supplement Yoker and the imminent Sandhills. However, it would take another 20 years to get a resignalling plan for many interurban routes. Having taken stock of OfQ, Gordon Pettitt felt it prudent to observe, 'No business can ever say, "This is the last change."'

Next day, 7 April 1992, Sir Bob Reid II formally opened Regional Railways' Birmingham headquarters. Meridian accommodated 340 staff, most brought from London, Derby and Crewe over the previous two months. Gordon Pettitt paid tribute to the effort put in across the business during OfQ, saying, 'Some people have been doing two or even three jobs, and I am aware of the strain this has caused.'

## The decision to privatise
On 9 April Britain went to the polls. The Conservatives were committed to privatise the railways but, as John Major was generally expected to lose, the industry was not seriously unsettled – though Gordon Pettitt and his team were prepared for the possibility. Pettitt himself had for some time seen privatisation as likely, telling managers at the start of 1992, 'Investment is coming now, and I don't want to see discussions on ownership slowing that.' A late swing gave the Tories a fourth term, and John Major a mandate to privatise. And six weeks later the new Transport Secretary, John MacGregor, published his privatisation White Paper.

The voters' decision came as Regional Railways brought the service it offered them to its apogee – in Christian Wolmar's words, 'just as BR had got its act together'. With operations and engineering integrated at sub-sector level, line speed improvements to make the most of the 158s were teased out of more routes – not just offering faster trains but also enabling them to cover more mileage. Chris Gibb is proudest of the 1992 timetable: 'Our resource utilisation was light years ahead – down to giving our Portsmouth trains 37 minutes at Fratton so the driver could have his break.' David

**ABOVE** Sir Bob Reid II opening Regional Railways' HQ at Meridian, Birmingham with Gordon Pettitt on 7 April 1992. *Author's collection*

Mather reckons SW&W's crowning achievement to have been a two-day diagram running Canton-Gloucester-Penzance-Plymouth-Penzance-Truro-Penzance-Plymouth-Penzance-Milford Haven-Carmarthen-Canton: 'We only ran out of fuel once.'

## Gordon Pettitt hands over to Jim Cornell
On 14 August 1992 Gordon Pettitt retired after 27 months as the sector's Managing Director, having overseen changes far beyond the rebranding of the business; it was the end of a 42-year career with BR. He brought forward his departure to give Regional Railways continuity during the 'exciting and difficult' period as BR prepared for privatisation, rather than go at some critical stage. He told staff, 'I believe Regional Railways has a good future – I'm almost sorry it's time for me to retire.' On privatisation, he averred, 'The work we have done to improve efficiency and quality means we have the management and staff capable of change and able to adopt the proposals in the White Paper. What I hope will be lasting is the business Regional Railways has developed.' He left with the Manchester Airport link and Birmingham Cross-City electrification close to fruition and Class 323s on order – but with trans-Pennine electrification, for which he had lobbied hard, receding as ministers curbed new investment.

His successor was Jim Cornell, BR's last Director of Civil Engineering. Cornell's room for manoeuvre would be limited, with increasing pressure from the Board to economise. His team identified yet further savings, with operators encouraged to take as many units as possible out of service in quiet times. Each business found its own way of economising: SW&W substituted a taxi to Newquay deep into off-season,

## Chapter 4: REGIONAL RAILWAYS, 1990-97

handling all the passengers who turned up expecting a train. A plan was even drawn up to run a skeleton service on all the Cornish branches with a single Class 153. Yet this round of cuts would leave Regional Railways' component parts with very little, if any, of the fat that bidders for franchises would assume was there to be stripped out.

Jim Cornell's passion was staff safety. The year before, six Regional Railways staff had died in accidents (one following a heart attack), and there were 47 major and more than 2,000 minor injuries. Across BR, he declared, 'we kill almost 20 staff a year and injure 400. This is just not on.' 1993 would bring a rash of minor collisions; no one was seriously injured, but six Class 158 and four 'Sprinter' vehicles were out of traffic for collision repairs at once, something Regional Railways could ill afford.

The greatest demand on him, though, was 'the hassle with Hunslet', as the 323s failed to arrive. 'I spent most of my time trying to sort that out,' Cornell recalls. And for trains already in service, availability and reliability remained constantly an issue as he built on Gordon Pettitt's commitment to deliver an 'utterly reliable railway'.

In December 1992 Cornell appealed for voluntary redundancies, telling staff that, while Regional Railways was on budget, it had to help out BR's other passenger businesses, which were £100 million down. One of the benefits of privatisation would be the cessation of such cross-subsidy. Moreover, with recession biting and the cost of post-Clapham safety measures, BR's total call on the taxpayer had soared from £700 million in 1988/89 to more than £2 billion in 1991/92.

**BELOW** No 323224 stands in Manchester Piccadilly during October 1994 in its joint GMPTE-Regional Railways livery. *Dennis Lovett*

### Regional Railways' 'maintenance holiday'

Then on 6 January 1993, in one of the most drastic economy measures on the nationalised railway, Jim Cornell imposed a 'maintenance holiday'. Fortunately some major examples of deterioration had been dealt with, and standards raised further under OfQ. The 'holiday', Richard Bonham Carter was told, would last 'until times get better or you need to do it'. He was instructed 'to assess the labour resources required to carry out the minimum of safety repairs needed to enable the route to carry its traffic, at reduced speed if necessary', and agree with planning and marketing managers 'how severe TSR [temporary speed restriction] time losses can be allowed to grow before closure becomes the only practicable option.' Cornell, who knew BR's infrastructure inside out, added, 'I do not expect many TSRs to be required during the first year.' In Whitehall, however, Cornell – with backing from John Welsby – warned that the 'holiday' carried risks: 'I demonstrated to the Department that if you had a maintenance holiday on routes taking an 11.2-tonne axle load, if you suddenly increase that to 20 tonnes and you're running on flat-bottom jointed rail with soft sleepers it will actually drop to bits.'

That March John MacGregor set out objectives for BR pending privatisation: to stick to the safety and quality targets, while 'exploring all possible means of increasing passenger numbers and income.' Regional Railways' PSO was set at £411 million, reflecting its difficulties in improving the bottom line during a recession that was finally bottoming out.

### Paul King sets up the Train Operating Units

Jim Cornell's tenure lasted less than 11 months. On 1 July 1993 he was appointed BR's Director of Infrastructure Services, Paul King moving up to become Regional Railways' Managing Director. With privatisation now certain, King told staff, 'Under the leadership and guidance of Gordon Pettitt and Jim Cornell, Regional Railways managers and staff created a cost-effective and productive passenger business during a period of deep economic recession. This was a superb achievement, and you have a great deal to be proud of as you embark on a new era in railway history.'

During 1993/94 Regional Railways maintained income and expanded services while reducing operating costs by 9% and staff by 8.3%, achieving an operating profit of £15.9 million. There were several landmarks. One – belatedly – was the entry into service between Lichfield and Redditch on 7 February 1994 of the first Class 323 (deliveries trickled into 1995). The first section of the 'Robin Hood Line' opened to Newstead in May

*Chapter 4:* **REGIONAL RAILWAYS, 1990-97**

**ABOVE** The crew of No 153370 sights a rare passenger at Pilning on 5 April 1997. The 09.05 service from Cardiff Central to Bristol Temple Meads was then the only daily train. Subsequently the service has been further reduced to a Saturdays-only train each way. *Martin Loader*

1993, proving an instant success, and SW&W, backed by West Glamorgan and Mid-Glamorgan county councils, the Welsh Office and the European Regional Development Fund, launched in May 1994 a 'SwanLine' local service between Bridgend and Swansea, with five new stations. Sadly the line's faster trains prevented SwanLine operating a clock-face service, competing buses ran more frequently and traffic was slow to develop.

Not all of the 100 new stations and 150 miles of electrification Regional Railways hoped to introduce between 1992 and 1994 came to fruition. The Leicester-Burton reopening foundered on grounds of cost and complication. In Scotland reopening to Alloa, set for 1994, and to Leven, still not achieved, slipped off the radar. But electric trains from Liverpool reached Chester and Ellesmere Port in 1993 and the wires went up north-west from Leeds. Openings – though slowed – continued until the final days of the nationalised railway; in 1996 Baglan (on 'SwanLine'), Filton Abbey Wood and Kirkby in Ashfield ('Robin Hood') welcomed their first passengers, and Strathclyde PTE launched its Motherwell-Cumbernauld service. By then Regional Railways' network had expanded by 4.8% in eight years.

Stations were closing, too (see Factfile G5). Cargo Fleet went in 1990, averting a subway renewal, and nearby Grangetown (Teesside) and Greatham (Co Durham) in 1991. Minimally patronised Elsham and Brocklesby in north Lincolnshire closed in 1993. Several little-used PTE stations – Attercliffe Road, Brightside, Godley East, Miles Platting and Park (Manchester) – went in 1995. The yardstick was whether the extra fuel used in stopping and starting there exceeded a station's receipts. Retaining such stations forced economies elsewhere, but by this stage pushing through any but the most surefire closures was rated a poor use of management time.

From taking charge of Regional Railways to the end of vertical integration, Paul King had just nine months, spent 'restructuring the business into the form that it had to be. Another massive reorganisation of people – but also requiring an enormous amount of documentation so that Railtrack could be a separate legal entity linked to the TOUs by contractual arrangements. For example, every station required at least five legal documents creating ownership by Railtrack, operating and maintenance contracts and access agreements for each TOU using the station. For Regional Railways that meant more than 8,000 documents. People were so busy that it kept their mind off what was going to happen next. A tremendous amount of energy went into that period, and miraculously the finances kept going OK.' It helped, says Gordon Pettitt, that the sector's managers were 'already used to massive change'.

# Chapter 5
# THE TRANSITION TO A PRIVATISED RAILWAY

*'The transition period was unbelievable: every regional manager was trying to run the railway as a day job; prepare the railway for privatisation as an evening job – and many were also preparing their own franchise bids as a night job.'*

**ALEX GREEN**, DIRECTOR OPERATIONS, REGIONAL RAILWAYS NW

**ABOVE** A busy day at St Ives, Cornwall. *Dennis Lovett*

## Case study – privatisation expectations

Gordon Pettitt had assumed that Regional Railways would be privatised as a whole. 'We thought we were setting up the OfQ organisation in what would be a privatised business and Regional Railways took a form compatible with being privatised.'

Chris Leah reflects: 'If only the privatisation process had been built on this model, we could have done wonders.'

And John Welsby says, 'Despite what the Government said, I was not opposed to privatisation. I just wish they had done it on the basis of the profit centres we had established, instead of the unfortunate model adopted.'

But when the political decision to privatise was taken, selling off this vertically integrated and highly cost-effective operation intact was not seriously considered.

## Margaret Thatcher not keen

Privatisation was not in Margaret Thatcher's vocabulary when she took office in 1979, despite her distaste for nationalised industries. Early steps were hesitant – though Norman Fowler, her first Minister of Transport, set in train the disposal of BR's ancillaries: Hovercraft in 1981, Hotels between 1982 and 1984, Sealink in 1984, Advertising in 1987 and Travellers Fare in 1988. Only with the sale of BREL in 1989 – adding to Provincial/Regional Railways' headaches over the Class 158s – did privatisation impinge on the operational railway.

BR was keen to inject private capital, but was thwarted by Treasury theology. Hiving off Gatwick Express was considered in 1983, the Conservative MP David Evans pressed to run LT&S as a free-standing entity, the Vale of Rheidol narrow-gauge line – an outpost of Provincial – was sold to a consortium after a process of immense complexity, and in 1988 BR tried to find a buyer for the Settle-Carlisle line (see Postscript). But the success of sectorisation made the railway itself a candidate.

Mrs Thatcher reckoned that privatising BR would be a can of worms. When Nicholas Ridley suggested it, she told him, 'Railway privatisation will be the Waterloo of this Government. Please never mention it to me again.' The first public suggestion came from Paul Channon at the 1988 Conservative Conference. Cyril Bleasdale recalls taking charge of ScotRail 'expecting it to be tested as an option for privatisation', rather as the community charge was first tried north of the border, before Channon backtracked.

## The first stirrings

Cecil Parkinson, brought up in a railway home, told Bob Reid I in February 1990 that privatisation was 'no longer a subject for urgent consideration'. Yet the pace was quickening even before Mrs Thatcher's replacement by John Major that November; indeed,

**BELOW** *Llywelyn* looks very smart in British Rail branding in 1975 before the Vale of Rheidol line was deemed an unsuitable route for BR to continue operating. It was eventually sold to a consortium. *David Edwards*

**LEFT** No 150137 stands at Manchester Victoria in GMPTE's modified Regional Railways livery in September 1992. *Dennis Lovett*

OfQ was partly a response to this. A DTp-led summit at Chevening in September reopened matters, and late in 1990 a working group of ministers and officials was established, the Department (now under Malcolm Rifkind) hiring consultants to examine 'business-led' and 'track company' models. A further stimulus was the European Directive 91/440, which appeared to require the splitting of track from train. Work done on this for the Department by Coopers & Lybrand fed into Conservative thinking.

BR wanted to be privatised – if it had to be – as a whole or, failing that, by sectors; John Major favoured a return to the pre-nationalisation 'Big Four', while the Treasury wanted a track authority with individual train paths auctioned off. As for Regional Railways, John Welsby and Alan Nichols, BR's director of policy, wrote just after the event: 'It was possible to conceive of a core railway that could be transferred to the private sector without need of subsidy. There was no suggestion that the regional passenger services could ever be profitable, but there was a belief that while profitable and unprofitable services were operated by the same owner the good would degenerate to the level of the bad, and the potential for virtually unlimited calls on the public purse would remain.'

## John Major's commitment

The 1992 Conservative manifesto pledged to 'end BR's state monopoly'. It promised separation of track and operations, a public-sector infrastructure company, franchising of all passenger services, and privatisation of freight and parcels. Rail did not figure greatly in an election fought largely on the economy, devolution and the NHS, and until the final hours Labour looked set to win. But on 9 April John Major was re-elected.

The Queen's Speech on 6 May promised a privatisation Bill, and on 14 July, only weeks after BR completed its OfQ reorganisation, John MacGregor published his White Paper 'New Opportunities for the Railways'. Just 21 pages, it stated that 'no single solution is appropriate to all BR's businesses' and proposed ending vertical integration, with a track authority, passenger franchises, franchising authority and rail regulator. But there was no detail. As Gordon Pettitt observes, 'The political class had been wanting to do this, but had done no work on it.'

In six months before the Railways Bill appeared on 22 January 1993, the substance of how the railway would be privatised and would operate was worked up between BR and the Department. There was no enthusiasm in the railway for the Balkanised structure that emerged. Paul King felt that this was heavily influenced by the Government's slender majority, which 'effectively prevented franchising in a manner which left some levers open, and prevented innovation to service patterns. Options on what services could run were narrowed to avoid political arguments.'

In October the Department issued a consultation document to potential bidders, with a very tight deadline for responses. The Government wanted 'a substantial proportion of passenger services franchised within the lifetime of the current Parliament. This means taking early decisions on the grouping of the first services.' There would be 'no universal template' for a franchise contract, and the franchising authority would initially 'base the pattern of passenger services to be provided on BR's existing service levels.' Gordon Pettitt annotated: 'Who is responsible in the longer term?' Other operators might be permitted to compete, but only the franchisee could receive subsidy. BR managers would be 'encouraged' to bid for franchises through buyouts. It would be 'in the operators' own commercial interests' to continue network benefits like through ticketing. Rolling stock was initially to be rented from BR.

The document noted that Regional Railways, 'an extensive people-carrying business … has been successful in increasing revenue, and considerable cost reductions have been achieved by the introduction of modern cost-effective rolling stock, with associated reductions in infrastructure costs. Operations are, however, heavily dependent on the grants which it receives from Central Government, from local Passenger Transport Executives and from some county councils. Only interurban services generate sufficient passenger income to cover vehicle operating costs, and both urban and rural services are run at a significant loss.'

RIGHT No 158856 is seen at Boston in Central livery on 28 April 2007. *Dennis Lovett*

## The structure takes shape

In January 1993 Roger Salmon, a merchant banker, was appointed Franchising Director designate and John Swift QC Railway Regulator designate; Gordon Pettitt became part-time advisor to Swift, 'helping him to understand how the railway works'. Between then and August, the Department nominated Shadow Franchises for privatisation; the first seven included ScotRail, which would be the last to go. Five stages were set for franchising: interested parties asked to prequalify; Invitations to Tender issued; Salmon's Office of Passenger Rail Franchising (OPRAF) draws up a shortlist; a preferred bidder is announced; and, subject to contract, the franchise is awarded.

The Railways Bill made franchising and competition the key planks of privatisation, without acknowledging the conflict between the two. It was not well received at Westminster. Robert Adley, Tory Chairman of the Transport Select Committee and a serious railway author and photographer, denounced it as a 'poll tax on wheels'; Adley's sudden death would greatly weaken the opposition. Most of the argument concerned network benefits, pensions and the like; BR's scope to influence the legislation was limited, but the PTEs worked with Brian Wilson, Labour's deputy transport spokesman, to protect their interests by getting the Bill amended.

The PTEs feared the Treasury would use privatisation to disrupt their long-term funding, but in fact the Bill strengthened their hand. It gave them the right to be consulted before a franchise was issued; when OPRAF forgot to consult Centro about the Chiltern franchise, the PTE threatened a judicial review. It also empowered them to support not only existing rail and – inevitably – 'bus substitution' services, but 'additional' services, and after Greater Manchester briefly withdrew support Section 20 grants were extended to cover Railtrack's access charges. The PTEs' contribution, nearing £150 million per annum, was funded through an enhanced Rate Support Grant.

The Railways Act as amended received Royal Assent on 5 November 1993. Meanwhile the particulars of franchising were fleshed out. The Treasury wanted three-year franchises to match its own spending horizon, but was persuaded that no one would bid for them, and settled for a seven-year standard term, with some of 15 years. Revenues from interavailable fares were to be divided between TOCs by ORCATS, with ticketing matters and permitted routes handled by an Association of Train Operating Companies (ATOC), which would struggle to reconcile its twin roles of semi-statutory body and trade association. 'At OPRAF we had to write policies on everything,' recalls Chris Stokes. 'To the intense frustration of the Department, we took time getting our proposition to something that was robust. When we were ready we went like a storm, and sold all the franchises in 13 months, taking in a bid over the weekend and giving a decision the following Tuesday.'

The Rail Minister Roger Freeman had wanted 50 franchises, some of them 'micro' covering individual lines. The exact shape of the franchises had first to be settled. Regional Railways was asked to propose options for how its services might be split up for franchising. The end result of the study was that the franchises were formed around the existing operating units, but with the Cardiff Valleys and Merseyrail franchises being set up as separate franchises as a move toward some microfranchising. Paul King's study of three years before could have helped, as 'Regional Railways was the one where you could think outside the box, and we were the only people to ask the questions.'

Gordon Pettitt, asked by the Department for his opinion, suggested separating Strathclyde services from ScotRail to give a clear idea of where the money was going; this was ruled politically impossible. One decision, which to Chris Stokes created the 'ideal franchise', was to combine Central's East Anglian branches with InterCity's dominant London-Norwich service, forming Anglia. Another was to allocate the entire Norwich-Liverpool route to Central Trains; some other routes were swapped between operators. However, Regional Railways' interurban routes (and, crucially, its trans-Pennine services) stayed with regional Train Operating Units (TOUs) rather than going to the new CrossCountry TOU based on InterCity's NE/SW route through Birmingham.

**ABOVE** The 22.10 Euston to Fort William sleeper – nicknamed the 'Deerstalker Express' – nears County March summit on 1 May 1984. No 37026 is hauling an 'Ethel' (a converted Class 25 loco) to provide electric power for heating and lighting. *Gavin Morrison*

## The PSR

Franchisees were crucially to be bound by the Passenger Service Requirement (PSR), which set minimum service levels – but looked to the concerned passenger very like cuts. Roger Salmon, who devised it, set the London-Birmingham service at one train per hour when BR was running two, insisting that running more would be 'commercially worthwhile for operators'. He also excluded the Fort William sleeper from the ScotRail franchise – InterCity having sloughed it off – reckoning each passenger was subsidised to the tune of £450. After a furore in the media – which nicknamed the train the 'Deerstalker Express' – Scotland's High Court ruled that because only the sleeper used a curve east of Glasgow the full closure process must be invoked. The train was reprieved, economies being found by combining more of the sleepers south of Edinburgh.

Each PSR covered the entire span of train operation and most commercial activity; for Paul King the 'killer' was the limiting of season ticket and Saver fare increases to the RPI for the first three years, and RPI-1% thereafter. This formula resulted in the slow but inevitable decline in franchise profitability and a greater call on the public purse. The PSR also covered possessions and compensation from Railtrack for disruption, and set the performance regime, and procedures for changes to the timetable or the network.

As foreseen by many, the PSR ossified the detail of the railway, and in many respects its timetable, for nearly three decades, through fears over changing it. 'There was a premium on safeguarding what was there,' Stokes says, 'even if it was pretty silly.' Chris Gibb observes: 'In Regional Railways we were encouraged to try things, and see what happened. Then privatisation froze in time wherever we were with the trials.'

Table 5.1 Train service activities covered by the PSR

| Activity | Contractual |
|---|---|
| Frequency | Yes |
| Stations served | Yes |
| Maximum journey times | Yes |
| First and last trains | Yes |
| Weekend services | Yes |
| Through services | Yes |
| Acceptable levels of crowding | Yes |
| Season ticket and saver fare increases | Yes |
| Railtrack compensation | Yes |

The privatisers believed that, because costs had fallen after every other disposal, they would with the railways, which they supposed inherently inefficient. So, according to Sir Christopher Foster, one of the advisors who drove the process, rail's new structure was 'designed to reduce costs'. OPRAF, on the Treasury's instructions, built sharply declining subsidy profiles into the contracts. Offsetting this, open access was restricted, lest 'cherry-picking' by others discourage bidders. For regional franchises, revenues would be low and costs high; Stokes says that they were 'back-end loaded in the franchising programme because everyone wanted a share of the action' from subsidy and the fruits of heavy cost-cutting. The wisdom of the bidders' financial forecasts was not OPRAF's concern: 'They were big boys and it was not up to us to point out their errors. Nor did we owe them a duty of care.'

### Railtrack and access charges

Railtrack was created in March 1993 as a division of BR. Its Chairman, Sir Robert Horton, identified projects that could benefit Regional Railways as a cross-Glasgow link, new infrastructure opportunities with the PTEs, and trans-Pennine electrification. But Railtrack's priorities were the West Coast Route Modernisation – with pathing and disruption implications for regional services – and the Thameslink 2000 project, which would slip to 2018. Paul King explained to Horton what he was inheriting, highlighting the 'bow wave' effect of past bursts of Government-sanctioned investment: 'Thirty years after an investment, the need for it hits you again.' John Edmonds became Railtrack's Chief Executive, moulding it as 'engineering-free' with work outsourced; the break-up of vertical integration, he said, would enable train operators to 'focus much more sharply on their own activities'.

Roger Salmon negotiated access charges for each franchise with Railtrack. Operators then bid, with any shortfall made up in subsidy. Railtrack's relationship with each TOU was governed by a Track Access Agreement several inches thick, covering routes to be used, the needs of other operators, access for maintenance, quality of ride, diversionary routes, severe weather plans, the performance regime, the amount of competition and – critically – the charging structure. The first tariff of access charges, issued in February 1994, looked to a return of 5.6% on Railtrack's assets. When the Regulator set them a year later for the period to 2000/01, he concluded that for 1995/96 they should be lowered by 8% in real terms, and by 2% per annum thereafter.

### BR is split up

On 1 April 1994 BR was split into Railtrack, 25 TOUs, five Freight Operating Companies (FOCs), three Rolling Stock Leasing Companies (ROSCOs), six track renewal companies, seven track maintenance companies, and six rolling stock maintenance companies, plus Rail Express Systems (special trains and mail) and Parcels. (Regional Railways' Finance Director, David Rutherford, became Managing Director of Freightliner.) At first, BR remained in charge of these companies (bar Railtrack) and of strategy. Pressed to get the TOUs off the books, Roger Salmon ignored bids from BR, even though the Lords had amended the privatisation Bill to permit them.

Regional Railways' full authority ended after just two years with the vesting of Railtrack – as a public sector organisation – on 1 April 1994. It lost its civil engineers and infrastructure staff to Jim Cornell's infrastructure units and its signallers to Railtrack, and concentrated on running trains, Paul King telling staff it had to be 'business as usual'. Railtrack took charge of 14 major stations, including Birmingham New Street, Glasgow Central, Leeds and Manchester Piccadilly, and train operators gained a 'landlord' juggling the demands of a station's users, and an invisible barrier with station staff.

The momentum of OfQ enabled Railtrack to make a strong start, despite its lack of close control over maintenance and a steady dilution of qualified staff. Control Period 1 kicked in on 1 April 1996, covering Railtrack's spending for the next five years. After lobbying from Sir Robert Horton, John MacGregor's successor Brian Mawhinney announced that Railtrack too would be privatised. It was floated on 20 May, the sale raising £1.9 billion; by October 1998 the company was worth £16 billion. Privatising Railtrack slowed franchising – only two contracts were signed by the end of 1995 – by injecting fresh uncertainty.

Creating the ROSCOs – Angel, Eversholt and Porterbrook – to take on BR's locomotives and 11,000 carriages was logical, as much of the stock would outlive the franchises. Most TOCs had a relationship with at least two ROSCOs, governed by a 'master lease'. The ROSCOs were marketed in November 1995, their buyers taking over the following year. The sale raised only £1.8 billion – half the value Hambros had put on them – and there was an outcry when all three changed hands again for £900 million more. The BR managers who acquired Porterbrook for £528 million sold it on after six months for £826 million, leaving Sandy Anderson, the bid leader, a multi-millionaire.

## The PTEs' concerns

Strathclyde PTE came within a whisker of halting the Railtrack flotation, seeking a judicial review because the Department insisted that it hand over £230 million worth of PTE-funded assets to Railtrack. A deal was hastily struck. Difficulties over Strathclyde also threatened the ScotRail franchise. The Government planned to transfer ratepayer-funded assets to TOCs and ROSCOs without compensation, but the PTEs insisted that the stock they financed must run on their lines unless something better was offered. Eventually agreement was reached, but again only after a threat of judicial review.

The PTEs suspected access charges were not accurately allocated to the lines they were supporting. Railtrack refused the information, and it took a threat from the District Auditor for South Yorkshire to impose a fine on the responsible member of Railtrack's staff under the Audit Regulations before it was forthcoming. The PTEs brought in Arthur Anderson to check Railtrack's figures, finding 'stacks of mistakes'. Other objections from the PTEs had the political aim of delaying privatisation into the tenure of a Labour Government. But Labour leaders urged them not to obstruct franchising, as an incoming Labour Government would not wish to inherit a 'hybrid' railway.

## The Train Operating Units (TOUs)

On 1 April 1994 Regional Railways' profit centres became TOUs, to be franchised out as soon as bidders were selected – but they would continue under Paul King's suzerainty for two years or more. By the time Railtrack was privatised they had been turned into registered companies – TOCs – with the shareholding sold to the bidder.

Paul King recalls the period to February 1996 as one where management teams were running the shadow franchises increasingly as if they were private-sector companies, with the intention of bidding for them. 'John Welsby went through the process of choosing the people to run them. If you wanted to be the boss of one of these companies you had to be involved in putting in a bid, and we got bespoke training sessions for the TOC teams organised by the London Business School.

'My approach was to say, "We are going to run these TOCs as if they were private-sector businesses accountable to shareholders. I am your Chairman and some of my colleagues will be your non-executive directors. We will have monthly Board meetings where I will be asking how you are doing running the business, not simply how you are doing running the trains." That was part of the learning process. Even if you didn't buy the franchise and wanted to go on doing the job, whoever did buy it would want managers to run it. So there was a lot of personal motivation.'

The 25 TOCs were grouped into two sets; the plan was for John Nelson to become Managing Director for the Southern and Eastern set and Chris Green for Northern and Western, but Green went back to ScotRail before leaving the industry (temporarily, as it turned out). Instead, John Welsby asked Paul King to combine responsibility for the Regional Railways TOCs with that for the InterCity TOCs East and West Coast, Great Western, CrossCountry and Midland MainLine, together with On Board services – in total 13 companies.

Paul King's fledging TOCs were confronted with a rash of strikes by Railtrack signallers. The NUR had merged with the National Union of Seamen in 1991 to form the Rail, Maritime & Transport Union (RMT). In April 1993 its militant leadership called two days of strikes – coordinated with the miners – aimed at preventing redundancies on privatisation and the contracting-out of maintenance by Railtrack. With the new system in place, RMT brought the signallers out on 19 days between May and September 1994 over pay. Their pay had fallen behind, but left-wingers in the trade unions saw a last opportunity for a confrontation before the industry became fragmented. In fact, they had missed the bus; strikes in the vertically integrated railway of the previous two years might have been more effective. Yet they were tiresome to passengers, and irritating to managers who were trying to run as tight and efficient a ship as possible – and put together management buyouts.

## Selling off the TOCs

Major's Government was impatient to see the TOCs sold off. Another election was already on the horizon, and even though the economy was finally recovering it looked unlikely that the Conservatives would win. Tory ministers took no chances; Brian Mawhinney, with Roger Salmon, set a target of 51% of passenger services in the private sector by April 1996 – yet it was two and a half years before any Regional Railways service was privatised. During this time it was hard to avoid a deterioration in service, the effects of falling investment compounded by a shortage of reliable rolling stock as orders were frozen.

Nevertheless interest in the early franchises was greater than anticipated, with 28 outside bidders, eight management buyout teams, and BR itself (which eventually gave up). And when the dust had settled, the 25 TOCs had been let to 13 different operators.

## Chapter 5: THE TRANSITION TO A PRIVATISED RAILWAY

**ABOVE** The ten volumes of the pack required to sell Regional Railways North West totalled 2,050 pages. Alex Green, Operations Director, remembers these arriving by courier almost every Sunday for three months for repeated proof-checking and corrections while he also tried to keep his daily 1,600 trains running safely and punctually. *Alex Green*

For Paul King, the year from March 1996, during which the Regional TOCs were franchised, was 'extraordinary'. 'The documentation required was monumental. For each TOC there was a long form report of 1,000 pages-ish, and information memoranda, all covered by due diligence. Those months were hell on earth – reading 2-3,000 pages of documentation a week.

'The train operating guys were producing this lot, running the trains, and virtually all of them put in a bid. Luckily in virtually every TOC there turned out to be a star who could run that sort of process: for example, Mike Hodson, Mark Causebrook, Bob Goundry, Alex Lynch in Scotland. In the railways I realised I had more intellectual horsepower reporting to me than I had ever had in private-sector jobs; what was lacking was a bit of aggression.'

### How RRNE management put its bid together

Mike Hodson, commercial director of Regional Railways North East (RRNE), led its reporting process on what the franchise would comprise, and subsequently the mangement buyout (MBO) team. 'For us it wasn't a financial thing – this was an opportunity that was only going to come once. The things I should have been worried about – like the financial responsibility if we won – I wasn't worried about.' He formed a bid team of six including RRNE's production manager Stuart Baker and its finance and HR directors. 'Ian Yeowart wanted to bid, but was not in the senior team. Bob Urie, our director, was ready to retire. Another senior manager opposed an MBO on principle; the doubters left at the beginning.

'We held a beauty parade of advisors and ended up with Ernst & Young on a no win, no fee basis. Each of us would have put in an equity stake had we won; E&Y said we wouldn't need to mortgage our houses. They gave us a partner to oversee the bid, a senior manager to work with us, and another person half-time. We couldn't work up the bid on BR premises, so we went over to the E&Y offices in Leeds most evenings; there were a couple of overnights before the end. The whole thing probably lasted six months, with 12 weeks in the last, intensive phase.

**BELOW** It's 02.00 on Sunday 2 March 1997 in the RRNW Manchester Control Office as Alex Green hands over responsibility for the new franchise to Brian Scott, CEO Great Western Holdings. Left to right are Derek Jones, duty shift manager; Mike Eden, section controller; Knowles Mitchell, public affairs GWT; Ilona Morgan, corporate affairs RRNW; Dick Tudor, fleet controller; and Dominic Riley, maintenance controller. *Alex Green*

'E&Y said our chances would be greater with a strategic partner; they introduced us to venture capitalists and Martin Ballinger of Go Ahead. Chris Moyes and Martin had done the original Go Ahead buyout; we probably learned most from Martin, though we spent more time with E&Y. Martin came to the weekly meeting and paid for Halcrow to give us some revenue forecasting; we dealt with Chris on points of detail. We now had a pretty powerful machine – ourselves, E&Y, Go Ahead, Halcrow, together with Dickinson, Dees, who were Go Ahead's lawyers.

'We concentrated everything on "How low can you get the subsidy?" We carried out a huge manpower planning exercise. We went very hard on overheads – E&Y said, "You can't afford to be soft" – plus things like more efficient driver diagrams. Most of our cost reduction was, "Is the person driving a train/selling a ticket, because if not we don't need them." There were a few bits of cream on top about service enhancement to make the long term interesting, but not a huge amount of investment beyond improving fleet reliability. We proposed a Middlesbrough-Darlington-Newcastle-Sunderland service and talked to Railtrack about that, and had quite a lot of talk with the PTEs; they were polite, professional, some warmer than others. Their main worries were about costs, they wanted trains to be clean and on time – crowding was then less of an issue.

'We didn't know if ours was a good number or a bad number. E&Y and Go Ahead had urged us to go lower than the others; Martin Ballinger suggested comparing with the bid teams for other franchises. Towards the end we did a lot of work on risk against the Net Present Value price we were pitching.

## MTL the surprise winners

'The bidders were MTL, ourselves and Connex. There were strange meetings with the Department; on one side were the bidders, on the other the incumbent team. Connex came with 12 people, MTL with one, Peter Davison. We all sat there trying to say as little as possible. Peter had a lot of questions, but was not on the ball. We looked at Connex, thinking, "We're a minnow compared with them," but felt we had a reasonable chance.'

'Gary Backler gave me the call from the Department: "I'm sorry to tell you…" He told me the winner: MTL. If we'd been beaten by anyone we would have expected it to be Connex; as it turned out Connex were the most expensive, and we weren't much below them. The Department went for the lowest price and were too easily satisfied that MTL had the ability.'

Gordon Pettitt recalls, 'I was at Connex and when we saw the winning bid we were glad we were nowhere near it.' Alex Ritchie observed, 'The PTEs thought that MTL, who had developed as a transport organisation, were coming up with a package they could cope with. They answered all the questions on quality and service development, but unfortunately we were proved wrong.'

'MTL were an interesting outfit,' says Mike Hodson. 'Basically they were the buses in Liverpool, one of the biggest in the second division. Arriva – naturals for the North East – came on the scene too late to bid. Winning North East as well as Merseyrail made MTL a big animal.' Strangely, the MTL managers behind the bid 'had no railway experience at all – they were naval architects. They recruited Peter Coombs as chairman from the shipbuilding industry; Henry Stirman (operations) came from JCB.

'MTL took over on 2 March 1997. They put in Peter Davison, who sat next to Bob Urie. We went three to four months without much happening. Then Henry Stirman arrived and started to talk to people and Peter Coombs came to address the staff. Within a few weeks they said who they wanted to stay and who to go: Bob went, Peter Davison became MD. They said I needed a broader business education, and sent me to do an MBA in Manchester.'

## Readying Wales & West for privatisation

While John Mummery worked up the management bid for W&W, Chris Gibb was working with David Mather to set the franchise's PSR, as discussed earlier in the chapter. 'The PSR was adopted to enshrine a level of service that couldn't cover its costs. It was difficult to figure out whether it should be extremely constrained or extremely relaxed,' Gibb says. 'The first draft required trains on the Looe branch to stop at Coombe Junction in case the lady who lived next to it wanted to get on.'

Sugar Loaf Halt, a previously unadvertised platform, appeared in the timetable as a 'gift' from SW&W when the Central Wales line lost one of its five daily trains in 1993. Gibb says, 'It was very basic and had been opened for ramblers on Sundays on a shoestring. The DfT and OPRAF wanted to know if it was open or not; it was not really, but to speed the process it was decided the station should be "open". It crept into the PSR for the whole of the week, meaning it had to have lighting, a waiting shelter, an information system, bilingual signage.

'Under constant pressure, a lot of the stuff that was coming out went back in, and in the end the PSR

Chapter 5: **THE TRANSITION TO A PRIVATISED RAILWAY** 65

**LEFT** Sugar Loaf Halt, complete with 'rumble strips', white lining, signing, Information Point, lighting and handrails to a long staircase – all for an average of two passengers a day. *Wikipedia*

enshrined almost every element of the service. The daily Cardiff-Holyhead business train was rated "very marginal", and we held back from marketing it until its inclusion in the PSR. OPRAF asked us to consider running a second train or diverting the existing one to serve Wrexham, but we concluded that such journeys could not possibly cover their operating costs.'

### Prism's aggressive bid for Wales & West

Prism Rail – with a bid seen then as 'very aggressive' – took over at Wales & West and Cardiff Railway on 13 October 1996, the first franchises to go. Prism was not a bus operator like MTL or National Express, but a consortium of managers who had led MBOs from the National Bus Company, 'competing bus company owners who got together to bid for rail franchises,' as Chris Gibb puts it. 'Prism turned out to be a great bunch of people – Giles Fearnley, Len Wright, plus Dominic Booth and David Weir, who came from the railway. They were a pleasure to work for, listened and we made good progress. The bus people were good at running a business; they applied a lot of the same logic to running ours. Prism were determined to make it work, but they determined, like many bidders, that all train companies were equally inefficient. When they won, they found that some were extremely efficient – if not profitable – and others unbelievably inefficient. They quickly realised they'd got two franchises wrong one way and two the other; for the first x years they would balance out, but after that…

'The franchise agreement included a minimum sum of £200,000 to install lighting at each station without it, and we used solar panels in some locations to power one light, the only one for miles around. The stations all now have full lighting, meeting national standards, which in Regional Railways we'd have considered lavish and highly inefficient.' Gibb applauds Prism – which had imagined that most of the stations already had full facilities – for honouring their obligations 'even when it was obvious how much money we were losing. We spent a fortune on "Project Inform" systems at every station, which are still in use at many – bilingual in Wales, which was unprecedented at the time. We also paid BT to put in public phones at many stations, which was very difficult, miles from the phone network! "Regular cleaning" even became a problem, as we'd got many stations adopted by local people (for free, or a train ticket from time to time). OPRAF wanted all that put in legal agreements, which we drew the line at.' As for Sugar Loaf Halt, 'I pointed out to Prism that the investment would take 420 years' receipts, but we went ahead. It is now subject to the Disability Discrimination Act, the lot.'

Dominic Booth, put in by Prism as Managing Director, found at W&W 'a really great team of people who had years of experience and had the Regional Railways way about them. It was a pleasure to go

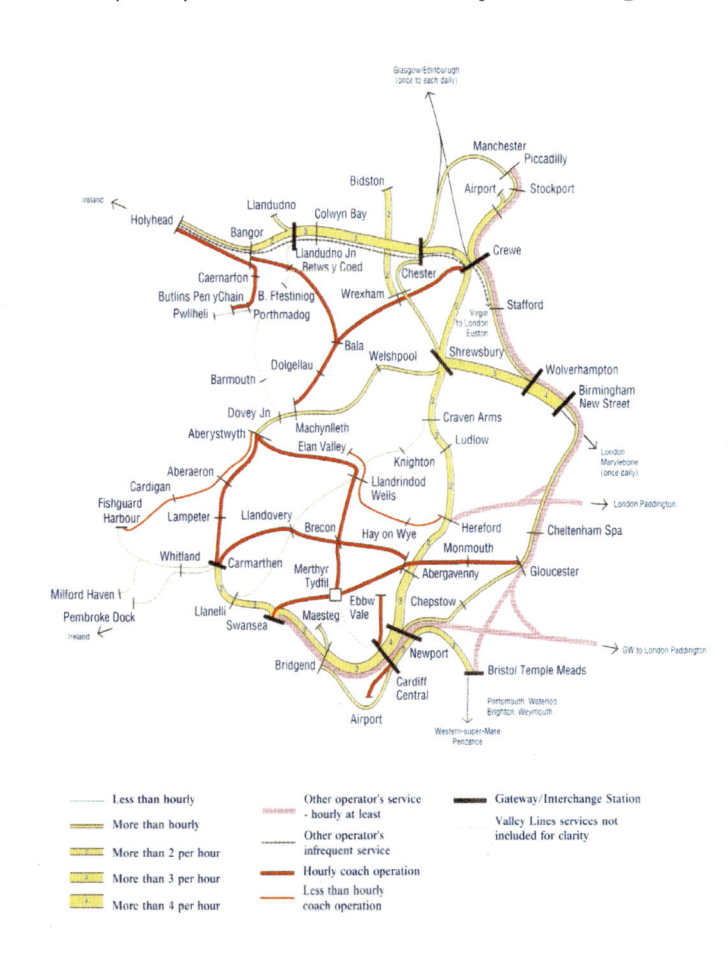

**RIGHT** Prism Rail's short-lived vision for integrated transport in Wales using their road and rail assets. *Chris Gibb*

# Chapter 5: THE TRANSITION TO A PRIVATISED RAILWAY

**ABOVE** No 47714 in Anglia livery waits at Yarmouth about to return with empty stock to Norwich Crown Point on Saturday 13 August 2005. *Chris Boon*

there, and every person I met knew their brief. They were incredibly dedicated and the strength in depth was excellent, but they needed strategic thinkers. I put Chris Gibb up because I could see he had some of that. When I went there he was Train Planning Manager; I first made him Operations Director, then MD. What also I didn't have (and it told on the Valleys lines) was any way to respond to what had happened in the bidding. They were fundamentally loss-making, and there was no way of fixing that.'

Both W&W and Cardiff Railway were chaired by Len Wright, Chairman of the coach company Q Drive. Giles Fearnley, Prism's Finance Director, was Chairman of Blazefield Holdings, which owned the bus interests. Their first decision was to move W&W's head office to Cardiff.

## GB Railways' 'kitchen table' bid captures Anglia

A very different winner was GB Railways, formed by two Canadian entrepreneurs, Michael Schabas and Max Steinkopf, with Jeremy Long, a senior executive at Grand Met. Long approached his boss, Lord Sheppard, to be GB's Chairman; also in the team was Jim Morgan, an early Railtrack director and now a partner in the rail consultancy First Class Partnerships. GB aimed to succeed by improving service, not slashing costs, and bid for LT&S and Anglia, with whom Sheppard's brother was a driver; its bids, says Long, were 'put together from three kitchen tables.'

Uniquely, GB – after early backing from Samuel Montagu – raised its funding through a share issue on the AIM market, the week after winning the Anglia franchise. 'You wouldn't do this today,' remarks Jeremy Long, now European Chief Executive of MTR, which has been awarded the Crossrail franchise and jointly operates London Overground. Told they had won in a call from franchise director John O'Brien, GB kept Andy Cooper as Anglia's Managing Director. And in January 1997 the company began operating a franchise that, uniquely for the time, combined former InterCity, cross-country and rural services.

## Incomers find they have overbid

The 'first train' under privatisation, on 4 February 1996, was a bus, replacing Great Western's 01.50 Fishguard-Paddington service as far as Cardiff. The actual first train was South West Trains' 05.10 Twickenham-Waterloo, whose nine passengers were greeted by a media scrum. The Great Western privatisation had also involved much of the spadework for Wales & West and Cardiff Railway; these were transferred to Prism Rail on 13 October 1996.

After that, Regional Railways' franchises all went within six months: Anglia on 5 January 1997; Merseyrail Electrics to MTL a fortnight later; and Central, North East and North West on 2 March to National Express, MTL and GW Holdings respectively. (Vesting dates for all the Regional Railways franchises are given in Factfile J.) Bidders became keener and made increasingly optimistic assumptions on getting down cost; MTL simply set percentage targets across the business.

None of the Regional Railways management bids were successful. Indeed, overall only Chiltern, Great Western and Thames Trains (Govia holding the majority share) were won by their managements; however, the GW team also – to their cost – acquired North West. Bid teams for Cardiff Railway (John Buxton), Central (Mark Causebrook), North West (Bob Goundry) and ScotRail (John Ellis) had also found financing partners and worked up plans for continuing to operate their railway, only to be frustrated by bus operators' readiness to gamble on cutting costs and an unstated reluctance in Whitehall to let railwaymen run trains.

Every regional franchise would turn out to have been bid too competitively, but at first the subsidies offset the higher costs of track charges, rolling stock and so forth than under BR. Great Western Holdings' bid for North West entailed a fall in subsidy from £100.3 million the first year to £69 million in year seven, and MTL's for North East from £224.5 million to £145.6 million. Government support to BR as a whole in 1993/94 was £1.09 billion; for 1994/95, in its new form pre-privatisation, £2.16 billion (not counting the £600 million that privatisation itself had cost, most going to lawyers, accountants and consultants). This was supposed to decline, but for 1997/98 – the first full year of private operation – total subsidies for former Regional TOCs alone were £930.1 million. Most went to ScotRail (£280.1 million), North East (£224.5 million) and Central Trains (£187.5 million).

All this occurred under the incredulous eye of Paul King. 'I was staggered by the seeming lack of effort among the bidders, and their failure to understand the economics of Regional Railways. They clearly thought we were a bunch of railway idiots, and they could do better marketing to bring revenue up, ignoring the fact that this would put the losses up. After a deal was done, I insisted on having a meeting with whoever secured a franchise. I was happy to talk about the team, the corollary being that they would honour BR severance terms if they decided not to keep people; almost all of them did.'

## Changing of the guard, then Regional Railways bows out

Sir Bob Reid II stood down as BR's Chairman in April 1995, John Welsby succeeding him. Mawhinney was replaced that July by the less abrasive Sir George Young for the final stages of privatisation. In October 1996 Roger Salmon stepped down as franchising director. His successor, John O'Brien, resolved outstanding differences with the PTEs; Paul King recalls 'trooping round all the PTEs to discuss and settle all their outstanding claims for financial compensation for non-delivery of services – difficult negotiations as they were not going to agree to the terms of the franchise until they got a final settlement.'

The final TOC to go, on 31 March 1997, was ScotRail, to National Express. Regional Railways' very last trains were ScotRail's 23.30 from Glasgow Queen Street to Edinburgh Waverley that evening, and reverse. The two pairs of 158s crossed between Falkirk High and Polmont and reached their destinations around 00.20. ScotRail held a party aboard the Queen Street departure through the moment of handover with champagne, whisky, jazz band and pipers. The same night InterCity's Caledonian Sleepers, before their transfer to ScotRail, departed from Glasgow Central, Waverley and Euston at 23.55 (Highland services having left earlier). Among ScotRail staff transferred to National Express was John Bowden, a booking clerk at Blairhill, who had joined the LNER as a lad and would retire in 1998, starting and finishing his career in the private sector.

Paul King cleared his desk on 25 April, and joined KPMG that October. 'My last task,' he says, 'was boxing up the documentation on which the franchise bids were made, as it was pretty certain BR would be sued by a successful bidder. To describe in a long form report a business that had hardly existed for any length of time but of great complexity inevitably left some options for people to come back at you. But remarkably that didn't happen.'

And on 1 May a Labour Government under Tony Blair was elected by a landslide, committed to keeping the railways accountable and supporting a shift from road to rail – but not to renationalise.

**ABOVE** No 158741 stands at Glasgow Queen Street in 'Express' livery under a commemorative banner celebrating 150 years of rail services in Scotland. *Dennis Lovett*

## Regional Railways' legacy

Regional Railways' legacy to the privatised railway was considerable. An operating structure was in place that could be privatised. The operating units were lean, but had revenues that, because of the high proportion of subsidy, were less vulnerable to the economic cycle. For Dominic Booth, now UK Managing Director of Abellio, the greatest legacy of all was a financial discipline that has stayed with the industry. 'How on earth do you get a quart out of a pint pot? If I look at the disciplines we enjoy today, a lot of that comes from those days. Regional Railways was brilliant at it: every single franchise was massively lossmaking in the first round of privatisation because the bidders "knew" that Regional Railways was not very efficient. They couldn't have been further from the truth – BR had put in its best people in terms of cost control and focus.' Theo Steel adds: 'The Regional Railways guys were absolutely focused on getting the most out of what they had. We all remember the big arguments over who was sponsoring one set of points; there was an absolute fixation with value for money.'

# Chapter 6
# UNDER PRIVATISATION, 1996 TO DATE

*'Railway privatisation begat a baby which was born critically premature and needed a long period of loving care in an incubator where it could develop into a properly functioning infant ready for the world. Instead John Prescott took the baby out to play political football with it.'*

**PAUL KING**

**ABOVE** No 142076 stands with two unidentified Class 143s at Canton Depot, Cardiff, in National Express 'Valley' livery with Arriva strapline branding. *Antony Christie*

## A record of success

Overall, Britain's railways under privatisation have gone from strength to strength. New services have been launched, new trains introduced, customer service improved – and passenger numbers have doubled. And former Regional Railways franchises have performed strongly, with TransPennine Express the star. The franchise map, however, looks very different from how it appeared in 1997, and the number of regional franchises has risen from eight to nine. A remarkable increase in business has been matched by a steep rise in subsidy, and while reliability also improved over several years, congestion on the network and the need to undertake more challenging infrastructure renewals and improvements has led to that improvement tailing off.

After the upheavals of the early years of privatisation, the creation of Network Rail and the redrawing of the franchise map completed in 2007 have enabled regional services to settle down, and operators' confidence has risen. Ironically, though, this settling down process has led to increased Government involvement in the minutiae of running the railway, with even the opening times of station booking offices decided in Whitehall. Such micro-management is a consequence of the taxpayer's contribution to the privatised railway being far higher than in the days of BR. The Department's 2004 Rail Study found that while BR drove down overheads by 15% during sectorisation, privatisation pushed them up again by 30%.

There have been bumps along the way: the failure of several franchises, the creation and abolition of the Strategic Rail Authority, micro-management by the Department, and the collapse of its system of franchising. For staff, privatisation initially meant trying to keep trains running against a background of cost-cutting and convulsions in the industry, then a steady increase in demand. Then there was Hatfield, which brought the collapse of Railtrack and disrupted the entire industry. The achievements of the train operators, and more recently of Network Rail, remain overshadowed by memories of idiocies from the first days of privatisation, early accidents on what is now Europe's safest railway, and continued overcrowding as some operators – notably Northern, with ageing rolling stock – struggle with rising demand on loss-making routes.

## A promising start

Punctuality and reliability improved into 1997. Railtrack showed ambition with major projects like the renewal of Standish Junction, south of Gloucester. Regional TOCs launched innovative interurban services before pathing problems and shortages of stock set in. Several drove

**BELOW** No 170204 forms an Anglia Railways Crosslink Ipswich-Basingstoke service at Woking on 3 September 2001. *Colin J. Marsden*

improvements in service delivery, catering, staff training and culture. In the first two years passengers using Central Trains increased by 13.1%, ScotRail by 11%, North East by 10.4%, and North West by 10%.

In September 1996 the Government ended its 1,064-day freeze on ordering new rolling stock. Over the next three years the ROSCOs purchased £2 billion worth of new trains, including 249 DMU carriages for National Express franchises, Anglia and North Western, and 168 EMU vehicles for North East and ScotRail. There was overdue investment in new maintenance depots, with in time the manufacturers – notably Siemens – maintaining its own trains. Central delivered Nottingham Eastcroft – the first specific 'Sprinter' depot – which had been part of the management's unsuccessful bid, and the Class 323 depot at Birmingham Soho – planned under Regional Railways – which ended the need to base Cross-City trains at Bletchley.

One intriguing new element was the involvement of the 'bus bandits' who had captured most of the TOCs. Most of them impressed; the election of Prism's Giles Fearnley to chair ATOC was recognition that the busmen (if not Prism) were there to stay. Highly motivated busmen like Fearnley, Martin Ballinger, Moir Lockhead, Brian Souter and Phil White would leave their mark on the railway.

## The glitter comes off

Then came the nonsenses, many stemming from slavish application or misunderstanding of the rules. At some stations only one TOC's trains were announced, platform staff saying the others were 'nothing to do with us'. Communication could be poor: as late as 2002 Railtrack control at Manchester Piccadilly was not aware of a possession that had halted through trains to South Wales. Signallers had not been notified and the National Rail Enquiry Service was still selling tickets; Wales & West staff took the heat from angry passengers. There was friction over 'ORCATS raiding' – the lesser operator on a route scheduling extra trains to capture a larger share of revenue. And there was the cost-inflating bureaucracy: a new public address system for Bargoed station required 168 sheets of paperwork and six architects' drawings.

Railtrack reported a £346 million profit for 1997, bolstered by a 'wonderful settlement' on access charges that the Treasury resolved not to let happen again. But punctuality and reliability were tailing off, and the company's intention to renew just 130 miles of track each year gave a worrying insight into its priorities. It also became evident that there were no contractual incentives to increase capacity to cater for growth.

Meanwhile the cuts the bidders had counted on making proved hard to deliver. Prism's bid for W&W had assumed that it could serve notice on the British Transport Police. Virgin had forgotten to budget for any drivers for empty stock in its CrossCountry bid, and First Group assumed that North Western, not the PTE, received the £38 million annual income from Merseyrail. Some incoming bus operators had imagined that BR's depots would be as inefficient as the garages they had taken over, only for cutbacks on maintenance to bring a 'sagging washing line' of punctuality and reliability.

Rising passenger numbers did not help. Paul King reflects: 'One of the things I didn't think anybody got their brain around with the regional franchises was that if you do better you make bigger losses.' Or as Gordon Pettitt puts it, 'If you need another vehicle, you're bound to lose more money unless the income covers at least the cost of providing the vehicle.'

With the PSR protecting basic services, hard-pressed TOCs looked for savings. At Merseyrail, MTL reduced almost all trains to one three-car unit. North East fell foul of OPRAF by raising fares more than it was allowed to. W&W cut Barnstaple's trains from 11 daily to seven – Devon County Council paying to reinstate two of them – and removed the Liskeard-Looe peak service in winter so its 153 could go into Plymouth and back.

'It became a constant exercise,' Chris Gibb says, 'to see if we could deliver the PSR with less services, crews, train sets, etc, and we did. This is mildly ironic, given that as BR people we had done a lot of the legwork for OPRAF to write the PSR. Changing the PSR was unbelievably difficult (and still is) as it needed the Secretary of State's consent, and no civil servant wanted to explain upwards why it was necessary.' The PSR did, however, have loopholes. 'Swanline couldn't cope with bus competition, and although it was in the PSR I managed to wriggle out of it. I bought the two "Pacers" from the local authorities – they're still in traffic, but owned by the TOC. We ran the bare minimum of service, with Cardiff-Milford Haven trains making the stops.'

The PSR also prevented station closures (see Factfile G). Etruria (track realignment) and Pendleton (arson) did go, but Barlaston, Norton Bridge and Wedgwood on the WCML remain served by buses; there is always the offchance that new business will appear, as it has for Atherstone and Broughty Ferry. A couple of dozen stations were left with a daily or weekly 'Parliamentary' train because it was too much effort to close them. Promoting new stations was also more complicated than under BR, but a few in the pipeline were delivered: Ashchurch and Euxton in 1997, and next year the final section of the 'Robin Hood Line' to Worksop.

Chapter 6: **UNDER PRIVATISATION, 1996 TO DATE** 71

**ABOVE LEFT AND RIGHT** Beautiful, graceful, historic and practical in western Scotland, but the enormous trainshed roofs in stations such as Glasgow Central (above) are a constant drain on railway finances. One solution can be the rebuilding of such iconic structures using modern materials that require less maintenance and cleaning. One example is Paisley Gilmour Street (above right), beautifully presented for the 21st century. *Both Dennis Lovett*

**RIGHT** In happier days, Managing Director Theo Steel and local mayors celebrate the launch of the 'Swanline' initiative. Difficulties in pathing services brought insuperable problems. *Theo Steel*

**BELOW** No 156406, in East Midlands livery, pauses at Worksop station. *Dennis Lovett*

### North Western in trouble

The Great Western MBO had been backed by a 24.5% shareholding from First Group. There was an early management clearout at North Western, and another after First bought out the GW team in March 1998, renaming the franchise First North Western (FNW); OPRAF secured a 'passenger dividend' of station improvements. Within days of MD Bob Goundry leaving, the operations director, finance director, human resources manager, planning manager and public affairs manager were also replaced. Performance subsequently dropped from 90% to 75% on a complex network that had been achieving all its targets right up to the end of BR.

FNW hit operational problems in Greater Manchester, having to suspend Oldham loop services for five days, and more heads rolled. Richard Peck, FNW's technical performance engineer and later its MD, attributes the strains in part to 'always being last in the queue for new trains. We had to have very flexible leases with the ROSCOs for stock that was life-expired – for Class 101s we ended up paying £1 per month.'

The pressures on FNW were such that First's rail management rebased to Manchester for a time, even holding First Great Eastern board meetings there. Mike Mitchell handed over to David Franks as Managing Director in 1999 (see Factfile H2), recruiting Vernon Barker as temporary Finance Director. Barker quickly ascertained that 'we were losing more money than anyone thought', and 'a lot of the focus on the customer had to be taken out. We were asking, "How much can we reduce cleaning of the trains by?" We had to, or the business was going to fail.' David Franks offset the cost-cutting by insisting his team got out on the barrier lines and met the customers while checking tickets. Vernon Barker went on to head TransPennine Express, where he would 'put things back in' with spectacular success.

**ABOVE** Franchise under pressure: First North Western-livered 150148 between duties at Bolton. *Dennis Lovett*

### John Prescott takes over

Labour came to power with the entire railway apart from RailFreight Distribution privatised. John Prescott, Deputy Prime Minister and head of a super-department including Transport, wanted a modal shift from road to rail, through more investment, and asked John Welsby, chairing the residual BR, to maintain a cadre of expertise to advise him on 'more effective use of our railway system'.

In July 1998 Prescott issued his White Paper 'A New Deal for Transport: Better for Everyone', proposing a Strategic Rail Authority to take charge of franchises, freight and track access grants and drive investment. Tony Blair's advisers kicked into touch Prescott's wider aspirations for a modal shift, reckoning 'anti-motorist' policies a vote-loser. That December Prescott asked John Welsby to stand down as Chairman of BR and John O'Brien as franchising director, in preparation for the SRA, which would absorb BR and OPRAF. And in February 1999 he appointed Sir Alastair Morton, who had famously got the Channel Tunnel built, as part-time Chairman of BR and prospective Chairman of the SRA.

Railtrack – and the railway – took a heavy blow when on 5 October 1999 a Thames Trains DMU pulled into the path of an HST from Cheltenham near Ladbroke Grove, killing 31 passengers and injuring more than 520. The local train had passed a red signal, and serious questions emerged both about how the accident could have happened on a line fitted with Automatic Train Protection and why Railtrack had done nothing about the signal's known poor visibility. The company's shares stopped their inexorable climb.

An unimpressive 'blame culture' around worsening punctuality and reliability was emerging between Railtrack and the TOCs. OPRAF figures showed only Island Line scoring A's for punctuality and reliability; North Western registered a B and a D. Then John Swift stood down as Rail Regulator, and in July 1999 Tom Winsor took over. A youthful Scottish solicitor as enthusiastic for complex contractual frameworks as he was for the railway, Winsor had been Swift's chief legal advisor during privatisation. Gerald Corbett, who became Railtrack's Chief Executive on John Edmonds's retirement, lobbied Winsor hard for more generous access charges as pressure grew for the company to spend more, and his eventual settlement for CP2 (2001-06) gave a 50% increase, which looked ample.

## A dysfunctional SRA

The Strategic Rail Authority only acquired its full status in February 2001. Mike Grant, formerly treasurer at Eurotunnel, became Franchising Director and the SRA's Chief Executive as it inherited 28 staff from BR and 222 from OPRAF; Gary Backler was responsible for regional networks.

It soon became evident that the SRA would have little power. Alastair Morton upset the Treasury and Railtrack by advocating 'investment, investment, investment', with 20-year franchises and 'special purpose vehicles' for major projects. Although it did gain in effectiveness, the SRA was a 'madhouse' according to Chris Stokes, who arrived there from OPRAF. Alastair Morton prescribed top-down solutions and was reluctant to listen, so 'silly ideas went unchallenged'. Mike Grant was not a strategic thinker, and had little influence on Morton.

It did not help that Morton believed John Prescott could deliver a massive modal shift, as set out in the DPM's Ten Year Plan for transport, launched in July 2000: £63 billion was to be spent on the railways (£29 billion of it from the private sector) to achieve a 50% increase in passengers and 80% in freight. On regional franchises, a 43% increase in journeys and 47% rise in passenger miles were achieved (see Factfile C3). Most of the spending was to be on mega-projects like the West Coast Route Modernisation (WCRM), High Speed 1 and Thameslink, with indirect benefits, if any, for regional services.

Progress on renewing franchises was slow, as the SRA first had to decide whether to negotiate with incumbents or launch a series of auctions. The only 20-year franchise it would award would be Chiltern's, in 2002 – leading to redoubling of track, reopening of a closed section, new stations and services, and recently a stretch of completely new line at Bicester to connect Marylebone and High Wycombe with Oxford. Capacity studies were initiated for the West Midlands and Greater Manchester. A Public Performance Measure was compiled 'better reflecting the passenger's experience'. Rail Partnership schemes worth £18 million were approved, though the reopening of Corsham station never happened as Great Western discontinued the Bristol-Oxford service that would have called there.

### Rail Partnership Schemes approved in 2002

Longer trains for Filton Abbey Wood
Edinburgh Crossrail
Faster Sheffield-Hull trains
Additional rolling stock for Leeds
Whitby Sunday service extended to winter
Secure cycle parking in Anglia
Reopening of Vale of Glamorgan Line
Reopening of Beauly and Corsham stations

The programme was short on investment and had little strategic thinking within it – the SRA rejecting the East-West Rail project between Oxford and Bletchley, now under way with electrification to follow. Meanwhile Railtrack increased provision for maintenance and renewals for Control Period 2 (1999-2004), but with little for regional routes – or for enhancement. Increased capacity was 'not on their radar,' says Stokes. 'There was a need for cultural change; we had spent most of our careers at BR ripping up track.'

**ABOVE** Multilingual signing at Welsh stations was provided by Prism as part of its commitment to improve stations – despite making heavy losses on the franchise. The re-signing was renewed by Arriva when they took over the franchise. *Alex Green*

### Welsh 20-year franchise

**Prism's vision**
Three daily Cardiff-Wrexham-Holyhead services
Sleeper service, Cardiff-Holyhead
Five trains daily on Central Wales line
Three trains per hour, Cardiff-Swansea
Hourly Vale of Glamorgan service
Eight trains per hour, Cardiff-Pontypridd
Line speed improvements
Reopenings to Bedlinog, Hirwaun, Ebbw Vale, Abertillery, Taffs Well, Coryton
40 new stations
Diesel tram-trains to Cardiff Bay
Coach links to Brecon, Cardigan, Elan Valley

## MTL and Prism bow out

The first train operator to collapse, in February 2000, was MTL, facing post-subsidy losses of £14 million on its North East franchise. Business had not increased as hoped and, more importantly, MTL's cost reduction targets had proved unrealistic. Arriva, the fast-growing Sunderland-based bus company, paid £34.7 million to take over North East and Merseyrail, relaunching the former as Northern Spirit (a brand thought up by RRNE). Arriva was paid £208 million to operate NS in 2001/02 – £55 million more than MTL would have received.

Then, that July, National Express bought out Prism for £166 million. The consortium gave up its four franchises because of heavy losses on W&W and Cardiff Valleys as the subsidy profile declined. Unlike MTL, Prism was missed; it had achievements under its belt, notably W&W's smooth operation during the 1999 Rugby World Cup.

Prism had been working up plans with the SRA for a separate Welsh franchise (see panel above right). Its 20-year vision for an area served by four TOCs and three Railtrack zones even included sub-post offices at rural stations.

'Why did we put all that effort into a Welsh train company?' asks Chris Gibb, by then Managing Director at W&W. 'We saw it as a route to terminating the franchise agreement because we had to prevent the costs putting us out of business. Welsh Assembly Government leaders were extremely helpful. We had over a year of discussions with the SRA, and in the end we agreed on termination of W&W and Cardiff Valleys and created two new companies: Wessex and Wales & Borders. I TUPE'd myself to Wales & Borders. National Express enquired if Prism was available a month later.'

## Creating Wales & Borders and Wessex

BR had been convinced that a Welsh franchise could not work, but in 2001 Wales & Borders was created, and National Express began operating it on 14 October. Gibb declared, 'Our image and style will be that of Wales: prosperous, fast-growing, successful and Welsh.' W&B initially comprised only the Valleys lines (which kept their own identity) and the Wales part of Wales and West, but would expand.

Wessex brought together local and interurban services in the West, and was intended to incorporate the reviving Waterloo-Exeter route. It was based at Exeter, with Charles Belcher in charge. There were difficulties over splitting W&W's stable of Cardiff-based 158s to meet Wessex's commitments, as numbers were tight. (Today there is nothing running in Cornwall between a 'Sprinter' and an HST, with gaps in the timetable.) Splitting W&W, says Belcher, was lucrative for National Express because Wessex was run on an annual management contract.

'Prism,' says Chris Gibb, 'was sold so quickly because Phil White was desperate to get his hands on WAGN and c2c. The key people at National Express were Ray O'Toole, Richard Brown and Phil; we had just as much freedom as under Prism, but we were more conscious of their presence. All nine MDs reported to O'Toole, who was a bus man. We must have looked to him like a highly intelligent sixth-form class. He couldn't really standardise anything between the likes of Midland Mainline, ScotRail and W&B. The only way for National Express was almost certainly downwards; even retaining all its nine franchises would have been overambitious.' And National Express, Gibb notes, took on Prism 'two weeks before Hatfield'.

**ABOVE** Barmouth Bridge represents key infrastructure in the Wales & Borders franchise. *Antony Christie*

## Hatfield leads to meltdown

The derailment of a northbound GNER express at 116mph near Hatfield on 17 October 2000, when a length of rail disintegrated under it, left four people dead and 70 injured; the fallout from it would fatally weaken Railtrack and leave several TOCs in financial trouble. Delays in replacing a rail known to be suspect and severe gauge corner cracking not fully detected were the cause; Terry Gourvish attributed the accident squarely to 'Railtrack's more commercial approach to the engineering function'.

The railway, in Alastair Morton's words, suffered a 'collective nervous breakdown'. Railtrack panicked, imposing 81 emergency speed restrictions that evening across the network; the British Transport Police and Health & Safety Executive kept the ECML closed through the offending section for 24 days. Over time 20mph restrictions were imposed at a staggering 6,821 locations pending a £200 million re-railing programme, much of it arguably unnecessary. Inter-City services were paralysed and, while regional services suffered less, passenger growth stalled and the £400 million compensation Railtrack paid the TOCs did not cover their losses. Railtrack, profitable hitherto, plunged £534 million into the red during 2000/01.

The fallout from Hatfield exacerbated financial problems for Central Trains, and for Anglia, whose parent company had launched Hull Trains over the affected route three weeks before. Anglia, however, kept up its customer offering despite the immediate pain in the belief that passengers would return; there was no reduction in train cleaning, and pressure to 'buy cheaper sausages' was resisted. Before long Anglia, Merseyrail, Northern Spirit, W&B and Wessex were all being run on a temporary, cost-plus basis.

## West Coast modernisation the final straw

Railtrack might have survived its post-Hatfield maintenance binge had it been managing to control costs. But it was not, and the project that brought it down was the West Coast Route Modernisation (WCRM), intended to deliver a 140mph railway for Virgin. Originally costed at £2.4 billion, the price rose relentlessly until £13 billion was talked of, and it would take hefty de-scoping – and new management – to deliver much of the job for nearer £8 billion.

WCRM disrupted the nation's trunk railway for a decade. Richard Peck, then running First North Western, recalls: 'There was a six-month blockade

# Chapter 6: UNDER PRIVATISATION, 1996 TO DATE

between Stockport and Crewe in 2002. It deprived our passengers of their trains for all that time, while Virgin's were just diverted – then the signalling work was cancelled for a redesign. An extra platform was put in at Stockport, but not used until it could be signalled. Even now there are manned signal boxes at Stockport, and the approach to Piccadilly is still not sorted.' Throughout the project FNW suffered from repeated route closures, having to appoint a full-time bus replacement manager, and compensation from Railtrack did not cover the disruption suffered. Peck notes: 'When you're going to work to satisfy the passengers and the passengers aren't getting any benefit, it's frustrating.

'Because of the concentration on the West Coast, other things in the North West got left; there were more speed restrictions as the track needed maintaining. On the Buxton line we couldn't keep time and, because of the weekend and overnight demands of the WCRM, work could only be done during the week – we eventually shut the line for three days.'

## Railtrack out – Network Rail in

John Prescott handed over Transport to Stephen Byers after Labour's re-election in June 2001. Briefed that both Railtrack and the SRA were 'deeply flawed', Byers told the SRA that its ambitions were 'unfocussed and unaffordable'. On 5 October he placed Railtrack in administration; lawyers and accountants combed over it and an offer – unsuccessfully challenged in the courts – was made to Railtrack's shareholders. Meanwhile the need for Railtrack to get a grip was reinforced by the fatal crash on 10 May 2002 of an EMU at speed on defective points at Potters Bar, and Jim Cornell was brought in. Railtrack had belatedly started spending on safeguarding structures and relaying track, but Cornell found that the company

**ABOVE LEFT** Stockport No 1 signal box, built in 1898 and still in use on the West Coast Main Line in 2015 despite an upgrade costing billions. *Alex Green*

**ABOVE RIGHT** A boom in rail replacement coach services took place after privatisation as a backlog of infrastructure renewals was tackled. Hundreds of coaches were hired by train companies through agents such as Fraser Eagle, which then passed the bill to Railtrack/Network Rail. *Trevor Hall*

had done little to maintain earthworks, 'all of which are structures and have a finite life', and 'did not believe in drainage'.

During the 363 days between Railtrack being put in administration and the formation of Network Rail, a 'not for dividend' company, to succeed it, the engineers regained control. Ian McAllister, formerly of Ford, became Network Rail's Chairman; John Armitt, who had been building HS1, Chief Executive; Ian Coucher, a veteran of London Underground, his deputy; and Cornell a non-executive director. Hatfield had torpedoed the access charge settlement for CP2, so Tom Winsor gave Network Rail a substantial increase, the Government picking up the tab.

## Change at the SRA

Sir Alastair Morton left the SRA in December 2001, replaced by Richard Bowker, the 35-year-old group commercial director of Virgin. After Morton's undelivered big ideas, Bowker wanted 'fewer TOCs with fewer interfaces', and his belief that there were too many operators into London's termini boded ill for Wessex. The franchise's management had worked hard to build community support for a railway no longer run from Cardiff, and 'our own company' had strong stakeholder support. Extensive planning had been done for taking on Waterloo-Exeter and basing the combined fleet of Class 158 and 159s at Salisbury. But Morton's departure left the project stillborn, and for Charles Belcher Wessex's fate was sealed when First Group persuaded the SRA that Thames Trains could be run more cheaply by merging it with Great Western; Wessex (minus Cardiff-Waterloo) had to follow.

The SRA finally published a Strategic Plan in January 2002. Importantly it included rolling out the TPWS train protection scheme across most of the network. It promised that regional networks would not lose out, with a £430 million Rail Partnership pot for small schemes. It committed the SRA to upgrade the core trans-Pennine route by 2010 and study rail links for Glasgow and Edinburgh airports, but overall it disappointed.

While advocating economies, the SRA upset operators by bidding up pay. When ASLEF's Mick Rix called for drivers to earn £35,000 nationwide, Chris Gibb said, 'We are supported by public money, and are part of the social infrastructure, like hospitals and schools. If the taxpayers invest in us it is because they want more and better trains, not higher-paid drivers.' To Paul King, the way the unions could leapfrog pay and allowances from one company to another while maintaining national rates stemmed directly from a flaw in the franchise agreements. 'Industrial action wasn't force majeure, and this handed immense power to the unions. Hence people were paid a lot more for doing the same thing.'

The Department has exerted sporadic pressure on operators to modernise working practices, but when this has resulted in disputes, notably involving drivers at East Midlands and London Midland over Sunday working and conductors on CrossCountry, this has turned to pressure to settle. Consequently there has been very limited extension of driver-only operation, in particular. Its application to the eastern end of the reinstated Glasgow-Airdrie-Bathgate-Edinburgh route brought RMT strikes on ScotRail that shut down the Far North line, and DOO in the new Northern franchise is being resisted tooth and nail by the union, which has not explained why a practice it accepted for Glasgow in 1982 is inherently dangerous for Manchester.

### Alistair Darling gets a grip

In May 2002 Blair re-created a stand-alone Department for Transport under Alistair Darling. He would stay four years, bringing continuity at the price of an at times unwelcome financial rigour; he began by cutting the SRA's budget. When a year later it updated its plan, schemes were de-scoped or delayed. TransPennine was downgraded to 'proceeding', and TOCs were urged to cut their most unremunerative trains, several trimming off-peak services that May and September. In *Modern Railways* Roger Ford declared of this recognition that costs were rising inexorably 'Boiling frogs ate my strategic plan' – and Terry Gourvish later

**BELOW** Two-car 158s, as seen at Huddersfield on 10 July 2008, struggled to keep up with growing demand on the trans-Pennine route. *Dennis Lovett*

concluded, 'The re-evaluation produced doubts as to whether regional railways could be fully supported within the existing service profile.'

The SRA did start fleshing out its redrawn franchise map. TransPennine Express was carved out of Northern Spirit and North Western, First/Keolis operating it from February 2004; Chris Stokes rates this as the SRA's 'big success'. But the residual Northern franchise – serving five of the six English PTEs – was saddled with its predecessors' heaviest loss-makers, and an assumption of nil growth. That December it was awarded to Serco/NedRail with a £2.5 billion subsidy for 8¾ years, the largest of any franchise. With the Department rating this 'unaffordable', the SRA brought in Steer Davies & Gleave to review its operations and consider the case for raising fares, and 'bustitution' or closure for eight marginal services (see panel below).

Little scope for savings was found, the consultants rating the franchise 'an efficient and well-managed operation' – albeit based on the DfT's service specification. Higher fares on the Leeds NW route would drive down rail use; eliminating the hourly stopping train between Doncaster and Hull and making the fast trains call at more stations would again be counterproductive; and closing Leeds-Morecambe would actually cost money through 'escapement' from the infrastructure. Nor could Northern's fleet be reduced as its commuter trains were full to bursting; indeed, an extra 60 vehicles would be found for Northern over the life of the franchise.

The Department may have reckoned Northern Rail a basket case, but its first Managing Director, Heidi Mottram, thought otherwise. One of a crop of outstanding 1980s BR management trainees, she 'started with the mindset that we could do better, even if we had no resources. What I and my team tried to do was say, "That's really lacking in ambition and Northern deserves more than this." Ultimately it was in our interests to expand the franchise.' Her recipe was innovative working and, above all, partnership.

Working with the PTEs, local authorities, Yorkshire Forward and the Department – which Heidi Mottram found 'in some respects no different to a PTE, with the same strategy, the same ideas, the same limitations' – Northern improved services and facilities through a 'web of bespoke deals'. Mottram subdivided Northern into three divisions, each aligned to one or two PTEs and under a senior director tasked with building relationships that could deliver. 'To make some of these deals fly we had to put something in, sometimes in kind. We levered in lots of people's money. We were very good at market segmentation – which lines are most likely to be grown. Often developing in urban corridors brought an outcome in rural because the train on its diagram cycle is going to go that way.'

Northern's status under Mottram – especially east of the Pennines – recovered despite continuing losses; in Gordon Pettitt's view this was 'one of the most important contributions post-privatisation. She started with very poor cards, and produced a winning flush.' In 2007 Northern Rail was named Public Transport Operator of the Year. In a decade under Mottram and her successors, Ian Bevan and Alex Hynes, its business would grow by 36%, fractionally more than its acclaimed counterpart TransPennine Express (TPE).

The SRA also split North Western between TPE, Northern and Wales & Borders. W&B was refranchised to Arriva, gaining the North Wales lines. Anglia was merged with Great Eastern to form Greater Anglia. First Group, the incumbent on Great Eastern, took

**Northern services reviewed for SRA, 2004**

Stockport-Stalybridge
Sheffield-Brigg-Cleethorpes
Knottingley-Goole
Morpeth-Chathill
Lancaster-Heysham
Helsby-Ellesmere Port
York-Sheffield local
Settle-Carlisle

**LEFT** Passengers flock back to rail for the 2014 Tour de France in Yorkshire, with many using Northern trains for the first time. Slaithwaite station is the scene. *Paul Salveson*

*Chapter 6:* **UNDER PRIVATISATION, 1996 TO DATE** 79

**ABOVE LEFT** West Anglia services were branded 'One' by National Express and were given a very colourful livery, as shown by No 170201 at Manea forming the 11.48 Peterborough to Liverpool Street service on 23 January 2005. *Martin Loader*

**ABOVE RIGHT** A revitalised Merseyrail electric scene, with No 507019 pausing at Ellesmere Port before returning to Liverpool. *Dennis Lovett*

over Anglia's parent GB Railways after being excluded from the shortlist for the franchise, but its subsequent bid was trumped by National Express. ScotRail was transferred – some said as a consolation – to First. And in 2004 Merseyside PTE awarded a 25-year Merseyrail Electrics franchise to Serco/NedRail.

That year Tom Winsor returned to private practice, eventually becoming HM Chief Inspector of Constabulary; meanwhile he contributed a column to *Modern Railways* explaining how the contractual system he had devised was really quite straightforward. His legacy was a settlement for Control Period 3 (2004-09) assuming that Network Rail would make economies of 8% per annum; nevertheless, this came to be seen by the Department as over-generous. To make sure Winsor's successors would be less assertive, the Government replaced the single Regulator with a revamped Office of Rail Regulation.

At this time Royal Mail ended its contract with EWS, halting all mail flows on rail and ending the Travelling Post Office trains immortalised in W. H. Auden's *Night Mail*. Some mail traffic would be regained over time by other operators, but 24-hour use of the railway for bulk mail ended at a stroke.

In addition, and of profound practical and reputational significance, Network Rail brought track maintenance, and some 15,000 workers, back in-house.

## The SRA gives way to DfT Rail

The SRA's payments to the TOCs had been rising again as more got into trouble and new franchisees took a realistic view of their costs. Overall the railway's cost to the taxpayer had increased in five years from 25% to 45% of turnover. Darling tempered this at the start of 2004 by allowing operators to increase regulated fares annually by RPI +1% over three years instead of RPI -1%. He went on to announce a further structural review of the industry, promising 'more fundamental reform' to match the creation of Network Rail. Irritated by the SRA's undisciplined approach to spending, cost overruns on the WCRM and the industry's continuing 'blame culture', Darling stressed the need for Government to reassert control over spending while maintaining independent regulation.

Darling's White Paper 'The Future of Rail' was published that July, and implemented in the Railways Act of 2005. The SRA was dissolved, 'not because it had failed, but because its remit had become impossible,' as Terry Gourvish put it. A unit within the Department, DfT Rail, took on its role, with First Group's Dr Mike Mitchell as its director. Holyrood was given full responsibility for the ScotRail franchise – passing it on to a new agency, Transport Scotland – and the Welsh Assembly Government for all Arriva Trains Wales services, with powers to fund improvements.

A new process for access charge reviews was mandated, the Government specifying both the railway services it wanted to buy for each Control Period (the High Level Output Specification – HLOS) and how much it was prepared to pay (the Statement of Funds Available, SOFA). Network Rail was given overall responsibility for the network, and the ORR took over the safety brief from the HSE, which had won few plaudits for its handling of the railways.

**ABOVE** The Central Wales line has many beautiful structures, such as the Cynghordy Viaduct. *John B. R. Davies*

## DFT Rail's prescriptive franchises

DfT Rail finally created a combined Greater Western franchise by merging Great Western, Thames and Wessex, and awarded it to First. Wessex's Waterloo-Bristol service went to SWT. Economies proposed by the SRA, including ending the Cornish sleeper and closing the Newquay branch, were not pursued, but the Department did impose some 'service synergies' and cuts in operating hours.

The first day of the franchise, 1 April 2006, was a baptism of fire. DfT Rail had specified an unrealistically small fleet of 100 DMU vehicles for FGW's regional services; today it needs 150. Serious overcrowding and cancellations ensued, especially in the Bristol area, the media gleefully reporting commuters' protests against 'Worst Great Western' while the trains previously used sat in sidings. Some were soon reinstated, but the East Midlands franchise – won by Stagecoach – would also experience severe overcrowding. When the Department told East Midlands' management it might receive three extra vehicles during the next control period, the response was, 'How are we going to cope if they all arrive at once?'

Finally, in November 2007 the Central franchise was dismembered (see Table 6.1), completing the jigsaw worked up by the SRA. Its East Midlands routes were merged with Midland Mainline to create that East Midlands franchise, and Silverlink's WCML services together with most of Central's in the Birmingham area became London Midland; a few passed to Chiltern. Its interurban services went to Arriva Trains Wales and CrossCountry. Patchy agreements with drivers on Sunday and rest-day working inherited from BR by Central Trains and never resolved brought continuing disputes and Sunday cancellations on both new franchises.

DfT Rail's determination of how much rolling stock the TOCs should have, and who should build it, would be a practical and political issue throughout its existence. The SRA had kept out of rolling stock issues, but the franchise structures it devised inevitably had implications. Combined urban/interurban/rural franchises like

**Table 6.1: Central franchise broken up, 2007**

| Central Trains | Reallocation |
|---|---|
| East Midlands-Lincolnshire | East Midlands Trains |
| West Midlands routes | London Midland and Chiltern |
| Cambrian services | Arriva Trains Wales |
| Cardiff-Nottingham | CrossCountry |
| Birmingham-Stansted Airport | CrossCountry |

*Chapter 6:* **UNDER PRIVATISATION, 1996 TO DATE**

**ABOVE** The new layout at Nuneaton, with the east-to-west flyover already in place and the new northern chord being built to link Felixstowe to the WCML Down Slow line. *Network Rail*

Central at the outset or East Midlands later allowed for stock flexibility, such as allocating a 'Meridian' to Norwich-Liverpool or an HST to Skegness on peak Saturdays. Stand-alone franchises like TPE were spared the temptation to put 'Pacers' onto interurban services, but experienced the headaches of an inelastic fleet.

FGW's travails focused attention on a steady increase in traffic — something the privatisers had not foreseen, and which nil-growth franchises still did not recognise. It was, however, reflected in planning to relieve the worst bottlenecks. One legacy of the SRA taken forward by Network Rail was a series of Route Utilisation Studies to identify pinch points and cost-effective ways of tackling them, and some significant schemes resulted. One of the few to benefit the regional railway in this period involved reinstating the Rocker Bridge flyover at Nuneaton to end conflicts between Virgin West Coast trains and interurban services between Birmingham and Peterborough. Another was the £11 million Allington chord, which removed Nottingham-Skegness locals from 3 miles of the ECML north of Grantham. It was a sign of how modest ambitions for the railway had become that the opening of the chord in 2006 merited a visit from the Secretary of State; fortunately the improvements would soon be coming thick and fast. (For a full – and impressive – list of infrastructure improvements made over time on the regional network, see Factfile F6.)

### Larkhall and Alloa at last

Railway development in Scotland had slowed with privatisation; since 1998 ScotRail has opened 19 stations – eight on reinstated lines – against 50 in the previous decade. Reopening to Larkhall (2005) and Alloa had been planned before privatisation, but costs for the latter rose, forecasts of demand fell, BR lost its ability to contribute, and ScotRail withdrew from its agreement with local councils. Post-devolution Clackmannan Council promoted reopening with Holyrood's Transport Minister Sarah Boyack, who had worked there as a planner. In 2002 Longannet Colliery closed, leaving the adjoining power station dependent on imported and opencast coal for which paths over the weight-limited Forth Bridge were scarce. Reopening not just to Alloa but on to Longannet became an imperative; trains to Alloa returned in May 2008, and the first coal trains ran that autumn. Passenger loadings were three times those forecast, and Stirling-Alloa is now programmed for electrification.

## Chapter 6: UNDER PRIVATISATION, 1996 TO DATE

**ABOVE LEFT** The reopened Larkhall station on 26 February 2007, with No 334002 in SPT livery. *Dennis Lovett*

**ABOVE RIGHT** Alloa station back in use in 2008. *Dennis Lovett*

**RIGHT** Lincoln station undergoing extensive infrastructure remodelling. *Dennis Lovett*

### Lord Adonis seizes the initiative

Alistair Darling was followed in May 2006 by Douglas Alexander, whose 13 months at the Department brought a commitment to 1,000 new carriages over five years, upped by his successor Ruth Kelly to 1,300; argument persists over how many were delivered. Ms Kelly stayed when Gordon Brown succeeded Tony Blair in June 2007. Soon after, the Department adopted a technical strategy ruling out further electrification until cab signalling was introduced – baffling technical journalists at its launch – and a White Paper 'Delivering a Sustainable Railway' set the agenda for CP4 (2009-14) and on to 2039. It rated HS2 as not a priority, and ruled out further closures for the time being.

In October 2007 Ian Coucher, Chief Executive of Network Rail, and Adrian Shooter, Chairman of ATOC, issued a joint response to the White Paper stressing the need for more electrification, sooner rather than later. Railtrack had shied away from electrification as its problems intensified, and Network Rail's readoption of it with the backing of the TOCs was of critical importance, not least for the urban and interurban railway in the regions. The Department's technical objections evaporated.

In October 2008 Geoff Hoon replaced Ruth Kelly. Though a railwayman's son from Derby, Hoon did not warm to the portfolio … but in an inspired move Brown gave him as Minister of State Lord Adonis, a former Liberal Democrat who had been a key advisor

**ABOVE** A temporary station was built in weeks at Workington North in September 2010 after a disastrous local flood destroyed a vital road bridge. *Network Rail*

to Tony Blair. Adonis knew about and liked railways – he had played a part in the rescue of Dilton Marsh Halt in Wiltshire (see Chapter 11) – and set up a National Networks Strategy Group with the Highways Agency, Network Rail and the Treasury.

By the time Adonis succeeded Hoon in July 2009, electrification (and HS2) was firmly on the agenda.

Aware that time was running out for the Labour Government (he was Transport Secretary for just 11 months), Adonis set a cracking pace, from commissioning Chris Green and Professor Sir Peter Hall to search out Britain's most dilapidated stations to, controversially, delivering the Department's new-generation inter-city train, the Hitachi IEP. Network Rail was encouraged to borrow more and electrification of the GWML and Manchester-Liverpool was approved, with more to follow when resources of money, plant and manpower permitted.

Remodelling of track and signalling at major regional centres was resuming, first at Lincoln, then at Nottingham. And Network Rail excelled when, after floods swept away the road bridge into Workington in November 2009, a temporary station, Workington North, was built in days to give access to the town by a Class 47-hauled shuttle. On the same route, Network Rail pioneered the 'Harrington hump', raising the height of enough of a platform to ease passenger access to a 'Pacer' or 'Sprinter'.

## The Coalition and McNulty scrutinise costs

The May 2010 election led to the Coalition under David Cameron; the Conservative Philip Hammond became Transport Secretary with a LibDem, Norman Baker – a campaigner for the Lewes-Uckfield reopening – in his team. Value-for-money reviews of HS2 and the IEP were ordered, and Lord Adonis had already commissioned one of the railway itself, which was consuming £4 billion a year of public money (down from £5.41 billion in 2006/07). Sir Roy McNulty, former Chairman of the Civil Aviation Authority, was 'to examine the overall cost structure of all elements of the railway sector, and identify options for improving value for money to taxpayers and passengers while continuing to expand capacity as necessary to drive up passenger satisfaction' – or identify ways of delivering the privatised railway less expensively.

McNulty's report, 'Realising the Potential of GB Rail', published in May 2011, reckoned that costs could be reduced by 30% over seven years to Continental levels, with the greatest savings from asset and supply chain management (up to £580 million) and 'people' (£260 million). It urged greater clarity on strategy and objectives, the alignment of incentives for Network Rail with those for the TOCs, less prescriptive franchises, system-wide DOO and fewer ticket offices, wider adoption of best practice, an independent change management team, a Rail Delivery Group of industry leaders, and 'new approaches to enable lower-cost regional railways'. Noting that 61% of Government support went on subsidising regional lines to the tune of 31p per passenger mile, McNulty recommended choosing several with different characteristics to pilot 'a more appropriate level for both infrastructure and operations that can maintain existing levels of safety, but reduce costs', as tried elsewhere in Europe, with PTEs and local authorities involved. (See Factfile K for McNulty's recommendations on lower-cost regional lines.)

Save for a chorus of outrage from the unions, McNulty was well received. The Department resisted those changes that would weaken its position, but a Rail Delivery Group was formed under First Group's Tim O'Toole. It made an encouraging start, then lost some of its momentum and merged itself with ATOC, being criticised within Network Rail as a 'talking shop' and elsewhere for excluding key players. Several of McNulty's other recommendations were taken forward, but nothing has come of his proposal for low-cost regional pilot schemes.

## Investment accelerates

Investment accelerated as Justine Greening succeeded Hammond in October 2011, then, from September 2012, under Patrick McLoughlin. These ministers' main concerns were not regional railways but the self-promotion of HS2 – resolved by appointing former Network Rail Chief Executive Sir David Higgins to head the project – fall-out from the award of the Thameslink rolling stock contract to Siemens rather than Derby's Bombardier, and the discrediting of the Department's refranchising process through a botched attempt to award West Coast to First ahead of Virgin on the basis of faulty data. A review by Richard Brown, Chairman of Eurostar, brought a far more professional approach, which benefited the entire railway.

In December 2013 the overhead between Manchester and the WCML was energised, enabling TransPennine Express to commence its Class 350 service to Scotland. Manchester-Liverpool followed early in 2015, cascaded Thameslink 319s arriving in driblets to supplant the line's 'Pacers'; Manchester-Bolton-Blackpool and Bolton-Wigan were to follow with similar stock. The GWML, Cardiff Valleys, Midland Main Line and an 'Electric Spine' between Southampton, Oxford and Coventry/Bedford joined the programme, and Patrick McLoughlin even urged Network Rail to electrify Hastings-Ashford.

The Department set up a task force with Network Rail on options for further electrification in the North, and its report in March 2015 prioritised Northern's unglamorous routes west of the Pennines, with the Calder Valley/Copy Pit line its first priority. Its

**84** Chapter 6: UNDER PRIVATISATION, 1996 TO DATE

**ABOVE** A possible diversion for future Dawlish closures would be a reopened Plymouth-Exeter route via Okehampton. The disused Brentor station lies on the closed section of the route. *Antony Christie*

**LEFT** Severe weather is becoming a growing hazard to the infrastructure of regional railways. The spectacular washaway at Dawlish in February 2014 points to future problems. *Antony Christie*

recommendations, based on ratings out of 100, are listed in Factfile F5. Twelve 'Tier 1' routes are proposed for electrification by 2024, comprising 450 miles; intriguingly the line between Manchester and Sheffield was lumped together with thinly patronised South East Manchester suburban services and missed the cut. Seven 'Tier 2' routes totalling 300 miles are recommended 'to be developed post-2024, but also considered for alternative approaches', one of which must be Tram-Train. Twelve routes covering 500 miles are categorised as 'other lines, to be considered for electrification in the longer term, but also for service enhancements using modern diesel trains in the interim'. The bottom five astonishingly includes Doncaster-Gilberdyke, used by inter-city, TPE and local traffic, which is outscored even by the Barton-on-Humber branch; Skipton-Lancaster-Morecambe-Heysham gets the lowest rating of all. One can be pretty certain that such lines will never be electrified.

Network Rail showed its growing confidence and versatility after heavy seas washed away a length of the GWML at Dawlish in February 2014, isolating Plymouth and Cornwall. Despite further slippages, the line was rebuilt and reopened within eight weeks. The risk of a recurrence, and regular problems with sea spray and the underfloor engines of 'Voyagers', led Network Rail to consider an alternative or supplementary route. Reinstating the Exeter-Plymouth line via Okehampton as a social railway and diversionary route was one option, another the more costly duplication of the Dawlish line through a tunnel set back from the coastal strip. Similar work to reopen the Cambrian Coast line after a series of washouts, notably at Barmouth, took months and cost £10 million, ten times the route's annual takings.

Control Period 5 (2014-19) dawned brightly for the regional railway. Together with electrification, work on the 'Northern Hub' was under way to transform connectivity across Manchester. Passenger numbers were still growing, if more slowly, increasing pressure for further investment in rolling stock, largely unrecoverable at the fare box. Network Rail was starting to take on the tougher and more complicated renewals, with higher costs and greater disruption, and capacity upgrades were falling foul of past economies; on the Wrexham-Chester line two bridges were inches too narrow for double track. The need to duplicate the ECML for freight led Network Rail to spend £280 million modernising the Joint line through Lincoln, enabling more than a skeleton passenger service, once single-shift opening was abolished on a route that had included 61 manned level crossings.

## The regional railway today

Today's regional railway carries far more passengers than at privatisation, when loadings were already well ahead of the low point of 1982 (see Table 6.2). Growth has not been uniform: since 1998 traffic into Liverpool has rocketed by 250%, in the West Midlands by 200%, in West Yorkshire by 180%, around Cheltenham by 148%, and around Bristol by 140%. But it has flatlined around Sunderland; around Hull it has risen by only 20%, around Blackpool by 22%, in Greater Glasgow by 30%, and around Grimsby by 45%. To an extent this reflects local economic conditions, Dick Fearn reckoning that 'this is not a railway story'.

The cost of the railway to the taxpayer nationally is back down to £3.8 billion, with income from fares £8 billion, and TOCs covering their costs in aggregate – all this despite continued Government regulation of many fares. In 2012/13 subsidy represented 27% of total industry income in England, 54% in Scotland,

## Chapter 6: UNDER PRIVATISATION, 1996 TO DATE

Table 6.2: Percentage growth in rail passenger journeys originating from, or made within, each economic region since privatisation and in the most recent year

| Region | % growth 1996/7-2013/4 Total | % growth 1996/7-2013/4 within Region | % growth 2012/3-2013/4 Total | % growth 2012/3-2013/4 within Region |
| --- | --- | --- | --- | --- |
| West Midlands | 190 | 252 | 5.6 | 6.6 |
| North West | 176 | 210 | 6.9 | 8.1 |
| Yorks and Humberside | 142 | 154 | 2.8 | 2.0 |
| East Midlands | 99 | 71 | 1.8 | -1.3 |
| South West | 95 | 133 | 1.8 | 3.3 |
| Wales | 94 | 107 | 1.6 | 2.9 |
| London | 93 | 120 | 6.0 | 8.2 |
| East of England | 89 | 142 | 4.0 | 2.4 |
| South East | 87 | 76 | 2.5 | 1.9 |
| Scotland | 82 | 83 | 1.2 | 1.0 |
| North East | 71 | 59 | 3.7 | 2.4 |

**ABOVE** No 380102 stands in North Berwick station in 2013 wearing Transport Scotland's colourful 'Saltire' blue livery. *Alex Green*

**RIGHT** An area of expenditure that has risen hugely but is directly funded by Government is the 'Access for All' programme. Colossal ramps and multi-lift structures are appearing across the network – seen here at Armadale (above right) and Perth (right) – to allow freedom of access to trains for all mobility-impaired citizens. While initial costs are covered by special funding, there will be further cost pressure on organisations to keep them safe and efficient. *Dennis Lovett/Alex Green*

and 56% in Wales. SWT and state-run East Coast took no public money; Northern Rail and ScotRail received 64% of their income from the taxpayer, and Arriva Trains Wales 65%. TransPennine Express, though receiving a £41 million subsidy, achieved a profit margin of 23.2% for Keolis and First.

In February 2014 Patrick McLoughlin announced the creation of a Rail Executive within the Department, eventually to become an arm's-length body, and within it an Office of Passenger Rail Services (a virtual rebirth of OPRAF, though with bidders now facing a far more costly and onerous process).

Investment in the railway infrastructure continues to accelerate, though it is questionable how long the Treasury will allow Network Rail – which returned to the Government's balance sheet in September 2014 with its Board in future appointed by the Secretary of State – to increase borrowings in excess of £30 billion. Big orders for (electric) rolling stock are also in the pipeline, with the benefit to the non-electrified regional railway mainly coming from cascading of ageing DMUs as the wiring is extended.

# Chapter 7
# THE URBAN CHALLENGE

*'What Provincial and latterly Regional Railways brought to the conurbations was focus. A focus of a senior empowered management team, a focus for solid partnerships with local authorities and PTEs, a focus for the introduction of new services and routes and for the introduction of purpose-built rolling stock. It evoked a new era of pride and trust in these urban areas, where rail now plays a key role.'*

**CHRIS LEAH,** MANAGING DIRECTOR, REGIONAL RAILWAYS NORTH WEST

**ABOVE** The disused terminal platforms at Birmingham Moor Street station in 1980. *Dennis Lovett*

## Trying to live with the car

Urban Britain in the post-war decades experienced increasing pressure on its infrastructure from a rise in car commuting against a background of inner-city decline. Initially most cities met that challenge by building new roads, as their rail networks contracted and once-extensive tram systems were abandoned. However, it became evident that the car caused as many problems as it solved, and that all modes of transport had to be considered if traffic congestion – which disadvantaged bus users as much as motorists – was to be overcome. The argument was not just a practical one; gridlock in Britain's cities had a deleterious environmental and economic effect, and breaking it would generate added value.

Up to the early 1980s the inner cities were subject to planning, transport and other policies that accelerated their decline, not least the 'decanting' of communities to estates some way out, which often lacked good public transport. Glasgow and Liverpool in particular were suffering, new suburbs mushrooming where there was no station, or away from the railway altogether. The young families moving out to them went everywhere by car.

In this context we are talking about every sizeable urban area in England, Scotland and Wales, not simply those that for political, administrative or geographical reasons have gained Passenger Transport Executives (PTEs). They have all faced the same challenges, and while the development of the PTEs forms a critical part of this story, the individual circumstances of each PTE are dealt with specifically in the next chapter.

Gradually pro-car policies were abandoned, and from the 1990s concerted efforts were made – more successful in some cities than others – to regenerate their central areas for commerce, shopping and eventually housing. Over time, the major conurbations made increasing use of the powers to coordinate and develop public transport granted to them by Barbara Castle's 1968 Transport Act, which established the first PTEs. The PTEs and their political sponsors looked beyond the municipal bus services they had inherited to foster not only the conventional urban railway, but also new-generation light rail. The railway, after a wary start, became an enthusiastic partner in choosing and delivering the mix of transport modes that would most effectively bust congestion and deliver an attractive and reliable high-capacity alternative to the car.

The success of the original PTEs brought pressure from other major centres to have PTEs of their own, but the Monopolies & Mergers Commission's recommendation in 1989 for Avon, Cardiff and Valleys and the East Midlands to have them was not implemented. Non-PTE councils were not permitted to assist local rail services until the Transport Act of 1985, after which some did so with enthusiasm, BR and its successors working increasingly to develop local railways with councils in non-PTE areas and with the Scottish and Welsh Offices. It is only since the Local Transport Act of 2008 that councils have been allowed to band together and create Integrated Transport Authorities. This has enabled the likes of Bristol and its environs, and industrial Lancashire, to drive forward initiatives of their own. They have been joined in this by the national capitals of Cardiff (even prior to devolution) and Edinburgh, and the results can be seen in new and improved rail transport systems generating revival and development.

## Creating the framework

The urban railways inherited by the Provincial sector in 1982 were largely run down and deficient in capacity even for the level of services then operating, let alone the expansion that was about to take place – an expansion driven initially by the policies of the PTEs and subsequently by a revival in demand. The closures of the mid- and late 1960s had stripped out many routes that lacked the high traffic levels and political sensitivity of London commuter services. Beeching had targeted 15 services into Manchester, 12 into Glasgow, 10 into Leeds, seven into Bradford, six into Edinburgh, and five each into Liverpool and Newcastle, and only a few survived.

**BELOW** Blackburn station in the 1990s, before its complete transformation into a new four-platform station in 2014. (Compare P. 149) *Dennis Lovett*

# 88 Chapter 7: THE URBAN CHALLENGE

### Table 7.1: City termini closed

| Birmingham Snow Hill | 1972 |
| Edinburgh Princes Street | 1965 |
| Glasgow St Enoch | 1966 |
| Glasgow Buchanan Street | 1966 |
| Leeds Central | 1967 |
| Manchester Exchange | 1969 |
| Manchester Central | 1969 |
| Nottingham Victoria | 1967 |
| Sheffield Victoria | 1970 |

For the terminal capacity put back in the decades since, see Factfile F6.

### Table 7.2: Creation of the PTEs

| Location and title | Year |
|---|---|
| Merseyside (MPTE, now Merseytravel) | 1968 |
| Greater Manchester (GMPTE, now TfGM) | 1968 |
| Tyneside | 1968 |
| Sunderland added (Tyne & Wear, now Nexus) | 1974 |
| West Midlands (WMPTE, now Centro) | 1968 |
| Coventry added | 1974 |
| Greater Glasgow (GGPTE) | 1973 |
| South-west Scotland added: Strathclyde (SPTE) | 1975 |
| South Yorkshire (SYPTE) | 1974 |
| West Yorkshire (WYPTE, now Metro) | 1974 |

PTEs shown on endpapers

At least as serious was the loss of city centre termini and the lines serving them. Some were redundant, but remodelling Leeds's remaining station in 1967 left just two platforms for all westbound local services; lines to Harrogate, Ilkley and Skipton were expected to close. Birmingham New Street and Nottingham struggled, while lack of capacity at Sheffield Midland prevented the Liverpool-Harwich boat train, rerouted from Victoria, from reversing and changing its engine; instead it had to continue eastward until it reached a connection that enabled it to turn south for East Anglia.

Mrs Castle's White Paper 'Public Transport and Traffic' concluded that the major conurbations should no longer comprise a patchwork of councils operating their own buses, but enjoy integrated public transport, with strategy set locally. The 1968 Act took the historic step of creating the first PTEs. Most important for the railways was Section 20, the mechanism for financing urban lines (until privatisation). It allowed a PTE to specify to BR the services it believed would aid integration, enabling conurbations to protect socially and economically useful lines. Under Section 20, security was given to the lines to Bury, East Kilbride, Ilkley, Southport and more. However, most services inherited by the PTEs were elderly, infrequent and filthy, and in Dick Fearn's words 'we had desperate inner urban stations all over the place'.

**BELOW** Bradford Exchange in the BR Eastern Region era. *Stuart Baker*

**ABOVE AND LEFT** A range of the early PTE logos when they were first introduced. All have since been changed or upgraded. *Author's collection*

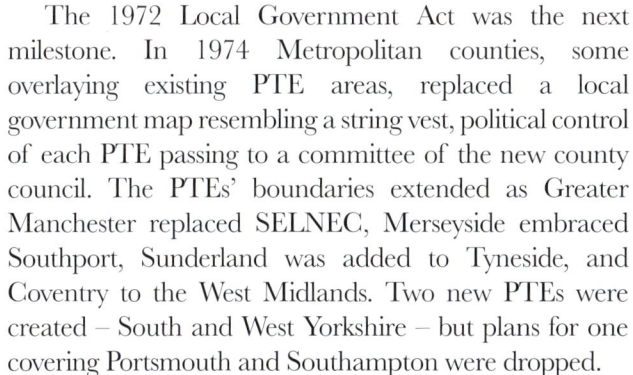

**ABOVE** Early linking of the West Yorkshire PTE and BR brands provided a cost-effective solution. *Dennis Lovett*

The 1972 Local Government Act was the next milestone. In 1974 Metropolitan counties, some overlaying existing PTE areas, replaced a local government map resembling a string vest, political control of each PTE passing to a committee of the new county council. The PTEs' boundaries extended as Greater Manchester replaced SELNEC, Merseyside embraced Southport, Sunderland was added to Tyneside, and Coventry to the West Midlands. Two new PTEs were created – South and West Yorkshire – but plans for one covering Portsmouth and Southampton were dropped.

Simultaneously, cities the size of Bristol and Nottingham lost their powers over transport planning to the shire counties that absorbed them. In Scotland the regional structure created in 1975 increased the reach – and clout – of the renamed Strathclyde PTE, which now stretched from Stranraer to the Highlands. While strong political personalities had driven some PTEs from the outset, notably Michael Campbell on Tyneside, new leaders now came forward who would include Malcolm Waugh in Strathclyde and West Yorkshire's Michael Simmons and Mick Lyons.

## The PTEs develop their priorities

Together the PTEs formed the railway's largest passenger sector after London & South East. They worked together, informally at first but from the early 1980s as the Passenger Transport Executive Group, comprising the seven directors-general. South Yorkshire's Alex Ritchie led negotiations with BR, trying to ensure that agreements between each PTE and BR were broadly uniform and did not undercut each other. The Association of Metropolitan Authorities' transport committee became the forum for the PTEs' political leaders.

One issue where the PTEs had different priorities from BR was the use of routes with limited capacity. From the 1970s to this day West Midlands PTE/Centro has sought better local services on the Coventry-Birmingham-Wolverhampton axis, heavily used by InterCity trains; the absence of quadruple track has disadvantaged stopping services. With fares, the PTEs' efforts to develop structures suiting them conflicted at times with BR's charging systems. PTEs' setting of fares below national levels may increase business (sometimes creating overcrowding, which the operator then comes under pressure to alleviate), but can leave less cash for investment. Lower PTE fares also have a 'halo effect' of undermining stations just outside PTE boundaries where the national railway's higher fares would apply, with commuters with access to a good road incentivised to head for stations within the PTE area; the A65/Aire Valley corridor into Leeds is an example.

Some local rail managers feared a PTE takeover after the 1974 reorganisation, and relationships took time to develop. Strains recurred as the PTEs experienced poor reliability from ageing DMUs; by the formation of the Provincial sector some were threatening to withhold Section 20 payments. And while the arrival of the 'Pacers' raised hopes, their early unreliability brought fresh tensions that were perpetuated by the Class 323 introduction saga.

By 1982 the PTEs had developed strategies showing varying degrees of commitment to the urban railway in one mode or other: Tyne & Wear with its pioneering Metro, Liverpool with its Loop and Link lines, Strathclyde with Glasgow's Argyle Line, and Greater Manchester with its abortive Picc-Vic scheme – all but the first promoted by BR or in close cooperation with it. While in a still difficult economic climate growth might seem unlikely, important foundations had been laid for it to occur.

## Chapter 7: THE URBAN CHALLENGE

### Expansion under Provincial

Sectorisation – and the subsequent creation of Provincial's sub-sectors – led railway management to devote more time to the PTEs, some areas of strain being tackled by special working parties. Generally, matters were resolved at regional or sector level; Alex Ritchie recalled only three instances when they had to involve the BR Chairman. Bob Reid I 'would never visit any of the metropolitan areas without ensuring that someone from the PTE was there so he could sit down and talk with them. Bob Reid II was a different kettle of fish. He understood what we were doing, he was happy to meet us, but occasionally you felt he was just taking the opportunity of saying "Thank you".'

The 1985 Transport Act, which deregulated bus services outside London from the following year, finished the PTEs as bus operators. They could only look on as a free-for-all broke out, with anyone possessing an operator's licence entitled to run buses on any route provided they gave 42 days' notice. They no longer had the powers to make buses call at interchanges, and the spread of integrated ticketing slowed. PTE and municipal bus operations became free-standing companies; some were forced out of business by predatory competitors, some were sold off, and others – notably Aberdeen's Grampian, the basis of First Group – were acquired by their managers, their first step to becoming train operators as well. Meanwhile congestion was exacerbated by throngs of competing buses; rush hours appeared in cities that had never really had one, bus use declined, and more commuters were pushed onto the roads.

Left with their rail networks, the PTEs began to take much more interest in them. West Midlands PTE relaunched itself as Centro, Tyne & Wear became Nexus, and West Yorkshire became Metro. Frank Beck-style maps started to appear on stations and in promotional leaflets. The PTEs – except South Yorkshire – arranged to have trains liveried with their own branding, West Yorkshire's Metro Train being a prime example. This caused headaches for operating managers if, as happened, they had to run a Metro unit into Sheffield or Manchester. Strathclyde liveried its trains orange – calling it 'Strathclyde red' because of sectarian sensibilities.

1986 also brought the abolition of the metropolitan counties as a concomitant to Margaret Thatcher's demolition of the Greater London Council. The English PTEs again became answerable to joint boards (PTAs) of councillors. Alex Ritchie recalled: '1986 was a horrendous year for the PTEs. How we got through it I shall never know.' Offsetting this, the 1985 Act also at last empowered councils outside the PTE areas to assist their railways, bringing a surge of reopenings and improvements in, especially, South Wales and the East Midlands.

### Regional Railways and the PTEs

When Regional Railways assumed its full powers in 1992, urban railways accounted for 55% of its income, and 56% of journeys made were in PTE territory. But PTE-specified services are costly: in 1995/96 each carriage deployed on Centro services earned £140,000, against £205,000 on East Midlands urban services, £290,000 on rural, and £388,000 on interurban. The reasons were that many vehicles were used during peak hours only, short distances giving low mileages, and lower fares.

**ABOVE LEFT** Tyne & Wear Metro unit No 4086 at the restored ex-BR Tynemouth station. *Antony Christie*

**ABOVE RIGHT** No 314209 at Lanark in early Strathclyde red livery. *David Burrell*

Chapter 7: **THE URBAN CHALLENGE** 91

Regional Railways' second source of income after central Government, the PTEs were also increasingly providers of investment funding. 'Each year,' recalled Alex Ritchie, 'the PTEs would bid to Government for approval to borrow. We were also able to tap the European market for grants, so we were in a position to build stations, buy rolling stock, assist in electrification, assist in resignalling.' Pressures on BR's External Financing Limit meant that if PTEs and local authorities wanted more intensive services – or, as in South Glamorgan early on, to fend off closures – they had to finance extra rolling stock themselves. By 1991 the PTEs funded 503 DMU and EMU vehicles, 40% of the fleet deployed on their local services. However, only West Yorkshire actually purchased rolling stock, which was eventually sold to the ROSCOs in 2012.

The PTEs also tried to keep Regional Railways up to scratch on station conditions and cleanliness, even putting in their own safety-accredited staff. 'They weren't allowed to clean the track,' says Alex Ritchie, 'but they did clean the stations and check that tannoy systems were working. Inspectors were put onto trains to make sure the correct destination was showing, and that the floor wasn't littered with the previous day's papers.'

Regional Railways appointed managers to interface with the PTEs in a genuine business environment. Gordon Pettitt saw urban railways generally as the key to 'congestion-busting', with even non-users benefiting from whatever modal shift could be achieved. Train mileage operated for the PTEs was increasing – by more

**ABOVE** The famous 'Club Trains' originally connected Manchester with Blackpool and Southport. They were also used on the North Wales Coast, where loco-hauled trains continued to be used spasmodically. Nos 31439 and 31465 head an immaculate rake of Regional Railways stock past Holywell Junction on 8 August 1995, forming the 17.24 Crewe to Holyhead service. *Phil Chilton*

than 15% between 1987/88 and 1990/91 – but Pettitt noted, 'The levels of business are well below the use made of rail in Network SouthEast, and it is the spare capacity which represents such great potential for solving road congestion and reducing transport demands on the environment.' Many routes were operated by two-car trains, so could accommodate far heavier traffic flows. Yet the ongoing shortage of DMUs hampered expansion; in 1991 Regional Railways reintroduced the 'Club' trains between Manchester Victoria and Blackpool/Southport with surplus carriages from NSE to free up stock for other routes.

By 1992/93 the PTEs were contributing £144 million a year – and expecting something in return. 'High-level meetings with BR were always, "Why are we not getting the service that you have signed up for?"' says Alex Ritchie. Friction over reliability continued until the total withheld again reached £20 million. When Chris Leah arrived to head North Western, he was tasked with engineering a settlement. Despite the common front presented by Ritchie, Leah found that each PTE showed a very different face. Tyne & Wear's involvement was limited, except over Metro, and West and South Yorkshire had 'no particular problems'. Merseyside's Director-General Roy Swainson was easy to deal with, West Midlands was 'mixed' because political control of Birmingham kept changing, but Greater Manchester, which considered itself 'a Labour government in exile', was

**BELOW** Wemyss Bay is a listed station built in 1903 by the Caledonian Railway and designed by railway architect James Miller. It was lovingly restored in 1994 to create an iconic Regional Railways terminus, supported by local staff who are renowned for their floral displays. *Dennis Lovett*

the grit in the oyster. Relations had got 'sourer and sourer', not helped by railway managers being 'suspicious, adversarial and get-off-my-turf' towards 'organisations wanting to pay us a shed-load of money'. BR had 'new people who were learning all the time,' while the PTEs had had decades to decide what they wanted. Leah eventually recovered enough of the £20 million to satisfy the Board. Through closer cooperation over the quality and reach of urban rail services, Regional Railways helped major cities become the focus of their conurbations; satellite centres, especially around Manchester, would struggle even when times were good. Although Section 20 set out to 'keep things as they are', Regional Railways tried to do better. This could mean rural lines making sacrifices. Mike Hodson, RRNE's Operations Director, noted: 'The nature of the peak in northern cities is different. There will be a peak train, or at most two, for each route, and most are two-car "Pacers". One reason we had trains on Saturdays only between Gainsborough and Grimsby, Stalybridge and Stockport was because we could use their "Sprinters" during the week to turn a two-car peak train into a four-car.' In 1992 each urban train carried just 14 passengers per vehicle averaged over the operating week, but when Regional Railways had to strip out its costliest services the PTEs' political stake left expensive urban peak-only resources untouched.

## Light rail enters the picture

During the early 1980s several urban areas began to consider the option of new light rail systems, which were cheaper than conventional rail. Most European cities east of France had kept their tramways, and they had played a significant role in shaping post-war residential development. Some, as in Brussels, had formed the basis of integrated networks of surface or underground routes. German experience had identified patterns of demand that buses could not handle without themselves contributing to congestion, but which did not warrant heavy rail lines. (A reluctance in Britain to resurrect 'archaic' trams led to the adoption of the term Light Rail, the traditional railway inevitably becoming Heavy Rail.)

The initiative came from France, with Nantes and Grenoble pioneering a policy designed both to attack congestion and sustain a French light rail vehicle manufacturing capability. These, and more than 20 subsequent French light rail schemes, benefited from cities' freedom to raise taxes specifically to finance such projects, and the planning of each tram route to be the spine of a coordinated and centrally controlled public transport system.

Although the Tyne & Wear Metro had been designed to be the main strand of local transport, the free-for-all of bus deregulation ruled out further integrated systems. Light rail schemes had to stand on their commercial merits; even the principle of giving trams priority at traffic lights was questioned.

By the late 1980s the specialist press could report that 49 areas from Aberdeen to Bristol were investigating light rail solutions, but very few came to fruition. Most could not prove that light rail's benefits could be delivered without the supportive Continental political and taxation model. Those that were built succeeded because they served a specific development need (as in London Docklands or Nottingham's NET), and/or made use of pre-existing radial rights of way (Midland Metro), penetrated further into city centres (Manchester Metrolink, Sheffield Supertram) or enabled BR to avoid major expenditure on re-equipping tired urban lines (Metrolink again). They also went ahead because they had relentless champions who could demonstrate that light rail was a more effective or less bad alternative to persevering with an inadequate status quo – though even that might not be enough, as witness the fate of Leeds Supertram.

The first regional light rail system promoted after Tyne & Wear was Advanced Transport for Avon (ATA), privately funded to ease congestion in Bristol and connect new suburbs with the centre. ATA aimed to use the dormant Portishead branch, then cross the city to parallel BR's main line to Bradley Stoke, not far from Bristol Parkway. Powers were obtained, but ATA met ideological opposition from Bristol's Labour council, despite support from the party nationally. Falling land values killed the project, and ATA went into liquidation in 1992.

Though BR was involved with ATA, the scheme never reached the stage at which formal agreements with BR were required. By contrast, Greater Manchester's development of Metrolink depended on a collaboration in which the PTE would take on ownership and responsibility for two BR routes (Altrincham to Manchester Piccadilly, and Bury to Victoria) and the costs of re-equipping them for and with trams, and providing the new link through the city centre that was crucial for commuters.

In 1988 the BR Board recognised that wherever light rail impacted on the railway it would raise issues of legal, commercial, operational and engineering principle, particularly for the Provincial sector. A review by BR's policy unit led to a decision to appoint a Project Director, LRT, to act as the central BR focus for all such schemes. Because Metrolink was the furthest advanced project, the post was made answerable to Sidney Newey as Director, Provincial. Martin Shrubsole, who was completing a secondment to the Highways Division at the DTp, was appointed that Spring.

With John Welsby taking the lead, the Board threw its weight behind Metrolink; it would make central Manchester more accessible for rail passengers, and could result in higher BR property values and consultancy opportunities. Transferring lines to the PTE would enable it to spend on light rail stock of its own choosing the funds BR would otherwise have had to devote to replacing life-expired trains.

This support came with crucial provisos:

- All works required to reconfigure BR's network, to permit the separation of light and heavy rail, had to be at the cost of the light rail promoter
- BR had to retain direct control over all elements of its train operations
- BR should not be left responsible for redundant land or assets severed from the rest of its network by construction of a light rail route

The chosen model for delivering Metrolink was a Design, Build, Maintain and Operate contract. Preparation of the Invitation to Tender documents required significant input from BR to protect its position and achieve clear demarcation between future PTE and BR responsibilities. Questions also arose – as they would at privatisation – of who held or retained risk. A 'wall of death' was constructed on the approach to Victoria to prevent a runaway tram bringing down the station's roof. The undercroft at Piccadilly also needed strengthening; the trams were far heavier than the wagons it was designed for, and the collapse of one underground pillar could have brought down the entire station.

A two-week shutdown between Timperley and Altrincham was needed for track and signalling works to separate a BR double track into two singles, one for trams and one for a continuing route for Chester trains to reach Piccadilly via Stockport, which commuters from beyond Altrincham now have to use. Not least because there were level crossings on this stretch, ownership and control of both lines was vested with BR, and subsequently with Railtrack.

### Regional Railways produces a light rail handbook

The decisions made over each new problem were recorded thoroughly, and the principles that emerged assembled into a single document. This, after Martin Shrubsole was succeeded by Martin Williams (who went on to head a formal light rail group within Regional Railways) became the basis for an 'LRT Handbook' published in 1992. The Handbook listed all the steps BR should take, from making contact the moment a feasibility study was commissioned. BR's civil engineers should coordinate, informing every relevant part of the organisation. The critical issue for BR was how heavy and light rail could coexist: 'Where total segregation is not possible, BR should retain the infrastructure and agree a method of joint working.' Issues included immunising signalling, shared structures, proximity running, risk assessments, light rail access to BR stations, light rail's impact on future BR schemes including electrification, and the cost of overhead attached to buildings versus free-standing poles.

Faced with the transfer of BR assets and services to PTE ownership, the rail unions pressed for BR to bid to operate Metrolink; the Board proposed operation by a discrete subsidiary – BR Light Railways Ltd – and a formal agreement on light rail conditions of service. Radical terms were thrashed out, but light rail operation by BR never proved politically acceptable. The terms would, however, be a useful reference point for the TOCs in the run-up to privatisation.

The Handbook also dealt with two other issues that Gordon Pettitt considered important. These were the scope for using light rail technology to develop cheaper and lighter trains, and how to enhance BR's service to the public by enabling vehicles running over city centre streets to reach outer suburbs on conventional railways (Tram-Train).

The former has belatedly been achieved, but only in one location; since 2009 a Class 139 Parry People Mover has operated the Stourbridge Town branch. In the frame now, however, is Very Light Rail, a national innovation centre for which is being established at

**BELOW** Parry People Movers Nos 139002 (foreground) and 139001 at Stourbridge Junction. *Antony Christie*

## Chapter 7: THE URBAN CHALLENGE

ABOVE NET tram No 214 pauses at the Hucknall terminus before returning to Nottingham station on 14 November 2014. *Alex Green*

Dudley with Government funding. The short section of railway between central Dudley and Dudley Port station on the Birmingham-Wolverhampton line is to be reopened, one track for a public service using such vehicles as are developed, and the other as a test track. This section of line had been intended as part of a longer Midland Metro route, plans for which are now in abeyance. Very Light Rail is being promoted as a cheaper alternative for urban areas, but could be valuable wherever the cost of conventional railway operation cannot be justified.

Several schemes beyond Metrolink involved the transfer of BR rights of way to new owners, but preserving BR's interests necessitated other works. To make space for a double-track Sheffield Supertram line along the Don Valley, BR's freight-only line was singled. Midland Metro raised issues over fitting a tram track into Snow Hill station, while to preserve BR access to a scrapyard at Smethwick an overbridge was insisted on where, arguably, a flat crossing would have sufficed. All such works – and the immunisation of signalling from electromagnetic interference – were chargeable to the light rail promoter. This spending, however, worsened the economics of light rail.

Tyne & Wear's aspiration to extend Metro to Sunderland and South Hylton, and NET's plans to access Hucknall, concerned routes with no room for third or fourth tracks. 'Parallel running' over single tracks offered insufficient capacity for one or both parties, so 'shared running' with trams and trains using the same track was investigated.

On Metro, freight trains ran until 1989 to an oil terminal on the Newcastle Airport branch, but only at times when no Metro services were running. The coast route could only accommodate the Metro service required to Sunderland, together with BR's own services, if both modes could share both tracks – a potential win-win for each. Shared running to Sunderland finally began in 2002; under the Metrolink precedent, control of the whole line from Pelaw lies with Network Rail's Tyneside IECC.

When the Nottingham scheme was proposed in 1988 it looked as though, without track-sharing, two lines would be needed for light rail services together with a single track for coal traffic from collieries further along the route. In the event the collieries closed, but the rebirth of that route as the 'Robin Hood Line' led to the tramway opening as a single line running beside a singled railway. The latter has proved a constraint to the level and punctuality of 'Robin Hood' services.

### Not all worked-up schemes delivered

The Treasury has never liked light rail. Either a system loses money, or its success encourages other cities to want one. However, light rail has proved more popular with the public – and notably car-owners – than buses. 'People are happy to use the tram where they're not prepared to use a dirty old bus, which is wrong,' observed a frustrated Alex Ritchie. Trams, with their extra space, would also be buggy- and wheelchair-friendly.

In 1995 Brian Mawhinney boasted of being the first Transport Secretary to approve two schemes in one year, but new systems only trickled into service. The promoters have not always helped their case; some estimates of usage have been over-optimistic, and costs have often soared once construction has begun.

John Prescott's Ten Year Plan promised 25 new light rail routes, and prior to the 2001 election his department approved four new systems. Sadly only Nottingham's NET, opened in 2004, came to fruition, and that after 16 years' gestation. A second scheme for Bristol was killed by disputes between Bristol Council and its neighbours; had work gone ahead it would have taken trackbed north from Bristol now needed for quadrupling. An enterprising project to link Portsmouth with Fareham via a tunnel under the harbour and the disused Gosport branch was torpedoed by the MoD's decision to base new aircraft carriers at Pompey, deepening the channel and increasing the cost.

The saddest outcome befell Leeds Supertram – an imaginative scheme for three radial routes from the city centre, largely on former tramway alignments. Funding was refused, but after Labour's election West Yorkshire PTA's leader Mick Lyons threw his political weight behind Supertram and the Department approved it. Two rival consortia were formed to build and operate

Chapter 7: **THE URBAN CHALLENGE** 95

**ABOVE LEFT** The West Midlands tram network took time to establish itself, but is now re-equipped with new trams such as No 23, seen here at The Hawthorns heading for Birmingham Snow Hill on 3 January 2015. *Trevor Hall*

**ABOVE RIGHT** Modern Blackpool tram No 016 en route to Starr Gate on 5 December 2014 running on newly upgraded infrastructure. An extension is planned to Blackpool North station. *Alex Green*

Supertram, with a view to the first trams running by 2008. But costs increased from £500 million to around £1 billion, and the scheme was scaled down to a single route south-east to Stourton. In 2005, with £40 million already spent, Alistair Darling withdrew Government support, saying Supertram had become poor value.

Darling's decision was driven by his civil servants, who were pressing for 'quality bus' schemes. But Leeds did need more than buses, and in 2012 the Department approved plans for a trolleybus route – Britain's first in 40 years. The significance for the railways of the rejection of Supertram was twofold: it would have been a feeder to heavy rail services from Leeds, and when tram-train operation was suggested for the line from Harrogate, there was no street tramway to run onto.

Other schemes did gain approval from the Blair/Brown Government, usually after initial rejection on financial grounds: Manchester's 'Big Bang', taking trams to Oldham and Rochdale, Ashton and Manchester Airport; the wholesale modernisation of Blackpool's seafront tramway; the extension of Midland Metro to New Street; and the extension of NET south and west of Nottingham. The 'Big Bang', with Metrolink taking over Northern Rail's Oldham Loop, had to wait on a raft of DfT-requested studies, including one into turning the line to Rose Hill Marple into a guided busway. Yet while progress has been slow, light rail is growing and proving its value, not least in feeding into and from the urban and interurban rail network.

Table 7.3: Tram networks serving Regional cities: as at 01.01.2015

| Network | Total route miles | Of which miles transferred from heavy rail | Passenger journeys 2013 (m) |
|---|---|---|---|
| Tyne & Wear[1] | 48 | 35 | 36 |
| Sheffield[2] | 18 | 2 | 13 |
| Nottingham[2,3] | 9 | 5 | 8 |
| Birmingham[2] | 13 | 12 | 5 |
| Blackpool | 11 | - | 4 |
| Manchester[2] | 57 | 28 | 29 |
| Edinburgh[4] | 9 | - | n/a |
| **TOTAL** | **165** | **82** | **95** |

1 Includes joint running, Pelaw-Sunderland
2 Currently being extended
3 One track taken from 'Robin Hood Line'
4 Opened 2014

Source: Theo Steel

**ABOVE** Newly commissioned Metrolink tram No 3041 calls at Rochdale station on 8 May 2013. The unique high-floor style of the Greater Manchester trams is dictated by the use of former BR stations with high platforms on the original Bury and Altrincham lines, now extended to include the Oldham Loop. *Stuart Ray*

### Tram-train finally tried

The development in Britain of through running between tramways and railways using dedicated vehicles has only recently begun, despite having been pioneered in Karlsruhe from 1979 onwards; the city's tramways initially absorbed independent railways before running through from city centre streets onto DB's urban railway. One of Gordon Pettitt's final initiatives at Regional Railways was to lead a study tour to evaluate the system as a possible solution for Cardiff and the Valleys, vehicles running to the outskirts as trains before making a circuit of the city centre streets as trams.

It was the mid-2000s before the Department decided to see if tram-train was also possible in Britain. 'Mike Mitchell was keen to get the technology in,' recalls Heidi Mottram, then Managing Director of Northern Rail. 'We looked at three or four routes, some in the west and some in the east, and chose the Penistone line because it had the potential for street running in Sheffield, interference with a main line and with freight, and was a "rural railway".'

However, while the Penistone line met Supertram at Meadowhall, a physical connection would have been complex and costly. Capacity was constrained by single-track sections with a 45-minute service the maximum (delivered in 2014 for the Tour de France), and special dual-powered vehicles would have been needed, accommodating fewer passengers than the line's DMUs. Nevertheless Northern pushed the concept as one way of getting rid of some 'Pacers', and Lord Adonis engineered the less challenging choice of the lightly used passenger and freight line beyond Meadowhall to Parkgate, an area ripe for regeneration that had lost its station in 1968.

The £60 million scheme, involving electrification, different platform heights for trams and trains at Rotherham Central, street running in Sheffield and vehicles from Vossloh, was approved in 2013, but is taking time to deliver. Some issues of inter-running remained after Metro's extension to Sunderland. Notably the interface between flange and railhead was different for railway and grooved tramway rail: much of Sheffield's tramway had to be relaid with track of a suitable profile. It also proved immensely difficult to rewrite and derogate from many established standards down to how much fresh air there is in the cab air-conditioning and the positioning of headlights. Once these have been settled for the pilot scheme, future tram-train projects will face fewer hurdles.

A further complication – and inflator of infrastructure costs – is that the chosen section of railway is being electrified for tram-train with full clearances for 25kV overhead because the Sheffield-Doncaster line is scheduled for electrification in Control Period 6. The trams are dual-voltage, so they can switch later from Supertram's power system when the feeder for AC electric supply – costing more than £30 million – is provided.

Tram-train is still being mooted for West Yorkshire, and in 2014 Cardiff Council adopted plans for tram-train between Cardiff Bay and the former Creigiau branch. Manchester is also keen, with several underused railways proposed for connection to Metrolink. Transport for Greater Manchester sees no reason why it need wait for the Department to declare the Parkgate experiment a success – but will probably have to.

### Service development slows after privatisation

Privatisation was bound to disrupt the relationship between the railway and the PTEs, and slow service development. The Department confirmed at the outset that the PTEs would 'continue to be responsible for deciding appropriate service levels, and for paying for them'. But it ruled out franchises contiguous with the PTEs, or the PTEs letting franchises themselves, as 'a sensible grouping of services for franchises will not necessarily fit within PTE boundaries'. A freeze on rolling stock orders did nothing for reliability and left trains for expanded services hard to find. New station openings stalled, and never fully recovered. Infrastructure projects took a back seat as Railtrack took over – not least because the company charged the PTEs 3½ times what BR had. Moreover, many urban lines remained heavy loss-makers: in 1999 every passenger mile on Merseyrail was subsidised to the tune of 33p – despite over-zealous economies by the franchise holder – and 31.2p on Cardiff Railways. The return in 1997 of a Labour Government promising to get people out of their cars augured well for Britain's cities, not least because most were under Labour control. Yet improvements were few as the new operators bedded in.

Railtrack did push through one landmark project: Leeds First. The previous remodelling had left Leeds station unable to cope as traffic revived, so between 1999 and 2002 additional tracks were laid to the west and the station rebuilt with a translucent roof and new entrance, and expanded from 12 to 17 platforms (a further, southern, entrance is now being added). When work was at its height, some trains used a temporary station named Leeds Whitehall.

Growth at Leeds (and elsewhere) demonstrated that cuts in terminal capacity had particularly disadvantaged regional urban services. Such thinking died hard; on the eve of privatisation BR passed up the chance to claw back space for two desperately needed tracks on the eastern approach to Birmingham New Street when an underground car park came up for redevelopment.

## Devolution on Merseyside and more widely – and now the Northern Powerhouse

In 2003 responsibility for Merseyrail was devolved from the Strategic Rail Authority to Merseyside PTE. This break with the national pattern was made because the self-contained third-rail network fell almost entirely within the PTE area. For other local services into Liverpool, Northern Rail enjoys a conventional relationship with the PTE. For Merseytravel, having its own railway raised the possibility of taking control of track and signalling as an exercise in vertical integration. Having a comparator on costs appealed to the Department, but not to Network Rail, which blocked the move. It looked all the more tempting to the PTE when Network Rail quoted a credibility-straining £207 million for electrifying the Bidston-Wrexham line. Then the RMT decided that transferring Network Rail infrastructure to a public authority amounted to privatisation; pressure was exerted on Merseyside's Labour politicians, and the idea was dropped.

As networks settled down after deregulation, development of bus/rail interchanges such as at Barnsley and Liverpool South Parkway made public transport more attractive. So did increasingly comprehensive smart ticketing schemes, offering variants and sometimes improvements on London's Oyster card. Merseytravel (inevitably) has the Walrus, Centro the Swift card; the Glasgow Subway went smart in 2013, and Nexus's Pop card is used for 60,000 journeys a day.

Under the 2008 Local Transport Act, England's PTAs became Integrated Transport Authorities (ITAs); they regained some powers to regulate and subsidise bus services, and became the transport planning authorities for their areas. They are responsible for setting rail fares and timetables, promoting light rail and funding concessionary travel. ITAs were also created outside the PTE areas; Lancashire's got off to an energetic start with a reinstated curve at Todmorden and redoubled track at Darwen for new Manchester-Blackburn and extra Bolton-Blackburn services. Under the Act there is scope for new PTEs, though none has yet been proposed.

However, with the development of the Northern Powerhouse – as discussed later – and with larger devolved units than the PTEs being canvassed, the role and even continuance of the PTEs is becoming a matter for debate.

**ABOVE** Class 319s were introduced to the 'Northern Hub' late in 2014, but delayed completion of the electrification prevented their deployment until the following March. No 319365 in newly applied Northern livery stands at Manchester Airport on 21 April 2015 before returning to Liverpool Lime Street. *Alex Green*

## Electrification resumes, but capacity still tight

The present stimulus to Britain's urban railways comes from electrification. In the 1990s few schemes were completed: Birmingham Cross-City, Leeds North West, and Merseyrail to Chester. Railtrack's reluctance, then the Department's opposition on spurious technical grounds, ruled it out in the 2000s; only in Scotland were the wires extended. It took the forcing of the issue by Ian Coucher and Adrian Shooter and an activist Transport Secretary in Lord Adonis to break the logjam.

Electrification to Bristol, Cardiff and the Valleys, Nottingham, Swansea and Sheffield will benefit local as well as interurban services. Wiring between Liverpool, Manchester, Preston and Blackpool, then the core trans-Pennine route, will enable lines now operated by packed DMUs to be served by faster, more capacious – if not necessarily newer – trains. And the units freed up will replace 'Pacers' or relieve overcrowding elsewhere.

Meanwhile capacity problems remain, and Table 7.4 (overleaf) shows just how busy the best-served of Britain's regional stations have become.

Services into Leeds and Manchester have the highest percentage of passengers standing outside London, 13% and 11% respectively in the morning peak, which, since privatisation, has started earlier. One reason why rail commuting into these cities continued to surge despite the financial crisis of 2008 was the steady rise in city centre white-collar employment at the expense of blue-collar jobs elesewhere. Another was that many of the offices where these commuters worked were

## Chapter 7: THE URBAN CHALLENGE

**Table 7.4: Regional's 25 busiest stations, 2013/14**

| Order | Station | Trips pa | Status |
|---|---|---|---|
| 1 | Birmingham New Street | 34.8m | Joint station |
| 2 | Leeds | 27.7m | Joint station |
| 3 | Glasgow Central | 27.4m | Joint station |
| 4 | Manchester Piccadilly | 24.4m | Joint station |
| 5 | Edinburgh Waverley | 20.0m | Joint station |
| 6 | Glasgow Queen Street | 15.8m | ScotRail sole user |
| 7 | Liverpool Central | 14.6m | Merseyrail sole user |
| 8 | Liverpool Lime Street | 14.2m | Joint station |
| 9 | Cardiff Central | 11.7m | Joint station |
| 10 | Cambridge | 9.8m | Joint station |
| 11 | Bristol Temple Meads | 9.5m | Joint station |
| 12 | Sheffield | 8.6m | Joint station |
| 13 | York | 8.2m | Joint station |
| 14 | Newcastle | 8.0m | Joint station |
| 15 | Manchester Oxford Road | 7.6m | Joint station |
| 16 | Manchester Victoria | 7.2m | Northern sole user |
| 17 | Liverpool Moorfields | 6.5m | Merseyrail sole user |
| 18 | Birmingham Moor Street | 6.2m | Chiltern/London Midland |
| 19 | Nottingham | 6.1m | Joint station |
| 20 | Coventry | 6.0m | Joint station |
| 21 | Leicester | 4.8m | Joint station |
| 22 | Huddersfield | 4.8m | TPE/Northern |
| 23 | Birmingham Snow Hill | 4.4m | Chiltern/London Midland |
| 24 | Paisley Gilmour Street | 4.0m | ScotRail sole user |
| 25 | Bolton | 3.7m | Joint station |

Note: Joint User stations include intercity passengers
Source: Theo Steel

constructed on former car parks, to which they could otherwise have driven.

Where PIXC (passengers in excess of capacity) is concerned, Sheffield (2.3%) and Leeds (2.2%) are worst in the morning peak, and Manchester (1.8%) and Leeds (1.5%) in the evening. And by 2018/19 an extra 2,800 high-peak passengers are expected to arrive in Leeds, and 2,600 in Manchester. It is a far cry from the 1960s, when many of these same lines were slated for closure.

### Away from the PTEs: Edinburgh

Edinburgh's local heavy rail services have enjoyed a revival in recent years but, as the pre-Beeching system largely comprised uncompetitive short branches, there has been limited scope for line reopenings. Exceptions have been the Bathgate line, reopened in 1986 and since extended, and the 'Crossrail' service from west of the city to Newcraighall, which commenced in 2002, the success of which has been less spectacular. Newcraighall is at the start of the 'Waverley' line, being reopened in 2015 as far as Tweedbank.

While reopening suburban stations on the Carstairs line in 1987 brought little traffic, others on the west of the city have thrived, including South Gyle (1985) and Edinburgh Park (2003), which handles 961,000 passengers a year. Edinburgh Gateway, interchange for the airport and the new tram route, should do even better. Intermediate stations on the ECML have opened for North Berwick services, Wallyford doing particularly well – and station reopenings at Reston and West Linton en route to Dunbar are proposed to serve these booming

**ABOVE LEFT** The Edinburgh trams were introduced the hard way – but they are now being well received by passengers and proving a useful feed to the rail network. *Nicholas Comfort*

**ABOVE RIGHT** The magnificent semaphore signal gantry at Radyr in the 1990s. *Malcolm McDonald*

commuter areas. However, efforts to reopen the Suburban line round the south of the city have come to naught; bus services are far more direct. And Holyrood in 2007 killed off the Edinburgh Airport rail link (EARL), which had grown to involve new spurs for Glasgow and Fife and a tunnel under the runway; Edinburgh Gateway will handle airport traffic instead.

Meanwhile few transport projects have aroused such controversy as the mismanagement of the tramway planned for Edinburgh. A three-route system costing £458 million was proposed in 2001, with powers obtained from the Scottish Parliament five years later. Escalating costs led to its being pruned to a single route between Leith, Princes Street and Edinburgh Airport. TIE, the agency set up to deliver the project, struggled because of the soaring cost of unplanned groundwork in the heart of the ancient city, and its refusal to listen to advice. With the SNP Government threatening to kill the project, the Leith section was dropped in 2009. Amid legal disputes between TIE and the contractors, ministers briefly withdrew funding, then in 2011 TIE was disbanded. With the cost of just the remaining section approaching £750 million, and far more trams delivered than would be needed, work resumed under the auspices of the City Council and the line finally opened in May 2014. While Edinburgh's trams now inspire pride and are carrying their projected level of traffic, the shambles around delivery of the scheme – now the subject of a judicial inquiry – did light rail untold reputational damage.

## Cardiff and the Valleys

The Cardiff Valleys network grew up with coal for the docks having priority, and several lines lost their passenger trains to accommodate freight. Beeching reduced the network to routes serving Rhymney, Merthyr and Treherbert in the north and Barry and Penarth in the south, with urban survivals in Cardiff to Bute Road and Coryton; some stations and track layouts were very restrictive operationally. By sectorisation in 1982 the passenger business in South Wales was on the slide, some lines surviving only because of poor roads. The decline of coal before and after the strike of 1984-85 freed up capacity, at the price of a major loss of revenue to BR.

The system was rescued by the Cardiff Valleys Rail Development Strategy, which produced 16 new stations, a loop at Ystrad Rhondda to allow a half-hourly frequency to Treherbert, and the reopening of three lines; Pontypridd station regained its second platform in 1990, and later a third. This revival was encouraged by John Davies, Provincial's, then Regional Railways', manager for Wales. Theo Steel, who was Director, South Wales & West, recalls: 'The Welsh Office and Mid, West and South Glamorgan were all involved. It was about providing better access from Cardiff's catchment area to support growth there, and better access to new jobs within the Valleys.'

The 'City Line' into Cardiff from Radyr and the west was reopened in 1986. 'It didn't have a case on its own,' says Steel. 'BR wanted to avoid closure, and saw a future role in decongesting Cardiff. The plan was to run Merthyr trains in that way, alternating with Aberdare trains, but having to tour south Cardiff to get to the centre met resistance; within 12 months Merthyr trains were diverted back via Cathays. "City Line" became a Cinderella route, with its trains the first to be cancelled. Peak business evaporated, and it took us years to get it back.' Today the line's four intermediate stations contribute just 1,000 passengers a day.

By contrast, the reopened Aberdare line now operates half-hourly; indeed, Aberdare has a larger footfall (558,000 passengers a year) than Merthyr (547,000). Next in 1991 came a Cardiff-Maesteg service, with successful new stations on the main line at Pencoed and Pontyclun; Ewenny Road, outside Maesteg, proved a turkey. Traffic volume and signalling on the main line precluded other stops, and Llanharan did not reopen until 2007. The main line from 1994 also saw 'SwanLine', born of the political need to benefit West Glamorgan.

The development of Cardiff Bay, now home to the Welsh Assembly, demanded better transport links. There was talk of trams to Bute Road and beyond, but the real issue was the railway embankment bisecting

**Chapter 7: THE URBAN CHALLENGE**

**ABOVE LEFT** The venerable Class 121 connects Cardiff Queen Street with the new Cardiff Bay development at Cardiff Bute Street station. *Alex Green*

**ABOVE RIGHT** Ebbw Vale Parkway station on 2 August 2008. *Roger Joanes*

the area; the line was saved by £600,000 from the Development Corporation to provide a second track south of Queen Street station, which regained its third platform in 1988 and now has five, handling 2.5 million passengers a year. A single-car shuttle operates to Bute Road – and there is reverse commuting from the Bay.

1994 saw the creation of the Cardiff Valleys operating unit, morphing into the Valley Lines franchise, run – at an unforeseen level of losses – by Prism. Meanwhile the Taff resignalling project was carried out from 1996 to 1998. Arising from a Welsh Office study into low rail usage and worsening traffic congestion in the Valleys, it involved the Government improving the A470 between Pontypridd and Cardiff, and councils paying for remodelled track layouts and resignalling to allow trains every 3 minutes if necessary against every 10 before. Tracks on former four-track alignments were slewed to raise line speeds.

Privatisation, the reorganisation of Welsh local government into single-tier authorities, and devolution brought a pause, except for the rebirth of the staff platform at Cardiff Central as Platform 0 for Millennium Stadium traffic (it is now used daily). Then the reopenings resumed: the Vale of Glamorgan line from Barry to Bridgend in 2005, and the Ebbw Vale line in 2008. The latter, South Wales's largest revival, was done to a high standard. It runs to Cardiff (the valley's traditional travel-to-work destination is Newport), has six intermediate stations and a dynamic loop for trains to pass. It terminates outside the town, yet its hourly service is healthily used – 760,000 passengers a year – with trains strengthened at times. A further station at Pye Corner has opened, and in May 2015 an £11.5 million extension to Ebbw Vale Town, and trains into Newport should follow … plus reinstatement of the Brynmawr branch as far as Abertillery.

Next for the Valleys is electrification, though some reckon tram-train more appropriate. New stations continue to open, most recently Energlyn (Cardiff's 21st), and there are aspirations to reopen to Llantrisant and Beddau. Meanwhile resignalling and further extra platforms (one at Cardiff Central) are increasing capacity; the main challenge is the shortage of DMUs.

### Bristol

Britain's other cities right down to Exeter (population 118,000) and Inverness (74,000) enjoy some rail commuting, but few possess a network. One exception is Bristol. Rail use doubled between 1987 and 1992 with new 'Sprinters' and better services to Bath and Cardiff. New housing and the high-tech boom continued the trend, and rail commuting's importance to the region made national headlines in 2008 with protests against overcrowding after First Great Western started its new franchise with too few DMUs.

That was an extreme example of rationing resources, but canny management has long been necessary. The peak service between Avonmouth and Severn Beach was suspended in 1995, Avon County Council supplying a bus to release a 'Pacer' for use elsewhere. David Mather, West of England manager in turn for Provincial, Regional Railways, Railtrack and Network Rail, notes: 'The Severn Beach service now needs three units, but usage has grown significantly – Clifton from 94,000 passengers in 1998 to 574,000 in 2014. Bristol as a whole has grown despite the double whammy of banking scalebacks and defence cuts.'

Filton Abbey Wood, opened in 1996 to serve the MoD complex just north of Bristol, has been a particular success. Local councils funded 'Sprinters' to serve the station, freed up by reorganising other

**ABOVE** No 143611 stands at Filton Abbey Wood on 19 January 2006. The line is currently planned for upgrading as part of the proposed Bristol Metro. *Chris McKenna*

services, the public responded and it has gained a third platform, with a fourth planned. It is now used by almost 1 million passengers a year.

Bristol Council has long pressed for further improvements, starting with reopening of the Portishead branch. Freight returned in 2002, but only when the Greater Bristol Metro consortium was formed in 2008 did the line find a sponsor. Metro, a grouping of Transport for Greater Bristol, local councils and campaigning groups, wants upgraded services from Bath, Weston, Severn Beach, Henbury and Yate, and several station reopenings, and in 2014 was promised Local Growth funding. During the current Control Period, Network Rail plans to spend £700 million on Bristol, including reinstatement of the original platforms at Temple Meads station and quadrupling of the main line into Bristol – something that would have been impossible had the formation for the extra tracks been handed over to light rail.

## Nottingham and the 'Robin Hood Line'

Nottingham is an important regional centre, but its limited suburban rail services did not survive competition from more direct trams and buses. The emphasis has always been on interurban commuting, and the present routes from Derby, Leicester and Chesterfield were duplicated by separate lines from Nottingham Victoria until their closure in 1967. However, that round of closures also deprived an important urban corridor – from Nottingham north to Mansfield and Worksop – of its last remaining rail passenger service. Mansfield, indeed, was left as arguably the largest town in England without a station.

What is now the 'Robin Hood Line' owes its genesis to the pit closures of the mid- to late 1980s and the need both to regenerate coalfield communities and open up employment opportunities in the cities nearby. Provincial and Nottinghamshire County Council – later with involvement also from Derbyshire, through which the line's northern section passed – worked up a plan to reinstate the Nottingham-Worksop route. Although three separate lines had run as far as Mansfield, parts of each of them had been lifted and tunnels blocked up; to offset the cost of reopening, the trackbed through the centre of Kirkby-in-Ashfield was sold off for development. As reconstructed, the line mostly followed the former Midland route to Worksop, but took over the trackbed of the Great Central main line near Annesley and a stretch of the old Great Northern at Kirkby.

The 'Robin Hood Line' opened between Nottingham and Newstead in 1993, to Mansfield Woodhouse in 1995 and through to Worksop in 1998. The trains were packed from the outset and, despite a continuing need for subsidy, the line is now, with 1.25 million passengers a year, England's busiest reopened railway outside London. It has a half-hourly and Sunday service as far as Mansfield Woodhouse, and an hourly weekday service on to Worksop.

The extension of the line spanned the end of BR and the birth of Railtrack, and it took determination by all concerned to see it through. Singling of the track between Bulwell and Hucknall to accommodate the NET tram route, opened in 2004, imposed a challenging limit on its capacity. However, Nottinghamshire County Council is pressing for trains now terminating at Mansfield Woodhouse to be extended to Edwinstowe and Ollerton on the long-closed Chesterfield-Lincoln line, to serve communities of 5,000 and 10,000 respectively left stranded by pit closures, together with the Center Parcs resort.

**BELOW** Whitwell station is one of many on the 'Robin Hood Line' that were launched with new livery and equipment. *Dennis Lovett*

## Chapter 8
# THE MAGNIFICENT SEVEN: THE PTEs

*'Sir Peter Parker called the PTEs the "Magnificent Seven". I could never quite figure out whether he was saying we were magnificent because we were providing money to BR, or whether he actually did respect what we were doing.'*

**ALEX RITCHIE**

**ABOVE** The Class 323 fleet had a difficult launch when computers were unable to cope with ice on the overhead line, but the units went on to become one of the most reliable in both the West Midlands and Greater Manchester fleets. No 323209 is shown in a joint Centro-Regional Railways branding at Hamstead. *Steve Hobson*

Chapter 8: **THE MAGNIFICENT SEVEN: THE PTEs** 103

The challenges facing each of Britain's major conurbations differ considerably, and the ways their railways have developed reflect this. So, too, have the policies followed …followed by their PTEs (see endpapers) – and the approach of BR and its successors towards them.

## Greater Manchester
### The inheritance

South-east Lancashire and north-east Cheshire boast England's largest rail passenger volume after London, but the area's network has not received the encouragement it deserves. Manchester's network developed with routes bouncing off the city centre rather than crossing it, suffered severely after Beeching, when it lost three of its termini, and inherited three incompatible systems of electrification. Inter-city and freight traffic has created pinch points, yet network usage is relatively low. Successive Governments have been lukewarm over investing in it, and the PTE, traditionally bus-orientated, moved on to promote the Metrolink light rail system, with those heavy rail lines not to be taken over low on its list of priorities.

**BELOW** A Class 142 'Skipper', withdrawn from use in Cornwall but deemed good enough for Manchester, stands in a decrepit Manchester Victoria in March 1990. *Dennis Lovett*

BR's Provincial sector, Gordon Pettitt recalls, was 'ambiguous in its attitude to the PTE' with its services into Manchester 'awful', and it took the managerial acumen of Chris Leah to improve matters. Moreover, apart from gaining Class 323s under Regional Railways, Manchester has always been at the back of the queue for rolling stock. Heritage DMUs ran until 2003, and even today demand on some electrified routes is suppressed because, with AC rolling stock in short supply, passengers are having to put up with 'Pacers'.

### North-south connections

To make up for the lack of a north-south connection crossing the city centre, BR and the PTE in the early 1970s promoted 'Picc-Vic', a £59 million, 2¾-mile tunnel linking Piccadilly and Victoria, with three convenient intermediate stops. Trains would have run through from Bury and Bolton (via a reopened branch from Radcliffe) to Alderley Edge, Hazel Grove and Macclesfield; flying junctions were planned at Slade Lane and Stockport. BR obtained Parliamentary powers for the tunnel – first proposed in 1839 – in 1972. Soon after the PTE submitted its grant application the economy nosedived and in 1974, with four platforms at Victoria cleared in readiness, the Labour Government refused funding. The rejection of 'Picc-Vic' is estimated to have set back the revival of Manchester's city centre by a generation.

BR returned in 1979 with proposals for a surface-level 'Castlefield curve' linking Piccadilly and Victoria; powers for this lapsed, and only now, with Network Rail's 'Northern Hub', is the renamed Ordsall Curve being constructed. Then in 1980 BR proposed a Windsor Curve enabling trains from south of Piccadilly to access Bolton and points beyond, with an interchange at Salford Crescent, as part of a scheme for electrifying to Blackpool (and running down Victoria station). Decoupled from that project when the Department cooled towards it, the connection was completed in 1988.

### Metrolink

BR's commuter lines to Altrincham and Bury needed new trains, the Bury line was electrified on a non-standard system, structures were ageing, and neither route went where commuters into Manchester wanted

**LEFT** The Manchester Victoria-Bury line was faced with a time-expired electric service with dwindling demand when Class 504 No M65457 was photographed awaiting departure from Manchester Victoria in November 1990. The route was transformed into a ground-breaking tram operation in 1992 and has been further upgraded in 2015. *Dennis Lovett*

to go. GMPTE's rail subsidy grew onerous, and in 1983 a Rail Study examined five lines – to Altrincham, Bury, Glossop, Marple/Rose Hill and the Oldham loop – together with the freight-only line through Didsbury. It concluded that conversion to light rail would be far cheaper (£75,000 per kilometre) than a guided bus system (£430,000), and Metrolink was born.

In 1984 BR, Greater Manchester Council and the PTE promoted a Bill for a 31km light rail system linking Altrincham and Bury through the city centre with a spur to Piccadilly, with 2.7km of street running. Paul Channon approved funding in January 1988, and a month later the Metrolink Bill received Royal Assent. A consortium was chosen to build and operate it, and high-floor trams ordered from Italy (most original stops were BR stations with high platforms). BR handed over the Altrincham and Bury lines 'as seen', the latter turning out to be in worse shape than supposed.

Trams first ran between Altrincham, Piccadilly, Victoria and Bury in August 1992, and the system has expanded steadily. Operated in turn by Serco, Stagecoach and RATP, and now on its second generation of trams, it carried 25 million passengers in 2013. A second route across the city centre is under construction.

**BELOW** The first-generation T-68 Metrolink trams in Manchester, with their unusual high floors. *Author*

## Manchester Airport, and the future

On Regional Railways' watch the Manchester Airport rail connection opened in 1993. This is a success story, with 3.3 million passengers in 2013 (after Piccadilly, Victoria and Bolton the conurbation's most heavily used station). There are trains to it from across the North, Metrolink has arrived, a fourth platform has just been opened, and interchange is planned with HS2.

Even after Metrolink's acquisition of lines to Altrincham, Bury and Oldham/Rochdale, Manchester has a significant heavy rail network. There are railways electrified under inter-city schemes (Glossop and the WCML, DMU-operated trans-Pennine, Calder Valley and local lines, and the newly electrified North-West Triangle. Transport for Greater Manchester (as it now is) hopes to see lightly used lines such as to Marple and Rose Hill connected to Metrolink with tram-train. On most of the network passenger volumes are not high, but peak overcrowding remains a problem, particularly on TransPennine Express and on the Bolton corridor.

But there is hope, at last, for heavy rail. The spread of electrification, with longer electric trains and the cascading of DMUs to the busiest services on Northern Rail, will bring more seats. Completion of the 'Northern Hub' will at last permit through travel between centres north of Manchester, the city's Cheshire hinterland and the airport. A driving force for further improvements will be the partnership that has developed the hub, embracing not only Transport for Greater Manchester, Network Rail and the train operators but also local authorities well beyond the PTE boundary that have a stake in new and better rail connections.

## Merseyside
### The 'Loop and Link'

Liverpool has suffered industrial decline and depopulation, but its railways have come through to drive regeneration. The most significant closures – the Liverpool Overhead Railway and the duplicate line to Southport – occurred in the 1950s. Merseyside PTE, now Merseytravel, has always been supportive of Liverpool's local rail services, though early plans for an eastern outer loop using then-available track came to nothing. And the long-term success of the network has been continued under privatisation, with NedRail/Serco bringing in innovations such as tickets sold from

**LEFT** An early success under Railtrack's short period of ownership was a revamp of Manchester Piccadilly including a new enlarged concourse, travelators connecting it to platforms 13 and 14 plus new retail outlets and a complete re-glazing of the vast trainshed roof and re-painting throughout the station. *Network Rail*

**ABOVE** The award-winning Liverpool South Parkway station was masterminded by Merseytravel as a hub for urban, interurban and airport traffic. *Jefferson Sheard, Architects*

shops and a conviction that Liverpool deserves the smartest railway possible.

The key initiative was the 'Loop and Link', worked up with the PTE but firmly BR's baby and constructed between 1972 and 1977. The Loop turned the line under the Mersey to the Wirral from a terminating stub into a one-way loop from James Street to Moorfields, Lime Street and Central and back out via James Street. The Link connected the lines northward to Southport, Ormskirk and Kirkby and south-east to Garston, its underground section meeting the Loop at Moorfields and Central. The 'Loop and Link' seemed to some an extravagance; they also involved relocating The Cavern, sacred to Beatles fans the world over. But these new connections boosted traffic by 30%, and extensions to Hooton, Ellesmere Port and Chester and of the Link to Hunts Cross paid off. Chris Leah remembers the post-electrification inspection saloon reaching Chester just as locals were stealing the new lineside fencing.

The only extravagance was the ordering in the late 1970s of 76 Class 507 and 508 EMUs; 17 were mothballed or sent south. MTL imposed severe cuts after privatisation: Hall Road depot was closed, and almost all workings reduced to a single three-car unit; overcrowding on the Southport line led to six-car trains being reintroduced. Since then traffic on Merseyrail serving the central business district has soared by 348%, and in 2011/12 Network Rail carried out a difficult expansion of Liverpool Central station, Britain's 28th busiest with 14.2 million passengers a year. This growth has been abetted by very low fares – an average of just £1.55 in 2013/14.

The Wirral Line faced problems because of a rise in the water table – 10 feet in the decade to 1990 – as industry's demand for water fell; corrosion to rails and chairs was forcing their replacement every two years. In 1995 Leah ordered a total closure, with complete rerailing and four massive pumps installed to shift 6,000 gallons a minute. The job was completed in just two weeks.

### Reclaiming the railway

Merseyrail's success story has in part been one of culture, of 'reclaiming the railway'. When NedRail/Serco took over in 2003 they installed as Managing

**LEFT** The street-level entrance to Liverpool Central has been transformed into a pleasant interchange experience in 2014. *Alex Green*

## An ambitious strategy

Merseytravel's 20-year Rail Strategy produced in 2014 is ambitious, stretching beyond the third-rail system to the lines to the east of Liverpool for which it has a PTE's conventional responsibility. It includes reinstating the Halton Curve to allow direct services to North Wales; a new line into Skelmersdale new town; electrification to Preston and Wigan and – at last – to Wrexham; and reopening Wapping Tunnel to the Dockland area. Beyond 2024 it wants reinstatement of the curves at Burscough to allow Liverpool-Ormskirk-Southport and Southport-Preston services; through trains between the Wirral and Northern Lines (a tunnel exists); reopening of the North Mersey and Bootle branches; a new line to the airport; Ellesmere Port-Helsby electrification; and an extra city-centre station.

Merseyrail must also replace its EMUs, which despite their age give more than 90% reliability. 'You could keep these trains running for 100 years if you wanted to,' says Dominic Booth, 'but shouldn't we have a step change?' The PTE's preference is for walk-through, dual-voltage stock … eventually.

## South Yorkshire
### The legacy

Sheffield's hilly geography militates against rail commuting, and much of what there is comes from Derbyshire. Most South Yorkshire rail corridors are served by interurban or CrossCountry trains; the PTE is left with stopping services from Sheffield to Barnsley and Leeds/Huddersfield, to Doncaster via Rotherham and to Worksop, and routes radiating out of the county from Doncaster. A useful Barnsley-Doncaster connection closed in 1959 and is beyond reinstatement. Buses were initially the PTE's main focus; the 'Socialist Republic of South Yorkshire' had the goal of eliminating fares, and a freeze between 1974 and 1986 led to much higher bus use – and eventually rail too. With bus deregulation, SYPTE finally concluded an orthodox Section 20 agreement, but fares stayed low. Until 2014 pensioners travelled free; ending the concession sparked sit-ins on Barnsley-Sheffield trains.

### Greater concentration on rail

When SYPTE was created in 1974 Gordon Pettitt, as BR's Sheffield Divisional Commercial Manager, detected 'no cooperation from BR on operations'. The PTE's dominant figure has been Alex Ritchie, who

**ABOVE** Network Rail completed a further award-wining restoration at Liverpool Lime Street in 2011. *Theo Steel*

Director Patrick Verwer, a former transport policeman from Rotterdam. 'He did a great job of saying we had to recapture the space – feet off seats, and so on,' says Dominic Booth, UK Managing Director of what is now Abellio. 'He had a major effect in terms of customer confidence – the trains are some of the oldest in Britain but passenger satisfaction is very high.'

Neil Scales's 12 years as Merseytravel's Director-General from 1993 produced many initiatives, culminating in the opening of Liverpool South Parkway interchange in 2006, replacing Allerton and Garston stations and connecting the Link (now Northern Line) with local and semi-fast trains on the WCML, with a bus connection to John Lennon Airport. Parkway is now used by well over 2,000 people a day. Liverpool also came close to gaining its own light rail line – to Kirkby, running beside a rail alignment through Croxteth. Merseytravel gained Transport & Works Act approval in 2004 but, with costs rising, Alistair Darling vetoed the expenditure; so confident had the PTE been that the first consignment of rail had been ordered.

**ABOVE** Sheffield station forecourt with its beautiful water feature. *Alex Green*

arrived in 1979 as Finance Director and left in 1998 as Director-General. Prior to bus deregulation, SYPTE's greatest concern over rail had been keeping the Penistone line, but in 1988 it agreed a three-year Railplan with Provincial, increasing supported stations from 22 to 34 and supported routes by three, and passenger journeys doubled. The second Railplan saw a move toward 20-minute frequencies on the Sheffield-Barnsley and Sheffield-Rotherham-Doncaster corridors (the former now has four trains per hour).

Mike Hodson, then Operations Director at RRNE, says: 'South Yorkshire had one of the earliest quality regimes; they saw us as a contractor, with them defining the standards, and some, like levels of litter on trains, were hard to quantify. They also wanted to take revenue risk; West Yorkshire and Nexus didn't. And their strategy involved new stations, not much on routes.' Most of these, like Adwick and Bentley, serve former mining communities to the east. Another was a platform at RAF Finningley (now Robin Hood Airport) for the annual air show; this was dismantled and brought back the next year.

SYPTE funded the diversion of trains in 1987 from Rotherham Masboro into the better-located Central station, and backed the new station at Meadowhall, which transformed travel patterns in South Yorkshire. It drove through a much-praised rail/bus interchange at Barnsley, flagship of its Transport South Yorkshire brand. It has also fought to keep in the 'Northern Hub' project an eastbound freight loop on the Hope Valley line, without which there can only be a 2-hourly local service off-peak despite heavy demand. South Yorkshire reluctantly accepted that routing HS2 via Sheffield Victoria would be unaffordable, and will capitalise on its planned interchange at Meadowhall.

### Trams and now tram-train

Consultants recommended light rail for Sheffield in 1973 – 13 years after its 'last tram' – but it took until 1994 to deliver. Meanwhile the buses were deregulated and the metropolitan county was created and abolished, leaving three districts out of four with no stake in the project. Supertram's eastern destination, Meadowhall, had gone from heavy industry to dereliction to mass retail. The Conservative Government was suspicious of the Labour (and at times Lib Dem) city council, so local businessmen

**LEFT** MetroTrain No 141114 stands at Doncaster in February 1997. *Dennis Lovett*

## Strathclyde
### Turning the tide

Greater Glasgow has Britain's most extensive suburban rail network outside London. The 'Blue Trains' inherited by Greater Glasgow PTE served east-west lines via Queen Street Low Level and routes south from Glasgow Central, electrified in 1960-62, but they reflected travel-to-work patterns soon changed by industrial decline. Jim Summers recalls: 'Glasgow had a particularly low car ownership, but the desire to move folk out had given rise to new towns such as Cumbernauld, East Kilbride and Livingston, designed without sensible reference to the railway nearby. So an active policy was moving people away from rail.'

The Greater Glasgow Transportation Study, inherited by the PTE that had been formed in 1973, gave rise to the next step in the network's development – the Argyle line – launched in 1979 and taking its name from the street above. This gloomy but still quite busy east-west route through Glasgow Central (Low Level) had closed in 1964 after electrification of the parallel route via Queen Street. The PTE saw a role for it in distributing commuters and shoppers across the city centre, and it was relaid as far west as Partick, electrified and given improved connections to the Subway. (Although Glasgow has two east-west routes, both north of the Clyde, it has, like Manchester, never had a north-south railway; while one has long been projected, the fact that it has not happened in part reflects a lack of obvious demand.)

Losses on SPTE rail services rose from £7.9 million in 1976 to £28.9 million in 1983, fares covering just 43% of costs. Chris Green says, 'The PTE was dependent on a cash-strapped PTA, who announced they would withdraw services unless costs could be significantly reduced; to show they meant business they closed the Glasgow-Kilmacolm line in 1983.' Malcolm Reed, later Director-General of SPTE and first head of Transport Scotland, says, 'That closure was very important politically because it sent out a message that the network was not sacrosanct. That was a very brave move by the regional councillors, especially as some were NUR or TSSA affiliates.'

### Making the network affordable

The PTE faced an 'excess of public transport provision' with a falling population, and matters were brought to a head by the realisation that the 'Blue Trains' contained blue asbestos. 'BR presented Strathclyde with a huge bill for taking asbestos out of the 303s,'

**ABOVE** South Yorkshire PTE found the answer to its urban transport development in Supertram – now operated by Stagecoach and planned to be extended to Rotherham. *Alex Green*

dominated Supertram's board. Eventually its £240 million cost was met by Government grant, borrowing and the European Union, with a contribution from the council and smaller ones from developers. Disruption as the mainly on-street system took shape brought protests from traders. Establishing an interface with BR, and running beside the Don Valley freight line, proved relatively simple. Supertram was delivered on time and within budget, then the franchise was sold to Stagecoach for money up front and a share of the profits. It has experienced modest growth to 15 million passengers a year, but efforts to extend it foundered on the Department's fixation with 'quality buses'. The tram-train experiment is now finally bringing an extension to Rotherham and Parkgate; services were to commence in 2015, but complications outlined in Chapter 7 have pushed this back two years.

**RIGHT** Thirty years on, a Blue Train soldiers on under Regional Railways. No. 303027 awaits departure at Glasgow Central in March 1992. *Dennis Lovett*

Reed recalls, 'and it was the shock of this unexpected and unmanageable capital claim among councillors – and finance officials – about the ongoing affordability of the network.' But the ensuing rescue constituted a further step in its improvement.

Chris Green continues: 'BR set up a joint group with Strathclyde Regional Council and the PTE, and I attended 23 working meetings with Mike Rayner of Provincial. The politicians, led by Malcolm Waugh, wanted to save the rail network, but the PTE was attracted to bus substitution. Our policy was to prevent closures by major savings, and we identified three big areas of cost: train service (£16m), track and signalling (£13m), and stations (£9m).

'The group reported in December 1983 that Strathclyde's rail network was "of critical economic importance" and should be retained by cutting the Section 20 subsidy from £29 million to £18.6 million by 1988 – a saving of 36% – through aggressive cost reduction, investment in modern equipment and filling off-peak seats.' Driver-only operation – possible because BR had just faced down ASLEF over its deployment between St Pancras and Bedford – would reduce annual costs by £2 million. 'The proposal led to strikes on the North Electrics; a sensible compromise retained conductors for on-train ticket checks and customer service, whilst the drivers took sole operating responsibility.' Station staffing would be reduced by conversion to Open Stations with ticket machines, travelling inspectors applying penalty fares. New signalling centres at Paisley and Yoker would replace 57 boxes. The threatened South Electric network was reprieved, at the price of two station closures and a 17-mile reduction in track. The diesel routes were the most expensive to operate, and the solution was to electrify Adrossan-Largs, Glasgow-East Kilbride and Coatbridge-Cumbernauld (the latter two not carried out). The Class 303 workhorse fleet was to be extensively refurbished. To Reed, the keys to the review's success were the toughness of its language, which satisfied the modernisers, and the Strathclyde Manning Agreement, 'really instrumental in bringing down costs.'

## Expansion since 1986

The uptick began in 1986 with electrification to Ayr, Ardrossan and Largs. Over seven years, 20 stations were opened. Yoker acquired its state-of-the-art SSI signalling centre and a washing plant; until then the North Clyde stock had been scattered, with only 60% of carriages

**ABOVE** Strathclyde No 318254, in the carmine and cream livery adopted in the late 1990s, departs from Anderston on the reopened Argyle Line through Glasgow. *Dennis Lovett*

washed each day. In 1990 the Kilmacolm line was reopened as far as Paisley Canal – by the same politicians who had closed it to bring matters to a head. The line to Whifflet reopened in 1992, the station there being rebuilt in just ten weeks. The Cowlairs chord opened in 1993, giving Cumbernauld its first direct Glasgow service since Buchanan Street closed 27 years before. The same year the line from Queen Street to Maryhill, used hitherto only by West Highland trains, reopened for local traffic; signalling constraints prevented it connecting with suburban services at Anniesland until 2005.

The network took on a new confidence as from 1995 its trains were outshopped in 'Strathclyde red' and black, later carmine and cream. With the creation in 2006 of Transport Scotland, Strathclyde PTE gained a new governing body: Strathclyde Partnership

**TOP** The promotional booklet on the Blue Trains, with Terence Cuneo's evocative painting. *British Railways Board*

**ABOVE** Airdrie station under reconstruction on 2 December 2010 prior to the reinstatement of the through route to Bathgate and Edinburgh. *Dennis Lovett*

for Transport (SPT). SPT gained responsibility for strategic non-rail transport planning, but lost some powers over franchising and concessionary fares.

Strathclyde's rail network is now almost the largest for which a case could be made. Frequencies are generous, and there have been suggestions that the Cathcart Circle in particular might be better served by light rail. The one extension in prospect will serve Glasgow Airport. The original scheme was cancelled by Holyrood in 2009 with work under way because of the cost of resiting the airport's tank farm; provision of a third track on the main line to Paisley and an extra platform at Glasgow Central went ahead. Five years later Westminster stepped in to promise funding. There is also ongoing pressure for the City Union line, closed in 1966, to reopen as a link between Ayrshire, the airport and points east of Glasgow.

## Tyne & Wear
### The Metro

Tyneside's concentration on its Metro system reflected in part the lack of ambition for heavy rail services in the area shown by successive BR managements over half a century. Lines were closed or de-electrified and handed over (grudgingly at first) to light rail operation, and those that remained were generally run with minimal services and correspondingly poor loadings. The situation today is little better, but there are some causes for hope.

The Tyne & Wear Metro was the most revolutionary – and unexpected – consequence of the 1968 Transport Act. The new PTE had recruited Tony Ridley, a Sunderland-born academic, as its Director-General to merge its three municipal bus operations. But Ridley took one look at the suburban network BR was running down – a sweeping and de-electrified loop between Newcastle and the coast, a freight-only branch running close to Newcastle Airport, and the line to South Shields – and conceived a metro system. Proposed in 1971, Metro would provide a fast and reliable way into Newcastle, beating congestion around the Tyne bridges, with a new Metro bridge and tunnelled sections beneath the city centre.

Ridley grasped from his contacts in the Department that the Act for the first time permitted grants for new infrastructure other than roads. He persuaded civic leaders to adopt the project and secured a £50 million grant – 75% of the estimated cost – from the Conservative Transport Minister John Peyton. BR was caught on the hop; when its leaders took their own hastily worked-up plans to Peyton, they were told that Tyneside had been promised its funding the previous week. There was bitterness at BR services being 'taken away', and this new operator – then Britain's third largest after BR and the London Underground – was even seen as a threat. Tensions continued for a time over who should own and operate the system. The Department, however, was happy to gain a comparator with BR in terms of operating and infrastructure costs.

Metro was opened by the Queen in 1980, having narrowly survived a cull of projects by a cash-strapped Labour Government and friction over which union's members should be in the cab. Completed in 1984, Metro's initial 34 miles (26 on railway alignments) thrived despite a 2.3% fall in population during construction and a 16.6% decline in employment. Metro helped make Newcastle's Eldon Centre a success, and kept firms in the city centre. Bus deregulation would cost it more than one-third of its traffic – but Metro survived, though today it carries 37 million passengers a year against 59 million at its peak.

**ABOVE** More regional investment in new capacity – the specially built Metro bridge over the River Tyne connecting the underground city centre section with South Shields and Sunderland. *Alex Green*

Ridley went on to bring Hong Kong's Mass Transit Railway into being, and head London Underground.

Since 2002 there has been full interworking with passenger trains over the 8-mile extension from Pelaw to Sunderland; risks are controlled by Metro's Automatic Train Stop system in conjunction with Network Rail's Train Protection and Warning System (TPWS). Onward to South Hylton, Metro runs mostly over BR's former Pallion branch. Mike Hodson says, 'An intensive heavy rail service would have been cheaper, but it wasn't what Nexus wanted.' An important consideration was a surplus of Metro cars. However, the branch is marked on railway atlases as 'Network Rail: for Metro trains only'.

### MetroCentre and potential reopenings

Tyne & Wear's conventional urban railway is vestigial – only six stations and 12 route miles are PTE-supported – and most improvements came in Provincial days. David Wharton-Street recalls, 'The line along the north bank of the Tyne ceased to carry freight, so we diverted the service to Hexham and Carlisle via the south bank, reopening Dunston station [not a long-term success]. This came in handy for the Gateshead Garden Festival, which was on the doorstep.

'MetroCentre was the UK's first out-of-town shopping centre. The Hexham line passed the site and in 1987 the developer threw down the gauntlet to build a new station for the opening. It was conceived and built in five months, and I twisted the developer's arm to contribute £100,000 of the £130,000 cost. With an enhanced train service, we clawed back our £30,000 in six months.' Served by Carlisle trains and a 15-minute service to Sunderland, traffic to MetroCentre boomed. But with Metro's extension most Sunderland trains were cut back to Newcastle, though MetroCentre is still served from Durham, Chathill, Hexham and Glasgow. Usage fell back to 1,000 passengers a day – one-seventh of the footfall at Meadowhall – but Northern Rail is now canvassing fill-in electrification to run through from the ECML.

Tyneside in the 1960s lost passenger trains to Ashington, Blyth and Washington – this last served by one a day towards the end. In 2009 ATOC named Washington, one of Britain's largest towns without a station, as a priority for reconnection to the network. Chester-le-Street, just over the border in Co Durham, also had one daily train in the 1960s, but today is served by three operators – mainly TPE – with 200,000 passengers a year using the station. Reopening to the Ashington area with a population of 80,000 would

## Chapter 8: THE MAGNIFICENT SEVEN: THE PTEs

**LEFT** The opportunity has been taken to transform the 1960s BR Sunderland station and make the underground station light and cheerful for both Northern and Metro passengers. *Alex Green*

**BELOW LEFT** Gateshead MetroCentre station. *Alex Green*

With James Isaac as the PTE's Director-General, the focus changed. A Development Plan recognised that the rail network could be revitalised, a Section 20 agreement was concluded, and in 1975 Stratford and Leamington gained extra trains, Moor Street station reopening for them in 1978 to relieve pressure on New Street. The local service was doubled to half-hourly between New Street and newly opened Birmingham International, and Stourbridge line services were improved with car parks extended and bus/rail interchanges.

### Cross-City triggers a revival

The most dramatic improvement came with the inauguration of the north-south Cross-City line – an upgrade of existing lines between Lichfield and Longbridge – on 8 May 1978. 'The LMR,' says Mark Causebrook, 'worked on this for the PTE with new points and crossings at New Street, upgrading of the freight line between Kings Norton and Longbridge, remodelling of Halesowen Junction, and new stations at Longbridge and University; Five Ways station (closed in 1944) was reopened. The total cost was £8 million. Twenty-four extra three-car DMUs were drafted in, and Tyseley depot enlarged. Cross-City was an immediate success, patronage quadrupling in two years. Services beyond the PTE boundaries to Redditch and Lichfield City were increased to hourly; Redditch previously had three trains daily (four on Saturdays).'

assist regeneration, but it is outside Tyne & Wear. Northumberland has long had an aspiration to reopen the line, but not the funds, while Nexus has seen little point as it parallels a heavily used bus route. Reopening to Ashington is, however, an option for the new Northern franchise.

### West Midlands
#### Focusing away from the car

The heart of Britain's motor industry saw the car as its future. Birmingham's 1960s ring road severed the city centre from its hinterland, and there was no overall transport plan for the region. West Midlands PTE came into being with WCML electrification to Wolverhampton, Coventry and Walsall recently completed, but it concluded early on that many short local rail journeys were better made by bus. This message was reinforced by the decline of Snow Hill station, in Mark Causebrook's words 'from the city's principal gateway to a weed-infested ruin with one platform'. Closure in 1972 saved £70,000 a year in operating costs. Fortunately its commuter lines to Leamington and Stratford survived, trains being diverted to New Street.

**BELOW** No 323218 in Centro/Regional Railways livery. *Martin Loader*

Chapter 8: **THE MAGNIFICENT SEVEN: THE PTEs**

**ABOVE** No 323219 waits at Alvechurch on 3 July 2014. The scene is a far cry from steam days when Redditch had three trains a day. The new double track from Alvechurch to Redditch allows three trains an hour today. *Robin Goundry, courtesy of Malvern Industrial Archaeology Circle*

With bus deregulation looming, BR relaunched its services in an area bounded by Stratford, Lichfield, Kidderminster and Northampton as 'Midline'. Provincial's local management cajoled councils to invest in the network – and the PTE refocused and renamed itself Centro. Warwickshire County Council financed reopening of the Coventry-Nuneaton line in 1987; it is now being upgraded as 'Nuckle', with extra stations.

**Snow Hill reopens**
On 5 October 1987 Snow Hill reopened to relieve a New Street struggling to cope. A four-platform concrete wind tunnel replaced the once stately Edwardian pile, but it was a station, and a useful one, Stratford and Leamington trains running on from Moor Street. In 1993 Network SouthEast, at the behest of Regional Railways, reintroduced direct services to London, routed into Marylebone rather than Paddington. Snow Hill became a through station again in 1995, and in 1999 the Midland Metro took over one of its platforms. It now handles 4 million passengers a year.

Next, in 1988, came Walsall-Hednesford, a Speller Act reopening with the PTE, Staffordshire County and district councils. The service soon became hourly, extended first to New Street and later to Rugeley. That November Cross-City services were extended to Lichfield Trent Valley, with a new park-and-ride and limited interchange with the WCML. Though many 35-year-old DMUs still worked Birmingham services, investment in 'Sprinters' was paying off, together with new signalling on the Stourbridge line and more robust timetabling; one month in 1991, cancellations had been reduced to 23 out of 2,600 peak trains.

**Cross-City electrification**
In 1993 the Cross-City electrification was completed, at a cost of £65 million including £34 million for new Class 323s. John Edmonds made the original case for it on the need to replace obsolete DMUs and mechanical signalling (with an IECC at Duddeston); the core section between New Street and Aston Junction was already wired. The PTE asked Provincial to plan for electrification between Blake Street and Longbridge, the last stations within its area, but they were not the natural terminals, so the scheme became Lichfield-Redditch. Cecil Parkinson's approval for the project in February 1990 was prompted by the death of Lichfield's Conservative MP; Labour still won the by-election.

Electrification caused three years of disruption, and when the full service was restored the use of unreliable 32-year-old Class 308 EMUs from NSE, and Regional Railways' own elderly 310s, did not give the start a newly electrified railway deserved. The route was also hard to operate through its central section until Proof House Junction was remodelled, but from the start 16 minutes were saved end to end.

When the 323s arrived belatedly in 1994, they too initially proved a problem. 'The clever software on the

**RIGHT** None of the glamour of the original station, but a valuable addition to Birmingham's infrastructure: an unidentified Chiltern Railways Class 165 awaits departure from Birmingham Snow Hill on 18 August 2010. *ReptOnix*

## Chapter 8: THE MAGNIFICENT SEVEN: THE PTEs

**LEFT** The number of rail passengers has doubled from an annual 750 million to 1.6 billion in the 16 years since privatisation. Urban stations such as Birmingham New Street have taken the brunt of this doubling of passenger throughput. *Network Rail*

**BELOW LEFT** Commencement of the Walsall-Rugeley electrification in 2013 was another opportunity to celebrate the rejuvenation of the regional railway network. *Network Rail*

trains – being used for the first time on an EMU – had a habit of shutting the train down,' Mark Causebrook recalls. 'The 323s particularly hated ice on the overhead lines, and on one fateful morning we had a line of them all shut down, in service, on the northern section of the line. However, over time the problems were fixed and they became a splendid unit delivering an excellent service. The fact that they were remotely maintained at Bletchley didn't help, but the subsequent opening of a proper maintenance facility at Birmingham Soho gave the units the love and ownership they deserved.'

### The 'Jewellery Line'

1995 brought the launch of the 'Jewellery Line', a second east-west route after Wolverhampton-Coventry. Worcester and Kidderminster services were diverted into Snow Hill over 4 miles of reinstated track, a new Smethwick Galton Bridge station providing interchange with the Wolverhampton line. New cross-city connections were offered and efficiency increased, paths for extra Walsall services were freed up at New Street and conflicting movements eliminated. The line's three new intermediate stations were soon attracting a million passengers a year.

The West Midlands rail system could have been transformed by the 'Birmingham Heartlands' station, a project worked up by BR in consultation with Centro in 1991/92. Sited near the M6, it would have taken inter-city and Channel Tunnel traffic, leaving New Street to Centro and Regional Railways. The three-level station would have had Birmingham-Derby trains at the bottom, local trains in the middle and WCML and continental services at the top. Opening was targeted for 1998, but privatisation put it into the 'too difficult' category.

Centro was the first PTE to negotiate a rewards and penalties package with a privatised TOC, Central Trains. The only difficulties concerned capacity on the Coventry-Birmingham-Wolverhampton axis. In 2002, with Virgin about to enhance its CrossCountry services, the Strategic Rail Authority tried to take away some of Centro's paths. They were repulsed, but the problem persisted. As Mike Hodson, later Managing Director of London Midland, explains, 'Virgin had 15-minute frequencies, which meant an all-stations service was difficult to fit in. They also made a 20-minute-interval service impossible if you wanted to go up from half-hourly.'

### Midland Metro opens

In 1999 the Midland Metro opened. Powers had been obtained for several routes, one involving joint running with freight trains through Dudley. But just one was funded, from Snow Hill to Wolverhampton St George's, largely following the former GW main line. Patronage built slowly, the AnsaldoBreda trams proved unreliable, and Centro struggled to gain funding for any extensions. Eventually, though, the Department approved one to the remodelled New Street station, to open in 2015, and on to Centenary Square. Further extensions to the HS2 station at Curzon Street, Edgbaston and Wolverhampton station, seem likely; Birmingham City Council wants Metro to run to the airport.

Meanwhile Walsall-Rugeley Trent Valley is being electrified. Cross-City – now England's busiest urban route outside London with almost 20 million passengers a year – is being extended down the Lickey Incline to a resited station at Bromsgrove, and part of the Redditch branch has been doubled. There are plans for new connections to divert more suburban trains from New Street to Moor Street. And HS2 will serve not only Curzon Street but Birmingham Interchange, linked to the airport and Birmingham International.

Birmingham City Council goes further in its 20-year plan, published in 2014. It wants to see reopening to passengers of the Camp Hill and Sutton Park suburban lines and a £400 million upgrade to Snow Hill station to make it a genuine transport hub, together with three more Metro routes. The one missing piece in the jigsaw is an adequate urban service across Birmingham to the airport, and this can be blamed on the West Coast route through the city being limited to two tracks. HS2 will offer limited relief, but quadrupling this line seems essential; considered by Railtrack before being dropped on grounds of cost, it may be a project that simply has to happen.

**RIGHT** Grade I-listed Huddersfield station is a focal point on the revitalised trans-Pennine line, complete with a statue of local boy Prime Minister Rt Hon Harold Wilson. *Peter Hackney*

**BELOW** The order for new electric trains for the Leeds to Skipton electrification was cancelled before construction work started. A determined WYPTE drafted in 40-year-old cascaded units from Network SouthEast, including No 308137 seen here at Skipton in WYPTE-Regional Railways livery. *Martyn Hearson*

## West Yorkshire
### A clear vision

West Yorkshire has seen the greatest rail passenger growth of any conurbation, doubling from just 7.5 million journeys a year between 1982 and 1993 and tripling again on some routes since. Leeds has become an economic and commuter magnet, and Bradford (with two termini handling 5 million passengers a year), Huddersfield (4.2 million) and other centres have also seen growth on both Northern and TransPennine Express services. Indeed, West Yorkshire's success story is if anything even more of an interurban than an urban one.

Beeching brought the shoehorning of Leeds Central's trains into Leeds City, closures in rural areas which are now prime commuter territory (the Ilkley line only narrowly survived), a thinning of duplicate routes, and many station closures. On the plus side

**ABOVE** No 333011 calls at Guiseley with a Leeds service on 27 October 2012. *Antony Christie*

New Pudsey station opened in 1967, and by the time the PTE was established a relocated rail and bus facility (Bradford Interchange) had replaced the colossal but decaying Bradford Exchange terminus. By contrast, passengers at Bradford Forster Square had to negotiate derelict buildings frequented by glue-sniffers and muggers (according to Regional Railways' staff magazine) en route to the platforms. A deal between BR and a property company to develop the 15-acre site collapsed, so from 1990 Regional Railways North East created a new access, then spent £240,000 on a smart glass building at platform level.

WYPTE, says Dick Fearn, had a 'very clear vision' for its rail network, and much of the credit goes to the Leeds Labour councillors Michael Simmons, who chaired the PTA until 1990, and Mick Lyons, a BR driver 42 years in the cab when he took over. The PTE's expansionist policy for rail was based partly on Leeds's increasing magnetism for commuters (and the need for residents of former mining areas to travel to find work) and on a financial windfall. When the metropolitan county was abolished in 1986 WYPTE, alone among such bodies, inherited a sizeable sum in capital receipts, which it put into rolling stock and new stations. Meanwhile a partnership between the PTE, Provincial and some enlightened engineers pioneering a low-cost 'Meccano-style' station, enabling 18 new ones to be opened in a decade.

The first new trains were Class 141s, which Metro's former Director-General John Rhodes says it was 'suckered into taking'. However, Mike Hodson notes: 'The "Pacers" are now seen with disdain, but West Yorkshire pioneered narrow-bodied 141s as a low-cost solution. First used on the Harrogate line, they led to its first half-hourly service, plus new stations. This was seen as a great achievement.' By the time the Department clipped the PTE's wings, it had uniquely also acquired or financed Class 155 and 158 DMUs, centre cars for Class 144 'Pacers', and Class 321 EMUs.

## Systematic expansion

Service development in West Yorkshire owed much to a Rail Policy Review published in February 1987 by a joint working group taking its membership from the PTE, PTA and BR Provincial. This paved the way for many important developments, including the electrification to Skipton and Ilkley. Roger Cobb – who subsequently joined BR and was to become Managing Director of Merseyrail – was the driving force for the PTE, and Mark Causebrook led for Provincial. Continuing development was determined by five-year Railplans produced by councils, Metro and Provincial/Regional Railways. Railplan 3 of 1991 noted rises in patronage, train miles, fares and revenue offset by a shortage of S&T resources, poor reliability and delivery of only 61% of planned strengthenings of trains. It also brought a commitment to improve services between centres other than Leeds. Pontefract-Wakefield reopened in 1992; the service lost heavily and the three intermediate stations still only handle 200,000 passengers a year.

## The wires go up

The PTE's priorities were 'an acceptable balance between reliability, service levels and cost', improved passenger facilities especially for the disabled, better passenger information, expansion of park-and-ride, and electrification. In 1990 an electric Doncaster-Leeds local service was launched using surplus Network SouthEast Class 307s, soon replaced by new 321s. That year the £56 million Leeds North West electrification was approved. WYPTE picked up 90% of the electrification and 68% of the signalling costs; one extra panel replaced 13 boxes. The line speed was mostly raised to 90mph, the track layout at Skipton remodelled, and a new Leeds-bound platform provided at Shipley.

Electrification masts were already being planted when the Department blocked an order for Class 323s to operate the route. Mick Lyons determined that the project must go ahead, and Gordon Pettitt, John Rhodes and Richard Peck, the Leeds NW project manager, intervened with NSE to secure 21 redundant slam-door 308s. Repainted in Metro red and cream, they arrived in 1995, passengers used to sliding-door 'Pacers' having to be re-educated lest they fall out. Electrification brought a huge increase in train capacity and frequency; services out of Bradford were doubled. Patronage increased further after Siemens/CAF Class 333s arrived in 2000; a fourth car had to be added, the Department trying to reclaim these when short-term financial support expired. These lines now carry 13.7 million passengers a year, with new stations imminent at Apperley Bridge and Kirkstall Forge.

## Hiccups after privatisation – then growth resumes

Following privatisation, a shortage of drivers after MTL cut staff on taking over the North East franchise led in 1997 to Metro withholding performance payments. Mick Lyons said that one four-week period had seen 703 cancellations, yet the PTE was expected to pay £50 million a year in subsidy because the franchise's performance was good overall. As a result, he was left with 'no alternative'.

Privatisation delayed a Huddersfield-Halifax service via a reopened Brighouse station until 2000. Halifax, Brighouse, Wakefield Kirkgate, Mirfield and Pontefract Monkhill also benefited from the launch in 2010 of Grand Central's Bradford Interchange-King's Cross service. Wakefield Council and the Railway Heritage Trust helped fund renovation of the dilapidated Kirkgate station after Lord Adonis branded it 'the worst medium-large station in Britain'.

Growth of traffic, especially into Leeds, has continued to surge, and easing a shortage of rolling stock is a higher priority than new services; in 2014 Metro denied funding to a commuter service on the Keighley-Oxenhope heritage line, and just three new stations are in hand. In the short term Northern hopes to use DMUs freed up by electrification west of the Pennines to strengthen services or replace unloved 'Pacers' – though more modern and capacious trains could bring a further surge in demand. Trans-Pennine electrification, and to an extent completion of the 'Northern Hub', also offers both better and faster services and a further step change in comfort for TPE passengers. There could also be an easing of overcrowding on West Yorkshire's interurban services, at least until the improvements trigger a further surge in passenger numbers.

**ABOVE RIGHT** Saltaire station has proved a big success, with passengers tripling from 252,000 in 1997 to 807,000 in 2013 – equal to a home counties commuting station such as Thorpe Bay. *Theo Steel*

**RIGHT** It is costing £4 million to refurbish Wakefield Kirkgate to acceptable standards, and the total refurbishment of the building and platforms is taking shape in January 2015. *Alex Green*

## Chapter 9
# INTERURBAN SUCCESS STORY

*'Regional Railways has revitalised cross-country travel between the regions, enabling journeys to be made between main centres where there is no direct InterCity service. Overall, passenger income generates a surplus above operating costs'*

**THE FRANCHISING OF PASSENGER RAIL SERVICES**, DEPARTMENT OF TRANSPORT, OCTOBER 1992

**ABOVE** No 185127 is seen at Brough forming a TransPennine Express service on 19 March 2014. *Dennis Lovett*

## Making a success of a 'horrendous' inheritance

Britain's provincial cities are linked today by frequent, comfortable and fast-ish trains, but in 1982 this was far from the case. Apart from InterCity's HSTs linking Newcastle, Leeds, Sheffield, Birmingham and Bristol, relatively few interurban trains crossed BR's regional boundaries, and most that did offered unattractive timings and run-down stock. Some routes with potential had been lost in the 1960s: Southampton-Oxford, Oxford-Cambridge (now to be reinstated), and the direct line between Leeds and the North East via Ripon. Many services were composed of loco-hauled Mark 1 coaches for holidaymakers; one set worked Newcastle-Yarmouth one Saturday, returning the next.

Summer Saturday trains ran to Skegness hauled by pairs of Class 20s. Dick Fearn recalls, 'The running costs were horrendous. We had to turn it into a "Sprinter" railway like anywhere else and provide communities along the line with a railway that would serve them all the year round. We ended up with pairs of two-car units; they were besieged on summer Saturdays, but we stuck with it.'

The Provincial sector, then Regional Railways, seized the opportunity presented by sectorisation and the eclipse of the regions to develop a rejuvenated product. Today TransPennine Express – and especially its core Leeds-Manchester section – is arguably the most successful of all the privatised franchises. ScotRail's interurban services deliver a product of ever-higher quality and popularity, and across England and Wales a largely new web of services is thriving. Nearly all trains are three cars rather than the original two, and some are longer than that.

This achievement is largely due to John Edmonds who, says Chris Stokes, had 'an emerging vision of what might be done with the interurban railway. He was quite taken with improving the service, but nervous how the Board might react. He asked me, "How can I contemplate us going every hour from Birmingham to Peterborough if InterCity are threatening to reduce London-Manchester to every 90 minutes?"' New and accelerated services were introduced, with 'Pacers' first replacing loco haulage, and by 1990 Provincial's Organisation Simplification Team could report: '"Express" is BR's most successful growth product. A developing network of fast modern trains links major provincial cities with a speed and frequency never before achieved in so comprehensive a fashion. The trains … fulfil vital parts of the Board's PSO, [but] are successfully presented to the customer as an attractive and developing means of making journeys which are not served by InterCity's London-orientated route system and which are becoming increasingly difficult on the nation's congested road network. These interurban activities give very high productivity of trains and their staff, and as they are in part superimposed on infrastructure already required to meet PSO or PTE needs, they earn marginal receipts in excess of the long-term marginal expenses of train operation.'

**ABOVE** Eating into the profits are two unidentified Class 20s on Sheepbridge Bank hauling a train of empty stock back from Skegness to Sheffield on a summer Saturday. *Phil Sangwell*

### The 158s make the big difference

With the belated arrival of the 158s to become what Sidney Newey had called Provincial's 'flag carriers', services that could truly be branded 'Express' were rolled out. By 1991/92 interurban services accounted for 31% of Regional Railways' receipts, or £91.3 million, with 16% of the vehicle diagrams – the sector's only business to cover its direct costs and make a contribution toward fixed costs. Even during the recession, which hit BR hard, growth of 30-40% was registered on routes newly operated by 158s.

Regional Railways' aspirations for a 'Tees-Tyne Express' linking Middlesbrough, Darlington and Newcastle were thwarted by the onset of privatisation. A Swindon-Peterborough service via Oxford, Bletchley, Kettering and Stamford was costed, and a 158 made a trial run. Efforts to raise the line speed to 90 mph were foiled by antiquated signalling and level crossings between Bletchley and Bedford, but what sank the service was the diversion of the trains earmarked for it to Waterloo-Exeter, where earnings per coach far exceeded what Regional Railways could offer.

# Chapter 9: INTERURBAN SUCCESS STORY

**LEFT** No 322484, repainted into North Western livery, passes Stafford on 1 June 1998 forming one of the short-lived Open Access services between Euston and Manchester Airport. *Tim Horn*

services to previously served centres will continue under the new East Coast franchise, with trains for London from Dewsbury, Middlesbrough and Sunderland and more from Bradford, Harrogate and Lincoln. Obviously both open access and, indeed, franchised incursions abstract revenue from regional services, to the extent that they are being provided. But some connecting regional passengers will find them useful, and Hull Trains is now starting a London train back from Beverley.

## Initiatives under privatisation

Privatisation brought some services that had not been on Regional Railways' radar. Anglia launched a fast Norwich-Cambridge service (an immediate success) and an Ipswich-Basingstoke 'Crosslink' with Class 170s via the North London Line. An erratic service pattern prevented the latter taking off; Anglia's CEO Jeremy Long recalls, 'It was very difficult to persuade Railtrack to free up even the paths we got, even though there was a real passenger benefit.' Rochdale-Warrington-Euston with a Class 158, Manchester Airport-Euston using 322s (both North Western), and Great Western's more popular Bristol-Oxford service were launched, then discontinued through a shortage of paths, unsuitable rolling stock or simple lack of demand. North Western's planned Crewe-Carlisle semi-fasts using 'Clacton' Class 309s fell foul of work on the West Coast route upgrade. Meanwhile Liverpool – Britain's fourth most visited city in terms of overnight stays – lost its through trains to Cardiff and Glasgow, and for several years to Newcastle.

Open access competitors under privatisation aimed not to run regional services but connect poorly served centres with London. They too were frustrated by lack of paths, but Hull Trains built a business with some benefit also to regional passengers, and, after setbacks that inspired a television series, so did Grand Central, from Sunderland via the Durham coast and from Bradford Interchange via Halifax. But they were hobbled by restrictions. Wrexham, Shropshire & Marylebone, prevented from abstracting passengers at Birmingham New Street and Wolverhampton and obliged to cross Birmingham at a snail's pace, went under.

Repeated efforts to connect Blackpool and Shrewsbury with London via the WCML failed because of pathing issues and special clauses in the franchise agreement of Virgin – which since December 2014 has belatedly obliged. This return of inter-city

## The trans-Pennine legacy

Core trans-Pennine services were rescued from steam in 1961, dedicated DMUs with a 'Griddle Car' making seven round trips daily between Liverpool and Hull, covering Manchester-Leeds in a then impressive 67 minutes. But by 1979 a study found that trans-Pennine trains were slow, worn out, unreliable and no longer went where most people wanted to go. Just 3% of revenue came from 1st Class. No one in BR was sure whose responsibility they were or whether they should be classed as inter-city. The Class 45 locos hauling most of them were only 65% reliable, had a track-punishing weight and were inconveniently based at Toton. By 1984 there was still only an hourly Leeds-Manchester service, of alternating loco-hauled Newcastle-Liverpool and Scarborough-North Wales trains, the latter largely empty at start and finish except on summer Saturdays. Custom was falling on what the market saw as a 'tertiary' route, with the service resource-based.

**ABOVE** An original trans-Pennine Class 124 unit at Hessle with a Hull to Liverpool service in September 1966. *The late John Ford, David Ford collection*

**RIGHT** No 47475, the only Class 47 to be repainted into Provincial livery to match rakes of coaches, crosses Saddleworth Viaduct on 16 April 1990 with the 14.20 Newcastle to Liverpool trans-Pennine service. *John Hooson*

Provincial Eastern took charge in 1985, and did what it could. Better carriages appeared on the core services, accompanied by an 'Up and Over' campaign fronted by the Rugby League icon Eddie Waring. To speed these up, Provincial persuaded Freight to divert all but three of its 17 daily trans-Pennine trains to the easier-graded Calder Valley line.

## The network is created

Today's TransPennine Express network connecting England's second, fourth, fifth, seventh, ninth, 15th and 23rd largest urban areas has its origins in a meeting Edmonds convened in Huddersfield in February 1986, and a subsequent strategy paper from Mark Causebrook. From these emerged a coherent strategy for route development, timetabling and rolling stock, Edmonds saying, 'We've got the "Sprinters" coming along – let's see what we can do with them.'

Causebrook assessed the basic route as Newcastle-Liverpool, with unmet demand from Hull and none between Yorkshire and North Wales. He proposed more York-Manchester trains, restoring Hull to the network and diverting North Wales services to Liverpool. With locomotive reliability below 50% and most of the stock due for major repairs, half-HSTs and ScotRail-style push-pull operation were considered, both failing the test on cost (the latter required more platform staff).

The strategy involved some loco haulage, then 'Sprinters' (Class 150) from 1986, 23-metre 'Sprinters' (156s) from 1987, and 'Super Sprinters' (158s) from 1989. The public would be told that the 'Sprinters' were only a temporary expedient. 'It set the model for short-train, high-frequency interurban services outside London, resource-efficient and revenue-generative,' says Causebrook. 'Putting a standard "Sprinter" on an interurban railway may seem stupid, but it got us in the door.' (And its operating costs were half those of a loco-hauled train.)

## Improving the offering

In 1987 the Class 45s were replaced by Gateshead-based 47s and refurbished stock – for which Provincial sponsored a briefly reopened depot at York Clifton – though the timings still did not allow one crew to work Newcastle-Liverpool and back. These trains were supplemented alternately by a 150 between Hull and Chester or North Wales, and a Scarborough-Liverpool

**ABOVE** No 45130 with a rake of Mark IIs newly painted into Provincial sector livery passes Prestatyn on 28 April 1987 with a morning trans-Pennine service from Holyhead to Newcastle. *Martin Loader*

'Sprinter', giving a pioneering half-hourly 'walk-on' service between Leeds and Manchester. The reworked timetable increased train miles by 50%, reduced vehicle miles by 20%, and drivers' turns from 365 to 362 … and cut costs by £1 million a year.

1988 brought an airport coach link from Manchester Victoria, and with the 1989 timetable one train per hour was switched from Victoria to Piccadilly to improve connections and save 15 minutes, getting Liverpool services onto the more lucrative route through Warrington Central. David Prescott recalls, 'The Scarborough-Liverpool service had been strengthened to four cars between York and Manchester Victoria. Signalling changes at York and the move to Piccadilly (previously blocked by the LMR) meant that these attach/detach moves were no longer possible and two extra units were required to run the service, effectively empty at either end. The trans-Pennine team planned to run the strengthening unit as a separate train, offering two per hour York–Manchester and three Leeds-Manchester, with the revenue increase from the extra frequency more than covering the crew costs. Then an edict came from HQ to stop any increase in train miles. We resisted, as we would require more units to run more miles for no more revenue, and Sidney Newey saved the extra train operation on the core York-Leeds-Manchester section.'

Mike Hodson recalls, 'We changed origins and destinations with almost every timetable, ranking markets off trans-Pennine routes as the next we would like to serve. It would have been nice to get two trains an hour to Newcastle via Sunderland, but the speed restrictions via Stockton would have made it too slow. On the west side we played with Liverpool, Southport (we didn't stay long) and Blackpool, and had two attempts at North Wales.' Ideas not pursued were a trans-Pennine service to Chester via Stockport and Altrincham following the transfer of the direct route from Manchester to Metrolink – and connecting two existing services to run Hull-Manchester-Cardiff.

A virtuous circle was now in place: faster trains, higher productivity, more passengers, increased revenue (by 1989 the route accounted for 5% of Provincial's entire takings). Computer studies were run to show where track improvements would bring the biggest time savings; passing loops were added, line speeds raised from 75 to 90mph on the likes of York-Scarborough, and timetables reworked to improve reliability.

## Game-changing 158s bring a surge in business

The 'Sprinters' facilitated more and better services, but the 158s were the game-changer. Trans-Pennine took the second batch after ScotRail, replacing loco-hauled stock, following a pitch made by Regional Railways North East to Paul King highlighting overcrowding on the route.

Their introduction from the start of 1991 between Newcastle and Liverpool brought substantial time savings, thanks to those pre-planned track improvements. 'Linking' arrangements at depots were reorganised to concentrate drivers' knowledge on fewer routes, reducing cancellations. Middlesbrough was added to trans-Pennine in 1992, a reopened station at Yarm following. The service, which exceeded revenue forecasts by 36%, offset the withdrawal of Teesside's single HST as travel to London by ICI executives fell off.

In six years patronage had grown by 74% and receipts by 150%. Yet RRNE's Director Aidan Nelson noted that despite 'new trains, more trains, air-conditioning, telephones plus catering on the train, 90mph, etc' there was still 'only 8% awareness of trans-Pennine in the Leeds-Manchester corridor.' There were also seats to be filled, with an average 23 passengers per vehicle across the network – against 14 on urban and rural services.

Nevertheless the surge in business, the pressure on two- and three-car DMUs and the potential for further growth led the PTEs and shire counties involved, together with Regional Railways and the Department, to commission a study of electrifying York-Leeds-Manchester-Liverpool (for £53.2 million). Manchester-Blackpool was also considered, with less enthusiasm. Gordon Pettitt lobbied hard for approval, but the onset of privatisation cooled interest in Whitehall.

With the opening of the Manchester Airport link in 1993, hourly trains were scheduled from Blackpool – and soon from Barrow and Lancaster. Through services from Leeds, York – a 24-hour service introduced in preference to one from Hull after surveying travel agents – and Scarborough also proved an instant success.

Under privatisation trans-Pennine services gravitated to the North East franchise, under MTL, which, preoccupied with survival, took its eye off its most prestigious offering. Punctuality, reliability and customer service fell away as costs were cut, and the Newcastle-Liverpool link was lost. Arriva did implement the franchise commitment for a fourth hourly Leeds-Manchester train from May 2000, but little more.

**BELOW** No 158765 calls at Darlington on 27 July 2002 in Northern Spirit livery, as used by Arriva Trains when it rescued the North East franchise from MTL. It was later taken over and expanded by First TransPennine. *Richard Mackin*

## Table 9.1: Trans-Pennine improvements

| Year | Trains run, 0700-1900, Mon-Fri | Average journey time (hr-min) | Average speed (mph) |
|---|---|---|---|
| Leeds-Manchester | | | |
| 1982 | 13 | 1-06 | 39 |
| 1997 | 36 | 1-00 | 43 |
| 2014 | 48 | 0-56 | 46 |
| Leeds-Liverpool | | | |
| 1982 | 11 | 1-49 | 43 |
| 1997 | 12 | 1-52 | 42 |
| 2014 | 24 | 1-28 | 47 |
| Newcastle-Manchester | | | |
| 1982 | 5 | 3-23 | 44 |
| 1997 | 6 | 2-55 | 51 |
| 2014 | 12 | 2-22 | 60 |

Source: BR/NR timetables, Alex Green

### Revitalised under the TPE franchise

The Strategic Rail Authority carved a stand-alone TransPennine Express unit out of the North Western and North East franchises, involving three groups of services: North TransPennine, the core route continuing to Newcastle, Middlesbrough, Scarborough and Hull; South TransPennine, from Manchester to Sheffield and Cleethorpes; and TransPennine North West, from Manchester Airport to Blackpool, Barrow and Windermere.

First and Keolis won the franchise in 2003 promising quality, their first priority being Leeds-Manchester trains at regular intervals. TPE's launch Managing Director, Vernon Barker, who came from First North Western, set out to recruit a talented team 'focused on customer needs'. The timetable they devised not only delivered the promised service but also, through the remarshalling of 158s, increased capacity on peak trains. Previously, says Barker, promoting rail in the North had been a value proposition, and in the North West destination-led – cheap fares to Blackpool, Buxton or Southport. Now TPE launched a 'car key challenge', telling commuters 'Leave your car at home, you'll find rail a better proposition'. Leisure traffic was targeted with online advance tickets, and Barker took the campaign to TPE's passengers, walking the trains to 'give people the opportunity to challenge me. They told me, "This will never happen, will it?", but we delivered on our promises.'

Growth accelerated and, struggling to meet demand with its Class 158 fleet, First TransPennine Express (FTPE) hired in 175s. Overcrowding between

**TOP** No 185135, forming a Barrow to Manchester Airport service, crosses the now renovated Arnside Viaduct on 8 March 2010. *Network Rail*

**ABOVE** Class 185s have revolutionised comfort levels on the trans-Pennine route. No 185103 stands aside between services at York. *Dennis Lovett*

**124** Chapter 9: **INTERURBAN SUCCESS STORY**

**ABOVE LEFT** Dubbed 'Britain's worst station' by the Station Champions Chris Green and Sir Peter Hall in a report to Lord Adonis, Manchester Victoria was partially rebuilt in 2014. This artist's impression shows the stunning glazed roof concourse covering Metrolink trams and several local rail platforms. *Network Rail*

**ABOVE RIGHT** The new Ordsall Chord in Manchester will be the key connection to unlock the full benefits of the 'Northern Hub', allowing through trains to call at Manchester Piccadilly from Manchester Airport and proceed via the new line to Manchester Victoria and on to the North TransPennine route, with similar services eastbound – both avoiding conflicting movements across the Manchester Piccadilly 'throat'. *Network Rail*

Manchester and Preston was eased by omitting stops at Oxford Road, leaving commuters to the stop from Bolton to catch local trains. To create a dedicated fleet TPE ordered 56 Class 185 'Desiro' DMUs from Siemens; the SRA trimmed the order to 51 units, then the Department blocked a fourth carriage despite a low unit cost of £1.3 million. Though heavy and fuel-hungry, the 185s can cover Manchester-Leeds in 54 minutes with two stops, but the overcrowding resulting from the reduced order has dented customer satisfaction. With passengers unable to board some trains, and to get round weight/speed restrictions on the line to Hull, TPE acquired nine Class 170s from South West Trains.

### TPE the most profitable franchise
The new franchise had a provision for profit-sharing, which, Barker says, the SRA probably never expected to kick in. But with traffic surging 'we were giving a subsidy reduction back to the Department very early in the franchise.' TPE prospered through the banking crash of 2008, gaining popularity with business travellers, not least because of hold-ups on the M62. By 2013 TPE's average seat occupancy was 52% – a figure most inter-city operators would kill for – and its subsidy down to 7p per passenger mile. It was also the most profitable franchise to the operator, with a 23% margin on a £284 million turnover – despite low PTE fares on short journeys into Leeds and Manchester. Moreover, David Prescott reckons that 'of all the TOCs, TPE exhibited the most Regional Railways' flair for well-targeted operations, and efficient resource use.' Barker, now First Group's UK Rail Managing Director, puts 'delivering the TransPennine experience for customers and communities across the North of England' as his proudest achievement.

May 2014 brought a fifth hourly core train, giving a best time of 3 hours on a restored Newcastle-Liverpool service, a saving of 37 minutes and an average of 59mph. From 2016 six Leeds-Manchester trains an hour are envisaged, four stopping only at Huddersfield and the additional working starting back from York or Newcastle; stops either side of Leeds will be omitted to ease short-distance overcrowding, which has devalued the interurban offering.

Overcrowding on peak TPE trains into Leeds and Manchester is now more acute than on Northern; there is also a weekend student spike. An impressive 12% of TPE's business comes from Manchester Airport, justification for Provincial/Regional Railways having treated the link as more than a connection to the city – though until 2014 it was over-served compared with Liverpool. Business to Blackpool, Hull and Middlesbrough remains disappointing. But within the 'East-West conurbation' – West and South Yorkshire, Greater Manchester and Merseyside – TPE goes from strength to strength.

## Further benefits to come

The £600 million 'Northern Hub' project will benefit TPE further. Manchester Victoria will become a hub for east-west services, the Ordsall Chord, assuming it survives Judicial Review, at last creating a connection with Oxford Road and Piccadilly. This will both bring new journey opportunities and end Liverpool-Scarborough services blocking the station throat at Piccadilly twice an hour. Piccadilly also gains two more through platforms, as does Leeds. The Leeds-Manchester journey time should come down to 40 minutes, Leeds-Liverpool to 72 minutes, and Newcastle-Manchester to 2hr 4min. TPE will lose its Manchester Airport-Barrow (Blackpool) services to Northern on the electrification of Manchester-Blackpool – with 156s replacing 185s. TPE's success has also hastened the York-Leeds-Manchester electrification, though Network Rail is struggling to deliver this as early as politicians and the train operators would like. When it is achieved, through services to Scarborough will be at risk if the resort has still to be served by diesels.

Though Leeds-Manchester commuter travel is still 40% below that for other major city pairs, the rail infrastructure is nearing saturation. As Vernon Barker notes, 'when things go wrong, trans-Pennine is predominantly a two-track railway.' With the cost of upgrading the core route to 100mph prohibitive, the Coalition's Chancellor George Osborne upped the stakes in June 2014 by proposing a 'High Speed 3' between the cities, raising the prospect of radical journey time improvements right across the North; the five main northern cities, under the banner 'One North', came back with a call for a largely new 150mph trans-Pennine railway – which is now being studied. (These and other initiatives are covered in Chapter 13.)

## The Calder Valley line

The other Leeds-Manchester route, via Bradford, Halifax and Rochdale, has only recently become truly 'interurban'. It traditionally enjoyed a basic all-stations service, and had easier gradients for freight – the decisive argument against BR's proposal in 1983 to single sections at its Yorkshire end. Crucially, it survived after a train of petroleum tankers caught fire in Summit Tunnel in 1984, turning the brick lining to glass and closing it for eight months. There were fears it would not reopen, John Edmonds setting a £2.5 million limit for repairs, but fortunately Stephenson's innermost, third, lining had held.

Then the improvements began. In 1984, after running charter trains to shuttle National & Provincial Building Society staff between Burnley and Bradford, Provincial launched a five-times-daily Leeds-Preston service over the Copy Pit connection from Todmorden to Burnley, unserved since 1965, with one train extended to Blackpool. 'Pacers' were deployed, then 'Sprinters' running through to Scarborough (both PTEs considered the route overlong for a 'Pacer'). Next – a Metro project – was a Bradford-Halifax-Huddersfield service via a reopened station at Brighouse, launched in 2000. This too proved a success, the route being shared since 2010 by Grand Central's Bradford-Huddersfield-King's Cross trains.

When franchises were redrawn, the line – still without semi-fast trains between Manchester Victoria and Leeds – fitted logically into Northern. The step up came with the December 2008 timetable, giving three trains hourly, one stopping only at Rochdale, Todmorden, Hebden Bridge, Halifax, Bradford Interchange and New Pudsey, one at all stations, and the third fast via Brighouse and Dewsbury. The Blackpool trains now start back from York, the Brighouse line trains from Selby. The former, and most of the Manchesters, are 158s. Timings remain slowish, though New Pudsey passengers can get to Manchester more quickly this way than via Leeds.

Money is now being spent on the line, which will be invaluable during trans-Pennine electrification. The third side of the Todmorden triangle has been relaid for an hourly service between Manchester, Burnley and Blackburn. Holme Tunnel, on the Copy Pit line, was closed for 20 weeks in 2013-14 for £16 million of award-winning reconstruction. The Ordsall Chord will allow through running to Manchester Airport. There is an aspiration for four trains per hour (two

**BELOW** In a joint ceremony to commemorate the reopening of Summit Tunnel some eight months after the disastrous fire, Greater Manchester-liveried No 142001 breaks the tape while a West Yorkshire PTE Class 141 joins in the fun at the other end of the platform. *David Wharton-Street*

**LEFT** The new station at Burnley Manchester Road opened on 17 November 2014 and is designed to attract more custom to the route by its eye-catching exterior design and comfortable staffed ticket office area. The previous station was reopened in 1986, but as an almost invisible staffless halt. The new station, with its colourful blue fin, was heavily promoted by Citizens' Rail. *Community Rail Lancashire*

To improve punctuality and cut costs, Provincial made gradual changes. Cleethorpes-Doncaster-Sheffield-Manchester was strung together from separate daytime workings, creating new journey opportunities. Norwich-Liverpool services were begun, duplicating the boat train north of Ely. In 1989 an upgrade of the Sheffield-Manchester axis (a Cinderella route since the closure of the Woodhead line in 1970) enabled trains from east of Sheffield to access Manchester Piccadilly or continue to Liverpool by capitalising on the new Hazel Grove chord.

Regional Railways Central rationalised the service into hourly Norwich-Liverpool trains and a 2-hourly Ipswich-Peterborough 'feeder' to the ECML. At a stroke, says Glen Kennedy, 'we were able to pull out of buying in train crew at Manchester Piccadilly, Peterborough, Ipswich and Liverpool. Norwich-Liverpool was virtually all worked by Nottingham crews, with just four diagrams at Norwich.' Longer formations were run between Nottingham and Liverpool to match the heavier demand on this section, and the attraction of an hourly service (half-hourly between Sheffield and Manchester) more than compensated for its extra cost. The deployment of 158s from 1992 paid further dividends. On privatisation Manchester-Cleethorpes went to Northern, marking time until the creation of the TPE franchise, and Norwich-Liverpool first to Central, then to East Midlands Trains.

Regional Railways North East had high hopes for a Nottingham-Sheffield-Leeds service and, recalls Mike Hodson, tried it for two years, 'but South Yorkshire PTE said we had to stop everywhere.' In 2002 Midland MainLine ordered seven nine-car sets of Class 222 'Meridians' for a fast service between the cities. Why this required trains longer than on its principal route was never explained; the 'Meridians' were shortened to strengthen the fleet operating out of St Pancras, and the Nottingham-Leeds service began with two-car 158s operated by Northern. Heavily patronised, it provides with the Norwich trains a half-hourly service between Nottingham and Sheffield, and valuable extra capacity on to Leeds; extension to Carlisle or Glasgow, reinstating a link lost in 1982, has been canvassed.

**ABOVE** The Hazel Grove chord allows South TransPennine services to run via Manchester Piccadilly from Sheffield to Liverpool. The effect on the Buxton line's formation can be seen by the hump-back track alignment required to match the heights of both the chord line and the bridge. *Peter Whatley*

semi-fast) between Victoria and Leeds, though infrastructure work will be needed and paths are getting scarce again at the Leeds end. To fit in with TPE services there, some Calder Valley trains have to skip stops – not ideal, as intermediate business is brisk. And with traffic buoyant and the line's DMUs coveted elsewhere, the government's Electrification Taskforce has put the Calder Valley at the top of its list for wiring.

## South TransPennine to the east

At sectorisation, only a daily Liverpool-Harwich boat train and a Manchester-Cleethorpes newspaper train connected the North West with the East Coast south of the Humber, with irregular, resource-inefficient and unreliable services like the summer Saturday Newcastle-Yarmouth train linking other destinations.

**ABOVE** A Class 170 in hybrid livery: the leading coach is No 170207 in 'One' livery, while the rear car is from No 170101 in Central Trains livery. The train is the 11.40 Norwich to Cambridge passing Eccles Heath near Thetford on 27 November 2006. *Martin Loader*

Strong growth on Norwich-Liverpool continued, and after much pleading the Department allowed East Midlands Trains extra 158s to make the Nottingham-Liverpool section a four-car operation, with 'Meridians' brought in for the Grand National; similarly, an HST is deployed on summer Saturdays between Nottingham and Skegness. This could not have been done by Central, which had no inter-city stock. In 2014 the Department and Rail North controversially revived a

**BELOW** New Nos 350404 and 350410 in First TransPennine livery pass Euxton on the Up Slow line during a test run on 17 May 2014. *John McIntyre*

decade-old proposal to split the service at Nottingham, transferring the northern half to TPE and diverting TPE's Cleethorpes service beyond Doncaster to Hull (both proposals were soon dropped in the face of strong stakeholder opposition). There could also be a third hourly train between Manchester and Sheffield, with the single-line bottleneck at Dore on Sheffield's western approach due for redoubling as part of the 'Northern Hub'. But electrification even of Manchester-Sheffield is off the agenda at present.

Ipswich and Harwich have drifted off the interurban network. However, a Cambridge-Nottingham portion attached to trains from Norwich at Ely is now being considered, and in the medium term electrification between Felixstowe/Ipswich and Peterborough could benefit passenger services as well as freight. Meanwhile the fast Norwich-Cambridge service has benefited from the upgrading to 90mph of much of its route. Since its launch, intermediate stops have recorded a 395% increase in traffic. The acceleration gave time for Brandon stops that brought a surge in commuting to Cambridge; station usage rose from 3,117 in 1998 to 89,522 in 2012. However, patronage took a hit in 2013 when problems with a new signalling system torpedoed reliability.

## TPE to Scotland

Traditionally the route between Manchester/Merseyside and central Scotland was InterCity territory. Services were poor, and Regional Railways planned trains of its own for 1994, using the last handful of 158s awarded to ScotRail and North West. However, Headquarters transferred the service (minus Liverpool) to become part of the CrossCountry TOU.

# Chapter 9: INTERURBAN SUCCESS STORY

**LEFT** Push-pull working an Edinburgh-Glasgow train with Class 27s at each end and Mark II stock. *Tom Heavyside*

**BELOW LEFT** An immaculate Class 47 and Mark III coaches with a Mark II DBSO dramatically improved levels of comfort on the flagship Edinburgh-Glasgow service in May 1985. *Eastbanks*

In 2007 the Department accepted First TransPennine's bid to take over Manchester-Glasgow/Edinburgh, growing the market by starting from Manchester Airport. Electrification between Manchester and the WCML created a new opportunity, and late in 2013 TPE deployed new Class 350s – eight cars at busy times – on the route; greatly improved frequencies and timings followed. The new TPE franchise could bring a Liverpool portion for its Scottish trains, joining at Preston.

## Scotland forges ahead

The Edinburgh-Glasgow shuttle, and services from both to Aberdeen, are ScotRail's 'jewel in the crown'. Like trans-Pennine, the former received dedicated DMUs in the 1960s. Again the novelty faded, and by 1982 rail between Edinburgh and Glasgow faced serious coach competition – as indeed is still does. To meet it, rakes of Mark III carriages with a Class 47 and a driving trailer replaced older carriages topped and tailed by 27s. The service's popularity, and the ScotRail brand, survived the Polmont accident of May 1984 when the DBSO leading the 17.30 Edinburgh-Glasgow service hit a heifer, killing 13 passengers. From May 1985 Glasgow/Edinburgh-Aberdeen services were rebranded 'ScotRail Express', with Glasgow and Edinburgh linked by 100mph trains every half-hour. That summer Class 47 No 47716, with Charles Rankine of Haymarket at the controls, covered Queen Street to Waverley in 36min 27sec, just over 78mph start to stop (for timings see Facftfile D2).

The first 158s went to 'ScotRail Express', giving a half-hourly Edinburgh-Glasgow service, generally of six-car trains. After prolonged teething troubles, revenue took off strongly. Haymarket-based 158s were soon working between Edinburgh, Glasgow, Aberdeen and Inverness; the Highland line still covered only one-third of its costs, but after an irregular Glasgow-Aberdeen schedule was replaced by hourly departures, revenue there shot up by 34%.

Edinburgh-Falkirk-Glasgow electrification was considered; a 1993 report from Oscar Faber recommended wiring the route for £75 million, but privatisation put it on hold. Councils on the East Coast pressed for electrification to Aberdeen, but poor economics and a constricted infrastructure ruled this out.

Scotland's interurban services have since privatisation been not only a matter for the operator of ScotRail – in

**BELOW** No158708, in National Express 'Whoosh' livery, arrives at Inverness forming one of the highly successful ScotRail interurban 'Express' services linking Edinburgh, Glasgow, Aberdeen, Perth and Inverness. *Dennis Lovett*

## Table 9.2: Interurban Scotland

| Year | Trains run, 0700-1900, Mon-Fri | Average journey time (hr-min) | Average speed (mph) |
|---|---|---|---|
| Glasgow Quen St-Edinburgh Waverley | | | |
| 1982 | 26 | 0-46 | 62 |
| 1997 | 27 | 0-50 | 52 |
| 2014 | 55 | 0-51 | 56 |
| 2017* | 55? | 0-35? | ? |
| Glasgow Queen St-Aberdeen | | | |
| 1982 | 5 | 2-50 | 46 |
| 1997 | 12 | 2-41 | 49 |
| 2014 | 12 | 2-34 | 51 |
| Glasgow Queen St-Inverness | | | |
| 1982 | 3 | 4-05 | 44 |
| 1997 | 3 | 3-26 | 52 |
| 2014 | 5 | 3-15 | 55 |
| Edinburgh Waverley-Aberdeen | | | |
| 1982 | 2 | 2-35 | 60 |
| 1997 | 9 | 2-33 | 61 |
| 2014 | 10 | 2-22 | 64 |
| Edinburgh Waverley-Inverness | | | |
| 1982 | 2 | 4-04 | 44 |
| 1997 | 3 | 3-26 | 52 |
| 2014 | 4 | 3-18 | 55 |

* post-electrification  Source: BR/NR timetables, Alex Green

turn National Express, First Group and now Abellio – but since 2005 for the Holyrood Government, and now for Transport Scotland. The Edinburgh-Glasgow frequency has doubled since 1997; the journey time for the pairs of three-car 170s has eased to 51 minutes for the 47 miles with extra stops (Falkirk being Scotland's fifth largest urban centre), but 42 minutes is planned after electrification. Although four lines now connect the cities (via Falkirk, Bathgate, Shotts and Carstairs) Holyrood has aspirations for a completely new high-speed connection.

Frequencies generally have improved and Glasgow-Aberdeen is now 60mph end-to-end, but long single-track sections on the Highland line preclude an hourly, or a faster, service to Inverness; Holyrood has preferred

**RIGHT ABOVE** Edinburgh Waverley forms the main hub for Scottish interurban services to Glasgow, Perth, Inverness and Aberdeen, and formed the basis for regular services throughout Scotland from the 1980s. *Dennis Lovett*

**RIGHT** No 170470 waits at Edinburgh Waverley before departing for Glasgow Queen Street on 20 August 2014. *Alex Green*

**LEFT** No 47467 heads the 10.38 Inverness to Aberdeen train through Nairn on the bi-directional line on 17 September 1988. Signallers used to transfer between the signal boxes at each end of the loop by bicycle. The line was modernised and the signal boxes abolished in 2000. *Gordon Thomson*

to invest in doubling the A9. Abellio plans to draft in upgraded and shortened HSTs for these routes from 2018 but, for the radical improvement Transport Scotland seeks, track stripped out in the lean years will need to be relaid. Longer-term, electrification would greatly improve trains' climbing capabilities, increasing capacity by cutting time taken on the single-line sections.

### Aberdeen-Inverness headaches

The Aberdeen-Inverness line, mostly single track, has long posed problems. Jim Summers says of the early 1980s, 'The road was very poor and we expanded services, particularly on a Sunday, putting on loco-hauled stock. We had been running DMUs with automatic tablet exchangers, in charge of the guard with bell signals to let the driver know it had been received or – dammit – missed again.' This was one of the last routes to receive AWS – and at Nairn, until 2000, the signalman had to cycle the length of the platform for the token exchange.

The service remained 2-hourly despite steady growth (commuting from Inverurie trebled between 2007 and 2013); increasing the frequency was prevented by passing loops being in the wrong places. Finally in 2014 the Scottish Government announced a £170 million five-year investment, restoring double track between Aberdeen and Inverurie, new stations at Dalcross (for Inverness Airport) and Kintore, relocating Forres station, signalling improvements, and platform extensions for six-car trains. A 2-hour journey time was promised (20 minutes faster), but a full hourly service will require further improvements. As a bonus, some services will be provided by shortened HSTs, some of these running through from the East Coast and Highland lines.

### Routes from Birmingham

Birmingham is the hub not only of the CrossCountry franchise, but increasingly of regional interurban services. At sectorisation there were just four trains daily to Norwich, loco-hauled, which suffered from a 10mph restriction through Arley Tunnel (lifted after a nine-month possession in 1993); conflicts with InterCity at Nuneaton; poor junction layouts at Whitacre and Water Orton; and low speeds over the Fens. In 1986 the services were 'Sprinterised', increased in frequency and diverted to Cambridge.

The service still met problems at Nuneaton, where Regional Railways trains crossed the WCML on the level until reinstatement of the Rocker Bridge flyover. Conflicts at New Street reached the point where, in 1990, a 'West Midlands Charter' was concluded

### Table 9.3: Interurban cross-country

| Year | Trains run, 0700-1900, Mon-Fri | Average journey time (hr-min) | Average speed (mph) |
|---|---|---|---|
| Norwich-Nottingham | | | |
| 1982 | - | - | - |
| 1997 | 10 | 2-36 | 52 |
| 2014 | 12 | 2-36 | 52 |
| Bristol-Portsmouth | | | |
| 1982 | 9 | 2-30 | 41 |
| 1997 | 12 | 2-27 | 42 |
| 2014 | 12 | 2-32 | 41 |
| Birmingham-Stansted Airport | | | |
| 2014 | 12 | 3-18 | 48 |

Source: BR/NR timetables, Alex Green

**RIGHT** The pilot ERMTS signalling brought new life to the Cambrian line. The old steam shed at Machynlleth was partially restored as the diesel light maintenance shed for the Class 158 fleet. No 158839 rests on shed, while No 158841 arrives on 19 October 2014 forming the 11.26 Shrewsbury to Aberystwyth service. *Martin Loader*

between BR businesses on turnround times, headways and the like. Extra platforms at Cambridge and Peterborough have recently eased the pressure, but Leicester, with just four platforms and low approach speeds, remains a bottleneck.

The opening of the North Curve to Stansted Airport brought the extension of the Birmingham-Cambridge service – by now hourly – in 1993, but business was poor and it was dropped after a year. Central Trains reintroduced the airport service in 1998, and it broke even within 12 months. In 2007 it became part of CrossCountry, as did Cardiff-Birmingham-Nottingham, into which more effort was put post-privatisation.

Under Regional Railways, hourly Birmingham-Shrewsbury trains were extended alternately to Chester and Aberystwyth and accelerated. This offset the ending of a daily Aberystwyth portion from one Euston-Shrewsbury train, and of Euston-Shrewsbury services at the depth of the recession. Shrewsbury was an example of Regional Railways' ability to provide a cheaper, and sometimes quicker, service than InterCity, having more flexible stock and better-sited depots. However, the timing through Birmingham New Street of a train between Birmingham International and Pwllheli depended on when schoolchildren needed to board or alight at Harlech.

Regional Railways proposed, but could not introduce, Birmingham-Manchester semi-fasts and a Birmingham-Portsmouth service. But 1993 saw Regional Railways Central and Network SouthEast launch a Snow Hill-Marylebone service, which passed to the Chiltern shadow franchise. This linked existing trains, restoring a connection between Solihull, Leamington Spa and London as well as between High Wycombe and Birmingham; before long Leamington was Chiltern's busiest intermediate station. Chiltern Railways under Adrian Shooter developed it further: 'We inherited a few trains per day, which were taken over by Central crews at Banbury and stopped at all stations to Snow Hill. We wanted a good semi-fast service. We started, from the December 1994 timetable, with our crews throughout, running hourly and mostly only stopping where we wanted. We had a running battle with Centro, who were always trying to get us to stop at places we didn't want to.

**ABOVE** Chiltern Railways shares services into Birmingham from the Warwickshire commuter belt with London Midland. 168216 – the first Turbostar DMU in the new Chiltern Mainline livery – calls at Dorridge on 29 September 2013. *John Binch*

'Later we did deals with Central Trains to take over stations on the Birmingham line, also Moor Street when we rebuilt it (reinstating two disused terminating platforms). Terminating all Chiltern services at Moor Street would have given a more coherent service, and better and more profitable use of trains and crews, than going off to Kidderminster; this was forced on us by Centro.' The Strategic Rail Authority, Shooter adds, were 'as unhelpful as possible' over Chiltern's opening in 2000 of a new station at Warwick Parkway.

## Radiating from Cardiff

Cardiff's ability to host a range of interurban services fit for a capital has been handicapped by geography. Only one of Wales's three east-west routes serves the city, and the only surviving north-south line (the North & West – Newport-Shrewsbury-Crewe) transits large swathes of rural England. Yet interurban services now

# Chapter 9: INTERURBAN SUCCESS STORY

**ABOVE** No 158821, an early branded unit in Provincial livery with an 'Alphaline' branding logo on the side, waits at London Waterloo to form the 19.17 service to Cardiff on 14 June 1999. *Michael Taylor*

fan out from Cardiff not just westward to Milford Haven but also south to Portsmouth and Brighton and north to Manchester … and to North Wales all the way to Holyhead. However, services to Liverpool and Penzance did not long survive privatisation.

The low point for Wales's north-south services came in 1967 when Cardiff-Manchester trains were diverted from the N&W to run via Birmingham. Closure of that route was considered, and in the 1980s singling of the double track for its six daily Class 33-hauled Cardiff-Crewe trains was narrowly averted. But under Provincial and Regional Railways South Wales & West the line recovered to the point where, says Chris Gibb, 'while not our biggest volume route, it was our best bottom-line performer.' When in 1988 an hourly 'Sprinter' was introduced through to Manchester or Liverpool, traffic shot up by 60%. Class 158s followed, with 90mph timings from October 1991, and by privatisation there were 12 Cardiff-Manchester trains a day taking a minute over 3 hours, 56mph end-to-end. Under unified Welsh management, some started back from Milford Haven.

'The route gave birth to through trains such as Manchester-Penzance and Liverpool-Portsmouth,' says Gibb. They were all successful, particularly on the Liverpool/Manchester-Bristol flow, which Virgin CrossCountry neglected. The summer Saturday 09.33 Manchester-Penzance was always fully booked with a four-car 158 and was one of our best-earning trains. Virgin tried everything to stop us. The dispute went to the ORR, but we were advised by Tom Winsor and we won – I was reminded of that every day after I joined Virgin! Sadly none of those trains is recognisable today, but at least the likes of Manchester-Milford Haven still run, making good sense for rolling stock utilisation, long-distance revenue and station capacity in Cardiff.' Passenger numbers on the N&W have doubled since

## Table 9.4: Interurban developments – regional routes from Cardiff

| Year | Trains run, 0700-1900, Mon-Fri | Average journey time (hr-min) | Average speed (mph) |
|---|---|---|---|
| Cardiff-Birmingham New Street | | | |
| 1982 | 7 | 2-10 | 52 |
| 1997 | 11 | 2-14 | 50 |
| 2014 | 13 | 2-00 | 56 |
| Cardiff-Manchester | | | |
| 1982 | No service | No service | No service |
| 1997 | 12 | 3-01 | 56 |
| 2014 | 11 | 3-15 | 52 |
| Cardiff-Nottingham | | | |
| 1982 | No service | No service | No service |
| 1997 | 6 | 3-35 | 47 |
| 2014* | 13 | 3-19 | 51 |
| Cardiff-Wrexham | | | |
| 1982 | No service | No service | No service |
| 1997 | No service | No service | No service |
| 2014 | 8 | 2-39 | 52 |

Source: BR/NR timetables, Alex Green

**ABOVE** Just two years old on 5 March 1994, No 158820 passes through Bitterne between Southampton and Fareham on the newly introduced Cardiff Central to Brighton service for Regional Railways South West & Wales. *Martin Loader*

1988, and nowadays Class 175s provide the Manchester service.

A loco-hauled Holyhead train was trialled either side of privatisation, initially via Wrexham. 'There wasn't enough through traffic to justify fast trains, so stops were judiciously added,' notes Chris Gibb. 'There was no way we could get North Wales-South Wales to cover its costs, even with a souped-up 153.' But since 2008 Arriva Trains Wales has run a nation-building 'Premier Service' between Holyhead and Cardiff under contract to the Welsh Government. With 1st Class and a dining car, the loco-hauled 'Parliament Train' – originally named 'Y Gerallt Gymro' ('Gerald of Wales') – departs from Holyhead at 05.30, returning at 17.16. Since 2012 it has run via Wrexham, though this lost it connections at Crewe and necessitates reversal at Chester; it covers Shrewsbury to Newport at 67mph, surely the longest non-stop run on any regional line.

## Better services across the Severn

With air-conditioning, on-train catering, seat reservations and a cardphone, the 158s dramatically improved SW&W's interurban services (and some of Central's), which were rebranded 'Alphaline'. By adding a Cardiff-Paignton service to Milford Haven-Cardiff-Portsmouth, the 1992 timetable doubled the Cardiff-Bristol frequency to two trains an hour days after traffic chaos when new toll equipment – with higher tariffs – was installed on the Severn Bridge. SW&W sent an Advan back and forth across the bridge to be seen by the media. 'They assumed we had moved smartly to introduce the new service,' recalls SW&W's marketing man Andy Pitt.

The Cardiff-Portsmouth axis generated 25% of SW&W's income, and serious overcrowding until an hourly Bristol-Southampton stopper was added. SW&W created 27 train crew posts at Westbury for this and a revamped Westbury-Weymouth offering. A weekend Plymouth-Portsmouth service aimed at naval personnel was pulled after one season, but SW&W briefly gained a toehold at Paddington with a late-night service from Cardiff.

SW&W ran through from Cardiff to Brighton after £420,000 of platform work at Shoreham. Chris Gibb recalls, 'The 158 clearance at Shoreham was a big job, which NSE were not keen on. The service went on to be a great success, requiring four-car 158s, and running right through as a portion train to Pembroke and Milford Haven. The "stock movements" became popular too, arriving in Brighton at 08.20 and leaving at 17.00, enabling people to commute at speed from places like Southampton and Havant.'

On the Cardiff-Portsmouth route now operated by First Great Western, 13 extra vehicles have been deployed since 2006. Recent efforts to provide a better service and ease overcrowding have run into a series of practical difficulties, notably over how to serve smaller stations if trains are accelerated.

# Chapter 10
# RURAL LINES

*'In many areas it would be more cost-effective to meet the limited demand for public transport by providing bus rather than rail services. Many of the trains on the Provincial sector carry very few passengers; and average loading of less than 30 people per train is quite common.'*

**SERPELL REPORT**, 1983

**ABOVE** Unit No 153325 in London Midland livery passes Terras Crossing on the First Great Western Looe branch. *Antony Christie*

## The conundrum

Railways are at their best when carrying large volumes of goods and people over long distances – but rural lines – especially those through thinly populated areas – are at the opposite end of this equation. Put another way, profits are impossible on rural services, and external funding for capital and running costs is essential. The conundrum is what level of support should be given to provide rural rail services – and whether this should be decided at national or local level.

Britain's rural lines were built in great numbers in the mid-19th century to connect remote areas to the national network before the advent of motor transport – but the rationale for their existence had largely disappeared by the First World War. This led to continuing closures of uneconomic rural lines and stations. Clinker's *Register of Closed Passenger Stations* records closures for every year from 1930 to the time of the Beeching Report in 1963. This reveals that rural closures only paused during the Second World War, while Table 10.1 shows that stations closed in large numbers from 1948 to 1963 – and at an annual rate 57% higher than in the Beeching era.

The development of the motor bus and the lorry had caused the wholesale closures of rural lines well

**Table 10.1: Station closures**

| Years | Stations closed | % |
|---|---|---|
| 1930-39 | 792 | 15 |
| 1940-47 | 256 | 5 |
| 1948-62 | 2,368 | 45 |
| 1963-82 | 1,838 | 35 |
| **Total** | **5,254** | **100** |

Source: Gordon Pettitt

**Table 10.2: Rural railways with long single lines, 2015**

| Line | Route Miles | Trains/day (Regional) |
|---|---|---|
| Inverness-Thurso/Wick | 161 | 4 |
| Dingwall-Kyle of Lochalsh | 64 | 4 |
| Helensburgh-Mallaig | 141 | 4 |
| Crianlarich-Oban | 42 | 6 |
| Craven Arms-Llanelli | 91 | 4 |
| Shrewsbury-Aberystwyth | 81 | 8 |
| Dovey Junction-Pwllheli | 58 | 8 |
| East Suffolk Line | 44 | 17 |
| Middlesbrough-Whitby | 35 | 4 |
| **Total** | **657** | |

Source: Gordon Pettitt

**ABOVE** Anthony Ghafour issues tickets on the first day of Paytrain operation on the Newcastle to Carlisle service in January 1969. *Rememberwhen*

before Beeching, and these accelerated as car ownership mushroomed and a new motorway network was built across the nation (see Table 1.2). Car ownership was undoubtedly the largest single cause for the post-war decline of both the rural passenger railway and of secondary main lines. The unremitting increase of car ownership almost to saturation point, and more recently the impact of fuel prices, remains a major factor in determining market share for railways today.

Two other strands ran through the post-Beeching history of Britain's rural lines. The first was attempts to get operating costs down – and the second was the pressure from Whitehall for buses to replace trains.

The drive to reduce operating costs led to a number of national initiatives. One focused on reducing station staffing through the introduction of Paytrain services, where the guard became responsible for checking and issuing tickets. A pilot scheme was introduced on the East Suffolk line in 1967, and over time Paytrains went nationwide, leaving the majority of rural stations unstaffed.

Another initiative tackled the problem of long single-line railways with numerous costly-to-staff signal boxes, such as those listed in Table 10.2. The solution emerged from an unexpected direction when a severe storm in 1978 destroyed the telegraph poles on the Far North line, which carried the communication for signalling the trains. The Scottish Region discovered that a BR research team was developing a radio-controlled train dispatch system (Radio Electronic Token Block – RETB) to eliminate the need for tokens or intermediate signal boxes on long single lines, and they joined forces to make the Far North line the pilot scheme for this new RETB signalling.

## Chapter 10: RURAL LINES

### Case study – the Far North line

Chris Green recalls that 'in the financial crisis after the ASLEF strikes of 1982, the new Provincial sector challenged the costs of retaining and modernising the long Scottish rural routes. ScotRail reacted with "Operation Phoenix", which identified two major areas for cost-cutting – signalling and track standards – and was widely supported by railway staff, local authorities and communities. We discovered that Derby Research was developing a new radio train dispatch technology (RETB) and we worked with them to introduce a new signalling centre at Dingwall – and later at Banavie on the West Highland line. Automation of the busier level crossings allowed every intermediate signal box to be eliminated, but at the price of 67 jobs. Trains were given permission to move by radio, and the points at loops were spring-loaded with a 15mph speed restriction. In return, ScotRail invested in a new Highland hub at Inverness with a new signalling centre, maintenance depot and station upgrade.'

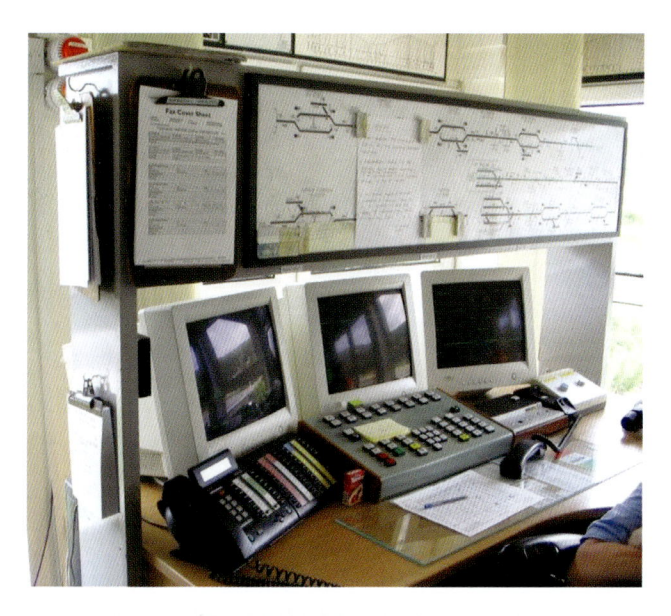

All the lines listed in Table 10.2 were converted to RETB, apart from Craven Arms-Llanelli (the Central Wales line) and Middlesbrough-Whitby. Signal boxes on these latter routes were also closed, through investment in the cheaper No Signalman Key Token (NSKT), which required drivers to leave their cab to operate a token machine at every station passing point.

The big disadvantage of RETB was the slow 15mph approach and exit at intermediate loops because of the unlocked points required. The Far North line (see panel) requires trains covering a similar distance as London to Crewe to slow to 15mph at 12 such loops, and this makes the journey slow and uncompetitive. The market position has been made worse by road improvements, which allow six express coaches to reach Thurso every weekday in just 3 hours – compared to the four trains that take 3hr 40min for the same journey. A similar position exists on the West Highland Line between Fort William and Glasgow, where buses take an hour less than the trains – albeit missing much of the best tourist scenery.

Despite these initiatives, costs continued to rise faster than income across the rural lines. By the time the Provincial sector came into being in 1982, a new conundrum had arisen over how to justify the large capital expenditure needed to clear the backlog of renewing their life-expired trains and track, or replacing labour-intensive semaphore signalling on the many lines not suitable for RETB, or the multitude of manned level crossings. There was a growing belief that this would lead to another wave of closures – yet over time this has not proved to be the case.

### Closures still threatened

The 1974 Railways Act established the Freight and InterCity businesses as commercial activities, with commuter and local passenger services becoming part of a social railway based on the concept of the PSO. The establishment of the PSO was accompanied by an equally important decision to replace grants for individual lines with a simple block grant.

Even so, joint studies of closures continued because the Board remained under severe pressure to keep

**ABOVE LEFT** The Banavie RETB signalling centre, showing the South workstation controlling Helensburgh to Upper Tyndrum and Crianlarich to Oban, with the adjoining North workstation controlling Upper Tyndrum to Fort William and on to Mallaig. *Scot-rail.co.uk*

**LEFT** The 15mph speed restrictions over spring-loaded points on RETB signalled routes mean slow journey times. *Dennis Lovett*

**Extract from Norman Fowler's letter to Sir Peter Parker, November 1979**

*'I thought that I should write to you immediately, following the stories in* The Guardian *yesterday and today about the Board's Corporate Review, to make it quite clear that it is my firm policy that there should be no substantial cuts in the passenger rail network. I thought it only right to also make it absolutely clear to you and your colleagues that this is the policy I shall pursue. I shall want to talk to you about the Corporate Review that you sent to me on October 25, but you will understand that the options of closing 40 passenger services is one that the Government have rejected.'*

**ABOVE** A busy summer's day at Sheringham with No 150257 arriving from Norwich in August 1998 before the stop blocks were removed for through rail access to the private North Norfolk Railway beyond. *Dennis Lovett*

reducing costs. In 1976 it published 'Opportunities for Change', which identified 10% of passenger train miles that could be withdrawn and replaced by guaranteed bus services. In February 1979 BR presented the unions with its latest thinking on bus substitution – replacing the largest loss-making services with BR bus services crewed by members of the rail unions rather than the Transport & General Workers' Union.

That October there were press reports – which were not denied – suggesting that around 700 miles of network were targeted. *The Guardian* then reported on 7 November: 'It is increasingly possible that British Rail will decide to close down some more local services. Plans to shut some 41 services running over 900 miles have been circulating between Whitehall and BR.' (For the list, see Factfile F7.)

This speculation was only quelled by the Transport Secretary, Norman Fowler, publicly issuing BR with clear policy guidance against such closures, as shown in the panel above.

### The mirage of bus substitution pursued

Despite Fowler's unequivocal statement, it would take a further decade of tension and wasted management effort before the devotees of bus substitution threw in the towel. There were attempts to study 'bustitution' involving the Provincial sector and the Department in 1982, 1985, 1987 and 1989. Darlington to Bishop Auckland was examined each time – John Welsby seeing it as a candidate – and is today one of a very few lines to have a worse service than then. Another route studied was Shrewsbury-Chester, now being partly redoubled. So was Norwich-Sheringham, by a unit in the Department that second-guessed BR's operation of individual routes until John Palmer shut it down as redundant; resignalled, this line is now thriving with an hourly service (see Table 11.1). The 1989 study included Lancaster-Barrow, though any replacement bus would have had to find a way of crossing two estuaries.

The first of these reviews stemmed from the Serpell inquiry and a follow-up request from the Transport Select Committee; John Welsby led for BR. Just over 40 lines were considered, roughly the rumoured hit-list. And in 1984 BR and the Association of County Councils published a 'Review of Rural Railways', which made 25 recommendations on their development, proposed more flexible funding, but also saw scope for 'bustitution'.

Nicholas Ridley's 1985 Transport Act empowered BR to subsidise rail replacement bus routes and gave them the same protection from closure as railways. His successor John Moore, in an otherwise supportive 1986 letter to the Chairman, asked BR to consider substitution before approving investment decisions, writing: 'The new powers which Parliament has provided for you to subsidise guaranteed substitute bus services connecting into the rail network give the opportunity to review those cases where attractive bus services could meet the needs of travellers as conveniently and often at markedly less cost… The Government will continue to support your efforts by approving worthwhile investment and by grant for socially necessary services: we are not asking for a programme of major route closures.' Bob Reid may not have minded; he knew that if the ensuing fuss rendered substitution politically impossible, ministers would have to ease BR's cash limit.

### The studies continue despite proof of limited savings

Provincial estimated that replacing with buses 24% of its mileage generating 5% of its business – effectively all its rural routes – would save around £33 million. A preliminary study of 33 lines under John Edmonds

**ABOVE** Class 153s were designed for deep rural lines such as the Central Wales line between Shrewsbury and Llanelli. Here No 153327 rolls through the stunning countryside forming the 13.12 Shrewsbury to Swansea service on 26 May 1997. It will call at 32 stations and take 4 hours to cover the 110 miles, giving plenty of time to compare the number of humans to sheep. *Martin Loader*

identified 1,200 route miles with combined operating losses of £17 million (£9 million in Scotland). Fuller investigation showed far lower savings, and nothing like the £100 million the Treasury had hoped for. Moreover, only 125 DMU vehicles would be saved. The alternative put to Whitehall was splitting Class 155 DMUs to create single-car 153s – a far more palatable option all round.

In 1988 Sidney Newey warned that Provincial might be 'over-trading'. 'The Provincial revolution will not be complete until we know whether guaranteed bus services on good roads, fully included in our timetable, and protected by standard TUCC procedures and ministerial review, are perceived to provide an alternative which customers will use, and which prove also to be politically acceptable.' Newey now says, 'The Ministry were really pushing bus substitution, and there was a chairman-level decision that we had to try it. Doncaster-Gainsborough was chosen; the Tory county council were very supportive of the railway and they objected. We had to have a session with the chairman's office where the decision was rescinded.' Proposals to replace trains with buses between Sleaford and Spalding were also shelved when the county council offered £1.5 million for level crossing and signalling improvements and two new stations (not delivered), together with £125,000 towards operating costs over four years.

Sidney Newey told David Wharton-Street that he 'wanted to really test the concept' of substitution. 'I had one or two routes looked at, telling David's people to pretend their car was a bus. "Start when you need to start, and drive like a bus. See how long the journey would take, what sort of services would be possible." It didn't seem to have been tested, but before we had got very far with it the heat went out of the issue.'

### The MMC effectively kills 'bustitution'

The 1989 the Monopolies & Mergers Commission (MMC) inquiry into Provincial was triggered by National Express's claim that the sector was unfairly subsidised. The coach operator said it could replace most rail services without subsidy, as Provincial's fares were the lowest of the three passenger sectors. (They also varied widely: on the East Suffolk line they were half those on the Barnstaple branch.) Third-party evidence to the MMC opposed 'bustitution', and the Commission concluded: 'Only a major programme involving … the withdrawal of all rail services from parts of the country could yield substantial savings, and this would require a considerable change in Government policy.' Instead it suggested – as would McNulty 28 years later – simplified low-cost services on the most heavily loss-making rural lines. The MMC also said the possibility of bus substitution should not be a factor when investment in rolling stock and infrastructure fell due; this was important to BR, as ordering the Class 158s had been held up for this reason.

Bus substitution ceased to be a serious issue for Provincial management from September 1988 when it was no longer included in the Secretary of State's annual letter to the Chairman. The running debate was effectively ended by the political fear of committing to unpopular rail closures, and Provincial's championing of cost reductions and growth through its new lightweight trains. Moreover, bus services too were struggling with patronage declining, and deregulation brought more casualties – especially in the countryside – with rural bus operators becoming over time increasingly dependent on local authority support.

With privatisation, much was made of the arrival of the 'bus bandits' as owners of rail franchises – yet joint ownership of bus and rail services seldom led to integration; Stagecoach stubbornly timed its first bus from Midhurst to arrive in Petersfield just after its peak train left for London. There were exceptions, Chris Gibb at Wales & West applauding Truronian's service from Redruth station to points along the former Helston branch.

The 'bustitution' debate was revived in 1999 by the junior transport minister Glenda Jackson. Up to a point she found an ally in Gordon Pettitt, who had said in a conference speech some years before: 'The demand for the majority of rural rail services will not rise and, in many cases, will fall further. People living in rural communities – particularly those without cars – must have good-quality public transport to meet work, educational and recreational needs. Public transport should also provide access to the main rail and bus networks. Local authorities should decide where a rail service should provide some/all of public transport needs of an area based on agreed criteria of service quality and value for money – and following a proper evaluation of options. I am clear that local communities can have better public transport for less money. Savings can then be made by investing in the 21st-century railway rather than preserving parts which still only meet 19th-century standards.'

## The Provincial sector and Serpell

As John Welsby started to develop his strategy for rolling stock replacement, passengers were badly affected by the 1982 industrial disputes that mainly concerned pay and flexible rostering. The resolution of these matters was important for the rural railways, partly because Government had lost faith in BR's ability to control costs and was limiting investment funding – and partly because flexible rostering was urgently needed to reduce traincrew costs and allow more imaginative operation.

The Serpell Report that followed begged the question of how closures could be back on the agenda so soon after Fowler's assurance on the subject. John Palmer, as we have seen, was adamant that the initiative came neither from ministers nor their civil servants, but from the hijacking of the committee by Alfred Goldstein, who intriguingly had strong ties to anti-rail elements in Number 10, among whom was Mrs Thatcher's advisor Alfred Sherman, a rail-into-roads campaigner who in 1984 nearly succeeded in having Marylebone converted into a coach station.

Serpell could have eliminated the rural railway altogether, with its most radical option a 'commercial' network of just 1,600 miles, comprising only the East Coast (as far as Newcastle), Great Western (only to Bristol and Cardiff) and West Coast main lines and a limited number of London commuter services. But the sheer political unacceptability of this extreme conclusion prevented serious discussion of the less drastic options, and it would be 28 years before another report on the economics of the entire railway (McNulty) appeared.

By the time Serpell was published in December 1982, the setting up of the Sector organisation and the favourable settlement of the industrial disputes had demonstrated that the railways had turned a corner and were able to manage their own affairs. The fact that the report's conclusions were pigeonholed so quickly demonstrated that ministers had set their minds against wholesale closure of railways.

However, one high-profile battle over a closure still lay ahead. In December 1983 BR advertised proposals to close the Settle & Carlisle line, arousing an unprecedented level of opposition. Full details of the campaign to save the line and of BR's unique commitment to maximise traffic during a five-year period of grace pending closure are set out in the Postscript. Closure was finally refused by Paul Channon in April 1989, and the line – while still attracting light intermediate traffic despite vigorous promotion – earned its reprieve many years later by again becoming for a time a trunk route for coal traffic. Since then, only the most fragmentary closures have gone through, involving a disproportionate amount of management time.

The Settle & Carlisle was not the only secondary main line to lose long-distance passenger and freight services and become a Regional Railways long rural route. Table 1.3 sets out the other routes that are no longer used by long-distance passenger operators – or indeed Regional Railways interurban services.

**Table 10.3: Secondary main lines as long-distance rural lines**

| Route | Route miles | Value as diversionary route | Trains/day (Regional) |
|---|---|---|---|
| Ayr-Stranraer | 59 | No | 6 |
| Kilmarnock-Carlisle | 82 | Yes | 8 |
| Carlisle-Newcastle | 62 | Limited | 14 |
| Carlisle-Settle Jc | 87 | Yes | 8 |
| Carlisle-Barrow-in-Furness | 85 | No | 24 |
| Settle Jn-Carnforth | 25 | No | 4 |
| Doncaster-Peterborough via Lincoln | 88 | Yes | 7 |
| Swansea-Fishguard/Pembroke Dock | 96 | No | 17 |
| **TOTAL** | **584** | - | |

Source: Gordon Pettitt

**140** Chapter 10: **RURAL LINES**

**LEFT** The closed locomotive inspection depot at Stranraer Harbour makes a forlorn site next to the closed car shipping facility. *Alex Green*

Taken together, the lines in Tables 10.3 and 10.5 total 1,241 route miles – or 13% of Britain's total network. None are used by interurban passenger services and less than half carry an appreciable amount of freight, yet they are mostly double track, except for Ayr-Stranraer.

## A closer look

The service beyond Ayr to Stranraer no longer connects with the boats for Larne, which now sail from Cairnryan, and Stranraer's station – on the pier – is not handy for the town. The advent of low-cost airlines in the 1990s killed the traditionally strong through traffic from Newcastle. The service has been refocused to cover the now very limited traffic to and from Stranraer. Ferry connections are now made by coach to and from Ayr, and its frequent Glasgow trains are coping much better with changes in sailing times.

In recent years the Glasgow-Kilmarnock-Carlisle and Settle & Carlisle lines were integrated to meet demand for heavy flows of imported coal. Most of these have now been diverted to other ports – or replaced by biomass although some opencast traffic from Ayrshire remains. As a result, only one or two freight trains a day were using the Settle route by December 2014. The combined route represents about 170 miles of lightly used railway with limited potential for passenger traffic. The lack of electrification will make it increasingly difficult to use as a West Coast diversion route.

The Doncaster-Peterborough 'Joint' line has recently been upgraded as an alternative route for East Coast freight. In December 2014 the number of freight trains using the line still only averaged 25 a week, though a weekend of diversions can bring the town of Spalding, with its many level crossings, to a standstill.

Some lines listed in Table 10.3 have limited real capability as diversionary routes for long-distance passenger services, as speeds are low and the routes remain unelectrified. The cost of maintenance and renewal for diversionary purposes requires higher standards than those required for a rural railway, and these costs should fall on the businesses that use them,

**BELOW** HSTs pass at Yeovil Pen Mill while on diversion from the Great Western main line due to flooding in the Bridgwater area on 21 January 2014. *Alex Green*

### Table 10.4: Support for Regional Railways Train Companies

| Company | Support per passenger km 2008/09 (p) | Support per passenger km 2013/14 (p) | % increase |
|---|---|---|---|
| Arriva Trains Wales | 11.13 | 13.07 | 16 |
| ScotRail | 8.60 | 17.47 | 103 |
| Northern | 4.00 | 7.79 | 75 |

Source: Gordon Pettitt

### Table 10.5: Rural line passenger usage

| | Distance (miles) | Passengers, 2013/14 | Average passengers per week |
|---|---|---|---|
| Truro-Falmouth | 12.25 | 750,690 | 14,436 |
| St Erth-St Ives | 4.25 | 588,308 | 11,255 |
| Plymouth-Gunnislake | 15.00 | 185,502 | 3,745 |
| Par-Newquay | 20.75 | 116,750 | 2,245 |
| Liskeard-Looe | 8.75 | 110,510 | 2,125 |

Source: ORR Joining & Alighting figures, 2013/14

which is not the case at present. All the routes listed lie within Scotland, Wales and the North of England – and Table 10.4 shows these to be the very networks that receive the largest amount of Government support.

## Rural branches

Some stations in rural areas lie on routes into the larger towns and cities and are categorised as 'urban'. Those remaining are mainly on branch lines connected to the long-distance routes, which fall into several groups with a total mileage of 265 miles:

- Devon and Cornwall branches: 61 miles
- South Wales branches: 73 miles
- Norwich branches (arguably urban): 48 miles
- Lancaster branches: 48 miles
- Hull-Scarborough: 54 miles
- Whitby branch: 35 miles

The Devon and Cornwall branches are a good example of the problems and the opportunities for rural branch lines today. Table 10.5 lists the five branches off the main line between Plymouth and Penzance in the order of the number of passengers using them.

The St Ives branch benefits from a park-and-ride station opened at Lelant Saltings in 1978. In the first year 130,000 people used the station, with 46% saying they would not otherwise have visited St Ives. The summer peak loading, however, remains a challenge, and currently the Class 150 that operates the half-hourly service is strengthened with another unit freed up by a seasonal pause in heavy maintenance. Community Rail designation brought innovations including clockface timetables, resulting in nearly 600,000 people using the line in 2013. In the medium term the branch could benefit from conversion to light rail, with a passing loop midway.

Unfortunately the much quieter Looe and

**ABOVE** No 150263, in First Great Western livery, works the highly successful St Ives branch. *Antony Christie*

### Case study – the Falmouth branch

The Falmouth branch now has a £7 million EU-funded loop at Penryn, which has allowed innovative deployment of rolling stock to double the service to half-hourly. University traffic contributed to a surge in usage to 710,000 passengers in 2012, compared to just 197,000 in 1998, and this has visibly eased traffic congestion on the A39. The line has benefited from county council funding and is supported by a Devon & Cornwall Rail Partnership.

Gunnislake lines have the same level of costs as Falmouth and St Ives – but with less than a quarter of the passengers. The Looe line is likely to remain highly seasonal, but Devon County Council is keen to supplement the Gunnislake branch by reinstating the line forking off it to Tavistock to cater for new housing development. The site of Tavistock station has been built on, but the developers are ready to contribute to bring the line up to a new terminus, with an hourly service to Plymouth.

## Chapter 10: RURAL LINES

**ABOVE** No 153372 pauses at Coombe with a Looe to Liskeard service. Coombe station is the fifth least used on the entire rail network – averaging just 42 passengers a year. *Antony Christie.*

The Newquay branch is the longest of these routes, but with severe speed restrictions and a basic signalling system, the service is very unattractive. Passenger numbers include those using the long-distance summer trains, which require withdrawal of the local services. Weekday traffic levels are so low that the service is based around when a DMU is available rather than the needs of customers.

### Urban one end, rural the other
Moving north, the Hull-Scarborough line is a busy route south of Bridlington with a half-hourly service, supplemented by some peak-time short commuter workings from Beverley. North of Bridlington the service is every 90 minutes to Scarborough. The heady summer Saturdays with through trains from industrial Yorkshire to Butlins at Filey did not survive the closure of the camp and its station in 1977. But there is a local and through demand that has been tapped by the extension of some Bridlington-Hull trains via Doncaster to Sheffield – and more recently by an open access train from Hull to King's Cross starting back from Beverley. Growth on the line has been steady but relatively modest; ever since the closure in 1965 of the direct lines between York and Hull via Beverley and from Bridlington and Driffield to the East Coast Main Line at Selby, travel from points along it has involved two sides of a triangle, leaving it not very competitive with road travel.

**RIGHT** A Class 153 calls at New Holland station en route to Barton-on-Humber in 2009. *David Wright*

### Deserted in winter, overcrowded in summer
An extreme example of a rural branch with minimal winter traffic and chronic overcrowding in the tourist season is the Esk Valley line from Middlesbrough to Whitby; the remnant of a series of closures, its single track serves villages with poor road access. Under Provincial and Regional Railways the line received the heaviest subsidy in the North East, costing £10 for every £1 taken, and in 1991 the service was halved to a single DMU making four round trips daily. Then North Yorkshire County Council declared it dangerous for children to stand for the last few miles into Whitby, and laid on school buses to the very villages said to have roads inadequate for them.

A Community Rail Partnership is encouraging use of the branch, and a second platform at Whitby has been reinstated for use by the North Yorkshire Moors Railway. Since a station serving James Cook Hospital opened in 2014, the short Middlesbrough-Nunthorpe section has enjoyed 17 trains daily, but North Yorkshire declines to support more services to Whitby. However, the new Northern franchisee will be required to run a morning commuter service from Whitby.

The line's fortunes are monitored by *Modern Railways* columnist Alan Williams, who has retired to the area. Traffic off-season can be very thin, not helped by there being no early-morning train into Middlesbrough. But overcrowding on summer weekends is the norm, with Williams reporting 307 passengers crammed onto one 150-seater Class 156, with many unable to purchase a ticket and scores more left behind en route.

### A surprising survival
An unexpected survival is the branch to Barton-on-Humber. Built to connect Grimsby with the ferry to Hull, it lost its purpose with the opening of the Humber Bridge, and in 1986 BR proposed closure. A senior

**RIGHT** Beauly station now attracts 55,000 passengers a year with minimal but sensible investment. *Dennis Lovett*

figure from the Department arrived at Barton by special train and, says David Wharton-Street, 'visited the famous early Anglo-Saxon church, which I gather was one of his personal hobbies. In due course I was informed that the closure was not to be progressed.'

Today a single Class 153 provides a 2-hourly weekday and summer Sunday service; an outpost of Northern Rail, it is due for transfer to East Midlands. All but 3¼ miles is double track, and the line is due for resignalling in 2016 with its level crossings automated – a surprising investment, given that use of the branch's six stations has fallen below 300 passengers a day.

## Provincial stability

Overall, BR's sector management brought about positive changes for rural lines. To everyone's surprise, the rolling stock replacement programmes progressed by John Welsby and John Edmonds included sufficient vehicles to eliminate all the 1950s-built heritage DMUs from these routes. The rural lines benefited because the sector had built an economic case around the overall savings made by renewing the entire Regional fleet – rather than attempting this for the rural railways fleet in isolation. Rural passengers won new trains on the back of the wider network benefits.

Thereafter, support grew for rural railways both among local authorities and the public at large. Instead of a continuous reduction in the size of the network, there were to be no line closures. Just five small stations were closed in the Provincial and Regional period, but 25 were opened or reopened on rural lines, including the S&C stations closed in 1970 (see Factfile G for details). The PORTIS portable ticketing system enabled most of these to be unstaffed; Muir of Ord (74,000 passengers yearly) and Melton (63,000) have done best. The latter, on the East Suffolk line, was reopened in 1984 at a cost of just £4,000.

Another successful rural reopening was frustratingly difficult to achieve. At Beauly, just north of Inverness, ScotRail proposed a platform just 15 metres long, passengers using one centre door of a 'Sprinter'. This satisfied one arm of the Health & Safety Executive, then another demanded a far more lavish scheme. It took several meetings involving ScotRail, Railtrack, the SRA, the HSE and ministers at Holyrood and Westminster before heads were banged together. The 15-metre-long station reopened safely in 2002, and now sees 55,000 passengers a year from a tiny population base – thanks to increasing road congestion in Inverness.

## Regional Railways

Yet despite cost savings ranging from the introduction of Paytrains to radio signalling and new train fleets, the small number of passengers on rural lines meant that the gap between revenue and costs continued to increase.

The problem was becoming critical again when Gordon Pettitt first became Director of the Provincial sector, then Managing Director of the new Regional Railways. The objectives set for BR by Cecil Parkinson in December 1989 (see Chapter 3) were good news for the sector as a whole. But with the rural lines representing only 9% of the income and remaining largely static markets despite their new train fleets, the only logical conclusion with steep urban and interurban growth was to save costs on the rural lines and transfer as many trains as could be freed up to satisfy demand in these areas.

However, this transfer of resources to lines where demand would lead to 1950s DMUs being pressed into service for a further decade resulted in many rural routes being reduced to just one train set providing the entire daily service – sometimes with opening hours for the line also cut back to a single shift. The longer rural secondary main lines faced similar cutbacks – with the Far North line to Wick limited to three trains a day each way despite no longer having signaller costs thanks to the earlier investment in RETB equipment.

Clearly this type of situation could not continue in the long term. Reducing the service on some lines to a level that failed to meet most local needs had made the rural conundrum even more apparent. In effect, the taxpayer was now being asked to pay for lines to remain in service for less social benefit – or even none at all.

Concern grew that a prolonged slashing of costs across the rural lines could do more harm than good, as some routes offered future potential as urban areas

**ABOVE** No 158734 stands at Wick station in August 2001. *Dennis Lovett*

expanded into the countryside and congestion grew. A further concern lay in the hidden infrastructure costs of maintaining rural lines over a long-term horizon. Major investment became inevitable at random moments – sometimes due to the age of the assets and sometimes due to legislation or political direction. For example, following the Ladbroke Grove accident major signalling investment was needed to install TPWS safety equipment across the UK network – including all the rural lines.

Gordon Pettitt was determined to provide detailed costs and income for all parts of Regional Railways' business before the Government set the next set of financial objectives in 1992. His intention was to highlight prior to then all the options available to Government. There were choices to be made if funds were limited – should growth be encouraged on urban routes, or should little-used rural lines be kept open with little benefit to the common good?

He set up a review led by Paul King, Planning & Marketing Director, which is described in detail in Chapter 4. Dr King found that services on most rural lines did not earn sufficient income to cover the daily costs of running the trains – train crew, fuel, cleaning and fleet maintenance – let alone any contribution to the costs of leasing the trains and paying for the infrastructure they used.

The review took place during a major economic recession, and resulted in what Theo Steel recalls as 'quite a lot of surgery' to rural services. The winter peak service to Looe was withdrawn; Gainsborough-Cleethorpes services went Saturdays-only to free up a 'Sprinter' for weekday use on urban services; Sheffield-Pontefract-York became off-peak only, and Leeds-Morecambe was reduced from two units to one.

Paul King gave a presentation to the DTp and the Treasury setting out the findings, but by this time the Government's priority had moved on to rail privatisation and ministers did not set the usual three-year Objectives that would have forced them to identify the level of subsidy they wished to spend on rural rail services – as distinct from the growing PTE urban services or the highly successful interurban network.

## Privatisation

It was widely expected that privatisation would result in closures and reductions in service, particularly on the heavily subsidised rural lines. But ministers' determination to complete privatisation within a single Parliament led to a structure that gave greater long-term security than had existed under nationalisation, especially through the stipulations of the Passenger Service Requirement (PSR). This was probably not the original intention, but an outcome that helped to soften the strong opposition that existed to privatisation at the time. However, the panel shows why potential

### Extract from the Department of Transport's 'The Franchising of Passenger Rail Services', 1992

'Rural services have a load factor of 14 passengers per vehicle, but with less peakiness than urban routes because of the low population base served. The journey speeds are often slow with frequent stops, but average mileage per vehicle is higher than urban at 120,000 miles per vehicle. However, the small size of the market means that the losses incurred are larger than urban.'

**ABOVE** Fishguard & Goodwick station reopened on 14 May 2012 and has been adopted under Arriva's 'adopt-a-station' scheme by the local community group POINT. The station cost £325,000 to build and now has seven trains a day each way. The operation has been supported and subsidised by the Welsh Assembly. *Alex Green*

**RIGHT** ScotRail started innovative marketing schemes on its rural lines. Here the passengers on the 10.10 Inverness-Kyle of Lochalsh service, hauled by No 37414 on 2 September 1988, had the choice of a Mark I DMU vehicle converted into an Observation Car to view the magnificent scenery. Transport Scotland stipulated that the latest franchise in 2015 must include innovative ideas to boost rural line tourism. *Gavin Morrison*

franchisees were worried at the fragile nature of the rural railways at privatisation.

So despite the low traffic base, there has as a result of the PSR been unprecedented stability for rural lines. Subsequent devolution of responsibility to Scotland and Wales has led to unexpected increases in service levels on some long rural lines such as that to Oban. Wales, with fewer devolved powers to date, has still managed to expand services to Fishguard and open a new station serving the town. Even the Central Wales line got an extra daily train each way from December 2014.

Devolution of control over rail services does seem to be the right answer for rural routes. Higher funding for the Kyle of Lochalsh and West Highland tourist routes has contributed to 68% and 30% growth respectively, and Transport Scotland sponsored an expanded train service into Oban from 2014. Since the Skye Bridge opened in 1995, the Kyle has acted as a focus for onward bus connections, while summer steam specials operate between Fort William and Mallaig. These seasonal specials, operated by West Coast Railways, carry more passengers than the local all-year service achieves annually.

The full story of Community Rail is told in Chapter 11, but the rural railway since privatisation has benefited from the engagement of community groups, Community Rail Officers appointed by local councils – and more recently from Community Rail Partnerships. The Community Rail movement has fostered local involvement, often very successfully, which centres primarily on stations and their upkeep and development.

Some rural train operators have responded to societal change through the expansion of Sunday services. These were traditionally few in number, with the exception of lines serving summer holiday resorts, but use of the railways on Sundays where a service is provided has risen sharply in recent years. Some routes still lack them either because of management inertia, perceived lack of demand, difficulties over crewing – or the demands of Network Rail engineers.

## Summary

With increasing Government support, the rural railway network's size has been maintained since 1982. Unfortunately traffic growth has been modest compared with the urban and interurban businesses. Apart from isolated cases at peak periods, loadings per vehicle remain low.

The biggest problem facing train operators and community organisations is therefore making the case for services that require additional rolling stock and staff. In the case of urban and interurban services, revenue generation will normally cover these basic running costs – but this is rarely the case for rural services.

This means that to carry additional passengers, which trains of existing length cannot accommodate, involves increasing the subsidy. The question that inevitably follows is: can these extra costs be offset by local social and economic benefits, such as reducing the effect of road congestion? Paul King ascertained in 1992 that each such journey was costing the taxpayer between £17 and £28 – and the cost today must be proportionately higher. So the rural conundrum has not gone away, though rural railways now only account for about 7% of the total regional business.

**LEFT** The 'Jacobite' steam-hauled service from Fort William to Mallaig crosses Glenfinnan Viaduct on 4 September 2014. *Alex Green*

# Chapter 11
# ENGAGING WITH COMMUNITIES AND STAKEHOLDERS

*'Community rail development has provided politicians with a practical and beneficial alternative to the constant pressure from civil servants to shrink the network further. Whilst it has not made local lines profitable, it has helped stabilise costs and increase passenger numbers, in some cases doubling them.'*
**CHRIS AUSTIN**

**ABOVE** While many stakeholders are councils and PTEs, many local stations such as North Berwick rely on devoted local residents to look after the gardens and general upkeep. *Alex Green*

## A record of growing engagement

The growing involvement of local councils, community and user groups, pro-rail campaigners and other stakeholders has been one of the strongest factors in the revival of Britain's regional railways. This mutually beneficial strengthening of the railway's engagement with communities and customers reflects fundamental changes in the industry as it has progressed from a near monolith through decentralisation to a franchised structure with such engagement obligatory. But it also reflects changes in society.

From nationalisation, the travelling public was represented by appointed Transport Users' Consultative Committees (TUCCs), whose more customer-facing successor is Passenger Focus. Local user groups flourished from the 1970s, then decentralisation within BR and privatisation were matched by the rise of a line-by-line Community Rail movement, backed by councils, train operators and ultimately the Department, which has delivered strong benefits at grassroots level.

BR management had always known that the right word from a sensible MP could help the railway's cause, and the Board conducted a sophisticated lobbying operation at Westminster. This reached its height as Sir Peter Parker and his PR man Will Camp rallied MPs and the media against closures to the point where the Department felt it was being outflanked. Tory backbenchers with threatened branch lines tended to work alone, but the railway gained useful support from the North Western group of Labour MPs, who extracted a line to Manchester Airport from BR as their price for not opposing the expansion of Stansted. It had generally helpful friends in, among others, Labour's John Prescott and Peter Snape, a former railwayman, and the Conservatives Patrick McNair-Wilson, who steered through BR's private legislation, and Robert Adley, and in time gained a nucleus of peers such as Lords Berkeley and Bradshaw with experience of the industry.

There had always been engagement between railway managers and individual MPs, even if the latter's expectations were sometimes unrealistic. Gordon Pettitt met them regularly on issues such as timetabling and electrification when Divisional Manager at Liverpool Street; as General Manager of the Southern Region, covering 62 constituencies, 'I always read all their letters and personally signed all the replies.' Much of the contact with and pressure from MPs concerned closures, standards of service and fares. As late as 1987 Alan Beith, Liberal MP for Berwick, intervened with Whitehall in concert with the Duke of Northumberland to frustrate an attempt by David Wharton-Street to close Chathill station. Today two DMUs daily trundle beyond Morpeth over electrified track to Chathill (which in a good year originates 5,000 passengers), then continue to the site of Belford station (which the local council wants to reopen) to reverse; their presence and low speed limit capacity on the ECML.

As BR – and especially Regional Railways – showed signs of recovery, MPs stepped up the pressure for improvements. Chris Gibb recalls, 'We had a lot of criticism over the Weymouth Quay line from Paddy Ashdown. We put on something very close to a charter train once a week. We set some success criteria, and brought in a catering company at their own risk. Running it wasn't easy; the police had to come and physically move cars from the section that ran through the streets. Some people were prepared to pay a premium, but we couldn't attract enough regular passengers. We did it for two summers, it didn't meet the criteria and we pulled it.'

Liaison with the wider business community has also been important to the railway, both to position itself and state its case as a key sector in the economy and to demonstrate to its peers how rail has been changing to meet Britain's needs. Nationally and through its regions, BR had strong links with the CBI, and these were inherited by the inter-city TOCs. However, the bulk of the owning groups now belong to, and work through, the Institute of Directors.

There have always been strong links between the railway and community business groups such as Chambers of Commerce; in Sheffield in the mid-1970s Gordon Pettitt was the conduit. BR managers recognised even during the darkest days that connecting with local business leaders and opinion formers could undo negative impressions and bring in business. From his time as Area Manager in Fife, Jim Summers recalls: 'I can't count how many Rotaries, Business Clubs and so on I addressed trying to defend the faith and keep the public interested in us.'

## The role of pro-rail lobbying groups

The formation in 1973 of Transport 2000 – now the Campaign for Better Transport – gave rail a valuable endorser, with its long-standing Chief Executive Stephen Joseph credible and persuasive. Set up on the initiative of the NUR General Secretary Sid Weighell and initially part-funded by BR, it addressed 'the threat of widespread rail closures [and] concern over environmental damage done by heavy lorries.' Such an organisation could speak with less self-interest than the

# Chapter 11: ENGAGING WITH COMMUNITIES AND STAKEHOLDERS

unions themselves, who have always had job protection principally in mind – even before the RMT began presenting any move for more economic staffing as an attempt to endanger the passengers.

Another independent voice for the railways is RailFuture, founded in 1961 as the Railway Invigoration Society and for a time called the Railway Development Society. It made its reputation saving the North London Line in the late 1960s, and has been a tireless advocate of 'missing link' projects like East-West Rail, Lewes-Uckfield and Colne-Skipton, working on this last with the local campaigning group SELRAP (Skipton East Lancs Rail Action Partnership). Another is the National Council on Inland Transport, formed to counter Beeching by the Labour peer Lord Stonham; in 50 years of campaigning, much of it by the indefatigable Roy Calvert, it failed to save the Great Central main line, but did twice prevent closure of the Romford-Upminster branch.

## Contacts with councils

BR's contacts with local authorities were traditionally overshadowed by the latter's lack of powers to support their rail services. However, councils' strategies could still be highly relevant to the railway; Beeching himself, before compiling his report, contacted them about any planning work they might have done on population growth to justify future rail service provision. Most counties outside South East England did not reply – and the communities they represented paid the price.

Not that every council appreciated its railways; some lobbied hard for lines to be reprieved from closure, but to others, coveting railway land for redevelopment or road schemes, closures were an opportunity. Blackpool notoriously gave up its Central station and the line to it for car parking and the M55, and many station sites were redeveloped as a consequence of (sometimes council-encouraged) closure. Bath Green Park, Bradford Exchange, Cheltenham St James's, Glasgow St Enoch, Gloucester Eastgate, Morecambe Promenade, Nottingham Victoria, Southport Lord Street and others found new uses as shopping centres or bus interchanges; Manchester Central was reborn as G-Mex.

**RIGHT** Manchester Central in 2007, beautifully restored as the GMex exhibition hall. *Southport News*

**BELOW** No 142070 waits at Okehampton to return to Exeter on 8 June 2008. *Antony Christie*

**ABOVE LEFT** The Huntington-Cambridge busway in action at Swavesey. *David Beardmore*

**ABOVE RIGHT** Rt Hon Jack Straw MP, the Mayor of Blackburn and officials from DfT, local county and town councils celebrate the rebuilding of the disused Platform 4 at an expanding Blackburn station. The £1.7 million scheme included DfT funding for 'Access for All' and a £200,000 contribution from Blackburn with Darwen Council. Mr Straw unveiled the community artwork by pupils at Daisyfield Primary School. *Network Rail*

Barbara Castle's creation of the PTEs gave some cities a stake in their rail services for the first time. But away from the conurbations, councils – even those with a responsibility for transport – still had no such powers; Fife Regional Council discovered this in the 1970s when it attempted to purchase DMUs. In 1973 the Department set up a working party to review the scope for devolving loss-making passenger services in England to local authorities. However, it was admitted internally that the aim was to 'produce an incentive for them to close services the Department has been unable to get rid of', with Government grant covering only three-quarters of the cost.

While some non-PTE councils did find ways of making small contributions – such as Norfolk funding the resleepering of the line through Berney Arms – they only received statutory powers to support local railways with the Transport Act of 1985. Even then they had no obligation to do so. Some shire county and district councils jumped at the opportunity presented by the Act; others did not, and the Provincial sector/Regional Railways found itself having to create stakeholders to represent and promote railways with few customers and heavy losses.

Cumbria, Durham, Lincolnshire and Norfolk negotiated joint plans with BR. Durham's aspiration to revive passenger services to Consett foundered on the indifference of a PTE, but it did in the late 1980s support a revived service between Bishop Auckland and Stanhope. Devon financed new stations or gave political backing to Provincial's plans for them. In 1997 the county secured Sunday reopening of the line to Okehampton; the council had guides on board, and in 13 summer weeks the six trains each day carried 10,661 passengers. Cornwall has been vocal, but no new station has opened in the Duchy since Lelant Saltings in 1978; the council did facilitate the new loop at Penryn, but spurned an opportunity in the 1990s to divert the Par-Newquay branch to start more usefully from St Austell. Avon and Gloucestershire helped deliver stations for Worle and Yate, and Avon after the opening of Filton Abbey Wood used offenders on probation to maintain the station buildings. Somerset pressed for a 'Somerset Spine' local service between Taunton and Westbury, which, says Theo Steel, 'would have lost money hand over fist'. Wiltshire paid to reopen the Chippenham-Melksham-Trowbridge line for school travel; it wanted several station reopenings, and under the SRA nearly got Corsham. Hampshire was supportive, though it has blocked reopening of the Fawley branch to ease acute road congestion. Warwickshire and Staffordshire worked with West Midlands PTE on line reopenings. North Yorkshire financed new stations and pressed for reopening to Ripon, but disadvantaged the line to Whitby by switching its school traffic to buses.

In some authorities the politicians took the lead; others were officer-led with councillors acquiescing. The development of the Cambridge and Luton busways on former railway alignments has been proof that councils – and their officers – have agendas of their own. In recent times some councils have appointed railway or transport development officers, with varying budgets and levels of political commitment behind them, to promote rail use and badger the TOCs into improving services. Richard Watts at Lancashire, and John Kitchen and his successor Sam Wheelan for Cumbria, have been highly rated, and Devon,

Hertfordshire, Lincolnshire, Sussex and – at district level – Darlington all currently have good stories to tell.

County councils, having more powers and covering a larger area than their district counterparts, have from the 1980s played a decisive part in reviving stations and entire lines. The Valleys saw several examples, while the 'Robin Hood Line' is a tribute to the persistence of Nottinghamshire (and Derbyshire, which supported its extension). The Settle & Carlisle would today be a path for hikers had it not been for the determination of Cumbria and North Yorkshire to prevent its closure. However, with lines within one county being the exception – save for Cornwall and Norfolk – results can be hard to achieve. A scheme that makes sense to one council may even be seen as a threat by another. It has long been accepted that Gloucester station is in the wrong place for the Birmingham-Bristol trains that pass through the city; a park-and-ride on Gloucester's northern fringe seemed the logical solution until councillors in Cheltenham decided that it might supplant their own station.

Nevertheless there are wins to be achieved. After a shaky start, the service through Melksham backed by Wiltshire County Council has proved a success. For councils and communities campaigning for and then financially supporting such services, the critical point is the one at which it is incorporated within the PSR for the franchise operator, thus achieving permanence.

## The 'Ivanhoe' setback

A major local authority initiative that largely came to grief, however, was the 'Ivanhoe Line' project, to reinstate local services between Leicester and Burton-on-Trent and into Leicester from the north. The Burton line – closed in 1964 – looked a useful regional link, and Leicestershire and Derbyshire worked up plans for an hourly Leicester-Coalville-Ashby-Burton-Derby service requiring four 'Sprinters', with the first trains running in 1992. But there were problems. The curve giving direct access from Leicester had been lifted; reinstatement would cost £9 million, and was made harder by resignalling at Leicester having been de-scoped. The 12 stops planned ruled out competitive journey times, and local politics made it hard to omit any. And just enough freight remained to dictate a more lavish infrastructure than needed by a passenger-only railway.

Leicestershire trimmed the scheme to Leicester-Coalville-Ashby with just four stations, still requiring £880,000 in subsidy. Privatisation pushed it back, and when the county revisited the project in 2009 it baulked on grounds of cost and difficulty. All that has come of the 'Ivanhoe Line' is three stations north of Leicester – Syston, Sileby and Barrow-on-Soar – with 277,000 passengers a year between them (and nearly empty trains off-peak), and a little-used station at Willington, between Burton and Derby, all opened in 1994.

## Smartening the stations

Provincial began working with councils and PTEs not just to open new stations but smarten up old ones, in Dick Fearn's words 'making them part of the philosophy that the sector was looking up'. It had 347 listed buildings, many unsuited for railway use and needing costly repairs, and 135 stations in conservation areas; one station in five was subject to at least one preservation order. The alternative was ripping down expensive-to-maintain buildings and replacing them with something worse, as had happened in the 1960s and '70s with the CLASP prefabricated steel stations.

**BELOW LEFT** Just a small part of the stunning annual floral displays at Bridlington courtesy of the station buffet proprietor supported by Northern Rail and ISS, the station facility management company. *Dennis Lovett*

**BELOW RIGHT** Thirty years on and the interest in floral displays lives on at many ScotRail stations. This is Ayr forecourt, a riot of blooms. *Alex Green*

**RIGHT** Bishop Auckland, where the ticket office is privately run, is well used and popular on Saturday 24 January 2015 as No 142071 forms the 11.25 service to Darlington and Saltburn. *Alex Green*

But with next to no money, BR looked to the councils for help. (For all the listed stations see Factfile G7.)

Chris Green, who did have a little to spend, says, 'Stations were at the heart of the ScotRail revolution because they were so terrible. The decision to make ScotRail an open station railway with ticket checking done on the trains provided the opportunity to completely renew the station furniture and brought in a house style of red seats (as later on Network SouthEast), modern cafés and electronic information displays. The crowning success was to use flowers extensively to brighten up the stations. This triggered a new alliance with towns and villages across the network; by 1985 61 stations were entering the Best Kept Garden competition.'

## Formalising the ties

Provincial's contacts with local authorities were on an ad-hoc basis, except where the PTEs were concerned. But Gordon Pettitt saw the need for a coordinated approach aimed at improving quality by monitoring public perception. That perception was threefold: what people experienced; what they imagined other passengers were experiencing; and what those who didn't use the railway thought it was like. Regional Railways, centrally and locally, built up contacts with MPs and community groups, fielding 'real people' as well as directors. And in 1992 it opened conversations with every local authority with a population of more than 250,000 on the scope for working together.

Formalising relations with the Association of Metropolitan Authorities, which represented the metropolitan county and district councils and hence the PTAs, led under Jim Cornell to Regional Railways and the AMA publishing 'Signals for Change', which underlined the case for partnership to deliver rail investment to 'beat traffic congestion and maintain healthy local and regional economies'. It emphasised the cooperation between the PTEs and surrounding districts necessary to deliver mutually beneficial improvements, and the shire counties' role in promoting rural and commuter services, pointing out that the countryside too was under threat from traffic.

Devon was applauded for promoting rail into Plymouth and Exeter, Avon for supporting the Severn Beach line, Cumbria for its help over Ribblehead Viaduct, Durham for backing the Bishop Auckland branch, Harrogate borough for facilitating the new Hornbeam Park station, Humberside for backing Barton-on-Humber and Hull-Bridlington services, and Hereford & Worcester for supporting Redditch services. Mid and South Glamorgan were praised for sponsoring Cardiff Valleys improvements, Dyfed and Powys for their support for the Central Wales line, and Gwynedd for backing the Conwy Valley line.

## Role of the regions

There has been continued tinkering by Governments of all parties with the structure of English local government, and Regional Development Agencies were set up by the 1997 Labour Government as a step towards elected regional assemblies. Seven English RDAs had the potential to benefit regional railways through their transport strategies. These turned out to be mainly directed at improving the road network, but Yorkshire Forward did get involved in rail through the stakeholder engagement programme developed by Northern Rail's Heidi Mottram. With the RDA and West Yorkshire PTE, in 2006 Northern put together a unique package to secure the 'Yorkshire Six' Class 158s spare from First Great Western for the Leeds-Sheffield-Nottingham service originally planned by Midland MainLine.

With the Coalition's abolition of the RDAs, the regional advocacy and development role moved to leaner Local Enterprise Partnerships, 38 of which cover areas ranging in size from London to Teesside. The first full wave of 'city deals' with the LEPs, in 2014, gave commitments to assist with Selby-Hull electrification; Cornish resignalling; reopening to Henbury, Portishead and Wisbech; short tramway extensions; and several new stations the funding for which had stalled in the recession.

Some English councils are now clubbing together to emulate the former PTAs in forming Integrated Transport Authorities. There is a political will, notably in Lancashire and the Bristol area (which has also had a vocal rail passenger group), to push through some railway schemes that previously lacked a sponsor with clout. Then there is

**LEFT** On 4 October 2009 the railhead treatment train, hauled by No 66116 and tailed by No 66153, manoeuvres through the clever new loop arrangement at Penryn, where the platform was split into two separate sections, eliminating the need for expensive access ramps or lifts to connect a second platform, thus allowing a doubling of the service between Truro and Falmouth at very low cost. Passenger numbers have grown by 91% in five years.
*Nigel Tregoning*

Rail North, formed by councils across the North of England to drive the improvement of rail links as part of wider regeneration and, in particular, to secure the devolution of franchising from Whitehall. Its ambitions and strategy, and those of its counterpart West Midlands Rail, are dealt with in Chapter 13.

### Councils in Wales and Scotland

Councils and other bodies in Wales have done much to improve rail services. The Wales Tourist Board in 1991 found £500,000 to help fund a resumption of winter Sunday services on the Cambrian line. West Glamorgan purchased two 'Pacers' for the 'SwanLine' service. Mid Glamorgan's transport committee chairman – 'Soapbox' Williams – was a BR guard, and Sidney Newey built a partnership with the county through him. One of the council's last acts was to sign up to the resignalling of the bulk of the railway between Pontypridd and Cardiff. Replacing the counties in 1996 with 28 unitary authorities, nine of them covering the Cardiff area, in Theo Steel's view made Wales 'very difficult territory' for working at this level to deliver a better railway. Lack of devolution of powers from Westminster is now cited by the Welsh Government as the reason for five planned station reopenings being deferred for at least five years; under the counties they would simply have happened.

The situation in Scotland has been different, partly because of the dominance of Strathclyde and also because for two decades from 1975, the principal unit of local government was the region. BR's contact with the Scottish Office in Edinburgh was particularly close, having in the view of David Cobbett, Scottish Region General Manager in the late 1970s, a 'greater impact on Government spending' than south of the border, notably delivering a redoubling of parts of the Highland line between Blair Atholl and Dalwhinnie ahead of expected growth in North Sea business. But relations with the regional councils produced less, though Highland fostered the regeneration of the Far North line. The creation of smaller unitary councils in 1996 produced more positive results than in Wales.

### Europe chips in

Europe has also played its part in regional rail investment, mainly in the areas that have at various times held special development status: principally Scotland, Wales, Cornwall and depressed parts of northern England. BR did not generally accept funding from Brussels because the Treasury would simply deduct it from the PSO; it was better to let local authorities apply for it, and work with them. Wales did particularly well; of £41 million invested in its rail infrastructure up to 1991, £23 million came from local authorities and from Europe. Part-funding for the Taff resignalling of 1996-98 came from the European Regional Development Fund. EC funding also went toward the Ayr/Largs and Hooton-Chester/Ellesmere Port electrifications. Several PTEs could play the European card, Alex Ritchie recalling, 'Most of us were in supported areas from Europe, therefore we were able to tap the European market for grants; a lot of the Glasgow lines were electrified or developed by this means.'

Railtrack, once privatised, had no problem in accepting EU money; nor (so far) has Network Rail. Two Cornish schemes have been assisted: the Probus-Burngullow redoubling and the Penryn loop on the

Falmouth branch (also backed by the county council); the recent rebuilding of Pont Briwet north of Harlech was also backed by the ERDF.

## The TUCCs

Despite theoretically owning the nationalised railway, the travelling public did not have a stake in it. But they did have statutory representation from the TUCCs, which crucially had to recommend whether or not closures should proceed. The Central (National) and nine Regional Users' Committees (reduced to seven in 1986) were formed under the 1947 Transport Act. In the Provincial sector's early years the CTCC's Chairman was the formidable Dame Alison Munro, who had been PA to Sir Robert Watson Watt, the inventor of radar, and later Headmistress of St Paul's Girls School. 'She could pick out the essential issues, and led BR a merry dance when she chose, but was extremely supportive when she felt there was a case,' Theo Steel recalls. She was succeeded in 1986 by Maj-Gen Lennox Napier, and he in turn by David Bertram, a retired businessman who had chaired the Eastern TUCC. All stamped their authority on the CTCC while leaving the regional groups as a largely self-governing federation.

The Munro era and the Settle & Carlisle closure case marked the final days of the TUCCs' detailed testing of applications for closures. Otherwise, appeals over complaints from passengers formed their major work. Their quarterly meetings also featured presentations from BR directors. Gordon Pettitt notes, 'I spent a lot of time during my career attending TUCCs despite having greater priorities most of the time. The problem was that some members never travelled by train and were prone to take too much time relating irrelevant anecdotes, and others used the opportunity to bolster their personal interests in railways.'

Regional Railways directors had responsibility for liaison with six of the TUCCs, each with its own flavour. As an example, in South Wales & West Steel was dealing with Sir Bob Wall, the ex-leader of Bristol Council, and his committee in the West of England, while Charles Hogg, a consumer champion, was Chairman in Wales. Typically the Committees comprised a mix of rail experts and representatives of worthy organisations, selected by the DTI. Latterly their Secretaries were appointed from outside the industry.

The TUCCs became Rail Users' Committees in 1993, the regional bodies were abolished by the 2005 Railways Act, and the national body morphed into Passenger Focus. Colin Foxhall has chaired Passenger Focus since its formation, and has driven its emergence under Anthony Smith as a respected research-based organisation with responsibilities for bus as well as rail. The data it has produced has added to the TOCs' understanding of customer views, and is used by the best of them to monitor their own performance. Like the ORR, Passenger Focus's remit is now being extended to roads.

## The origins of Community Rail

The notion of a community promoting – or even running – its own railway dates back at least to the classic 1952 movie *The Titfield Thunderbolt*, but in practice community activism took longer to gain legs. While preservationists began running their first ex-BR branch line – between Horsted Keynes and Sheffield Park in Sussex – in 1960, commuters took several decades to gain a formal voice in how their services were run.

Community Rail originated in a number of scattered and spontaneous initiatives driven either by a desire to see improvements that BR could clearly not afford, or to secure a line's future by reversing declining patronage. It also built on BR's growing willingness to engage.

The Cotswold Line Promotion Group was formed in 1978 as a proactive user group dedicated to encouraging growth in demand and an improved train service and stations. The line was in poor condition, with run-down stations and a thin service, many trains requiring a change at Oxford. The state of the track led to plans to replace all loco-hauled trains with DMUs, and minor stations faced closure; the CLPG campaigned for a reversal in the line's fortunes, and ultimately secured the redoubling of most of it.

Numerous commuter groups sprang up during the 1970s and '80s, mainly in the South East, in response to a relentless cycle of fare increases and perceived declining quality of service. In 1985 the East Suffolk Travellers' Association, with Gerard Fiennes a central figure, lost its battle to keep the line's daily through train to Liverpool Street. Most, however, were understandably more concerned with the interests of the passengers than with actively promoting the railway.

## Dilton Marsh and Yorton

The saga of Dilton Marsh Halt, between Westbury and Warminster, showed what grassroots action in concert with the railway could achieve. Opened by the GWR in 1937, it survived a Beeching-era closure attempt, inspiring a John Betjeman poem beginning: 'Was it worth it keeping the halt open?' Fewer than 20 people a day were using it when, in 1991, BR declared that the waiting room was unsafe and would have to be demolished unless £25,000 could be raised locally, then that DTp requirements obliged it to rebuild the platforms as well, at a cost of up to £250,000.

**LEFT** Dilton Marsh station, complete with its 15-metre platform, lighting, Help Point and shelter. *Alex Green*

Chris Gibb told the parish council – who had obtained a quote of £5,000 – that he was trying to keep Dilton Marsh open, but new Health & Safety Executive standards meant that the platforms were too short, and therefore 'unsafe'. The HSE insisted that all platforms must be as long as the longest train that might stop there, which meant 58 metres, although only 'Sprinters' called. The council launched a high-profile lobbying campaign, and the Secretary of State ruled that 15 metres would do. The station was completely rebuilt for £80,000, stakeholders contributing. At its reopening on 28 April 1994 Betjeman's daughter Candida Lycett-Green recited the poem, and Chris Gibb was offered the freedom of the village. Gibb notes: 'Yes, Dilton Marsh was a remarkable victory over the HSE, aided by Betjeman's poem on the front page of the *Telegraph*, and Wiltshire Lib Dems including their councillor Andrew Adonis! Fifteen-metre platforms made huge sense, and they have had a safe history since, serving 100 or so people a day.'

Yorton station, between Shrewsbury and Crewe, also faced closure 30 years after surviving Beeching.

There were just 20 passengers a day, the barrow crossing was no longer safe, and BR would only contribute £7,000 for new access. Local councils and the community rallied round, the Hardwick Estate donated land and the station gained a new lease of life. Today it is used by 30 passengers a day.

Privatisation disrupted relationships, but new ones soon formed, with the added inducement that the TOCs' contracts committed them to better customer service. Expectations rose among passengers, MPs and councillors, requiring new attitudes among customer-facing staff and a determination to reach what Adrian Shooter termed 'Japanese levels' of punctuality and reliability.

## Promoting better stations and information

One of the keenest demands, which the TOCs have generally met – apart from the occasional spectacular lapse at times of major disruption – has been for better passenger information. A crucial improvement, from the early days of privatisation, is the recorded information system bringing details of how the trains are running to almost every station. In Wales & West, Chris Gibb recalls, 'it was Project Inform, a huge undertaking which made a very big difference to what customers experienced. The announcements were done by real people: a man called Eryl who did the Welsh ones, and a lady from the booking office in Truro called Ruth who did the English. You can still hear their voices via that information system, 16 years after we installed it.'

In 1991 the Devon & Cornwall Rail Partnership was formed in the University of Plymouth's geography department to promote the use and development of local trains and stations. This became the largest and one of the most successful partnerships under the management of Richard Burningham, who ran the Travel Centre at Barnstaple before moving to the Southern Region public affairs team at Waterloo. Over 25 years Burningham, in the words of former Wessex Railways Managing Director Charles Belcher, did 'an awful lot to show the railway was a local railway'. In the North West, Lancaster University developed a similar initiative.

Community rail also has its roots in the takeover by locals of station gardens as staff were withdrawn. (Charlbury, on the Cotswold Line, retained its garden

**LEFT** No 142001 stands at a lovingly cared-for Barnstaple station, complete with restored Southern Region signing to give it a local feel. *Anthony Christie*

*Chapter 11:* **ENGAGING WITH COMMUNITIES AND STAKEHOLDERS**    155

**ABOVE** Denby Dale station in West Yorkshire is now well-maintained and well-patronised. *Dennis Lovett*

**RIGHT** Every red line indicates ACoRP's involvement in promoting community partnerships. *ACoRP*

through the enthusiasm of Sir Peter Parker, a local commuter.) In 1993 volunteers at Penmere on the Falmouth branch persuaded SW&W to let them smarten up the station and create a garden; they have since won national awards. The Friends of Handforth Station, formed in 1996, did the same in an urban setting on an electrified route.

## The Penistone Line Partnership

In 1993 came the formation of the Penistone Line Partnership, driven by Paul Salveson who had been a signalman and guard in Manchester before setting up a transport consultancy; he was given his first office on Huddersfield station by Regional Railways North East. Spanning two PTEs, this had been a problematic rural route. The Huddersfield-Penistone branch's six trains a day, connecting to the Woodhead line into Sheffield, were reprieved by Barbara Castle, and after Woodhead closed a through service struggled on, reversing to access Sheffield Midland. In 1977 South Yorkshire refused to fund its portion, and three years later BR proposed closing all but the section between Huddersfield and Denby Dale. Despite a record number of objections, closure was set for 1983. Then SYPTE offered to fund a service diverted via Barnsley. This attracted new business, then West Yorkshire withdrew support for the Denby Dale-Penistone section. Closure notices were reposted, but the TUCC detected a legal flaw and, by the time they were reissued, the metropolitan counties were being abolished and in 1987 WYPTE agreed to restore funding.

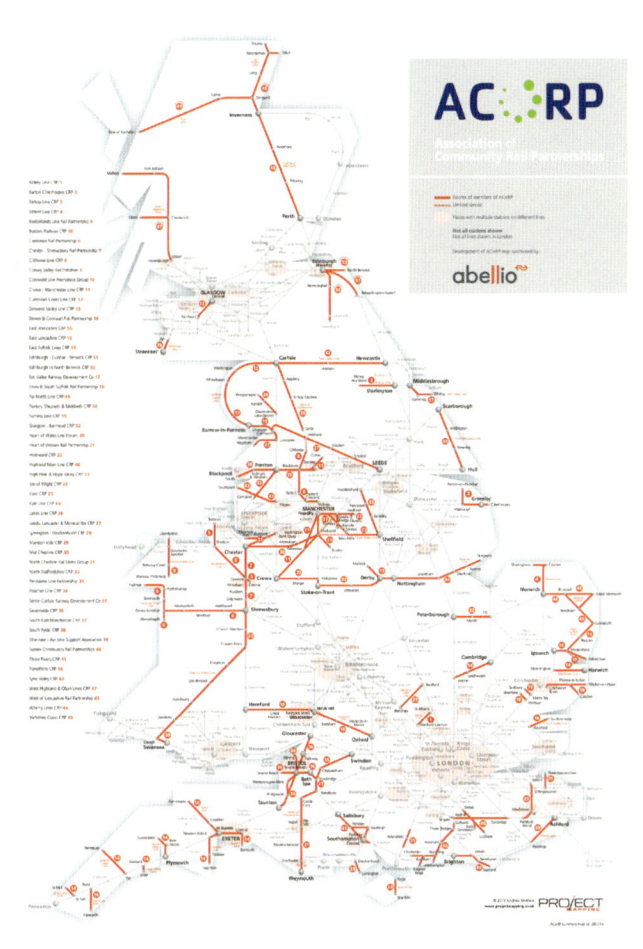

An hourly service was introduced and, with the opening of Meadowhall station in 1990, loadings surged. Despite its circuitous route, slow speeds and overcrowding at peaks, growth on the Penistone line continued as it moved from the 'rural' to the 'urban' column. By the time the DfT initially chose the line in 2008 for its tram-train experiment, there were doubts whether such vehicles could handle the traffic.

The tide had already turned in the line's favour when the Partnership was formed to promote it and press for service improvements. The introduction of the celebrated 'Jazz Trains' in 1993 was the first of several initiatives to raise its profile.

## The founding of ACoRP

Supporters of other lines, such as Carlisle-Newcastle with its 'Curry Train', followed suit, and in 1997 Salveson formed the Association of Community Rail Partnerships (ACoRP). Progress had been limited by the focus on privatisation, but Salveson was quick to build a relationship with the Strategic Rail Authority. Inspired by visits to Germany, and particularly tram-train developments, he presented ideas for microfranchising to Chris Stokes.

Chris Austin says, 'When I arrived at the SRA at the end of 1999, I picked up this work and the concept was developed further. The SRA became one of ACoRP's sponsors, with the objective of driving the spread of community rail partnerships to a wider range of local lines. [The SRA also introduced Rail Partnership funding, which Charles Belcher says enabled operators to 'squeeze in a little extra'.]

'In 2003, with the Northern Rail Review under way and the search for big economies, Richard Bowker asked me to develop a strategy for local railways whose future might otherwise be in doubt. A small team of us produced a consultation paper drawing on good practice from existing partnerships, and from train operators and Network Rail contractors (Andy Savage of Carillion was a particular help).'

## The Community Rail Development Strategy

Chris Austin continues: 'The Community Rail Development Strategy was published in November 2004 just before the abolition of the SRA, but was adopted by Government and remains the definitive statement of policy. The Department took over sponsorship of ACoRP, and Network Rail has embraced the concept.' Some train operators have from the outset proactively supported CRPs, 'to get local interest in the railway back' in the words of Jeremy Long, who worked with local communities to build support for Anglia's 'Bittern Line'; traffic on the line has, appropriately, boomed (see Table 11.1). For some TOCs, support for Community Rail Partnerships is now a franchise requirement.

The strategy,' says Chris Austin, 'had the objective of providing a framework for local and rural routes, services and stations, within which they can develop and be put on a sustainable basis for the medium to long term. It had three elements – increase use of the line and fares income, reduce costs, and encourage

Table 11.1: 'Bittern Line' usage figures, 1998 v 2013

| Station | 1988 | 2013 |
|---|---|---|
| Sheringham | 72,000 | 190,000 |
| West Runton | 5,000 | 24,000 |
| Cromer | 66,000 | 187,000 |
| Roughton Road | 2,000 | 12,000 |
| Gunton | 6,000 | 17,000 |
| North Walsham | 78,000 | 241,000 |
| Worstead | 10,000 | 22,000 |
| Hoveton & Wroxham | 49,000 | 123,000 |
| Salhouse | 2,000 | 9,000 |
| **Total** | **290,000** | **825,000** |

**ABOVE** The 'Bittern Line' is a Community Railway Partnership line running from Norwich to Sheringham via Cromer. The line has seen phenomenal growth: more than 185% at North Walsham. *UKrailways1970till today*

community involvement – to which the Department added a fourth: support social and economic regeneration. The strategy has been very successful in increasing ridership and income, and annual growth for Community Rail lines is above the national average for local services (in the first ten years of Community Rail, passenger growth of 61% was recorded on the 33 lines participating, against 55% for regional services as a whole and 51% for the entire network).

'Community Rail has been very successful in involving the community, and the value of community volunteering is put at £27 million per annum. Station adoption now embraces hundreds of stations; in East Anglia and Scotland almost every station has been adopted. This has brought benefits in terms of station appearance, gardens and landscaping, better security, a reduction in trespass and vandalism, and better maintenance: faults are reported and acted on quickly.' The Friends of Dronfield Station secured, then publicised a better train service, developed an attractive garden and organised litter patrols, helping achieve a quadrupling in footfall over four years; a more convenient location for the station is now being considered.

Austin adds that Community Rail has been less successful in reducing costs. 'These lines are run on a minimalist basis anyway, often with simplified signalling, one or two units and unstaffed stations. There is limited scope for further economy without breaking away from national agreements. The big costs for community lines occur infrequently and relate to renewals, and emergency repairs when earthworks or structures fail, such as the periodic washouts on the Conwy Valley line.'

## Impact of the CRPs

The Community Rail Partnerships – thanks to strong local authority support – have been particularly effective in Lancashire, with Preston an important node for potential growth. A 14% increase in traffic between Manchester, Blackburn and Clitheroe in 2012/13 was largely attributed to Partnership activity; Sunday services were reintroduced, subsidised from a 'levy' on weekday fares. Local schools (the next generation of travellers) have been engaged, together with ethnic groups, some without a culture of rail travel. The Accrington eco-station, promoted by the East Lancs CRP, and the reborn station at Burnley Manchester Road, where the Partnership has been allocated an office with staff of Northern Rail, and several others in the North West where the local authority operates a booking office that would otherwise be closed, are further examples of what can be achieved.

ACoRP, until recently with Richard Burningham on its committee and now headed by Peter Roberts, has pioneered community use of empty railway property, most remarkably an art gallery in a disused Gents at Worcester Foregate Street. It is also a conduit for small grants to CRPs, for everything from minor redecoration to leaflets and mince pies. ACoRP has set out – with Northern Rail and Transport for Greater Manchester – a template for starting a station adoption group and keeping it going. Notwithstanding Scotland's divergent political course, 2014 saw its first CRP – for the Stranraer-Ayr line – with backing from Holyrood, and there will be over a dozen more under the new ScotRail

**BELOW** Accrington is a new-style Eco Station with solar panels, toilets flushed with collected rain water and cycle parking. The £2 million project was funded by Lancashire County Council, Hyndburn Borough Council and Network Rail. *Community Rail Lancashire*

**ABOVE** A North Yorkshire Moors Railway service with Stanier 'Black Five' No 45428 *Eric Treacy* supports the Whitby community. The heritage line has now built its own run-round facilities to enable a more comprehensive and attractive service pattern. *Dennis Lovett*

franchise. However, efforts to improve the service on the Central Wales line with a radical rethink on costs have fallen foul of the Welsh Assembly Government's limited powers over rail, as any savings funded from Cardiff would be clawed back by Network Rail and Whitehall.

ACoRP has been directly involved in setting the specifications for both the new ScotRail and Northern franchises; with the latter it opposed the removal of little-used stops, and supported driver-only operation as giving train conductors more time to sell tickets.

Local user groups still have a role, though Paul Salveson rates these 'highly variable in quality'. The Hope Valley Rail Users' Group, for a line also covered by a CRP, recently persuaded Lafarge to retime one of its cement trains to allow an additional Sheffield-Manchester commuter service; however, the Woodland Trust then blocked plans for a loop at Grindleford that would permit even more. The rural CRPs also engage with the National Parks, the National Trust, the RSPB, wildlife trusts and other stakeholders. Cycling and disability groups have been increasingly involved, over the provision of adequate facilities or assistance at stations and on trains.

Britain's enthusiast-led heritage railways have also developed a working relationship with the train operators; those with rail connections, as at Aberystwyth, Alton, Aviemore, Blaenau Ffestiniog, Bodmin Parkway, Keighley, Lydney, Paignton, Sheringham, Tywyn and, most recently, East Grinstead, not only stimulate local tourism but encourage their visitors to arrive by National Rail. The North Yorkshire Moors Railway now shares the track with Northern Rail between Grosmont and an expanded terminus at Whitby, and occasionally provides (steam) replacements for timetabled services. But no such railway has yet run a year-long daily service.

# Chapter 12
# CHOOSING THE TRAINS

*'Since 1982, over 1,400 vehicles have been built to replace much older rolling stock. At no time in their history have so many new trains been available outside London and the South East for urban, inter-urban and rural travel. By 1993, 88% of Regional Railways' diesel and electric vehicles will be under eight years old.'*

**'THE FRANCHISING OF PASSENGER RAIL SERVICES'**, DFT CONSULTATION DOCUMENT, OCTOBER 1992

**ABOVE** The dawn of a new age – newly completed 'Sprinter' No 150001 stands outside Derby in 1985. *Colin Boocock*

## Making the choice

One of the biggest issues facing the new Provincial sector in 1982 was how to justify a fleet of new trains to replace the 2,500 ageing 'heritage' DMU vehicles that were riddled with asbestos – not to mention the 1,000 life-expired Mark I and II coaches together with the locomotive-hauled services.

This was a critical decision for the future success of the sector, as locomotives and carriages have a long life, where 30 years in front-line service is quite normal. InterCity had inherited the right train for the job through BR's inspired development of the HST and the Mark III coach. These vehicles were first introduced in 1976 and are still popular 40 years later – having undergone interim refurbishments that have proved so successful that passengers often believe them to be new trains. Quite a few of the HSTs are now to be given a further lease of life with ScotRail.

A robust Provincial specification that looked to the future was inevitably going to be a compromise in technical development and passenger expectation. Affordability, particularly first cost, would be central to the choice, not least because of the substantial and escalating losses being made by BR at the time, which were triggering worries of a second round of Beeching-style closures.

The Provincial sector did not have the HST option of sourcing a standard coach through a single supplier, as the Board had already established new procedures for competitive tendering before the first order for 'Pacers' was placed. A single coach body suitable for urban, interurban and rural services was also an unrealistic expectation. Nevertheless, the story that follows is one of moving, albeit slowly, towards standard designs suitable for use by a diverse range of customers in the future.

## Developing the 'Pacer'

BR had already been working to develop a new generation of DMU, and in 1981 the Class 210 diesel-electric multiple unit emerged – essentially a 90mph Class 317 EMU body as developed for the St Pancras-Bedford line, with traction equipment occupying half the forward carriage. A four-car unit powered by a 1,140bhp above-floor MTU engine and a three-car unit powered by a 1,125bhp Paxman were built. The hope was that performance would match that of an EMU, but this was unrealistic. The trains settled into diagrams around Reading, but no follow-up order was placed. They were too heavy and too expensive, and were withdrawn in 1987.

The search was on for something that would be better than the diminutive railbus of the 1950s, but cheaper than the Class 210. Five four-wheel railcar prototypes (LEVs) were built between 1978 and 1984, having been jointly developed by Leyland and the Railway Technical Centre at Derby. Each comprised a

**RIGHT** Heritage EMU No 3044006 at Manchester Piccadilly. *Dennis Lovett*

**BELOW LEFT** Heritage Class 101 DMU at Betws-y-Coed. *Dennis Lovett*

**BELOW RIGHT** No 27102 looks very sorry for itself at Falkirk Grahamston. *Dennis Lovett*

# Chapter 12: CHOOSING THE TRAINS

**TOP LEFT** New prototype No 210001 passes Royal Oak, Paddington, in 1981. *Colin Boocock*

**CENTRE LEFT** LEV 1 was the first of five lightweight railcar prototypes based on a new two-axle design. *Colin Boocock*

**BOTTOM LEFT** LEV 4. *Colin Boocock*

Leyland National bus body mounted on a wagon chassis. LEV 1 and LEV 3 briefly entered traffic, but LEV 3 soon ended up in Northern Ireland and the other three were shipped across the Atlantic in the hope of securing export business (which never came). LEV 1 and 4 are preserved in this country.

The LEVs did, however, lay the groundwork for the lightweight Class 140, a two-car Leyland bus, apart from cabs and chassis, which both had to meet BR crashworthiness requirements. This first 'Pacer' had a Leyland engine, a Self Changing Gears mechanical automatic gearbox, and a Gmeinder final drive unit on each car driving only one axle. Built at Derby, it entered traffic on the Central Wales line at the end of 1981 and is now preserved on the Keith & Dufftown Railway.

Just after this, John Welsby was appointed Director at Provincial and his priority was to make a start with renewing the ageing DMU fleet. He had a clear idea of what he wanted and summarised this in a recent interview: 'I wanted a DMU with power units under each carriage – the only question was how rigid the specification should be. I went to consult the DM&EE [Director of Mechanical & Electrical Engineering] at Derby and asked to see their Engineering Intelligence Library: there wasn't one. Lots of learned opinions from senior engineers, but no consistency and no demonstrable analysis of relative performance of different bits of kit – though some information on the performance of existing equipment, such as the average life of engines and gearboxes. I was appalled. Before going to university, and during all vacations, I had been a lorry driver. I knew a lot about the expected performance of automotive equipment. Any haulage firm that only obtained the levels of performance BR were experiencing would have gone bust in double-quick time.'

Despite the reservations of others, particularly in relation to the absence of bogies causing excessive wear on wheels and rails, John Welsby decided to go ahead on the basis that one 'Pacer' vehicle would replace two DMU carriages. The cost savings were enough to convince Government to approve an immediate build – and the initiative was further speeded on its way when David Kirby, MD London & SouthEast Sector, agreed to transfer some of his allocated funding to accommodate the 'Pacer' order. A further three orders were subsequently placed for 'Pacers', bringing the fleet to a total of 164 units, as detailed in Table 12.1.

Many observers still believe that the 'Pacer' family was built for use on branch lines, but this was not the case. John Welsby was adamant that 'they were built to replace lightly loaded trains wherever they could be found.' This, together with the PTE pressure for newer

Chapter 12: **CHOOSING THE TRAINS** 161

**ABOVE LEFT** The early 'Pacer' prototype No 140001 outside Springburn Works, Glasgow. *Colin Boocock*

**ABOVE RIGHT** The 'Pacer' family: from left to right, a Class 144 in WYPTE livery, a 142 in BR Provincial livery, a 141 in experimental green, and a 141 and a 140 both in BR standard blue and white, stabled at Leeds. *David Wharton-Street*

**LEFT** No 144002 in West Yorkshire PTE livery. *David Wharton-Street*

## Shortcomings and durability

Thirteen Class 142 'Pacers', locally branded as 'Skippers', were sent to work on the Devon and Cornwall branches, but did not prove a success. The two-axle trains quickly wore out both wheels and rails as they screamed their way round the sharply curved lines, and were transferred to routes in the North East and North West to be reunited with the majority of the fleet.

and cheaper trains, meant that the majority were actually sent to work in urban areas around the main cities in the North – or on longer routes such as trans-Pennine or Newcastle-Carlisle later in their career.

**Table 12.1: The 'Pacer' family**

| Class | 141 (two-car) | 142 (two-car) | 143 (two-car) | 144 (two-car) | 144 (three-car) |
|---|---|---|---|---|---|
| No of units | 20* | 96 | 25 | 13 | 10 |
| Seats | 120 | 103-122 | 104 | 87 | 145 |
| Weight (tons) | 42.5 | 49.5 | 49.5 | 48.5 | 72 |
| Horsepower | 410 | 460 | 460 | 460 | 460 |
| Original engine | Leyland TL11 (-) | Leyland TL11 (205hp) | Leyland TL11 (205hp) | Leyland TL11 (205hp) | Leyland TL11 (205hp) |
| Current engine | - | Cummins LTA10 | Cummins LTA10 | Cummins LTA10 | Cummins LTA10 |
| Axle load (tons) | 10.6 | 12.3 | 12.1 | 12.1 | 12.0 |
| Max speed (mph) | 75 | 75 | 75 | 75 | 75 |
| Body | Leyland bus | Leyland bus | W. Alexander | W. Alexander | W. Alexander |
| Underframe | BREL Derby | BREL Derby | A. Barclay | BREL Derby | BREL Derby |
| Assembly | BREL Derby | BREL Derby | Kilmarnock | BREL Derby | BREL Derby |
| Built | 1984 | 1985-87 | 1985-86 | 1985-86 | 1985-86 |

* Class 141 fleet withdrawn (1997)
Source: Theo Steel and Colin Marsden

## Chapter 12: CHOOSING THE TRAINS

LEFT No 143013 stands at Carlisle in BR Provincial livery.
*Dennis Lovett*

### Case study – early 'Pacer' memories

David Wharton-Street, Director North East:
'The "Pacers" were based on the premise that they would be so reliable you could out-stable them overnight and they would start up. They didn't. The main user of the "Pacers" was West Yorkshire PTE and quite rightly the main criticism was from them. We were not only letting them down – we were letting the public down.'

Dick Fearn, Resources Manager, Provincial North Eastern:
'The "Pacers" were ordered when there was no money. People actually lobbied for them as a "bus on wheels". Tyne & Wear and Lincolnshire were keen to use the "Pacers" – but not for long!'

Alex Ritchie, Director-General, South Yorkshire PTE:
'Everything about a "Pacer" was wrong: gearboxes, doors, driving units, brakes.'

Sidney Newey, MD Provincial:
'The gearboxes were a sad surprise – but the brakes were the show-stopper.'

Ian Walmsley, Fleet Engineer:
'We would have been better off in hindsight if the whole idea had been dropped and we built hundreds of Class 150s – but the longer wait might have been fatal for some lines.'

Meanwhile a new problem was appearing as a result of the new BRB procurement policies referred to earlier. The Board was keen to give the established train builder BREL – part of BR – some external competition, but this was not readily compatible with Provincial's quest for a standard HST-style production line. In the event, about 85% of the 'Pacer' fleet was to be assembled at the BREL workshops in Derby, but the bodies were to be supplied by Leyland Bus and Walter Alexander at Falkirk. Table 12.1 shows the variety of manufacturers that became involved in delivering the bodies and underframes for this 'standard' product.

Despite these problems, the 'Pacer' represented a radical change in technology and succeeded in bringing significantly lower running costs. Sadly, however, bus technology did not transfer well to the more demanding rail environment and the fleet turned out to be very unreliable. The technical problems involved key areas such as the brakes and gearboxes, and the units' availability in traffic fell as low as 50% by 1989. The northern PTEs were highly critical of the poor service being delivered, and for a time even withheld payments to BR in protest. The case study (left) recalls those days.

When Gordon Pettitt arrived in May 1990, he ordered a review of 'Pacer' performance from external consultants to identify the problems and make recommendations on what needed to be done to bring about a lasting improvement. This was essential both to give the PTEs some confidence that action was in hand and also to make the financial case for the resulting modifications. The major programme that followed included modifications to door operation, replacement of Leyland bus engines with more robust Cummins engines, and the replacement of mechanical gearboxes with a Voith hydraulic transmission. These changes by a team led by Ian Walmsley achieved significant improvements to fleet availability and reliability.

To everyone's surprise, the 'Pacers' have remained in service to this day – with the exception of the original Class 141 units, which were withdrawn in 1997. Impressively, the Class 141 workload was covered by the improved availability of the remaining 'Pacer' fleet, but 'Pacer' reliability remains below the level of the 'Sprinter' fleet to this day.

Since privatisation, a number of TOCs have initiated substantial refurbishment of 'Pacer' interiors. These have improved the passenger environment, but the ride characteristics and general ambiance are still below passenger expectations, with the possible exception of a refurbished 144 for short trips.

The question now is how much longer 'Pacers' will remain in service. Under the Disability Discrimination Act of 1995, all public transport must be accessible by 2019 and the implication is that the fleet will have to be withdrawn from service unless still further expensive modifications are made. The most likely solution is that the future electrification plans outlined in Chapter 13 will create a cascade of 'Sprinter' units that will finally allow the 'Pacers' to be retired. The scope for a

## Table 12.2: The 'Sprinter' and 'SuperSprinter' family

|  | 150 (three-car) | 150/1 (two-car) | 150/2 (two-car) | 153 (single-car) | 155 (two-car) | 156 (two-car) | 158 (two-car) | 158 (three-car) |
|---|---|---|---|---|---|---|---|---|
| No of units | 2 | 50 | 85 | 70* | 7 | 114 | 165 | 39 |
| Seats | 240 | 124-141 | 130-149 | 69-72 | 156 | 140-152 | 140-150 | 202 |
| Weight (tons) | 105.8 | 76.4 | 74.0 | 41.2 | 77.7 | 76.5 | 77.0 | 155 |
| Horsepower | 855 | 570 | 570 | 285 | 570 | 570 | 7-800 | 1,050 |
| Axle load (tons) | 8.9 | 9.5 | 9.2 | 10.3 | 9.7 | 9.9 | 9.6 | 9.6 |
| Speed (mph) | 75 | 75 | 75 | 75 | 75 | 75 | 90 | 90 |
| Body | Steel | Steel | Steel | Steel | Steel | Steel | Aluminium | Aluminium |
| Built | 1984 | 1985/6 | 1986/7 | 1991/92 | 1988 | 1987-8 | 1989/92 | 1989/92 |
| Assembly | BREL York | BREL York | BREL York | Leyland* | Leyland | Metro-Cammell | BREL Derby | BREL Derby |

* Rebuilt from Class 155 units by Hunslet-Barclay
Source: Theo Steel and Colin Marsden

**RIGHT** No 150145 passes Duffield forming the 15.52 Matlock to Nottingham service on 10 July 1986. *Colin J. Marsden*

**BELOW RIGHT** Metro-Cammell No 151001 at Derby in 1983. *Colin Boocock*

new build of DMUs to replace them is considered later in the chapter. One intriguing proposal is that redundant London Underground District Line stock acquired by Vivarail, refurbished and fitted with diesel engines giving a maximum 50mph, could come in as a stopgap. There is some resistance in the North to replacing 'Pacers' with even older second-hand vehicles from London, but Vivarail's Adrian Shooter, former head of Chiltern Railways and progenitor of the highly successful 'Turbostar', is pushing the idea hard.

## Developing the 'Sprinter'

John Welsby recognised long before all the 'Pacers' were delivered that there was a need to create a higher specification of DMU to replace the remaining heritage DMUs and loco-hauled fleets. But he remained of the view that Derby Research's Class 210 option was too expensive, with the above-chassis engine taking far too much valuable passenger space. His solution was the Class 150 'Sprinter', which took the best features of the 210, such as its Mark III bodyshell, but created a more affordable train with underfloor engines. But this was not to be achieved without competition.

The sector decided to trial two alternative prototypes to stimulate the market – the Class 150 from BREL York and the Class 151 from Metro-Cammell. The two Metro-Cammell prototypes were the first to arrive and represented a complete break from the BREL tradition.

They were built of lightweight aluminium, which made each 8 tonnes lighter than a traditional steel train. A new transmission system gave 15% efficiency improvements in performance. But Metro-Cammell failed to secure the order on two counts – first because the first cost of aluminium trains was too expensive, and second because of the poor reliability of its new transmission system.

## Chapter 12: CHOOSING THE TRAINS

So the first 'Sprinter' orders were won by BREL York, following the success of its two Class 150 prototypes, both of which three decades on were still working intensive diagrams with First Great Western. John Welsby knew that the only hope of winning more Government investment in new fleets lay in further dramatic cost reductions – and the Class 150 would do just that. But it did more than simply reduce capital investment costs – it generated more income, created new markets, and heralded a new era in which Provincial trains would become more attractive and reliable.

Introduced in 1985, the 'Sprinters' had steel bodies, Cummins 285hp underfloor engines, Voith transmissions and Gmeinder final drives. This formula would dominate the DMU business until the arrival of the 'Turbostar' 12 years later. Thirty years on, it is a tribute to the robustness of the Class 150 fleet that the units are still operating at high levels of utilisation and reliability. The class raised availability in traffic from the traditional 75% level to an impressive 90% – a feat supported by a transfer to night-time maintenance and the ending of maintenance exams measured in days. Henceforth maintenance would be broken down into 8-hour night shifts called 'Balanced Exams'.

The Sector vision was still built around a two-car unit fleet, with three cars only provided for proven demand. John Welsby has since spoken of his pride in creating a quality train in the Class 150 that was to become the workhorse of Regional Railways for a whole generation. He confirmed that the key factor in getting the first 'Sprinters' authorised was the elimination of the expensive loco-hauled fleets that were still operating many of the Provincial routes. Indeed, he envisaged the 'Sprinters' as a replacement for the longer-distance routes, and this explained their early appearance on interurban services such as Scarborough/Hull to Manchester. The 'Sprinter' had hit the right balance between cost, performance, reliability and availability. A total of 276 vehicles were built by BREL at York, with some re-formed later into three-car trains for busy routes around Birmingham.

### The 'Super Sprinter' fleet

When John Edmonds became Director of Provincial in 1984 his mind was focused on developing the technical reliability behind the Class 150 'Sprinter', based on its underfloor engine and hydraulic transmission, but his vision was a train with higher standards of comfort for passengers, which would attract more business than the austere 150 with its 2+3 seating. At the same time he wanted lower unit costs, despite specifying 2+2 seating, which reduced the capacity of a traditional 20-metre carriage. This was to be achieved by increasing the length of each vehicle to 23 metres. This major change of policy increased the space available within each coach by 15% – and therefore reduced the number of new vehicles needed. There was considerable opposition from civil and rolling stock engineers at the time, but 23 metres has been adopted as standard ever since.

John Edmonds's vision for the 'Super Sprinter' was taken forward in two phases. The first was an order for 42 Class 155 two-car units from British Leyland at Workington, and the second for 114 Class 156 two-car units from Metro-Cammell in Birmingham. Both builds were manufactured with steel bodies.

In 1991 all but seven of the Class 155 fleet were converted into single-car Class 153 units with a cab at each end. This created a new flexibility, as they could operate as single cars on rural routes – or strengthen

**TOP** No 155343, owned by West Yorkshire PTE, leaves Selby in WYPTE livery as the 11.18 Hull to Manchester Piccadilly service on 12 April 1997. *Martin Loader*

**ABOVE** No 153317 is seen at Hunslet-Barclays while being converted from a 155 unit. *Colin J. Marsden*

**Chapter 12: CHOOSING THE TRAINS** 165

**ABOVE LEFT** No 156434 in Provincial 'Sprinter' livery at Carlisle. *Dennis Lovett*

**ABOVE RIGHT** No 154001, modified from No 150002, is seen at Leicester on its first test run for 90mph with 350hp Cummins engines. *Steve Dentith*

existing two- or three-car units into longer formations on urban routes at busy times. The downside of the 153s was of course their dependence on a single engine, but this was more than balanced by the significant cost savings on vulnerable lines, together with the easement of overcrowding on the busier routes. Gordon Pettitt regarded the 153 conversions as 'absolutely vital', but the small size of the cab was a serious problem and it took a meeting at the Kilmarnock plant between himself and ASLEF for the union to accept that there was no practicable alternative.

The Class 156 followed, also aimed at the busier urban and interurban services and becoming the bedrock of routes such as Birmingham-Nottingham and Glasgow-Mallaig. These units, together with the Class 158s, retained the Cummins-Voith-Gmeinder transmission package.

But the pinnacle of the 'Super Sprinter' range was to be the 'Express' Class 158 unit, first delivered in 1989. John Edmonds was determined to produce an inter-city unit that could sustain 90mph running over long distances, while offering air-conditioning and carpeting throughout, seat reservations and on-board catering.

### Class 154 prototype

Steve Dentith, the Class 158 Project Engineer, explained that the evolution from the Class 150 to the 155/156 had used the same power equipment, but that the next step to the 158 was much more difficult. If the 158 was to have the performance required and a top speed of 90mph, the power-to-weight ratio needed to be significantly increased. The existing Cummins engine and Voith transmission were rated at 285hp and neither were proven in service above this rating, nor were any other suppliers able to offer anything higher.

To prove the higher-rated power equipment necessary for the Class 158, one of the original Class 150 prototypes – No 150002 – was used as a test bed. Initially, just the driving cars were modified, while the original Rolls Royce engines were replaced with 350hp Cummins engines. In place of the mechanical gearboxes one car was fitted with a Voith transmission and the other with a twin disc transmission to compare the two. Both end cars were fitted with air-conditioning, which had not previously been tried but was specified for the Class 158, together with 2+2 seating.

The converted unit was re-geared for 90mph running and reclassified as Class 154 to differentiate it from the rest of the fleet. Later, the centre car was fitted with the newly developed Perkins engine, matched to a Voith transmission. This car was not air-conditioned, which was useful as a comparison to the other cars – especially on hot days. The Class 154 unit was thoroughly tested, then ran in revenue-earning service. It also made several demonstration runs to prove the principle of the 90mph diesel railcar. John Edmonds followed the development personally and rode on a number of the test runs.

The 350hp power equipment was not enough on its own to meet the performance specification for Class 158s. This would require the power-to-weight ratio to be no greater than 38 tonnes. This led the manufacturers towards aluminium body shells, lightweight interiors and lightweight seats. They were also required to offer both 23- and 26-metre vehicle

**166** Chapter 12: **CHOOSING THE TRAINS**

**ABOVE** No 158707 under construction in Derby Litchurch Lane Works on 30 May 1990. *Colin J. Marsden*

lengths, but the longer version was ruled out by the BR gauge restrictions.

BREL was awarded the contract and chose to offer its Series 4 bogie rather than the Series 3 used on all other 'Sprinters'. This was because the crush laden pivot load on the 26-metre option was too much for the Series 3 bogie. And nobody wanted to have different bogies for the two options.

### The Class 158 production train

The Class 158 contract was the largest single order placed by Provincial/Regional Railways for one class of train, totalling 204 units (447 vehicles) – of which 39 units were three cars. It was placed with BREL at Derby at a time of great upheaval for management and staff. The company was put up for sale in November 1987 and a Management and Employee Buyout (MEBO) was concluded in April 1989. This had a profound effect on the delivery timescales and quality for the 158 fleet, which is discussed in some detail in Chapters 3 and 4.

When Gordon Pettitt took over in May 1990 he was surprised to find that only two Class 158 units had been delivered against the 200 planned by that date. The full consequences of this crisis, together with the transfer of the final 22 units to Network SouthEast as Class 159, are discussed in Chapter 9.

The Class 158 procurement process and the construction and reliability issues played out against a rapidly changing background. As noted by Terry Gourvish in his history of British Rail, there were over 170 variation orders, which were among the causes of a claim for £150 million liquidated damages from BREL/Trafalgar House. These were settled at £65 million by BR in 1993 at the time when BREL was sold on to ABB and the Government was seeking to form the rolling stock companies.

The late delivery of the 158s – coupled with the unreliability of 'Pacers' – remained a constant cause of concern at all levels of the business. Both problems created unexpected increases in cost, losses of income and poor performance for Regional Railways' customers. These issues, combined with reorganisation and the effects of a gathering recession, put enormous strain on the management team at HQ and in the profit centres.

The tide eventually started to turn with Class 158 deliveries, and a demonstration run was arranged between Derby and St Pancras for 11 September 1990. This was a great success. Gordon Pettitt was delighted with the quality of the customer features, in particular the smooth and quiet running when seated over the engines. The 90mph design speed was demonstrated in style throughout, but in particular between Leicester and Luton, where the average start-to-stop speed was 79.6mph. A detailed log of this journey is at Factfile D3.

Despite all the initial issues, the Class 158s, and more particularly the 159s, have proved a remarkably successful train that developed the initial focus of the interurban renaissance and growth, becoming the mainstay of interurban services such as the ScotRail Express network, Liverpool-Norwich and the TransPennine routes.

Even today Abellio has included refurbishment and aligning seats with windows for the 158s' use on the Far North and West Highland lines in its plans for the new ScotRail franchise.

### The 'heritage' legacy

The 'Pacers' and the 'Sprinter' family did not quite replace all the 'heritage' DMUs, as might have been the case had traffic not begun to surge. In 1981 there were approximately 2,500 'heritage' DMU vehicles in use on lines that were to become Provincial, of 21 different classes of unit ranging from single-car 'bubble cars' through to the quasi-InterCity trans-Pennine DMUs. By 1991 the number of first-generation vehicles in service was less than 700, mainly Class 101, Class 108 or the Class 116-118 suburban family. About 100 Class 101 vehicles survived to privatisation, with the final withdrawal taking place in First North Western on Christmas Eve 2003. Latterly a 'bubble car' Class 121 was reintroduced on the Cardiff Bay shuttle for a while. (Details of Regional rolling stock over the years are given in Factfile E.)

### Post-privatisation – diesels

Privatisation brought about great changes in the ownership of trains, and the capacity of workshops in the UK to build them. The BREL works at York, Derby and Crewe were sold as a Management and Employee Buyout in April 1989. The undertaking was subsequently bought out by ABB to form ABB Transportation Ltd, and subsequently recently became Bombardier Transportation. Both the BREL York and Metro-Cammell Birmingham works – having been acquired by Alstom – have since closed, leaving Derby Litchurch Lane as the only UK manufacturing plant for rolling stock until the arrival of Hitachi in 2012 (referred to later).

At privatisation the rolling stock owned by Regional Railways was sold to the three rolling stock leasing companies (ROSCOs). From this point onward the ROSCOs leased rolling stock to the TOCs, which were initially responsible for the day-to-day maintenance of the trains that were leased to them (over time the train makers, and especially Siemens, would take on train maintenance themselves). The ROSCOs remained responsible for heavy overhauls and refurbishment. Under this arrangement the ROSCOs had a substantial interest not only in keeping their fleets in good order but also in ensuring that they would have a good residual value at the end of the contracts. In total contrast to the BR era, standard designs appealing to a variety of customers were the way forward.

A perfect example is the 23-metre 100mph Bombardier 'Turbostar' range of DMUs, which accounts for 67% of all DMU orders since privatisation and is probably the train Regional Railways would have specified had it still been in existence. They were available in two-, three- and four-car versions, together with a mix of high-density or inter-city seating. These units also have

**ABOVE** No 170410 awaits departure from Aberdeen in a smart National Express ScotRail 'Whoosh' livery in May 2000. *Dennis Lovett*

the benefit of double doors at one-third/two-third positions, unlike the 158 with its single doors at each end. Details of these and other DMUs used by Regional Railways' successor companies are shown in Table 12.3.

Since privatisation, two other DMU designs have been purchased. Twenty-seven 'Coradia' interurban Class 175 units were built by Alstom and are currently based at Chester depot for use on Arriva Trains Wales services. Like other Alstom products of the era, reliability did not become right for a very long time, but they have since become excellent.

In addition, 51 interurban Class 185 trains were built by Siemens, based on the company's highly successful electric 'Desiro' fleets. As explained in Chapter 9, these 2,260hp 100mph units were to revolutionise travel across the Pennines – and subsequently from Manchester to Scotland.

**Table 12.3: Diesel fleets purchased by regional operators post-privatisation**

| Class | 170 (two-car) | 170 (three-car) | 172 (two-car) | 172 (three-car) | 175 (two-car) | 175 (three-car) | 185 (three-car) |
|---|---|---|---|---|---|---|---|
| No of units | 30 | 77 | 12 | 15 | 11 | 16 | 51 |
| Seats | 122* | 196* | 114 | 188 | 118 | 186 | 15/154 |
| Weight (tons) | 90-92 | 133-34 | 84 | 121 | 102 | 149 | 163 |
| Horsepower | 844 | 966 | 966 | 1,455 | 900 | 1,350 | 2,250 |
| Axle load (tons) | 11.3 | 10.5 | 10.5 | 10.0 | 12.5 | 12.4 | 13.6 |
| Speed (mph) | 100 | 100 | 100 | 100 | 100 | 100 | 100 |
| Body | Aluminium | Aluminium | Aluminium | Aluminium | Steel | Steel | Aluminium |
| Builder | Adtranz | Adtranz | Bombardier | Adtranz | Alstom | Alstom | Siemens |
| Year built | 1998-01 | 1998-2001 | 2009-11 | 2009-11 | 1999-00 | 1999-01 | 2006 |

\* Varies between operators
Source: Theo Steel and Colin Marsden

# 168 Chapter 12: CHOOSING THE TRAINS

While privatisation has led to standard designs like the Class 170, it has also resulted in progressive increase in axle load weights – and therefore to increased track costs. The Class 185 is 'worst of class' with a 42% increase in axle load over a three-car Class 158. But it is not just about a train's impact on track maintenance costs, but also its fuel consumption that has led to the operators issuing instructions to drivers to cut out an engine wherever possible.

The Class 172, however, has started to reverse the trend down to 10.5-tonne axle weights – thanks to the use of the B5000 inside frame bogies used on the 'Voyager' fleet. The continued growth in business since privatisation is underlined by the fact that 72% are three-car trains and all have been justified by the need to meet expanding markets.

One other type of DMU is set to enter regional service later in this decade: the Class 165/166 'Networker Turbo' built by BREL in 1990-92 for Thames Valley and Chiltern commuter services. Many freed up by the Great Western electrification will be transferred to routes in the South West (or Wales) where diesel services will continue and which can accommodate the more ample GW loading gauge to which they were built. This in turn will release 'Sprinters' to provide extra capacity elsewhere on the network … or to replace 'Pacers'.

## Electric fleets

Not all Provincial fleets were diesel-operated. The sector inherited suburban electric networks in Glasgow, Manchester and Liverpool – and two more in the planning stage in the Birmingham and Leeds areas. Provincial and Regional Railways faced over time three major challenges:

**TOP** No 172345, in London Midland livery, on a special working for employees from Great Malvern to Birmingham Snow Hill on 31 August 2011. *Andrew Smith, courtesy of Malvern Industrial Archaeology Circle*

**ABOVE** No 310108, in three-car formation, is seen at Wolverhampton in October 1999, with Regional Railways livery still applied but the logo removed post-privatisation. *Dennis Lovett*

### Table 12.4: Provincial/Regional Railways' electric train family, 1982-91

| Class | 303 (three-car) | 311 (three-car) | 314 (three-car) | 318 (three-car) | 320 (three-car) | 321/9 (four-car) | 322 (four-car) | 323 (three-car) |
|---|---|---|---|---|---|---|---|---|
| No of units | 91 | 19 | 16 | 21 | 22 | 3 | 5 | 43 |
| Seats | 236 | 236 | 212 | 216 | 227 | 307 | 291 | 284 |
| Weight (tons) | 126 | 127 | 102.5 | 107.5 | 114.5 | 138 | 138.2 | 114.7 |
| Horsepower | 829 | 829 | 880 | 1,328 | 1,328 | 1,328 | 1,328 | 1,565 |
| Axle load | 10.5 | 10.5 | 8.5 | 8.9 | 9.5 | 8.6 | 8.6 | 9.5 |
| Speed (mph) | 75 | 75 | 75 | 90 | 90 | 100 | 100 | 90 |
| Body | Steel | Steel | Steel/aluminium | Steel | Steel | Steel | Steel | Aluminium |
| Built | 1959-61 | 1967 | 1979-80 | 1985-86 | 1990 | 1991 | 1990 | 1991 |
| Assembly | Pressed Steel, Paisley | Cravens, Sheffield | BREL York | BREL York | BREL York | BREL York | BREL York | Hunslet, Leeds |

Source: Gordon Pettitt

- To order new trains to replace life-expired stock on the existing electrified lines in Manchester – where there were different systems of electrification – and Strathclyde
- To order a new fleet of trains for the Cross-City electrification in Birmingham and the Leeds North West electrification, with options for additional trains
- To identify suitable life-expired electric stock from Network SouthEast to provide temporary cover when deliveries of new trains were delayed – and during the hiatus in new rolling stock orders from 1993-97

## The new Class 323

The Birmingham Cross-City electrification between Redditch and Lichfield was planned to open in 1993, and the project triggered a radical new electric train that was destined to break the custom of Provincial/Regional Railways piggy-backing onto the latest Network SouthEast electric builds. The obvious solution for a 25kV EMU lay in the emerging aluminium 'Networker' fleet, but John Edmonds was determined to extend his policy of 23-metre vehicles – not feasible on most lines in the London area – into this new electric fleet. BREL chose to quote an unexpectedly high price for the new build, so Regional Railways decided to break with the 'Networker' and procure its own 23-metre vehicle from Hunslet TPL of Leeds.

The resulting Class 323 EMU was the first truly European train to be assembled in the UK. The aluminium extrusions for the body travelled from Switzerland to be assembled in Belgium. The bodies were then transferred to Leeds to be fitted with RFS bogies and HOLEC traction motors from Holland.

**ABOVE** No 323226, in GMPTE livery, arrives at Crewe forming the 14.45 service to Manchester Airport on 3 April 1999. *Matt Taylor*

Not surprisingly, there were severe delays in getting the train certified for use in the midst of the transition to privatisation, but with time the trains have come to give good, reliable service. Indeed, in 2014 the Class 323 fleet operated by Northern was awarded a 'Silver Spanner' in *Modern Railways*' annual train maintenance awards for the most improved fleet in the new-generation EMU category – a tribute both to the train and to Alstom Traincare, which maintains these 323s at Longsight.

The 323 order for the Birmingham Cross-City electrification included 17 units to replace life-expired Class 310s operating in the West Midlands and Manchester areas over routes electrified in the 1960s. A further build for the Leeds North West electrification fell foul of the Government's pre-privatisation freeze on new rolling stock orders. The final fleet totalled 43 units when a further three sets were ordered with 2+3 seating and extra luggage space for the opening of the Manchester Airport link in 1993. (Hunslet also developed a 'Sprinter' sister to the 323, the Class 157. Strathclyde placed a £36 million order for 21 two-car 157s in 1993; more were expected, but the 157 fell victim to the rolling stock freeze and the project was stillborn.)

## Electrics in the North West

The introduction of the Class 323s allowed the ageing Class 304/5 units to be withdrawn from local services into Manchester Piccadilly, although some were retained until 2000 to provide emergency cover for the new fleet. It also enabled 310s from Birmingham area services to be pensioned off.

## Chapter 12: CHOOSING THE TRAINS

**LEFT** A smart No 305511 stands in Manchester Piccadilly on 5 October 1993, wearing a GMPTE livery adapted from the Regional Railways standard. *Dennis Lovett*

**LEFT BELOW** Class 504 No M77177 arrives at Crumpsall forming the last BR service on 16 August 1991. This unit provided a shuttle between Bury and Crumpsall to allow the line to be converted for the new tram service. Note the new masts ready for Metrolink trams. *Antony Guppy*

for TransPennine Express services, Siemens Class 350s being provided in the short term for trains to Glasgow and Edinburgh. Otherwise history is repeating itself, Class 319s from the late 1980s being cascaded from the London area to Northern Rail as Thameslink gains brand new rolling stock. At four cars, these outer-suburban units will provide more seats, and political pressure is bringing steadily more of them to the North West than the handful originally promised. During a considerable refurbishment, they are having the door controls altered to rule out continued driver-only operation.

### Electric stock for Yorkshire

Regional Railways was desperate to maximize the number of services that could be covered by electric trains in order to reduce overcrowding on its DMU fleet. Doncaster-Leeds was covered after electrification of the main line in 1989 by use of Class 307 units made surplus by Network SouthEast. But South and West Yorkshire PTEs were opening more stations on the route and wanted increased frequency. Faster trains were needed to make this possible and West Yorkshire funded three four-car Class 321/9 units to operate an enhanced local service.

**BELOW** Former Great Eastern No 307105, in WYPTE livery having been transferred from London, stands at Doncaster before working the 15.41 Doncaster to Leeds service on 22 October 1990. *Graeme Phillips*

This still left equally aged two-car Class 504 units operating over a very non-standard 1,200V DC third-rail route from Manchester Victoria to Bury. The solution proved to be the ground-breaking agreement with Greater Manchester PTE to incorporate the Bury (and Altrincham) lines into what became Metrolink, as detailed in Chapter 7. This allowed the 26 Class 504s to be scrapped in 1991 without Provincial having to fund their replacement.

Manchester also had one of the first modern overhead electrifications in the country with the Woodhead line, where eight Class 506 units continued to operate local services from Piccadilly to Glossop and Hadfield after the closure to passenger traffic of the line onward to Sheffield in 1970. The original 1,500DC overhead electrification was converted to the new standard 25kV in 1984, enabling standard BR EMUs to be used.

With the wave of electrification from 2014 in the North West, new rolling stock has only been considered

*Chapter 12:* **CHOOSING THE TRAINS** **171**

## A reliable workhorse for Merseyrail

The Merseyrail third-rail DC fleet had been renewed by BR from 1978 with Class 507 and 508 units. These were derivatives of the larger fleet of Class 313, 314 and 315 units built by BREL at York; indeed, the 508s were originally ordered for London Waterloo suburban services as four-car sets and were sent north minus one carriage, which was inserted into later NSE formations. The new Provincial sector soon discovered that the number of units allocated to Merseyrail was well in excess of requirements and, even after the route to Chester had been electrified, 15 units were put into store until early privatisation initiatives transferred 12 south to Southern and a further three to Silverlink. The remaining fleet received a highly successful and popular refurbishment that has kept it in front-line service, but after nearly four decades the scope for new stock is now being canvassed (see Chapter 8).

## Electrics for Scotland

The Paisley to Ayr electrification scheme had been authorised prior to the creation of Provincial, and the 21 Class 318 units became the first electric trains to be delivered to Shields Road Depot in Glasgow in 1985. The design for these attractive 90mph three-car units was based on the Bedford-St Pancras outer-suburban Class 317 fleet, and they were to revolutionise travel on both the Ayr and Largs corridors.

The original Glasgow 'Blue Train' fleet proved to be the next challenge. It comprised the original Class 303 units built in 1959-61, supplemented in 1967 by the more advanced 311s. Both fleets were found to have extensive asbestos problems and the best financial solution proved to be the premature withdrawal of the 60 worst-affected units and the extensive refurbishment of the remaining 50 at BREL's Springburn works.

**TOP** No 321901, also in WYPTE livery, waits at Leeds as the 11.21 service to Doncaster on 21 June 1993. *Graeme Phillips*

**ABOVE** Possibly the best ever commuter train – No 333001 passes No 333016 at Frizinghall on 27 October 2012. *Antony Christie*

When the Leeds North West electrification scheme was authorised in 1994, provision was made for 17 Class 323s as an option in the submission for the Birmingham Cross-City fleet, but a 1,064-day ban on the ordering of any new trains intervened. A personal appeal by Gordon Pettitt to the Transport Minister, Roger Freeman, failed to gain any concession. So to ensure that the opening date for WYPTE's electrification was achieved, 21 more redundant Class 308s were secured from NSE.

It would be 2000 before new trains arrived, in the shape of 16 four-car Class 333 units built by Siemens to the same basic design as those already in service on Heathrow Express. The original order was for three-car trains, but the DTp was persuaded that demand was such that it should be increased to four cars – though in 2006 it did briefly attempt to claw back the extra carriages it had paid for despite the trains being packed. These units remain one of the best fleets in the country for commuter use.

**ABOVE** No 318250 stands at Hamilton Central on 1 August 1980. *Dennis Lovett*

**172** Chapter 12: **CHOOSING THE TRAINS**

**ABOVE LEFT AND RIGHT** The revolutionary Glasgow 'Blue Train' in 1961, complete with sliding doors and wrap-around windows; the passengers enjoyed a scenic view through the driving cab. Note that the driver is still wearing the traditional steam-age uniform. *BR Scotland*

**RIGHT** No 320312 is at Glasgow Central for the *Sir William A. Smith, Founder of the Boys' Brigade* naming ceremony on 27 October 2004, performed by Sir Alec Ferguson. *Dennis Lovett*

**CENTRE RIGHT** 'Juniper' No 334006 stands at Ayr in Strathclyde livery in August 2002. *Dennis Lovett*

**BOTTOM RIGHT** A quality post-privatisation EMU, No 380107 stands at Carstairs on 1 August 2012. *Dennis Lovett*

The gap left by the missing 'Blue Trains' was filled by an order for 22 Class 320 three-car units with a top speed of 100mph. These were procured at a favourable price on the back of a large Network SouthEast order from BREL York, and brought still higher standards to the Scottish electric fleet. The final 'Blue Trains' were to survive privatisation and were not withdrawn until 2002, supplanted by 40 Class 334 'Juniper' units ordered from Alstom.

The same degree of passenger comfort change experienced in West Yorkshire with the Class 333s has now been brought to Scotland with the delivery of the 23-metre 380s in both three- and four-car formations. These are based on the Siemens 350/360 'Desiro' family and offer the very latest commuting comfort with 2+2 seating, air-conditioning and an exceptionally smooth ride, bringing a new perspective on the 'North-South divide'.

However, the new franchise holder, Abellio, has selected Hitachi to provide stock for the Edinburgh-Glasgow electrification to replace some of Strathclyde's older trains – supported by seven Class 321s from the

### Table 12.5: Regional electric fleets post-privatisation

| Class | 333 (four-car) | 334 (three-car) | 350 (four-car) | 380 (three-car) | 380 (four-car) |
| --- | --- | --- | --- | --- | --- |
| No of units | 16 | 40 | 30 | 22 | 16 |
| Seats | 360 | 183 | 183 | 208 | 282 |
| Weight (tonnes) | 186 | 125 | 179 | 133 | 167 |
| Horsepower | 1,877 | 1,448 | 1,341 | 1,000 | 1,000 |
| Axle load (tons) | 11.65 | 10.41 | 11.18 | 11.08 | 10.47 |
| Speed (mph) | 100 | 90 | 100 | 100 | 100 |
| Body | Steel | Steel | Aluminium | Aluminium | Aluminium |
| Built by | Siemens/CAF | Alstom | Siemens | Siemens | Siemens |
| Built | 2000 | 1999-2002 | 2004-05 | 2009-11 | 2009-11 |

Source: Theo Steel and Colin Marsden

London area. The order is for 70 100mph EMUs formed into 46 three-car and 24 four-car trains. The AT 200 is a new 23-metre design fitted with cab-end gangways for multiple unit operation. It should enter service in 2017.

### Summary

The 30-odd years from 1982 to 2015 have seen Provincial's inheritance of run-down and thinly patronised train fleets transformed into one where demand often exceeds capacity – particularly in the North-West. It was not clear as recently as 2011 where the extra trains were going to come from to match this welcome growth. However, where Government saw little future for the rail industry 30 years ago, it has in more recent years approved and funded a major rolling electrification programme for the nation that will be of the greatest benefit to the regional networks as well as the inter-city spine.

As an example, the electrification of the Great Western main line and the Cardiff Valley lines will bring refurbished electric trains to both the Cardiff and the Bristol urban networks. The imaginative 'Northern Hub' electrification plans will bring extensive new electric services to an area where growth has been limited in the last decade by a lack of train capacity. And Scotland is seeing its flagship Glasgow-Edinburgh route electrified.

Even the quieter regional lines that are not destined to be electrified will benefit from the national rolling programme, with longer-life DMUs cascaded from newly electrified routes. And yes, the iconic HST, shortened and with yet further refurbishment, is to feature as the preferred train to cover the ScotRail inter-city network north of the Central Belt, until these routes too can be electrified.

Despite the extensive network of electrification now planned, new DMUs will be needed, some maybe for rural services where new solutions to reduce costs of operation are also necessary. The market for tram-train remains unclear at present, but this will become clearer following the Meadowhall-Parkgate pilot.

Looking to the future, electric rolling stock operators will be seeking higher acceleration rates to create more capacity, and lower weight to reduce fuel costs. As the costs of trains increase, higher availability will be ever more important, and this will be best done through competition in international markets; Chinese manufacturers have had their eye on possibilities in Britain for several years now.

The extension of the Great Western franchise and First's selection of Hitachi as preferred bidder to displace its HSTs from their final stamping ground on Devon and Cornwall services has thrown up intriguing possibilities. With stiff gradients, single-track sections and low line speeds at the western end of the route and electrification east of Bristol and Newbury, a truly versatile train is needed and Hitachi has come up with the AT300: a bimode IEP with extra large fuel tanks and uprated power units. The order about to be placed as we went to press was for seven 9-car and 22 five-car sets, the latter capable of being operated in pairs and split at Plymouth with a portion going forward into Cornwall. Because of the early delivery requirement (2018) they will almost certainly be built in Japan.

While the AT200 for ScotRail and the AT300 were conceived away from the public gaze, Hitachi had wider operation in mind and has kept other operators in the loop. The manufacturer sees Greater Anglia, with its need to replace loco-hauled trains between London and Norwich and for a new generation of outer suburban EMUs, as ideal territory for a 'mix and match' of both trains.

## Chapter 13
# THE WAY AHEAD

**ABOVE** The rebuilding of the Borders line at Stow in December 2014: the contractors were laying a mile of track a day at this time. *Dennis Lovett*

## Nothing is for ever

Most readers of investment and pension documents have at some time been unnerved by the warning, 'Please note that past performance is not a good guide to future performance'. This wisdom applies to all fields of human endeavour – not least to regional railways. Looking back to the start of the Regional Railways story in 1982, we have to accept that if Government had based its future investment decisions on the declining performance of the previous 20 years, we would most certainly not have the railway that we enjoy today.

Similarly, in looking ahead beyond 2015 we should recognise that neither the investment levels of recent years, nor the growth in passenger numbers can be taken for granted. The biggest change for regional railways in the last generation has been the change of ownership – yet this change was unforeseeable in 1982. It is a reminder that unexpected political decisions will continue to dominate in future years.

Indeed, these changes in ownership continue to take unexpected twists and turns. In 1992 Regional Railways was a business sector of the BR Board and responsible for all the infrastructure, trains, timetables and staff. From 1994 the track would be the responsibility of first Railtrack, then Network Rail as a not-for-dividend company. Then in September 2014 the same infrastructure was transferred back onto the Government's books. It seems that nothing lasts for ever.

Any review based on the track record of the past 30 years would take a very rosy view of the future. Table 1.4 shows that that the regional network has been a growth business in network size, trains run and passengers carried. But it would be foolhardy to extrapolate this golden age into the future without a more detailed analysis.

## Population

The forecast increase in Great Britain's population will be a key feature in the size of the rail market in the years ahead. The current population of 61 million is forecast to increase to 73 million by 2050 – an increase of 20%. But of equal significance for regional railways is that by then 89% of the population will be living in urban areas, compared to 82% today. A key challenge for the regional train operators will be to increase its market share from this growing urban population.

**RIGHT** While being preparing for electrification of the Manchester to Preston route, Chorley Tunnel and its approaches have had to be relaid and the flying arches restored ready to support the contact wires. *Network Rail*

## UK National Debt

Investment in the railways and money to make up the difference between cost and revenue – subsidy – has to be paid for by the Government and taxpayers in one form or another. A recent review by the Office for National Statistics suggests that the Government owes its creditors a total of £1.4 trillion. New accountancy rules have recently led to Network Rail being reclassified as part of central government, adding a further £33 billion to the nation's debt – a sum roughly equal to the GDP of Uruguay. At the time of writing, the National Debt is still increasing by around £90 billion per annum.

Very large investments are planned for rail, and most are now associated with supporting economic growth. It is not surprising, therefore, that most of these schemes are in support of large urban and interurban routes. Nevertheless, the state of the nation's finances will almost certainly involve a revision of current priorities, the lengthening of timescales and, in some cases, even the cancellation of projects.

## Devolution

Significant moves towards devolution of responsibility for railways – first to Scotland, then to Wales – turned out to be the start of a wider movement for change, and the future effect on regional railways is likely to be profound.

The first significant such move in England has coincided with the renewal of the Northern and TransPennine franchises. The DfT has made it very clear that it is 'working together with Rail North, a consortium of local authorities covering the north of England, with the aim of setting up an integrated partnership structure including both local and central government, which would be capable of managing its franchise contract once it has been let.'

# Chapter 13: THE WAY AHEAD

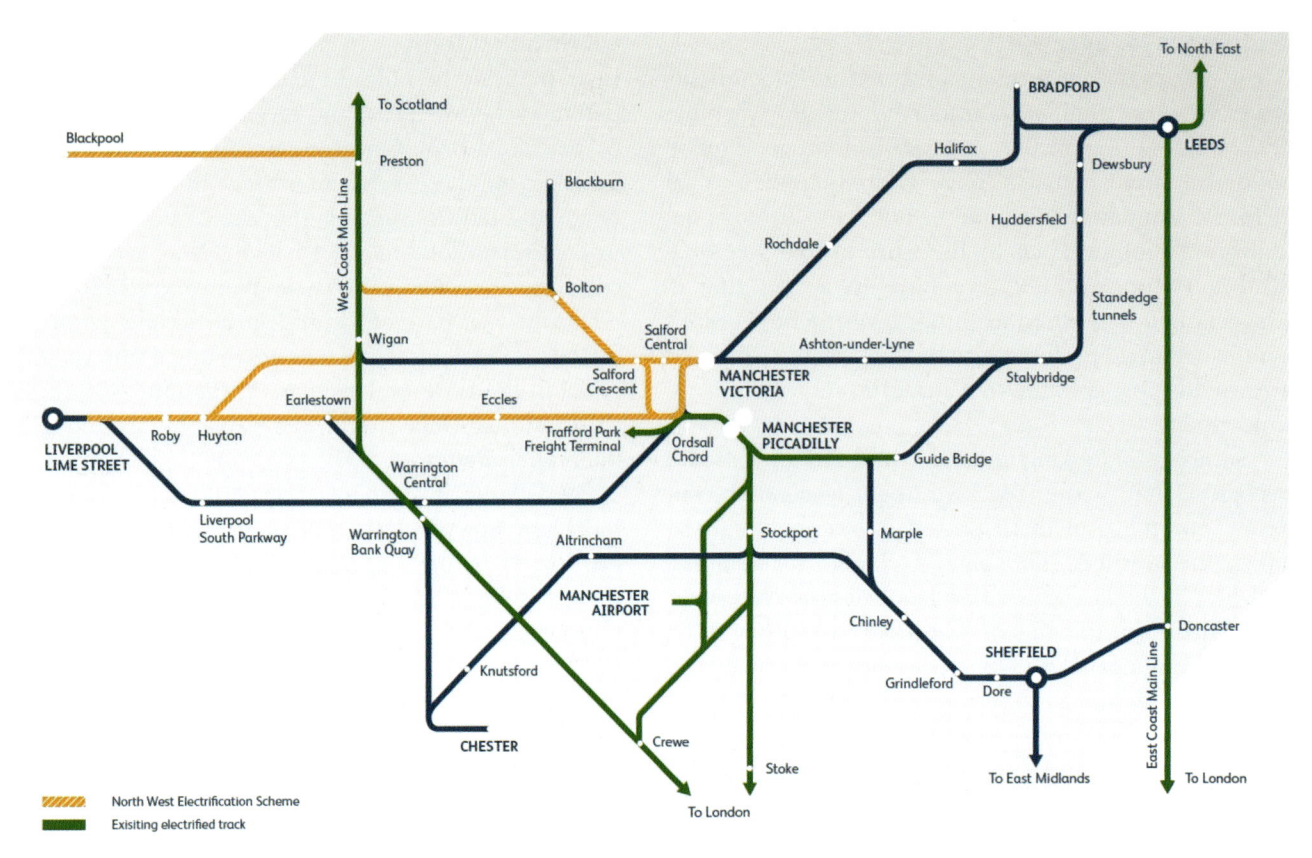

*ABOVE* A map of electrification work in the North West scheduled for completion between 2013 and 2018. *Network Rail*

## Rail North

Rail North's consortium of 33 local transport authorities stretches right across the territory to be served by Northern Rail and TPE. Rail North's 20-year strategy aims to encourage a higher market share for rail; more and faster trains; better travel-to-work opportunities; and more through services to London, Glasgow, Edinburgh and Birmingham – especially from centres in Lancashire. It also wants more peak capacity, better integrated services, newer rolling stock, greater reliability, improved ticketing, safer stations, fares more in line with buses, more cross-city services, and at least a nod towards higher productivity initiatives such as driver-only operation.

Every transport authority in the North backed Rail North's proposal to participate in the process. A Partnership of Principles was agreed between Rail North and the DfT for the renewal of both franchises, which would be 'collaboratively designed' with a single integrated structure to manage them. Under the partnership agreement, it is intended to give the local authorities a stronger role in determining future services and setting out a route to devolved decision-making.

Transport Secretary Patrick McLoughlin went to Manchester in January 2014 to sign the agreement, and its core objectives are set out in the next column. Rail North did not achieve its goal of outright devolution, but did secure a greater focus on multi-modal smart ticketing, replacement of 'Pacers', extra capacity and station

## Rail North

### DfT Statement of Objectives
- Having a platform for determining investment priorities within the partnership
- Risk and reward sharing between members of the partnership, including the potential for revenue or profit-sharing mechanisms that could allow re-investment into rail services
- A Partnership structure that allows the balance of risk to change over time
- Growing the railway to maximise the infrastructure investment and linking this to railway efficiencies

### DfT Statement of Structure
- These objectives imply that Rail North's members may contribute financially to projects, new services or rolling stock and that there will be a move over time to full or fuller devolved powers, once the baseline arrangement is seen to work as Rail North hopes it will
- Rail North's decision-making structures will be formalised, including a formal Leaders Committee. Rail North will also become a limited company with its own Board of Directors
- All this is to be achieved by May 2014, along with further refinement of Rail North's proposition. The integrated partnership will then assume direct responsibility for managing the franchises

Source: DfT

improvements. McLoughlin commented, 'I am determined to give local people a greater say in running their railways, and this will make sure that they are at the heart of the decisions.'

The DfT and Rail North published a substantial and detailed stakeholder and consultation document in June 2014. At the conclusion of the consultation the invitation to tender for both Northern and Trans Pennine were published in February 2015 (running to 201 and 193 pages respectively). It was clear from both documents that DfT and Rail North were looking for substantial change to services to reflect both the outcome of the consultation and national and local political policy in respect of the new Northern Power House and One North initiatives referred to again later.

The ITT formally sets out that whilst the franchise agreement is between the Franchisee and the Secretary of State, a 'Memorandum of Understanding' with Rail North is to be followed by a legally binding agreement setting out how the Dft and Rail North will work together to manage and develop both franchises. This new approach may turn out to be the first of many, enabling consortia of local authorities with a common economic interest to join together in the specification and subsequent development of a franchise. Such organisations should lead to greater devolution, although at present devolution of finance from central government is still an unresolved issue.

The franchise awards to Northern and Trans Pennine were to be made in June 2015, and it is only when they are that we can judge the full extent of the benefits of devolution and the partnership with Rail North. In the meantime it is significant that all bidders have been asked for more frequent and higher quality services, and in particular for a minimum of 120 new diesel vehicles to replace 'Pacers'.

## HS2

HS2 takes devolution and integration to new levels. In March 2014 Sir David Higgins, newly appointed Chief Executive of HS2, published his first report, titled 'HS2 Plus'. It included a number of proposals significant for the future of regional railways along its route, but particularly for urban and interurban railways in the North. Among these were:

- Government to accelerate Phase Two as soon as possible to take HS2 43 miles further north to a new transport hub at Crewe, which could be completed by 2027 – six years earlier than planned. This would bring together road and rail services for the whole region.

- More work to be done on integrating HS2 into the existing rail network together with potential improvements. HS2 should also be fully integrated into the plans that local authorities are making across the North to regenerate their particular economics and communities. It should revitalise the northern economy as a whole.
- Links to be improved in the north, both between regions and to other major hub cities such as London and Glasgow. Within the north, connectivity is especially slow between Liverpool and Manchester, and between Manchester and Leeds/Hull. The same is true between Leeds and Birmingham and Manchester and Birmingham.

The £600 million incremental schemes of the 'Northern Hub' are designed to improve this connectivity, but HS2 brings the opportunity to do so much more.

Sir David clearly believes that the transformative power of HS2 on the region has been underestimated and wants it to be considered as part of the wider transport network.

## The 'Northern Power House'

Just three months after the announcement of HS2 Plus, the Chancellor of the Exchequer, George Osborne, announced that he wanted to see a 'Northern Power House' formed of a collection of northern cities sufficiently close to each other that 'combined, they can take on the world'. He declared, 'Today the transport network in the north is simply not fit for purpose – and certainly not good enough. I want our cities to pool their strengths ... so step one in building this Northern Power House is a radical transport plan to make travelling between northern cities feel like travelling within one big city.'

It was from this speech that the proposal for a new fast rail link between Manchester and Leeds emerged – dubbed 'High Speed 3' by the media, but in reality a series of sections of new alignment.

## 'One North'

Just one month after the Chancellor's speech, a document titled 'One North – a proposition for an Interconnected North' was jointly published by the leaders of Leeds, Manchester, Newcastle and Sheffield city councils and the Mayor of Liverpool. The importance of this document cannot be overstressed, as it was 'a new Transport Plan developed by the key Northern cities for presentation to the Chancellor of the Exchequer and the Chairman of HS2 in response to the "Northern Power House" speech and the HS2 Plus report.'

## 'One North'

**By 2019**
- Electrification of Liverpool-Manchester-Leeds-Hull and Middlesbrough, and new rolling stock
- Midland Main Line electrification
- Complete all national pipeline strategic highway schemes

**By 2024**
- Further electrification to Scarborough, Calder Valley and Hope Valley/South TransPennine routes, together with new electric fleets and more rolling stock across the North
- 40-minute journey times between Leeds and Manchester, and improved services from Manchester to Sheffield
- Managed motorways complete across the M62/M56/M60 network and north-south on M1, M6 and M61
- Network gaps from the North East to South Yorkshire and northwards towards Scotland closed
- Rail/light rail connection to Leeds Bradford Airport

**By 2026**
- With HS2 reaching Crewe in 2026, provide additional capacity for onward links to Newcastle, Manchester, Liverpool (east-west), Manchester, Sheffield, Bradford (north-south link such as a tram-train or similar) using good-quality rolling stock

**By 2030**
- New tunnelled 125mph trans-Pennine route
- To the west, direct connectivity with Manchester Airport, Liverpool and Manchester
- To the east, connectivity with Sheffield, Leeds, Newcastle and Hull
- Recast HS2 in Yorkshire – bring forward Leeds-Sheffield section with new trans-Pennine route
- Integrate HS2 into existing Leeds station
- In Sheffield City Region create connectivity with an HS2 station with east-west capability

Source: 'One North – a proposition for an Interconnected North'

The original 'Rail North' was a partnership of local authorities with a specific interest in rail services provided by the Northern and TransPennine franchises. The new 'One North' had a much wider objective that it planned to implement over a wider area and with a longer timescale. A summary of the shopping list is shown above; it includes both rail and road schemes in a single document.

In March 2015 the DfT, HS2 and Highways England jointly published 'The Northern Power House: One Agenda, One Economy, One North'. The stated strategy is 'about using transport to aid change in the pattern of land use and economic growth with the goal of creating a single economy in the north. Rather than forecasting the future from current trends, we aim to change that future.'

Fine words, and not those we are used to hearing. But they did come from a joint body with a foreword from the Secretary of State for Transport after a year of political pressure for 'The Northern Power House' from a Conservative Chancellor – but, importantly, also supported by Labour locally. Clearly devolution from Westminster is on the move. And the railways of the North, starved of capital improvements for so long, are in a stronger position than ever to benefit.

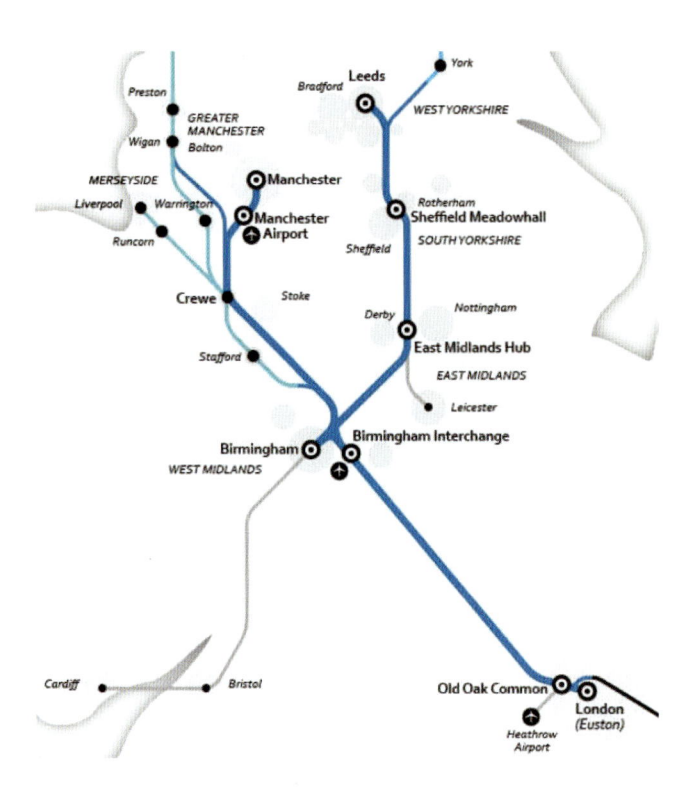

**ABOVE** The proposed HS2 network as at January 2015. *HS2Ltd*

## Rebalancing Britain

The message is now clearly about rebalancing Britain by transforming the HS2 spine railway into a wider national transport strategy. Sir David Higgins was back in Leeds with a new report on 27 October 2014, and with the Prime Minister, Chancellor of the Exchequer and the Secretary of State for Transport present. He had a number of key messages for this high-level audience:

- As with motorways, the critical issue today is that HS2 should fit into a wider transport strategy within which central and local government can develop detailed plans for the future.
- Rather than having to develop a series of business cases for individual projects in contrived isolation from the bigger picture, the strategy would be informed by clear data on how transport investment between towns and regions can release untapped economic potential and relieve congestion.
- The Manchester-Leeds-Sheffield triangle is central to the Northern Power House economy,

and the lack of high-performance road and rail links between Manchester and Sheffield should be a matter of national concern.
- Reducing Leeds-Manchester journey times is the first step in what should be a clear strategy to address poor connectivity across the North from Liverpool to Hull, as well as to Sheffield and Newcastle (as demonstrated below).
- HS2 and proposals for the new west-east line across the Pennines require a rethink to secure a combined station at Leeds and for the wider connectivity package to provide good access to the HS2 network for Bradford with its population of 500,000.
- A new organisation 'Transport for the North' representing the City Regions across the north – including Liverpool, Manchester, Leeds, Sheffield and Newcastle – should be set up.

This concentrated level of activity by national and regional leaders, together with the management of HS2, is impressive and almost unprecedented. While it is quite clear that the political focus has moved from London following the large Thameslink and Crossrail projects, it remains to be seen to what extent the current preoccupation with the 'Northern Power House' and related projects will develop into firm and funded projects under the Government elected in May 2015.

In support of the plans for a 'Northern Power House' and to maximise the economic potential of the North referred to earlier, the Chancellor announced in November 2014 that Greater Manchester is to get its own directly elected conurbation-wide Mayor with powers over transport, housing, planning and policy. Specifically, the Mayor will be responsible – as in London – for a 'devolved and consolidated transport budget', with a multi-million settlement to be agreed at the annual Spending Review. The Mayor will also be responsible for franchising bus services subject to consultation with Greater Manchester, and for integrating smart ticketing across all local transport modes.

## West Midlands Rail

Another devolution proposal has emerged from West Midlands Rail, which represents the region's metropolitan, shire and unitary authorities. It plans to gain greater influence and control over local rail services from 2017 when the current London Midland franchise is re-let. WMR proposed a remapping of the existing franchise, with itself taking responsibility for local rail services in an area bounded by Northampton, Hereford, Shrewsbury, Rugeley and Nuneaton, as shown in Table 13.2.

West Midlands Rail is keen to create a small West Midlands franchise out of the overstretched London Midland franchise (excluding its Euston-Northampton and Birmingham-Liverpool services), which could be awarded to run initially from September 2015 to June 2017 as a prelude for its more ambitious proposals. (Some Chiltern services might also be included.)

The final outcome of the discussions on devolution for both Rail North and West Midlands Rail at the time of writing is uncertain. The amount of central government funding involved is substantial and there must be some doubt as to how responsibility for this scale of funding could be transferred to local authorities while insulating the Treasury from excessive expenditure; Patrick McLoughlin was quick to warn West Midlands Rail that devolution would not mean more money.

Table 13.1: Trans-Pennine journey time improvements

| Route | Current (hr-min) | With new route (hr-min) |
|---|---|---|
| Liverpool-Leeds | 1-28 | 1-00 |
| Leeds-Manchester | 0-49 | >0-34 |
| Manchester-Hull | 1-51 | >1-30 |
| Manchester-York | 1-14 | >1-00 |
| Manchester-Newcastle | 2-22 | >2-00 |

Source: HS2 Rebalancing Britain, October 2014

Table 13.2: West Midlands Rail – proposed membership

| City Councils | Metropolitan Boroughs | Shire County Councils |
|---|---|---|
| Birmingham | Dudley | Hereford |
| Coventry | Sandwell | Northamptonshire |
| Wolverhampton | Solihull | Shropshire |
| | Walsall | Staffordshire |
| | Telford & Wrekin | Warwickshire |
| | West Midlands Integrated Transport Authority | Worcestershire |

Source: DfT

**Chapter 13: THE WAY AHEAD**

**RIGHT** The shape of the future is shown in computer images of Hitachi's new AT200 commuter train for Abellio ScotRail. *Hitachi*

## ScotRail

The ten-year contract worth £6 billion awarded to the Dutch state rail operator Abellio to operate Scotrail services from April 2015 is the biggest single contract awarded by the Scottish Government. Central to the franchise award is the completion of four major investment schemes by Network Rail amounting to more than £1 billion, namely:

- The Edinburgh-Glasgow electrification project (EGIP) resulting in four trains an hour offering a journey of just 42 minutes by 2016 – an acceleration of 8 minutes. Other services on this route to benefit from accelerations to provide paths for the fast services.
- Rebuilding Glasgow Queen Street station to give greater capacity for trains of up to eight coaches by 2019.
- Reinstatement of the 30-mile Borders Line from Newcraighall (Edinburgh) to Tweedbank, due to reopen in 2015.
- The £170 million upgrade of the Aberdeen-Inverness line by 2019.

The outcome of a long consultation period was reflected in the invitation to tender, from which it was clear to bidders that high standards of operation were called for. In particular, they were asked to start from a base where all the existing rolling stock leases were terminated – with the exception of the contractually committed Class 380 electric fleet. Fleet specifications were very detailed and required bidders to take into account the public preference for more space for luggage and cycles, toilets, catering and WiFi. Furthermore, trains on the West Highland and Kyle of Lochalsh lines should include 'Premier' coaches suited to encourage tourism.

Abellio's bid covered all these requirements and was certainly innovative – particularly in respect of the re-use of the iconic HST for the 'Scottish InterCity routes' from Edinburgh/Glasgow to Aberdeen/Inverness – together with the upgraded Aberdeen-Inverness corridor. While the HSTs were built in 1975-82, interim refurbishments over the years have created a range of options to suit customer requirements. It is likely that these HSTs, which had new MTU engines fitted from 2006, will be cascaded from the front line Great Western fleet upon electrification, after a further refurbishment to suit their new market.

The use of HSTs – albeit in four/five-car formations – should revolutionise long-distance travel in Scotland, with their quality interiors, greater frequencies and shorter journey times.

Devolution has already delivered significant improvements for railway passengers in Scotland, but the changes already financed will bring about another step change and offer one of the best services in the UK.

## Wales

South Wales is to see a major enhancement of services on the route from the Severn Tunnel to Swansea, which is to be electrified by 2019 when the HSTs to London are to be replaced by a fleet of new Hitachi-built high-speed electric bimode trains. These trains will be serviced at a new depot in Swansea and will provide a much-needed improvement in journey times within, to and from Wales. But the electrification will open up opportunities to introduce electric trains on services to and from Bristol, as well as for local services between Newport and Swansea. The original plan was to electrify only as far as Cardiff, but pressure from the Welsh Government and the local community resulted in a change of mind in favour of Swansea.

Another dispute between the Welsh Assembly Government and Westminster arose over who would pay for the planned Valley Lines electrification. This was finally resolved with Westminster taking over sponsorship and funding the Cardiff-Bridgend section of the main-line electrification to Swansea – worth £105 million. Westminster also contributed £125 million towards the cost of the Valley Lines electrification. The Cardiff Bay-based Government took on sponsorship and delivery for the remainder of the Valley Lines at an estimated £170 million – though this costing is likely to prove optimistic.

A 2013 Impact Study identified the need for a long-overdue Cardiff Metro network, which could include a wide range of transport improvements from heavy rail to trams and tram-trains. This initiative is likely to be stimulated by the arrival of the main line and Valley electrification schemes, which will raise the issue of how to disperse the additional passengers from Cardiff's rather poorly situated stations around the city centre.

The Swansea-Severn Tunnel electrification provides the foundation stone in South Wales, but a balancing investment may emerge in North Wales. This could take the shape of a continuation of the trans-Pennine electrification from Manchester to Holyhead – with a link from Chester to Crewe. This would have the strategic advantage of locking North Wales into the national HS2 network at both Manchester and Crewe. However, Network Rail's initial costing of £764 million in 2015 was coupled with the assessment that line speed improvements offered far better value than electrification.

Mid-Wales aspires to an hourly 90mph service from Aberystwyth to Shrewsbury – and on to Birmingham, where it too will feed into the HS2 network at both Birmingham Curzon Street and Birmingham International Airport. The key issue then will be to lock North, Mid and South Wales together with a high-quality interurban route linking Bangor with Chester, Wrexham, Shrewsbury and Cardiff and making hub connections to England. The embryonic services exist, but they deserve to expand into at least a 2-hourly service across the Principality.

This leaves the Central Wales line, which must represent the ultimate rural route challenge in the country. One solution might be to recognise its primary role in opening up tourism in this beautiful area and turn it into a microfranchise – effectively a Swiss-style private railway – which would be encouraged to develop innovative solutions for its infrastructure, trains and marketing in return for a regional subsidy. There is plenty of scope for creative management in both urban and rural Wales.

**LEFT** An artist's impression of the new Glasgow Queen Street.
*Network Rail*

LEFT Regional services in the Bristol area and elsewhere will benefit from the main line deployment of the new Inter City Express (IEP) train being built in the UK by Hitachi. *Hitachi*

## West of England

The Great Western route to Exeter and beyond is currently undergoing a massive upgrade, with electrification and resignalling between Paddington and Bristol. Regional railways will see a direct benefit in the Bristol area where an intensive service of modern IEP inter-city services will generate new travel opportunities for their feeder services. Local authorities envisage a 'Bristol Metro' network that will provide cross-city transport from a reopened Portishead branch via Temple Meads to Bath, and from Bristol Parkway across the city to Weston-super-Mare. Further west, Exeter is likely to follow Bristol with its own Metro providing significantly upgraded services on both the Exmouth-Paignton and Axminster-Barnstaple axes. Both Bristol and Exeter have some of the most overcrowded commuter services in the country, and additional rolling stock will be needed – probably Class 165 DMUs cascaded from Paddington outer suburban services – before either expansion programme can progress.

Services to and within Devon and Cornwall should also benefit from First Great Western's announcement following the four-year extension of its franchise to 2019 that it had appointed Hitachi as preferred supplier of a new fleet of AT300 bimode main line trains to replace the 40-year-old HSTs. These have provided not only the long distance trains but the spine of the regional network within Devon and Cornwall, Regional Railways' Class 158s having given way to less frequent 'Pacers' and 'Sprinters'. There is every likelihood that the service on that spine will be enhanced to twice hourly, an AT300 to or from Paddington stopping only at major centres and a 165 providing an all-stations service between Plymouth and Penzance. Both would share an upgraded sleeper maintenance facility at Penzance.

Inter-city services west of Plymouth are already an integral part of the timetable, and the secret lies in maintaining the balance with local services. This further move to amalgamate service provision across adjacent counties is a welcome step, but the low line speeds west of Exeter also need to be addressed. In the meantime new stock with better acceleration will be the answer.

Chancellor George Osborne just before the May 2015 election urged councils in the far South West, who had already created a Peninsula Rail Task Force, to build the case for improvements to the route, to form a Rail South West organisation similar to Rail North. This, he said, could 'play a part in the design and management of a new local rail franchise, so we have decisions on local transport taken by those who know what is right for the South West'.

There is much to be said for a separate Devon and Cornwall franchise, covering all but the Paddington services, provided the service on the main line remains co-ordinated. The counties' branch lines are classic rural routes, most of them providing short but effective feeder services into the main line, and it is vital that robust connections are maintained. Costs will always be a key issue, and, while congestion-busting routes such as St Ives and Falmouth obviously justify their futures, there must be some challenge to the all-year need for the slow and rambling branch to Newquay – unless it can be rerouted. However, the possibility of a new park-and-ride station by the Moorswater cement terminal could give a greater purpose to the Looe line.

The strategic hot potato is whether to reinstate the route between Exeter and Plymouth via Okehampton and Tavistock to provide a resilient alternative to the coastal line through Dawlish, severed with disastrous consequences in 2014. Another option is to construct a diversion to the section of line through Dawlish that would be immune to depredations from the sea and not be seen by councils in south Devon as a threat to the long-term future of the existing route.

There are already sporadic summer weekend trains between Exeter and Okehampton (pop. 6,000), and at the other end of this route plans are well advanced to reinstate the 6½ miles of track between Bere Alston and Tavistock (pop. 11,000) to provide a commuter service into Plymouth; a Section 106 planning agreement requires the developer of 750 new homes at Tavistock to contribute £13.2 million toward reinstatement of the line. This leaves a gap of 16 miles, which would be costly to reinstate not least because the iconic Meldon Viaduct is said to be beyond economic restoration.

The economics of reinstating the Okehampton-Tavistock line for what would be a heavily lossmaking social railway except when needed as a diversionary route are not attractive, but neither are those of boring a tunnel to bypass Dawlish. The final decision will be political as much as economic.

### East Anglia

East Anglia already has two electric spine routes through its area – the London to Norwich main line and the London to Cambridge/King's Lynn route. An area for growth remains at Stansted Airport, for which a more intensive interurban service is planned to Cambridge and Peterborough. The missing link is an electric route from Ipswich/Norwich to Cambridge and the East Midlands. This could emerge as a DfT investment in freight services from Felixstowe to the Midlands to divert them away from the congested London area. If this happened, electric interurban services could improve connectivity along a route that suffers from severe road congestion. London services could also be extended to Bury St Edmunds from both Cambridge and Ipswich with electrification in this fast-growing area.

Beyond that, East Anglia faces the classic regional problem of how to keep local diesel services running at minimum subsidy. Norfolk and Suffolk both face varying levels of challenge in a sparsely populated area with good alternative bus services. The future does not necessarily lie in joining these services up into even longer trans-Britain safaris. They may offer customers better value if they provide more frequent shuttle services that connect with their nearest main line.

The proposed east-west rail corridor from Oxford to Bletchley and Bedford is a big idea whose time has finally come. Reinstatement of the route to Bedford in 2020 will provide a strategic link between the Great Western, Midland and West Coast main lines – with the option to continue further to link to the East Coast and Anglia networks. This will provide a superb opportunity to connect fast-growing high-economic-value regional communities with fast interurban services, and has been the focus of strong local government support along the route.

### The Network Operating Strategy

The emerging Operating Strategy for Network Rail is the equivalent of the 1950s Modernisation Plan in size and ambition. The whole of the network infrastructure is affected, together with all the trains that run over it. But it should be remembered that a lasting criticism of the 1950s Modernisation Plan was that a large part of the money was spent before deciding what infrastructure was actually needed for the future.

## Proposed New Passenger Services on East West Rail Western Section

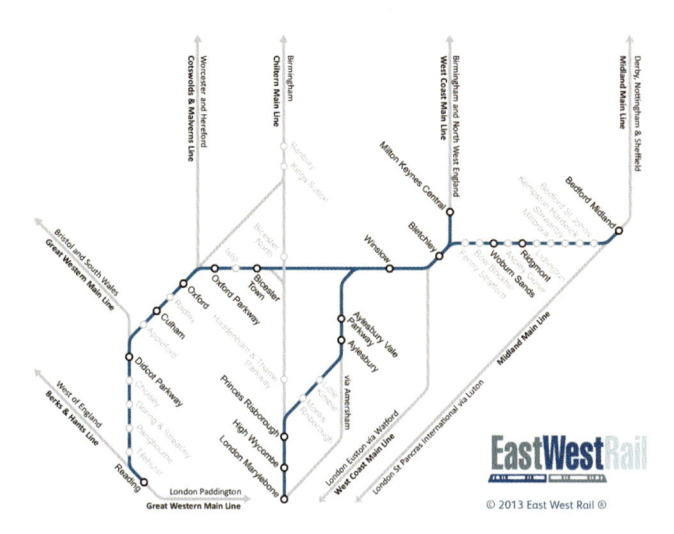

**ABOVE** Map of the proposed east-west rail corridor. *EastWestRail*

To avoid similar criticism, it now seems essential that the shape and size of the lower-cost regional railway identified in the 2011 McNulty Report is identified quickly so that abortive costs of removing infrastructure, signalling and conversion of trains is avoided.

It is clear that there is a large variation in the type of railway that would be included in a study of the 'lower cost regional railway' – from short branches to the long-distance rural and secondary main lines discussed in Chapter 10. The application of national standards to such lines needs urgent review, and there is some evidence that this is being done. The Government's decision early in 2015 to fund the development of Very Light Rail (see Chapter 7) could

**Table 13.3: Subsidy per passenger kilometre at 2012/13 prices**

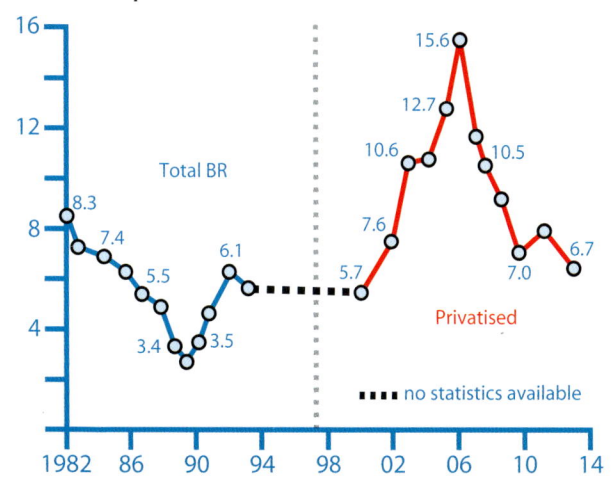

Source: Roger Ford and *Modern Railways*

### Table 13.4: Net cost of Government support by business sector

|  | Passenger km | Net cost to Government | Net cost per passenger km | Net cost to Government |
|---|---|---|---|---|
| Long-distance franchises | 9.4bn (30%) | £693m | 7.3p (17%) | 25% |
| London & South East | 15.7bn (51%) | £760m | 4.8p (11%) | 19% |
| Regional | 6.0bn (19%) | £1,873m | 31.1p (72%) | 61% |
| TOTAL | 31.0bn (100%) | | | |

Source: DfT McNulty Report, May 2011

have important repercussions for some of the shorter rural lines where present cost levels are hard to justify.

There is also the question of whether some of these railways would best be operated as devolved mini-franchises where local managers could develop new initiatives in operations, engineering and timetabling. It will be remembered from earlier chapters how savings and improved revenues were made by unleashing the power of local managers; it is time to do so again.

## The gathering clouds

So, the future looks good for the national network, with devolution of decision-making, more investment, more electrification, more opportunities for faster trains and more frequent services. What could possibly go wrong?

Some darker clouds are gathering in an otherwise clear sky. These dark clouds all have large £ signs attached to them and relate to both infrastructure and trains – particularly on routes where passenger numbers are low. Table 13.3 demonstrates how the subsidy per passenger on the national network remains stubbornly high despite the increase in passenger numbers. The 2011 McNulty Report concluded that the costs of the rail network were still 30% higher than might be expected, and drew special attention to the level of Government support for the regional railway. It included a specific section drawing attention to the worrying cost base for regional services. McNulty found that, compared to the other sectors, regional franchises 'convey lower passenger volumes, have lower fares and low overall revenues in proportion to their cost base'. Table 13.4 shows regional services catering for 19% of the passenger miles, but taking 61% of Government funding to provide them.

In the case of infrastructure, there are now many hundreds of miles that will require expensive track renewals and resignalling – and decisions should be made on the long-term role of each route before major expenditure is committed. For example, track renewals are unavoidably expensive when they have to be made. Commentators have criticised the way lines such as the Whitby, Windermere and Skegness branches have been relaid with deep ballast and continuous welded rail in recent times. The truth is that this is the most economical method now that bullhead rail is no longer available and flat bottom rail needs deeper layers of ballast to hold the track in place.

The effects of weather and increased traffic are starting to affect the stability of our 150-year-old cuttings and embankments. This, together with bridge renewals and level crossing removals, will have an increasing impact on budgets and access charges. Network Rail intends to implement its Network Operating Strategy – a policy of concentrating the signalling of all lines in Britain on 12 regional operating centres (ROCs) over the next ten years, which will close more than 600 smaller signal boxes. It will then introduce the European Traffic Management System (ERTMS) across the system, having already trialled it on the Cambrian line since 2011. This will increase capacity on main-line routes and increase flexibility in the way they are operated. But its impact will be seen fastest on regional railway routes because of the need to drive down operating expenditure on lines with the largest numbers of signal boxes, so routes like the Tyne Valley and Glasgow-Kilmarnock-Carlisle are a priority. The aim is to accelerate investment to get the maximum benefit in savings, but it remains to be seen whether the conversion of the entire national network can be justified.

## Final thoughts

The long list of new investment schemes in this chapter goes far beyond the wildest dreams of those who started to revive the regional railways in 1982, or even those who took over that challenge at privatisation. While this is immensely encouraging, there are worrying signs that the electrification schemes now under way – in particular – will not be finished as speedily, or at anything like the cost, as the Government has been led to expect.

Government, local authorities and others have shown great confidence in the railway by providing record levels of funding needed for these investments. To maintain this confidence two things matter: schemes have to be delivered on time and on budget, and forecast levels of use have to be achieved or exceeded.

**ABOVE** Many routes were established by Regional Railways managers in the 1990s and have become established success stories, whoever runs them. Recently rebranded from Central Trains to Arriva CrossCountry as the franchise was changed, No 170107 is seen at speed between Lydney and Gloucester forming the 09.45 Cardiff to Nottingham service on 3 September 2010. *Martin Loader*

# Postscript: The Settle & Carlisle line

## Proposed for closure

The Settle & Carlisle line feels interurban, but serves a very sparse population. In 1980 BR proposed closing it in return for investment in the Cumbrian Coast line as a diversionary route for the WCML. It lost its Nottingham-Sheffield-Leeds-Glasgow through trains in 1982, and Provincial inherited a railway with just two surviving stations (Settle and Appleby). But there had since 1975 been 'Dalesrail' charter trains, with some stations reopened for walkers. And in 1981 the Friends of the Settle & Carlisle Line was formed.

Despite the ministerial letters encouraging BR to maintain the network at its current size and the row over the Serpell Report, Jim O'Brien, General Manager of the LMR, in December 1983 had the S&C – and its connection from Blackburn to Hellifield – advertised for closure. Cyril Bleasdale, a later GM, says the Board were 'pretty cross', but to John Welsby the S&C 'appeared to be redundant. It played neither a significant Provincial role, nor an InterCity one. There was minor freight traffic, but that could be accommodated elsewhere.' Presented with an estimate of £6-7 million for urgent repairs to the majestic Ribblehead Viaduct, Welsby could see 'no justification for spending this level of taxpayers' money'. John Prideaux, head of BR's policy unit, termed the line a '73-mile museum', and Transport Secretary Nicholas Ridley reckoned that 'all the users of the line could be accommodated in a decent-sized minibus'.

## Interim maintenance issues

BR approved limited repairs to keep the line open during the closure process, and uniquely promised to retain it for five years. The LMR appointed Ron Cotton as project manager to implement the closure, but maximise any potential in the interim. More trains were run. Steam excursions were encouraged. Fares were cut. InterCity retimed its first train to Leeds to give passengers a chance of a day on the S&C. A 'Rail Aid' promotion was run, BR contributing £5 to Live Aid for every ticket sold (Bob Reid and Nick Ridley were confronted with the posters at Carlisle, but made no comment). Local councils in 1986 funded the return of the 'Dalesrail' stations to the timetable under the Speller Act, and the Friends – who collected objections to closure on the trains – invited members to adopt a station.

When at the Class 156 launch a journalist asked Sidney Newey, 'Why are you bothering with new trains when the Ministry wants bus substitution?' he replied, 'I will believe in bus substitution when the DoT agrees to closure of the Settle & Carlisle.' Bob Reid was furious. 'He sent me on a public speaking course to "learn to keep my mouth shut",' Newey recalls. But he adds, 'Keeping the S&C prevented us spending the money on something else. Nobody wanted to close it, but it was needs must.'

Provincial inherited costly-to-operate locomotive-hauled trains and steam specials that 'knocked hell out of the track'. Alex Green, then Area Manager at Carlisle, recalls the track as 'truly shocking', with the area civil engineer 'forbidden to touch it'. When Green accompanied him on a post-appointment saloon inspection tour, the young engineer attacked randomly selected sleepers with an ice axe and they all fell to dust. Showing the autonomy and enterprise present in the delegated BR lines of command, hundreds of new sleepers were put in under rail joints the very next weekend – without any reference upwards. The LMR S&T Department tried to have the line closed on safety grounds when the frame at Hellifield signal box developed cracks; Cyril Bleasdale ordered them to find a simpler replacement.

InterCity said it could manage without the S&C, and Freight claimed no long-term interest if that meant contributing to its maintenance – leaving Provincial 'prime user' under BR's new accounting regime. DMUs were the solution, but the Class 108s available could not keep time over the S&C's gradients, the new 'Pacers' were not suitable, and no justification could be made under Provincial's rolling stock bidding process for the S&C receiving 'Sprinters'. Yet eventually they were cascaded onto the route, lowering its maintenance costs. 'Part of the S&C we managed up, to remove speed restrictions,' says David Wharton-Street. 'Others were managed down. Getting down to a 12-tonne axle weight was critical.'

## Closure procedure

The closure was re-advertised after BR had inadvertently left out the Blackburn line and failed to involve the North East TUCC, into whose territory a small section fell. The Friends, the Railway Development Society and Transport 2000 formed a Joint Action Committee to save the line. After hearings at Appleby, Carlisle, Settle, Skipton and Leeds in March/April 1986, both the North West and Yorkshire TUCCs recommended against closure on grounds of hardship.

LEFT *A copy of the original – but flawed – closure notice as issued by the London Midland Region. David Wharton-Street*

BR estimated that closure would save between £156,000 and £956,000 a year on operation, while retention would involve heavy capital spending, mostly on Ribblehead Viaduct. The damage done to Ribblehead's limestone blocks, especially facing the prevailing westerly wind, by repeated freezing and thawing, water seeping through the trackbed, became the critical issue. The main problem was that each stone pillar was hollow in the centre where the wooden crane stems had been left in situ when the viaduct was completed. Over a century the timbers had rotted, allowing moisture to accumulate, then freeze in winter, expanding the pillars from the inside outwards and splitting the mortar joints further. Each column was bound with steel bands to stop it bursting open. In 1985 the track over the viaduct was singled to reduce pressures on it.

## Transfer to Eastern Region

During 1986 the S&C was transferred to the Eastern Region. 'The decision was taken by Provincial,' says Cyril Bleasdale. 'John Edmonds thought it was the logical thing and it seemed to me very sensible.' David Wharton-Street says, 'The S&C wasn't anywhere near the top of the list of lines you would close. But I was left in no doubt by John Edmonds that there should be no delay.' Wharton-Street gave Mark Causebrook the line to manage and told David Prescott to 'create a strategic plan for positive marketing of the S&C, to run in parallel with the closure process.' This he did in liaison with Cumbria County Council and the Friends.

Meanwhile Wharton-Street called on Lord Whitelaw, Deputy Prime Minister and formerly MP for the line's northern section. Whitelaw reckoned that with BR investing in the WCML and ECML, it was difficult to justify a lightly used third route. But when the line was saved, Whitelaw's intervention at the highest level was suspected.

Fare-cutting and higher costs from reopened stations that in 1989 took just £21,569 widened the losses. Yet passenger numbers rose, according to BR, from 93,000 in 1983 to 450,000 in 1989. David Prescott explains: 'The LMR had not put the APTIS ticketing system into Settle and Appleby, so takings were still allocated to services by percentages settled when the "Thames-Clyde Express" still ran, leaving only 40% to Leeds-Settle-Carlisle. I refused to certify the figures, APTIS was installed, and revenue and passenger numbers rose sharply. The data caught up with the facts.'

David Mitchell – who had told Bleasdale, 'The problem is how can I close the S&C and leave open the line between Inverness and Wick?' – announced in March 1988 that he was 'minded to consent to closure'. With 32,000 objections lodged, BR decided to run the process again, with further hearings at Appleby and Settle that September. Weeks later, Bob Reid restated that 'the line is no longer required by us'.

## Early privatisation proposals

John Welsby was now a Board member, and part of his remit was 'encouraging businesses to invest private capital in the railway'. He sold the Vale of Rheidol line as a going concern, and this struck him as a possible solution for the S&C: a golden opportunity for preservationists and supporters of the line to run a railway with tourist potential. Welsby secured a six-month deferral of the decision on closure. 'I thought that, provided a sufficient number of societies were prepared to cooperate together, privatisation of the S&C could be a practicable proposition. We might

**ABOVE** The ceremonial signing of the contract for repairs to Ribblehead Viaduct, with David Wharton-Street signing on behalf of Regional Railways. *David Wharton-Street*

**LEFT** A copy of the 'Information to interested parties'. *Alex Green*

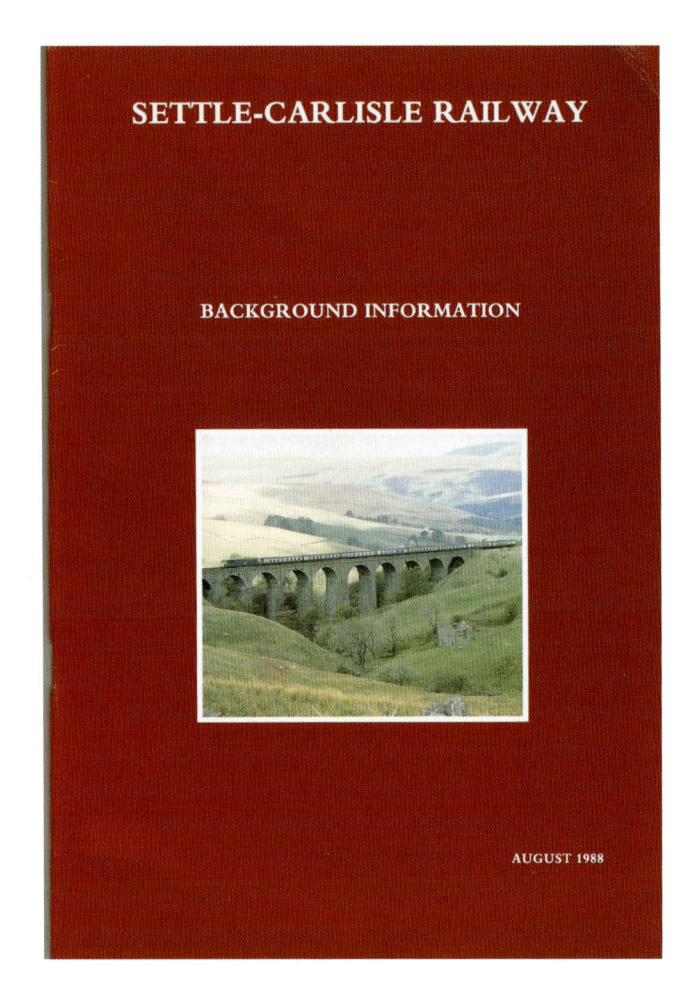

have been prepared to contribute a one-off payment towards its infrastructure costs and accept a negative sales price. Lazards were appointed to try and achieve a sale – but there was no interest worth mentioning.'

Meanwhile the Settle & Carlisle Railway Development Company was formed, backed by the Friends, the Rural Development Commission and the English Tourist Board. Twelve prospective purchasers came forward, two rated serious; a preferred bidder was named – Cumbrian Railways – and negotiations reached an advanced stage despite only a Hellifield-Carlisle service being proposed … and with disruptive interventions from West Yorkshire PTE.

### Portillo seeks compromise

Michael Portillo now arrived at the Department, convincing Wharton-Street that he was 'determined to find solutions'. He asked if Ribblehead Viaduct was listed; Wharton-Street told him it 'had not been considered worthy of listing'. Portillo recalled in 2014, 'The Government was asking BR to make savings so that it would require less subsidy, so why were we interested in saving the line? I think the Government, right up to and including Margaret Thatcher, had two contrasting points of view. We wanted more efficiency, but we also valued national heritage.'

A saloon trip studying the route's notable structures and stations was organised by Sir William McAlpine, chairman of the Railway Heritage Trust. On 23 November 1988 English Heritage listed Ribblehead Viaduct as Grade 2*, offering £1 million toward repairs. The Friends proposed a Trust – duly formed in 1992 – to assist with future restoration work. And on 11 April 1989, with a judicial review looming, Paul Channon refused permission. Strangely, most of the letter from the Secretary of State apart from the decision itself read like a refusal, heightening the impression of a last-minute, and political, U-turn engineered largely by Portillo.

With Portillo observing, 'The line may continue to operate at a loss, but not necessarily a large one,' BR committed itself to run at least the five daily trains then operating. The viaduct was repaired for £3.15 million, £1.9 million from outside bodies. David Wharton-Street set up a stakeholder committee led by Cumbria County Council, and appointed a liaison manager – Brian Hinchcliffe, who also covered the line to Morecambe.

In 1990 the Standing Conference for the Settle-Carlisle Railway published an agenda for increasing patronage to 1 million a year, with new services 'from places such as Manchester' and a luxury train from

**ABOVE** The crowning glory of the work undertaken by the FoSCL must surely be the extraordinarily detailed restoration work to stations, signal boxes and some footbridges. Garsdale is a wonderful example of this valuable work. *Steve Poole*

centres across the North, ordinary passengers paying a supplement. With the Railway Heritage Trust, it saw commercial potential for the line's station buildings, heritage railway connections at Appleby and Hawes, and much more. A new platform was opened in 1993 at Ribblehead station, where trains had only been stopping in one direction. The Development Company worked on projects with local businesses, and the Friends with train operators. Today the Friends run a shop at Settle, and share in staffing the station.

### Post-privatisation
Railtrack's West Coast Route Modernisation brought the S&C's revival as a diversionary route, then it unexpectedly regained its freight. Demand from Yorkshire power stations after pit closures generated a flow of imported coal from the Clyde ports. The line – only 36% of it then continuously welded – was not ready for the heavy trains which began heading south from Hunterston in 1998. Railtrack asked Richard Bonham Carter if the track could take them; he concluded that it could, but recommended work to ease a number of speed restrictions. As the traffic grew, Railtrack relaid the track with steel sleepers, but when it reached 18 2,000-tonne trains a day from 2005 Network Rail had to relay the up line again with concrete sleepers and deeper ballast. Colour-light distant signals were put in to break up signalling sections (though semaphores are still operated from seven boxes, some extremely remote) – and overall some £100 million was spent. The coal traffic has now fallen back from its peak as Drax power station has switched to biomass from ports in North East England.

Seasonal timber trains are running again from Ribblehead. Morning commuter trains resumed in 2011. Most passenger trains are formed by 158s. Commercial activity at the line's stations has blossomed,

## Postscript: THE SETTLE & CARLISLE LINE

**ABOVE** A Class 66 heads an empty coal train north over Ribblehead Viaduct. *Jason Cross*

**RIGHT** Heidi Mottram, former Managing Director of Northern Trains and a leading figure in partnership deals with organisations such as the Friends of the Settle & Carlisle Line, was one of the specially invited VIPs on the 25th Anniversary special train. *Alex Green*

**BELOW** A special peal of bells was rung from the church in Settle, where the station platform was crammed with local residents celebrating the line's continued good prospects. *Alex Green*

from a cycle hire shop to holiday lets. Ribblehead station boasts an award-winning visitor centre. The line's station gardens are so well tended that in September 2013 Gardeners' Question Time was broadcast from the 10.49 from Leeds and the 14.04 return. And the supporting bodies are coordinated by the Settle-Carlisle Partnership.

On 13 April 2014 the Friends chartered a train from Blackpool to Carlisle via Hellifield to mark the 25th anniversary of the reprieve. Ron Cotton was aboard, and Michael Portillo and Colin Speakman, one of the architects of the rescue, spoke at a celebratory lunch. The Friends could look to a line with a busy commercial life, a nationally acclaimed support network and a secure future. But they want a higher line speed than 60mph, and more services. Intermediate carryings have yet to reach 500,000, and the drives to develop the connection from Blackburn and even reinstate the further link to Skipton from Colne lack a heavyweight sponsor.

Has the S&C an interurban future? Even now, Leeds-Glasgow with a change at Carlisle can be quicker – just under 4 hours – than via Newcastle. Reinstatement of Nottingham-Leeds-Carlisle services was rejected by the SRA in 2001, but pressure for them, and for through trains from Manchester, continues.

**ABOVE** Class 153 unit No 153352 shows its usefulness in strengthening a Class 158 service, calling at the beautifully restored Appleby station on 10 July 2011. Dales-type weather looks to be setting in, but hopefully the Settle & Carlisle line will bask in the warmth of continued tourist growth and long-term freight usage. *Michael Bonser*

# Factfile A: Chronology

| Year | Events |
|---|---|
| 1979 | May: Conservatives return to power under Margaret Thatcher; Norman Fowler Minister for Transport |
| 1980 | August. First stage of Tyne & Wear Metro opens |
| 1981 | September: David Howell Secretary of State for Transport |
| 1982 | January: New BR business sectors introduced; John Welsby first Director Provincial Services |
| | May: Howell commissions Serpell Report |
| | May: Scottish 'basic interval' timetable introduced |
| | July: ASLEF strike over flexible rostering for train crews |
| 1983 | January: Serpell Report 'Review of Railway Finances' published |
| | June: Conservatives re-elected. |
| | Tom King Secretary of State for Transport |
| | September: BR Chief Executive Bob Reid succeeds Sir Peter Parker as Chairman; ScotRail brand unveiled |
| | October: Nicholas Ridley Secretary of State for Transport, sets Objectives for new sectors |
| | December: Ayrshire, Leicester resignalling commissioned; BR proposes closure of Settle & Carlisle line |
| 1984 | January: John Edmonds Director Provincial Services |
| | March: 'Rails into roads' conversion report |
| | June: Final closure of BR Divisions; Provincial sub-sectors created: Eastern, Midland, Scotland, Western |
| | October: BR Corporate Plan launched – large manpower and subsidy cuts |
| | December: First 'Pacers' delivered to Neville Hill depot; Joint BR/Greater Manchester Bill for light rail Altrincham-Manchester-Bury |
| 1985 | Transport Act creates bus deregulation in 1986 |
| 1986 | January: First Class 150 'Sprinter' introduced at Derby |
| | March: Reopening of Edinburgh-Bathgate line; Metropolitan Counties abolished |
| | May: John Moore Secretary of State for Transport, David Mitchell Minister of State |
| | October: Moore issues new Objectives cutting BR subsidy by 25%; 'Sprinters' introduced on some trans-Pennine services; sectors take over funding, investment and product specification from regions |
| 1987 | January: Ayrshire electrification launched |
| | February: Stansted Airport rail link authorised |

| Year | Events |
|---|---|
| | May: Launch of TransPennine Express; introduction of the first Class 155s on Portsmouth-Cardiff (also of first Class 156) |
| | June: Conservative Government re-elected, Paul Channon Secretary of State for Transport |
| | October: Sidney Newey Director Provincial, John Edmonds GM of new Anglia Region; Glanrhyd Viaduct collapses on 19th; Birmingham Snow Hill reopens; Class 156s introduced on TransPennine |
| | December: All rolling stock allocated by sector |
| 1988 | February: Manchester Metrolink authorised |
| | April: DTI announces MMC study into Provincial sector |
| | July: Michael Portillo appointed Minister of State |
| | October: Reopening of Aberdare line |
| | December: Clapham collision on 12th – 35 killed |
| 1989 | February: Ness Bridge collapses on 7th; MMC Provincial report published |
| | April: Channon refuses closure of Settle & Carlisle line. |
| | July: Cecil Parkinson Secretary of State for Transport |
| | September: First Class 158, Glasgow-Edinburgh |
| | December: 35 Class 155s split into 70 Class 153s; Parkinson sets new Objectives for Provincial |
| 1990 | January: John Welsby Chief Executive BR |
| | February: BR announces intention to introduce on-the-spot penalty fares |
| | March: Bob Reid II appointed Chairman of BRB |
| | May: Roger Freeman Minister of State; Gordon Pettitt Director, Provincial |
| | June: BR announces regions to be abolished by April 1991 and business sectors to own all assets |
| | July: Provincial announces sector to be renamed Regional Railways in autumn; First Class 323 EMUs ordered; NUR accepts BR national pay offer after bitter dispute; Paisley Canal line reopened |
| | September: Class 158 high-speed tests, Derby-St Pancras |
| | October: Bob Reid II takes over BR chair full-time; BR subsidy increased by 20% to fund post-Clapham safety investments; Board endorses transfer of 22 new Class 158s from Provincial to Network SouthEast; Forth Bridge Centenary celebrations; 12-car Class 158 special train for all staff involved in introduction of fleet and their families |

| Year | Events |
|---|---|
| 1990 | November: Margaret Thatcher resigns as Prime Minister, succeeded by John Major; Malcolm Rifkind Secretary of State for Transport |
| | December: Launch of Regional Railways with 'Prospectus for Quality'; Leeds NW electrification approved |
| 1991 | January: Dr Paul King joins Regional Railways as Planning & Marketing Director |
| | March: Stansted Airport link opened |
| | April: BR launches new OfQ organisation with Regional Railways gaining full ownership of its assets; first meeting of RR Executive Board; new corporate identity agreed |
| | May: Record Edinburgh-Glasgow run in 32min 9sec with top speed of 107mph |
| | December: Class 158 introduced on TransPennine; Devon & Cornwall Rail Partnership initiated |
| 1992 | April: OfQ reorganisation complete: vertically integrated railway; first stage of Metrolink opened; Bob Reid II opens new Regional Railways HQ at Meridian, Birmingham; Conservatives re-elected, John MacGregor Secretary of State for Transport |
| | May: Rail privatisation Bill promised |
| | July: White Paper 'New Opportunities for the Railway' |
| | August: Gordon Pettitt retires, Jim Cornell becomes MD Regional Railways |
| 1993 | North Clyde resignalling commissioned |
| | January: 'Passenger's Charter', delay compensation payments introduced; Railways Bill for privatisation published |
| | Mar: DTp sets out final Objectives for BR and announces future Shadow Franchises |
| | May: Three Rolling Stock Companies announced, to own fleets; 'Robin Hood Line' Stage 1 opens, Nottingham-Newstead; Birmingham Cross-City electrification inaugurated; Class 323 introduced on Greater Manchester services; Class 320 introduced in Scotland; Manchester Airport link opened |
| | June: Board announces Sectors to close 1 April 1994 |
| | July: Paul King MD Regional Railways |
| | November: Railways Act 1993 receives Royal Assent;: Director of Passenger Rail Franchising, Roger Salmon, takes up duties |
| | December: John Swift QC, Rail Regulator, takes up duties; Gordon Pettitt appointed his railway adviser |
| 1994 | February: First Class 323 on Birmingham Cross-City line |
| | March: First stage of Sheffield Supertram opens |

| Year | Events |
|---|---|
| 1994 | April: Railways Act takes effect; Regional Railways abolished; 25 Train Operating Units (TOUs) created (eight from Regional); BR rail infrastructure transferred to Railtrack plc |
| | July: Dr Brian Mawhinney Secretary of State for Transport |
| 1995 | April: John Welsby appointed Chairman of BRB |
| | July: Sir George Young Secretary of State for Transport |
| | September: 'Jewellery Line' reconnects Birmingham Snow Hill with Stourbridge line; Leeds NW electrification inaugurated with Class 308s from NSE |
| 1996 | April: Railtrack's five-year Control Period 1 commences |
| | May: Railtrack floated on Stock Exchange |
| | September: First rolling stock orders for 1,064 days (Class 168s for Chiltern) |
| | October: First franchises: Prism takes over Cardiff Valleys and South Wales & West |
| | November: John O'Brien appointed Franchising Director |
| 1997 | March: National Express takes over ScotRail franchise; last BR passenger services operate |
| | May: Labour Government elected with Tony Blair as PM, John Prescott Deputy PM, Secretary for Environment, Transport & Regions |
| | September: GW Holdings orders Class 175 DMUs from Alstom; Rail Regulator redrafts Railtrack's network licence to reflect concern that not enough spent on renewals and maintenance |
| 1998 | July: Prescott announces new Strategic Railway Authority |
| | December: John Swift resigns as Rail Regulator, Chris Bolt appointed; Class 170 DMUs introduced on Midland Mainline |
| 1999 | February: Prescott names Sir Alastair Morton as Chairman elect of SRA |
| | May: Mike Grant appointed Franchising Director; First Class 175 on NW services; First Class 334 introduced in ScotRail |
| | May: Midland Metro opens |
| | July: BRB and OPRAF merge as Shadow SRA with Alastair Morton Chairman and Mike Grant CEO; Tom Winsor appointed Rail Regulator |
| 2000 | February: MTL collapses, Merseyrail and NE taken over by Arriva |
| | July: Second casualty of privatisation: Prism purchased by National Express Group |
| | October: Hatfield derailment on 17th brings widespread speed restrictions across railway; Class 333 EMUs introduced by West Yorkshire PTE |

| Year | Events |
|---|---|
| 2001 | February: SRA takes up its powers. |
| | April: Railtrack Control Period 2 starts |
| | June: Labour Government re-elected, Stephen Byers Secretary of State for Transport and Environment |
| | October: Byers puts Railtrack plc into administration; South Wales & West franchise split to create Wales & Borders and Wessex |
| | December: Morton stands down, Richard Bowker appointed SRA Chairman |
| 2002 | May: Alistair Darling Secretary of State for Transport |
| | June: SRA Strategic Plan published |
| | October: Network Rail created as not-for-dividend company |
| 2003 | July: Merseyrail franchise devolved to Merseyside PTE, concession for 25 years |
| | October: Network Rail to bring maintenance in-house |
| | December: Northern and TransPennine franchises created |
| 2004 | January: Darling announces structural review of railway |
| | July: Railways & Transport Safety Act 2003 creates Office of Rail Regulation; White Paper 'Future of Rail' proposes abolition of SRA |
| | November: SRA launches Community Rail Development Strategy |
| | December: First Class 350s introduced |
| 2005 | April: SRA abolished under Railways Act 2005, powers transferred to DfT Rail. Rail safety transferred from HSE to ORR. New process for access charge reviews: Government to specify what service it wants to buy (HLOS) and how much it is prepared to pay (SOFA); Network Rail Control Period 3 begins |
| | December: Reinstated Larkhall line opened |
| 2006 | April: Scottish Government takes on full rail franchise funding; Welsh Assembly takes on responsibility for Wales & Borders; Greater Western franchise commences |
| | May: Douglas Alexander Secretary of State for Transport; TransPennine Express introduces Class 185 DMUs |
| | June: Transport Scotland becomes responsible for railways in Scotland |

| Year | Events |
|---|---|
| 2007 | June: Gordon Brown becomes PM, Ruth Kelly Secretary of State for Transport; White Paper 'Delivering a Sustainable Railway' published |
| | October: Joint letter from Network Rail/ATOC to Government puts case for more rail electrification |
| | November: Central Trains franchise broken into East Midlands Trains & London Midland |
| 2008 | May: Reinstated Alloa line opened. |
| | November: Local Transport Act renames PTAs as Integrated Transport Authorities |
| | October: Geoff Hoon Secretary of State for Transport, Lord Adonis Minister of State |
| 2009 | April: Network Rail Control Period 4 begins |
| | June: Lord Adonis Secretary of State for Transport |
| | November: Class 380 EMUs introduced on ScotRail; DfT announces Liverpool-Manchester electrification |
| 2010 | May: General Election produces Conservative/Lib Dem Coalition Government with David Cameron as PM, Phillip Hammond (Con) Secretary of State for Transport |
| 2011 | May: McNulty Report 'Realising the Potential of Rail' published, proposing creation of Rail Delivery Group |
| | October: Justine Greening Secretary of State for Transport |
| 2012 | January: Government commits to build Phase 1 of HS2; investment approved for 'Northern Hub' |
| | September: Patrick McLoughlin Secretary of State for Transport |
| | October: Refranchising on hold after West Coast challenge |
| 2013 | January: Rail Delivery Group formalised under licences of Network Rail and train operators |
| | December: Manchester-Earlestown energised, allowing electric TPE services to Scotland |
| 2014 | February: Rail Executive created within DfT; storms sever railway at Dawlish and on Cambrian coast |
| | April: Network Rail Control Period 5 starts |
| | May: Edinburgh tram opens; Task Force appointed to review further Northern electrification |
| | September: Network Rail becomes fully funded by Government – effectively renationalised; DfT creates new Office of Rail Passenger Services (for future franchising); DfT and Rail North launch consultation on future Northern and TransPennine franchises |

# Factfile B: Financial facts, 1982-94

### B1: Provincial/Regional Railways financial results

| Year | Income (£m) | Expenditure (£m) | Subsidy (£m) | Capital investment (£m) | Revenue investment (£m) |
|---|---|---|---|---|---|
| 1982* | 136 | 625 | 489 | n/a | n/a |
| 1983* | 164 | 653 | 489 | n/a | n/a |
| 1984/85* | 208 | 817 | 609 | n/a | n/a |
| 1985/86 | 209 | 713 | 504 | n/a | n/a |
| 1986/87 | 224 | 698 | 474 | n/a | n/a |
| 1987/88 | 247 | 720 | 473 | n/a | n/a |
| 1988/89 | 274 | 740 | 466 | 37 | 27 |
| 1989/90 | 276 | 770 | 494 | 90 | 36 |
| 1990/91 | 304 | 796 | 492 | 71 | 39 |
| 1991/92 | 313 | 808 | 495 | 87 | 35 |
| 1992/93 | 349 | 852 | 503 | 49 | 37 |
| 1993/94 | 359 | 801 | 443 | 44 | 39 |

* BR finances previously reported for calendar year 1984/85 with change to the financial year covered over 15 months
Source: British Rail 1974-97, T. Gourvish; BR Annual Reports

### B2: Provincial/Regional Railways Financial Key Performance Indicators, 1988-94

| Year | PSO subsidy per passenger mile (pence) | PTE subsidy per passenger mile (pence) | Costs per train mile (£) | Receipts per train mile (£) | Receipts per passenger mile (pence) |
|---|---|---|---|---|---|
| 1991 constant pricing | | | | | |
| 1988/89 | 20.10 | 8.25 | 10.74 | 3.79 | 9.30 |
| 1989/90 | 20.48 | 9.24 | 10.33 | 3.71 | 9.34 |
| 1990/91 | 22.48 | 10.51 | 10.11 | 3.63 | 9.32 |
| 1993 constant pricing | | | | | |
| 1991/92 | 17.66 | 10.62 | 9.85 | 3.82 | 9.75 |
| 1992/93 | 17.22 | 8.43 | 10.03 | 4.11 | 9.83 |
| 1993/94 | 14.96 | 8.63 | 8.89 | 3.98 | 10.02 |

Source: Rail Plan 1993

### B3: Provincial/Regional Railways pricing above inflation, 1984-91

| Year | Average yearly fare p.a. (%) | Inflation (average RPI p.a.) (%) | Real pricing (%) |
|---|---|---|---|
| 1984/85 | 6.7 | 6.5 | + 0.2 |
| 1985/86 | 5.8 | 5.3 | + 0.5 |
| 1986/87 | 7.5 | 5.6 | + 1.9 |
| 1987/88 | 6.2 | 2.3 | + 3.9 |
| 1988/89 | 6.2 | 3.7 | + 2.5 |
| 1989/90 | 7.8 | 5.8 | + 2.0 |
| 1990/91 | 6.8 | 6.0 | + 0.8 |
| 1991/92 | 11.0 | 8.0 | + 3.0 |

Source: *British Rail, 1974-97*, T. Gourvish

# Factfile C: The train/passenger interface

### C1: Train performance: Provincial/Regional Railways and Franchises

| Year | Punctuality (right time) | Punctuality (5 mins – PPM) | Trains cancelled | Customer satisfaction (%) |
|---|---|---|---|---|
| BR target | 87.5% | 90% | 1.5% | |
| **Provincial/Regional** | | | | |
| 1984/85 | | 90 | 1.9 | |
| 1985/86 | | 91 | 1.9 | |
| 1986/87 | | 91 | 1.6 | |
| 1987/88 | | 92 | 1.2 | |
| 1988/89 | | 92 | 1.4 | |
| 1989/90 | | 90 | 4.0 | |
| 1990/91 | | 90 | 2.1 | |
| 1991/92 | | 85 | 1.3 | |
| 1992/93 | | 88 | 1.6 | |
| 1993/94 | | 92 | 1.1 | |
| 1994/95 | | 90 | 2.1 | |
| 1995/96 | | 90 | 2.2 | |
| 1996/97 | | 89 | 2.6 | |
| **Franchises** | | | | |
| 1997/98 | 74 | 89 | 2.3 | n/a |
| 1998/99 | 69 | 89 | 2.8 | n/a |
| 1999/00 | 69 | 89 | 2.6 | 84 |
| 2000/01 | 58 | 86 | 4.8 | 83 |
| 2001/02 | 51 | 80 | 4.4 | 78 |
| 2002/03 | 53 | 80 | 4.1 | 80 |
| 2003/04 | 56 | 82 | 3.1 | 85 |
| 2004/05 | 55 | 83 | 3.2 | 90 |
| 2005/06 | 57 | 83 | 3.0 | 87 |
| 2006/07 | 62 | 87 | 3.0 | 88 |
| 2007/08 | 66 | 89 | 2.8 | 87 |
| 2008/09 | 69 | 89 | 2.4 | 86 |
| 2009/10 | 72 | 92 | 2.4 | 88 |
| 2010/11 | 71 | 92 | 2.5 | 86 |
| 2011/12 | 77 | 91 | 2.2 | 86 |
| 2012/13 | 74 | 92 | 2.2 | 85 |
| 2013/14 | 73 | 91 | 2.2 | 84 |

Source: BR Annual Reports; ORR Statistics; National Passenger Survey

**C2: Customer satisfaction, franchised train companies, 2014**

| Customer satisfaction (%) | | Value for money (%) | |
|---|---|---|---|
| Merseyrail | 95 | Merseyrail | 70 |
| ScotRail | 90 | ScotRail | 56 |
| East Midland Trains | 87 | First TransPennine Express | 54 |
| First TransPennine Express | 85 | Arriva Trains Wales | 54 |
| Arriva Trains Wales | 85 | Northern Rail | 54 |
| CrossCountry | 82 | CrossCountry | 52 |
| London Midland | 82 | London Midland | 50 |
| Abellio Greater Anglia | 81 | East Midland Trains | 49 |
| First Great Western | 80 | First Great Western | 48 |
| Northern Rail | 80 | Abellio Greater Anglia | 35 |

Source: Passenger Focus independent research, Spring 2014

**C3: Passenger miles travelled on regional routes (and journeys made, available only from 1989)**

| Year | Passenger miles (bn) |
|---|---|
| 1973 | 3.4 |
| 1974 | 3.4 |
| 1976 | 3.0 |
| 1977 | 3.0 |
| 1978 | 3.4 |
| 1979 | 3.2 |
| 1980 | 3.2 |
| 1981 | 3.2 |
| 1982 | 2.9 |
| 1983 | 2.9 |
| 1984/85 | 3.0 |
| 1985/86 | 2.9 |
| 1986/87 | 3.0 |
| 1987/88 | 3.3 |
| 1988/89 | 3.6 |
| 1989/90 | 3.5 |
| 1990/91 | 3.5 |
| 1991/92 | 3.4 |
| 1992/93 | 3.7 |
| 1993/94 | 3.6 |
| 1994/95 | 3.6 |
| 1995/96 | 3.3 |
| 1996/97 | 3.9 |

| Franchised train companies | | |
|---|---|---|
| Year | Journeys (m) | Passenger miles (bn) |
| 1997/98 | n/a | 3.9 |
| 1998/99 | 215 | 4.3 |
| 1999/00 | 228 | 4.3 |
| 2001/02 | 222 | 4.4 |
| 2002/03 | 219 | 4.3 |
| 2003/04 | 240 | 4.7 |
| 2004/05 | 251 | 4.9 |
| 2005/06 | 267 | 5.1 |
| 2006/07 | 276 | 5.3 |
| 2007/08 | 286 | 5.6 |
| 2008/09 | 302 | 5.9 |
| 2009/10 | 304 | 6.1 |
| 2010/11 | 318 | 6.5 |
| 2011/12 | 341 | 7.0 |
| 2012/13 | 341 | 6.9 |
| 2013/14 | 351 | 7.1 |

Source: DfT; British Rail, 1974-97, T. Gourvish

# Factfile D: Train services

**D1: Selection of interurban services, journey times and average speeds 1982-2014**

| Route | No of trains | | | Average journey time (hr-min) | | | Average speed (mph) | | |
|---|---|---|---|---|---|---|---|---|---|
| 0700-1900hrs Mon-Fri | 1982 | 1997 | 2014 | 1982 | 1997 | 2014 | 1982 | 1997 | 2014 |
| Birmingham New Street to: | | | | | | | | | |
| Aberystwyth | - | 6 | 6 | - | 2-56 | 3-02 | - | 42 | 41 |
| Liverpool Lime Street | - | 12 | 24 | - | 1-46 | 1-34 | - | 50 | 57 |
| Nottingham | 1 | 19 | 24 | 1-33 | 1-18 | 1-12 | 37 | 44 | 47 |
| Stansted Airport | - | 1 | 12 | - | 3-13 | 3-18 | - | 50 | 48 |
| Bristol Temple Meads to: | | | | | | | | | |
| Cardiff | 9 | 23 | 23 | 0-52 | 0-47 | 0-58 | 44 | 49 | 40 |
| Portsmouth | 9 | 12 | 12 | 2-30 | 2-27 | 2-32 | 41 | 42 | 41 |
| Weymouth | 4 | 6 | 6 | 2-29 | 2-23 | 2-20 | 35 | 37 | 37 |
| Cardiff Central to: | | | | | | | | | |
| Birmingham New Street | 7 | 11 | 13 | 2-10 | 2-14 | 2-00 | 52 | 50 | 56 |
| Carmarthen | 1 | 9 | 20 | 2-00 | 1-55 | 1-53 | 40 | 42 | 42 |
| Manchester | - | 12 | 11 | - | 3-01 | 3-15 | - | 56 | 52 |
| Chester to: | | | | | | | | | |
| Llandudno | 9 | 11 | 10 | 1-19 | 1-10 | 1-13 | 36 | 41 | 39 |
| Manchester | 13 | 14 | 25 | 1-07 | 1-02 | 1-07 | 36 | 39 | 36 |
| Edinburgh to: | | | | | | | | | |
| Aberdeen (excluding inter-city) | 2 | 9 | 10 | 2-35 | 2-33 | 2-22 | 50 | 51 | 55 |
| Inverness (excluding inter-city) | 2 | 3 | 4 | 4-04 | 3-42 | 3-25 | 43 | 47 | 51 |
| Glasgow to: | | | | | | | | | |
| Aberdeen | 5 | 12 | 12 | 2-50 | 2-41 | 2-34 | 54 | 58 | 60 |
| Edinburgh | 26 | 27 | 55 | 0-46 | 0-50 | 0-51 | 62 | 57 | 56 |
| Inverness | 3 | 3 | 5 | 4-05 | 3-26 | 3-18 | 44 | 52 | 55 |
| Inverness to: | | | | | | | | | |
| Aberdeen | 5 | 7 | 8 | 2-28 | 2-16 | 2-20 | 44 | 48 | 46 |
| Leeds to: | | | | | | | | | |
| Hull | 11 | 11 | 12 | 1-12 | 0-59 | 0-57 | 43 | 53 | 54 |
| Newcastle | 4 | 6 | 10 | 2-02 | 1-48 | 1-36 | 52 | 59 | 62 |
| Sheffield | 12 | 17 | 24 | 1-19 | 1-26 | 0-59 | 29 | 27 | 39 |
| Liverpool Lime Street to: | | | | | | | | | |
| Blackpool | - | 7 | 11 | - | 1-20 | 1-24 | - | 39 | 38 |
| Leeds | 11 | 12 | 12 | 1-49 | 1-52 | 1-47 | 43 | 42 | 43 |
| York | 11 | 12 | 12 | 2-21 | 2-25 | 2-13 | 44 | 43 | 53 |
| Manchester to: | | | | | | | | | |
| Hull | 9 | 12 | 12 | 2-41 | 2-02 | 1-53 | 35 | 46 | 50 |
| Leeds | 13 | 36 | 48 | 1-06 | 1-00 | 0-56 | 39 | 43 | 46 |
| Newcastle | 5 | 6 | 11 | 3-23 | 2-55 | 2-41 | 44 | 51 | 55 |
| Norwich to: | | | | | | | | | |
| Cambridge | 1 | 1 | 12 | 1-53 | 1-20 | 1-19 | 36 | 51 | 52 |
| Manchester Piccadilly | - | 9 | 10 | - | 4-36 | 4-39 | - | 47 | 47 |
| Nottingham | - | 10 | 12 | - | 2-36 | 2-36 | - | 52 | 52 |

Source: BR/NR Timetables

NB: Ex InterCity-type services are excluded from figures in this table

## D2: Edinburgh-Glasgow: record runs

| Journey | | 19 June 1985<br>47716 + five coaches<br>287 tonnes; 2,550hp<br>8.88hp per tonne<br>8.26hp per seat | | 6 May 1992<br>158708 and 158710<br>155 tonnes: 1600hp<br>10.3hp per tonne<br>5.8hp per seat | |
|---|---|---|---|---|---|
| Miles | Timing point | Actual (min sec) | Speed[1] (mph) | Actual (min sec) | Speed[1] (mph) |
| 0.0 | **Glasgow Queen Street** | 0 00 | - | 0 00 | - |
| 1.4 | *Cowlairs* | - | | 2 44 | 30 |
| 1.8 | Cowlairs box | 3 22 | 40/45 | 3 12 | 54 |
| 3.1 | Bishopbriggs | 4 41 | 78 | 4 29 | 75 |
| 6.2 | Lenzie | 6 53 | 92/43* | 6 38 | 93 |
| 11.4 | Croy | 11 11 | 62 | 9 51 | 101 |
| 12.8 | *Dullatur* | - | - | 10 40 | 104 |
| 15.4 | *Castlecary* | 13 57 | 96 | 12 11 | 105 |
| 17.2 | *Greenhill U Jn* | 15 05 | 97 | 13 13 | 103 |
| 18.3 | *Bobbybridge* | - | - | 13 50 | 107 |
| 21.7 | Falkirk High | 17 53 | 100/95* | 15 44 | 90* |
| 24.6 | *Polmont Jn* | - | - | 17 33 | - |
| 24.9 | Polmont | 19 57 | 86* | 17 44 | 101 |
| 27.1 | *Bo'ness Jn* | - | - | 19 03 | 106 |
| 29.6 | Linlithgow | 23 09 | 94/90* | 20 26 | 106/104 |
| 32.6 | *Philipstoun* | 24 31 | 92 | 22 03 | 107 |
| 34.6 | *Winchburgh Jn* | 26 24 | 101/87* | 23 17 | 105/95* |
| 36.4 | *Broxburn Jn* | - | - | 24 24 | 98 |
| 38.7 | *Newbridge Jn* | - | - | 25 46 | 107 |
| 39.0 | *Ratho* | 29 21 | 93 | 25 57 | 104 |
| 43.8 | *Saughton Jn* | 32 15 | 100/98 | 28 40 | 107 |
| 45.3 | *Haymarket Jn* | - | - | 29 32 | 102 |
| 46.0 | Haymarket | 34 01 | 38* | 29 59 | 65* |
| 47.1 | **Edinburgh** | 36 27 | - | 32 09 | - |
| | **Net time/speed** | **35. 00** | **80.7** | **32. 00** | **88.3** |

Source: The Railway Magazine, July 1992: Peter Semmens
[1] Figures in italics are averages from previous timing point
* Speed restrictions
Source: The Railway Magazine, July 1992, Peter Semmens

## D3: Derby-St Pancras – log of inaugural run, 11 September 1990

Four-car formation: 158711 and 158708 (155 tonnes loaded)

| Miles | Timing point | Actual min sec | Speed mph |
|---|---|---|---|
| 0.0 | **Derby station** | 0 00 | 5* |
| 2.6 | Spondon | 4 12 | 74 |
| 6.1 | Draycott | 6 28 | 87/78 |
| 8.1 | Long Eaton | 6 41 | 15* |
| 9.2 | Trent Jn | 12 00 | 53* |
| 12.1 | Kegworth | 15 43 | 61 |
| 16.8 | LOUGHBOROUGH | 17 13 | 90 |
| 24.6 | Syston | 24 27 | 89 |
| 29.4 | LEICESTER | 26 30 | - |
| 3.6 | Wigston Magna | 5 14 | 84 |
| 7.5 | Great Glen | 7 17 | 89 |
| 12.8 | East Langton | 9 47 | 90 |
| 16.1 | MARKET HARBOROUGH | 13 28 | 63* |
| 21.0 | Desborough | 17 34 | 79 |
| 23.5 | Glendon | 19 13 | 89 |
| 27.0 | KETTERING | 21 41 | 86 |
| 29.7 | Burton Latimer | 23 29 | 90 |
| 34.0 | WELLINGBOROUGH | 27 33 | 50* |
| 36.4 | Irchester | 28 30 | 78 |
| 39.3 | Sharnbrook Summit | 30 38 | 83 |
| 42.4 | Sharnbrook | 32 46 | 87 |
| 49.2 | BEDFORD | 37 56 | 85 |
| 58.9 | Flitwick | 44 26 | 90 |
| 61.8 | Harlington | 46 25 | 89 |
| 66.3 | Leagrave | 49 29 | 87 |
| 68.8 | LUTON | 51 50 | - |
| 5.6 | Harpenden | 5 12 | 91 |
| 10.4 | ST ALBANS | 8 23 | 89 |
| 15.0 | Radlett | 11 32 | 90 |
| 17.8 | Elstree | 13 23 | 90 |
| 20.9 | Mill Hill | 15 30 | 88 |
| 23.2 | Hendon | 17 06 | - |
| 25.1 | Cricklewood | 18 24 | - |
| 30.2 | **St Pancras** | **24 16** | - |

### Average speeds (mph)

Derby-Leicester 66.6
Leicester-Luton 79.6
Luton-St Pancras 74.7

\* Speed restrictions
Source: Peter Semmens

# Factfile E: Train fleets, 1981-2014

## E1: Diesel multiple units

| Class | No of cars | Built | Vehicles (1981) | Vehicles (1990) | Vehicles (1995) | Vehicles (2014) |
|---|---|---|---|---|---|---|
| 139 | 1 | 2008 | - | - | - | 2 |
| 141 | 2 | 1984 | - | 40 | 38 | 0 |
| 142 | 2 | 1985-87 | - | 192 | 190 | 188 |
| 143 | 2 | 1985-86 | - | 50 | 50 | 46 |
| 144 | 2 | 1986-87 | - | 56 | 56 | 56 |
| 150 | 2 | 1984-87 | - | 276 | 272 | 264 |
| 153 | 1 | 1991-92* | - | - | 70 | 70 |
| 155 | 2 | 1988 | - | 84 | 14 | 14 |
| 156 | 2 | 1987-89 | - | 228 | 228 | 228 |
| 158 | 2 | 1989-92 | - | 2 | 320 | 236 |
| 158 | 3 | 1991 | - | - | 51 | 99 |
| 170 | 2 | 1999-05 | - | - | - | 86 |
| 170 | 3 | 1999-05 | - | - | - | 267 |
| 172 | 2 | 2010-11 | - | - | - | 24 |
| 172 | 3 | 2010-11 | - | - | - | 45 |
| 175 | 3 | 1999-00 | - | - | - | 22 |
| 175 | 3 | 1999-00 | - | - | - | 48 |
| 185 | 3 | 2005-07 | - | - | - | 153 |
| Heritage units (1955-64) | | | 2,514 | 785 | 111 | - |
| New units (from 1984) | | | - | 928 | 1,289 | 1,848 |
| **Total units in service** | | | **2,514** | **1,713** | **1,400** | **1,848** |

* Formed by splitting two-car Class 155 units
Source: Theo Steel and Colin Marsden

## E2: DC electric multiple units

| Class | No of cars | Built | Vehicles (1981) | Vehicles (1990) | Vehicles (1995) | Vehicles (2014) |
|---|---|---|---|---|---|---|
| 502 | 3 | 1939 | 54 | - | - | - |
| 503 | 3 | 1939/56 | 129 | - | - | - |
| 504* | 2 | 1959 | 47 | 34 | - | - |
| 506* | 3 | 1954 | 24 | - | - | - |
| 507/8 | 3 | 1978 | 96 | 225 | 177 | 177 |
| Heritage units (1958-86) | | | 183 | 34 | - | - |
| New units (from 1987) | | | - | 225 | 177 | 177 |
| **Total** | | | **344** | **259** | **177** | **177** |

* 504 third rail side contact; 506 1,500V DC overhead
Source: Theo Steel and Colin Marsden

## E3: AC electric multiple units

| Class | No of cars | Built | Vehicles (1981) | Vehicles (1990) | Vehicles (1995) | Vehicles (2014) |
|---|---|---|---|---|---|---|
| 303 | 3 | 1959 | 273 | 186 | 144 | - |
| 304 | 4 | 1961 | 176 | 114 | 21 | - |
| 305 | 3 | 1960 | - | 24 | - | - |
| 305 | 4 | 1960 | - | - | 20 | - |
| 308 | 3 | 1961 | - | - | 72 | - |
| 309 | 4 | 1962 | - | - | 16 | - |
| 310 | 4 | 1965 | 28 | 44 | 47 | - |
| 311 | 3 | 1967 | 57 | 30 | - | - |
| 312 | 4 | 1976 | 16 | - | - | - |
| 314 | 3 | 1979 | 48 | 48 | 48 | 48 |
| 318 | 3 | 1985 | - | 63 | 63 | 63 |
| 319 | 4 | 1987 | - | - | - | 16* |
| 320 | 3 | 1990 | - | - | 66 | 66 |
| 321 | 4 | 1991 | - | - | 12 | 12 |
| 322 | 4 | 1990 | - | - | - | 20 |
| 323 | 3 | 1992 | - | - | 129 | 129 |
| 333 | 4 | 2000 | - | - | - | 64 |
| 334 | 3 | 1999 | - | - | - | 120 |
| 350 | 4 | 2004 | - | - | - | 64 |
| 350/3 | 4 | 2014 | - | - | - | 12 |
| 350/4 | 4 | 2013 | - | - | - | 40 |
| 380 | 3 | 2009 | - | - | - | 66 |
| 380/1 | 4 | 2010 | - | - | - | 64 |
| Heritage units | | 1959-90 | 598 | 509 | 509 | 225 |
| New units | | 1992- | - | - | 129 | 559 |
| **Total** | | | **598** | **509** | **638** | **784** |

*NB: the first of 80 coaches to be transferred from Thameslink
Source: Theo Steel and Colin Marsden

## E4: Loco-hauled coaches

| | Built | 1981 | 1990 | 1995 | 2014 |
|---|---|---|---|---|---|
| Mark I/II | 1955-75 | 1,075 | 392 | 71 | 40 |

Source: Theo Steel and Colin Marsden

## E5: Total number of Provincial/Regional vehicles

| | 1981 | 1990 | 1995 | 2014 |
|---|---|---|---|---|
| All | 4,537 | 2,873 | 2,286 | 2,849 |

Source: Theo Steel & Colin Marsden

# Factfile F: Infrastructure

**F1: Lines opened/reopened 1982-2014 (new construction/reinstatement marked *)**

| Date | Section opened | PTE | Miles | Passenger service |
|---|---|---|---|---|
| 1983 | Penistone Barnsley Jn – Summer Lane Jn | SYPTE | 5.8 | Huddersfield-Sheffield |
| 1986 | Newbridge Jn-Bathgate | SPTE | 10.0 | Edinburgh-Bathgate |
| 1986 | New Mills South Jn-Hazel Grove HL | GMPTE | 5.5 | Sheffield-Liverpool |
| 1986 | Holmes Jn-Rotherham Central Jn* | SYPTE | 0.7 | Liverpool-Sheffield |
| 1986 | Hazel Grove HL Jn-Hazel Grove East* | GMPTE | 0.3 | Norwich-Liverpool |
| 1987 | Coventry-Nuneaton | WMPTE | 9.6 | Coventry-Nuneaton |
| 1987 | Birmingham Moor Street-Snow Hill | WMPTE | 0.6 | Stratford-upon-Avon-Birmingham Snow Hill |
| 1987 | Ninian Park-Radyr | - | 4.2 | Coryton-Radyr |
| 1988 | Castlefield-Ordsall Lane | | | |
| | Ordsall Lane-Windsor Bridge* | GMPTE | 0.9 | Manchester-Southport/Blackpool |
| 1988 | Abercynon Jn-Aberdare | - | 7.4 | Barry Island-Aberdare |
| 1988 | Lichfield City-Lichfield Trent Valley | WMPTE | 1.1 | Redditch-Lichfield Trent Valley |
| 1989 | Cowlairs West Jn-Springburn | SPTE | 0.9 | Glasgow Queen St HL-Cumbernauld |
| 1989 | Airdrie-Drumgelloch | SPTE | 1.4 | North Clyde-Drumgelloch |
| 1989 | Walsall-Hednesford | WMPTE | 9.6 | Birmingham New Street-Hednesford |
| 1989 | Clitheroe-Hellifield Jn (seasonal) | - | 13.5 | Blackpool-Hellifield/Carlisle |
| 1989 | Crediton Jn-Coleford Jn | - | 4.7 | Exeter-Okehampton (seasonal) |
| 1990 | Stansted North-East Jn* | - | 0.6 | Birmingham-Stansted Airport |
| 1990 | Shields Jn-Paisley Canal | SPTE | 5.9 | Glasgow Central-Paisley Canal |
| 1992 | Bridgend Llynfi Jn-Maesteg | - | 8.0 | Cardiff Central-Maesteg |
| 1992 | Crofton West Jn-Pontefract West | WYPTE | 6.9 | Wakefield Kirkgate-Knottingley |
| 1993 | Heald Green South-West Jn* | GMPTE | 0.5 | Manchester Airport-Crewe |
| 1993 | Heald Green North-Manchester Airport* | GMPTE | 1.5 | Manchester Airport-Manchester Piccadilly |
| 1993 | Mansfield Jn-Newstead ('Robin Hood')* | - | 10.1 | Nottingham-Newstead |
| 1993 | Cowlairs South Jct-Sighthill West Jn* | SPTE | 0.4 | Glasgow Queen St HL-Cumbernauld |
| 1993 | Rutherglen East Jn-Whifflet | SPTE | 7.0 | Glasgow Central-Whifflet |
| 1994 | Daisyfield Jn-Clitheroe | GMPTE | 10.1 | Manchester Victoria-Clitheroe |
| 1995 | Newstead-Mansfield Woodhouse* | - | 8.2 | Nottingham-Mansfield Woodhouse |
| 1995 | Eaglescliffe South Jn-Northallerton East | - | 13.9 | Middlesbrough-Manchester Airport |
| 1995 | Birmingham Snow Hill-Smethwick Jn* | WMPTE | 4.0 | Birmingham Snow Hill-Worcester |
| 1996 | Coatbridge Central-Garnqueen North | SPTE | 2.3 | Motherwell-Cumbernauld |
| 1997 | Hednesford-Rugeley Town | WMPTE | 4.3 | Birmingham New Street-Rugeley Town |
| 1998 | Mansfield Woodhouse-Shireoaks East | - | 12.1 | Nottingham-Worksop ('Robin Hood') |
| 1998 | Rugeley Town-Rugeley Trent Valley | - | 1.3 | Birmingham New Street-Rugeley Trent Valley-Stafford |
| 1999 | Cumbernauld-Greenhill Lower Jn | SPTE | 5.7 | Glasgow Queen St-Falkirk Grahamston |
| 2000 | Dryclough Jn-Greetland Jn | WYPTE | 1.1 | Halifax-Huddersfield |
| 2000 | Greetland Jn-Bradley Jn | WYPTE | 4.8 | Halifax-Huddersfield |
| 2004 | Portobello Jn-Newcraighall | SPTE | 1.3 | Fife Circle-Newcraighall |
| 2005 | Maryhill Park Jn-Anniesland Bay | SPTE | 0.9 | Glasgow Queen St-Anniesland |

**F1: Lines opened/reopened 1982-2014 (new construction/reinstatement marked *) continued**

| Date | Section opened | PTE | Miles | Passenger service |
|---|---|---|---|---|
| 2005 | Haughhead Jn-Larkhall* | SPTE | 3.0 | North Clyde-Larkhall |
| 2005 | Barry Jn-Bridgend Jn | - | 19.0 | Cardiff Central-Barry-Bridgend |
| 2008 | Ebbw Jn-Ebbw Vale Parkway* | - | 18.4 | Cardiff Central-Ebbw Vale Parkway |
| 2008 | Stirling-Alloa* | SPTE | 6.9 | Glasgow Queen St-Alloa |
| 2010 | Allington East Jn-North Jn* | - | 0.3 | Grantham-Skegness |
| 2010 | Drumgelloch-Bathgate* | SPTE | 13.3 | North Clyde-Edinburgh |
| 2013 | Parkside East Jn-Golborne Jn | GMPTE | 1.1 | Manchester Airport-Wigan NW |
| 2014 | Hatton North Jn-Hatton West Jn | WMPTE | 0.5 | Birmingham Moor St-Stratford-upon-Avon |
| 2014 | Stansfield Hall Jn-Todmorden Jn* | GMPTE | 0.3 | Burnley-Manchester Victoria |
| 2015 (scheduled) | Newcraighall-Tweedbank* | - | 30.5 | Edinburgh-Tweedbank |
| Total | | | 280.4 | |

Source: Alan Taylor

**F2: Regional lines closed/transferred from national rail ownership, 1982-2014**

| Date | Section closed | Owner | Miles | Reason |
|---|---|---|---|---|
| 27.11.82 | Spalding-March | BR (ER) | 19.5 | Low usage |
| 16.08.91 | Aberystwyth-Devil's Bridge | RR | 11.7 | Line sold to Vale of Rheidol Railway |
| 27.08.91 | Manchester Victoria-Bury | GMPTE | 9.2 | Conversion to Metrolink tram |
| 24.12.91 | Deansgate-Navigation Road | GMPTE | 7.0 | Conversion to Metrolink tram |
| 30.03.02 | Derby Melbourne Jn-Sinfin Central | - | 0.7 | Failed experimental – service already discontinued |
| 17.11.12 | Miles Platting Jn-Oldham-Rochdale | GMPTE | 14.0 | Conversion to Metrolink tram |

Source: Alan Taylor

## F3: Regional lines electrified 1982-2014

| Date | Section electrified | PTE | Miles | Passenger service |
|---|---|---|---|---|
| 1983 | Garston-Hunts Cross | Mersey | 1.5 | Southport-Hunts Cross |
| 30.09.85 | Rock Ferry-Hooton | Mersey | 5.4 | Liverpool-Hooton |
| 01.09.86 | Paisley Gilmour Street-Ayr | SPTE | 34.3 | Glasgow Central-Ayr |
| 19.01.87 | Kilwinning-Ardrossan Harbour | SPTE | 6.5 | Glasgow Central-Ardrossan |
| 19.01.87 | Ardrossan-Largs | SPTE | 11.5 | Glasgow Central-Largs |
| 12.12.88 | Newbridge Jn-Bathgate | Lothian | 10.0 | Edinburgh-Bathgate |
| 01.05.89 | Airdrie-Drumgelloch | SPTE | 1.4 | North Clyde-Drumgelloch |
| 10.03.91 | Stansted North Jn-Stansted East Jn | DTp | 0.6 | Birmingham-Stansted Airport |
| 30.11.92 | Aston North Jn-Lichfield City | WMPTE | 16.8 | Birmingham New Street-Lichfield City |
| 17.05.93 | Heald Green North-Manchester Airport | DTp | 1.6 | Manchester Piccadilly-Manchester Airport |
| 06.06.93 | Birmingham New Street-Redditch | WMPTE | 14.5 | Redditch-Lichfield Trent Valley |
| 06.06.93 | Lichfield City-Lichfield Trent Valley | WMPTE | 1.1 | Redditch-Lichfield Trent Valley |
| 03.09.93 | Hooton-Chester | Mersey | 8.0 | Liverpool-Chester |
| 29.05.94 | Hooton South Jn-Ellesmere Port | Mersey | 3.5 | Liverpool-Ellesmere Port |
| 01.05.95 | Leeds-Skipton | WYPTE | 26.4 | Leeds/Bradford-Skipton |
| 01.05.95 | Apperley Jn-Ilkley | WYPTE | 9.2 | Leeds-Ilkley |
| 01.05.95 | Esholt Jn-Dockley Jn | WYPTE | 3.5 | Ilkley-Bradford Forster Square |
| 01.05.95 | Shipley East-Bradford Forster Square | WYPTE | 3.0 | Leeds/Ilkley-Bradford Forster Square |
| 01.05.95 | Shipley West-Shipley South | WYPTE | 0.2 | Skipton-Bradford Forster Square |
| 14.01.96 | Heald Green South-West Jn | GMPTE | 0.5 | Manchester Airport-Crewe |
| 27.05.96 | Coatbridge Central-Garnqueen North | SPTE | 2.3 | Motherwell-Cumbernauld |
| 01.12.05 | Haughhead Jn-Larkhall | SPTE | 3.0 | North Clyde-Larkhall |
| 14.12.08 | Crewe South Jn-Kidsgrove Jn | DfT | 8.4 | Crewe-Trent Valley-Euston |
| 12.12.10 | Newbridge Jn-Drumgelloch | TS | 23.4 | North Clyde-Edinburgh |
| 10.12.12 | Shields Jn-Paisley Canal | TS | 6.0 | Glasgow Central-Paisley Canal |
| 08.12.13 | Castlefield Jn-Golbourne Jn | DfT | 15.2 | Manchester Airport-Scotland |
| 01.05.14 | Coatbridge Central–Garnqueen North | TS | 2.3 | Motherwell-Cumbernauld |
| 01.05.14 | Springburn-Garnqueen North Jn | TS | 8.0 | North Clydeside-Cumbernauld |
| **Total mileage** | | | **218.1** | |

Source: Alan Taylor

Notes: DTp/DfT – Department of/for Transport  TS – Transport Scotland  WA – Welsh Assembly

**F4: Lines scheduled for electrification that could be used by regional railway services (as at 1/2/2015)**

| Date | Section electrified | PTE | Miles | Passenger service |
| --- | --- | --- | --- | --- |
| May 2015 | Bootle Branch Jn-Earlestown East | DfT | 13.0 | Manchester-Liverpool |
| May 2015 | Huyton Jn-Springs Branch Jn | DfT | 12.9 | Liverpool-Wigan |
| Jul 2016 | Barnt Green Jn-Bromsgrove | WMPTE | 3.7 | Lichfield Trent Valley-Bromsgrove |
| Dec 2016 | Manchester Victoria-Stalybridge | DfT | 7.8 | Liverpool-Leeds |
| Dec 2016 | Manchester Victoria-Euxton Jn | DfT | 25.4 | Manchester-Preston |
| Dec 2016 | Guide Bridge W Jn-Stalybridge Jn | DfT | 2.0 | Manchester Airport-Newcastle |
| Dec 2016 | Oxenholme-Windermere | DfT | 6.3 | Manchester Airport-Windermere |
| Feb 2017 | Preston-Blackpool North | DfT | 17.2 | Manchester-Blackpool |
| Mar 2017 | Glasgow Queen St HL-Newbridge Jn | TS | 38.9 | Glasgow-Edinburgh via Falkirk |
| Jun-Dec 2017 | Bristol Temple Meads/Parkway-Swansea | DfT | 86.3 | Bristol-Cardiff |
| Dec 2017 | Lostock Jn-Wigan | DfT | 6.8 | Manchester-Wigan Wallgate |
| Dec 2017 | Walsall-Rugeley Trent Valley | DfT | 15.3 | Wolverhampton-Rugeley Trent Valley |
| Dec 2018 | Stalybridge-Copley Hill West Jn | DfT | 34.9 | Manchester Airport-Newcastle |
| Dec 2018 | Marsh Lane Jn-Colton Jn | DfT | 20.0 | Manchster Airport-Newcastle |
| Dec 2018 | Micklefield Jun-Hambleton South Jn | DfT | 7.5 | Leeds-Doncaster |
| Mar 2019 | Oxford North Jn-Bletchley Flyover Jn | DfT | 30.2 | Oxford-Milton Keynes |
| Mar 2019 | Stirling-Alloa | TS | 7.0 | Glasgow Queen St/Edinburgh-Alloa |
| Mar 2019 | Rutherglen East Jn-Whifflet | TS | 7.0 | Glasgow Central-Whifflet |
| Mar 2019 | Cumbernauld-Greenhill Lower Jn | TS | 5.6 | Glasgow Queen St-Falkirk Grahamston |
| Mar 2019 | Greenhill Jn-Carmuirs-Polmont | TS | 8.6 | Glasgow Queen St-Falkirk Grahamston |
| Mar 2019 | Carmuirs West Jn-Dunblane | TS | 16.3 | Glasgow Queen St-Dunblane |
| Mar 2019 | Holytown-Shotts-Midcalder Jn | TS | 21.8 | Glasgow Central-Edinburgh |
| Dec 2019 | Trent Jn-Derby | DfT | 9.2 | Leicester-Derby |
| Dec 2019 | Leamington Spa-Coventry Sth Jn | DfT | 9.4 | Leamington-Nuneaton |
| Dec 2019 | Coventry Nth Jn-Nuneaton Sth Jn | DfT | 9.4 | Leamington-Nuneaton |
| Dec 2019 | Ebbw Jn-Ebbw Vale | WA | 18.4 | Ebbw Vale-Maesteg/Cardiff Cen |
| Dec 2019 | Cardiff Bay-Cardiff QSt Sth Jct | WA | 0.8 | Cardiff Bay-Cardiff Queen Street |
| Dec 2019 | Barry Island-Merthyr Tydfil | WA | 33.3 | Barry Island-Merthyr Tydfil |
| Dec 2019 | Cardiff Queen St N Jn-Rhymney | WA | 22.7 | Cardiff Bay-Rhymney |
| Dec 2019 | Heath Jn-Coryton | WA | 2.5 | Radyr-Coryton |
| Dec 2019 | Abercynon-Aberdare | WA | 7.5 | Barry Island/Penarth-Aberdare |
| Dec 2019 | Ninian Park-Radyr | WA | 4.2 | Coryton-Radyr |
| Dec 2019 | Pontypridd - Treherbert | WA | 10.8 | Barry Island/Penarth - Treherbert |
| Dec 2019 | Cogan Jn-Penarth | WA | 1.1 | Cardiff Valleys-Penarth |
| Dec 2019 | Barry Town-Bridgend Jn | WA | 19.0 | Cardiff Central-Barry-Bridgend |
| Dec 2019 | Bridgend-Maesteg | WA | 8.0 | Ebbw Vale/Cardiff-Maesteg |
| Dec 2020 | Bletchley North Jn-Bedford | DfT | 17.4 | Oxford-Bedford |
| **Total mileage** | | | **568.2** | |

Source: Alan Taylor

Notes: DfT – Department for Transport  TS - Transport Scotland  WA – Wels Assembly

## F5: Lines reviewed by Northern Electrification Task Force, March 2015

### Tier 1 schemes, recommended for electrification during Control Period 6 (2019-24):

| Route to be electrified | Operator(s) | Miles | Score (out of 100 max) |
|---|---|---|---|
| Leeds-Bradford-Halifax/Manchester/Preston/Brighouse, etc | Northern | | 84 |
| Liverpool-Warrington Central-Manchester | Northern | | 80 |
| Southport/Kirkby to Salford Crescent | Northern | | 79 |
| Chester-Knutsford-Stockport | Northern | | 75 |
| Northallerton-Middlesbrough | TPE, East Coast | | 73 |
| Leeds-Harrogate-York | Northern | | 70 |
| Selby-Hull | Northern, TPE, Hull Trains | | 70 |
| Sheffield-Barnsley-Leeds/Castleford and connections | Northern, East Midlands* | | 68 |
| Bolton-Clitheroe | Northern | | 67 |
| Sheffield-Doncaster/Wakefield Westgate | Northern, TPE | | 66 |
| Hazel Grove-Buxton | Northern | | 64 |
| Warrington-Chester | Northern | | 64 |
| **Total mileage** | | **450** | |

*Completion set by Network Rail for June 2021

### Tier 2 schemes to be developed post-2024, but also considered for other approaches'

| Route to be electrified | Operator(s) | Miles | Score (out of 100 max) |
|---|---|---|---|
| Manchester-Sheffield (Hope Valley) & Manchester south east local services | East Midlands, Northern, TPE | | 59 |
| York-Scarborough | Northern, TPE | | 53 |
| Bishop Auckland-Darlington-Saltburn/Sunderland | Northern | | 53 |
| Barnsley-Penistone-Huddersfield | Northern | | 50 |
| Sheffield-Retford-Lincoln | Northern | | 49 |
| Chester-Crewe | Wales & Borders, West Coast | | 47 |
| Colne-Burnley; Kirkham-Blackpool South | Northern | | 45 |
| Knottingley-Goole | Northern | | 45 |
| **Total mileage** | | **300** | |

## F6: Capacity enhancement schemes benefitting regional services

In operation and planned, 2014

| | Year | Miles | Comments |
|---|---|---|---|
| **Requadrification (4 tracks)** | | | |
| Leeds West End | 1997 | 1 | |
| Trent Valley four-tracking | 2007 | 13 | |
| Edge Hill-Huyton Jn | 2014 | 4 | |
| Lawrence Hill-Filton | 2016 | 4 | |
| **Re-doubling** | | | |
| Blair Atholl-Dalwhinnie | 1974 | 23 | |
| Probus-Burngallow | 2003 | 7 | |
| Gretna-Annan | 2008 | 8 | |
| Lugton-Stewarton | 2009 | 5 | |
| Uphall-Bathgate | 2011 | 6 | |
| Moreton in Marsh-Evesham | 2011 | 15 | |

## F6: Capacity enhancement schemes benefitting regional services (continued)

|  | Year | Miles | Comments |
|---|---|---|---|
| Charlbury-Ascott | 2011 | 4 | |
| Doncaster Sheffield Jn | 2011 | 1 | Sheffield line junction re-doubled |
| York Holgate Jn | 2011 | 1 | Leeds line junction re-doubled |
| Swindon-Kemble | 2014 | 12 | |
| Swansea-Gowerton | 2014 | 6 | |
| Chester-Wrexham | 2015 | 8 | |
| **Extra platforms** | | | |
| Bristol Parkway | 2007 | | New Platform 3 added |
| Bristol Temple Meads | 20?? | | Platform 13/14 restored to use |
| Cambridge | 2012 | | Two new platforms (new island) |
| Cardiff Central | 2000 | | Platform 0 for Stadium |
| Cardiff Central | 2015 | | New Platform 8 |
| Cardiff Queen St | 1987 | | Platform 1 restored (Cardiff Bay) |
|  | 2015 | | Two new platforms added |
| Chesterfield | 20?? | | New Platform 3 |
| Edinburgh | 2006 | | Four new platforms (1, 3, 10, 20) |
| Filton Abbey Wood | 2016 | | Fourth platform with fourth track |
| Glasgow Central | 2010 | | Two new platforms (12, 13) |
| Glasgow Queen St | 1991 | | One platform restored |
| Gloucester | 1984 | | Platform 4 restored to use |
| Haymarket | 2006 | | New bay Platform 5 |
| Leeds | 1987 | | Seven additional platforms |
| Manchester Airport | 2015 | | New Platform 3 |
|  | 2015 | | New Platform 4 |
| Manchester Piccadilly | 2017 | | Two new platforms (new island) |
| Newcastle | 1987 | | Platforms 5-8 |
| Newport | 2010 | | Down platform restored to regular use |
| Nottingham | 2007 | | One extra platform |
| Nuneaton | 2005 | | Two new platforms |
| Peterborough | 2014 | | Two new platforms (new island) |
| Pontypridd | 1990 | | New Platform 2 on freight lines |
|  | 2015 | | Bay Platform 1 (formerly 6) restored |
| Stockport | 2008 | | New Platform 0 to Buxton |
| Swindon | 2003 | | Down Main platform and Valley bay restored |
| **New passing loops** | | | |
| Llandrindod Wells | 1988 | | Replaced siding |
| Knighton | 1991 | | New loop |
| Mountain Ash | 2002 | | New loop |
| Penryn | 2007 | | New loop |
| Merthyr Vale | 2008 | | New loop |
| Beccles | 2013 | | Restored loop |
| Alvechurch | 2014 | | New dynamic loop to permit 20-minute service |
| Cross Keys-Llanhilleth | 2015 | | New 'dynamic loop' to permit half-hourly service |
| **Additional flyovers** | | | |
| Norton Bridge | 2017 | | Separation of Crewe and Manchester traffic to increase capacity of WC main line |
| Nuneaton | 2008 | | Restored flyover |

Source: Theo Steel

## F7: Lines proposed by BR Board for closure (leaked document, September 1979)

| Service | For closure in Beeching Report? | 1968 grant (£000) | Bus substitution studied | Serpell casualty? | Current position |
|---|---|---|---|---|---|
| Wrexham-Bidston | Yes | 155[1] | 1987 | Yes | Electrification proposed |
| Hooton-Helsby | Yes | 190[2] | No | No | Part electrified |
| Lancaster-Morecambe | No | 69 | No | Yes | Minimal facilities |
| Aylesbury-Princes Risborough | No | Yes[3] | No | No | East-west line potential |
| Bristol-Severn Beach | Yes | 81[4] | 1987/88 | Yes | 90% growth, 2007-11 |
| Harrogate-York | Yes | 172 | No | Yes | Half-hourly Leeds-Knaresborough |
| Darlington-Bishop Auckland | Yes | 120 | 1982/85/89 | Yes | Shildon Museum: Weardale Railway |
| Sinfin-Derby | No | Until 1974 | 1987/88 | Yes | Closed |
| Clayton West-Shepley | Yes | 140[5] | 1981 | Yes | Closed - No PTE support |
| Watford-St Albans | Yes | 45 | No | Yes | Electrified |
| Bletchley-Bedford | No | 89 | No | Yes | Closure revoked 1974 |
| Stourbridge Town-Junction | No | 30 | No | Yes | Class 139 Parry People Mover |
| Oldham-Rochdale | No | 454[6] | No | Yes | Metro light rail, 2014 |
| Stratford-Leamington | Yes | 73 | 1982 | Yes | Chiltern Railways |
| Colchester-Sudbury | Yes | 61 | 1965/69 | Yes | Established commuter service |
| Norwich-Sheringham | No | 44[7] | 1982/87/89 | Yes | Traffic doubled since 2004 |
| Peterborough-Spalding | Yes | See below | 1987 | Yes | Closed 1970, reopened 1971 |
| March-Doncaster | No | 363[8] | 1982/87/89 | Yes | March-Spalding closed, rest upgraded for ECML freight |
| Grantham-Skegness | Yes | 10[9] | No | Yes | Promoted as 'Poacher Line' |
| Retford-Barnetby | No | 70[10] | 1985/89 | No | Limited service Saturdays only |
| Par-Newquay | No | - | 1987/89 | Yes | 53% growth, 2007-11 |
| Falmouth-Truro | No | 89 | 1987/89 | Yes | New loop; 91% growth, 2007-11 |
| Exeter-Barnstaple | No | 148 | 1987/89 | Yes | 47% growth, 2007-11 |
| Plymouth-Gunnislake | Yes | 82 | 1987/9 | Yes | 22% growth, 2007-11 |
| Ashford-Hastings | Yes | 140 | No | Yes | Proposed for extension of HS1 electrification |
| Lowestoft-Ipswich | Yes | 173 | No | Yes | Hourly service with Beccles loop |
| Lowestoft-Norwich | No | 141 | No | Yes | Core service |
| Shrewsbury-Hereford | No | 81 | No | Yes | Hourly Manchester-South Wales |
| Worcester-Hereford | No | 319 | No | No | Core route |
| Ardrossan-Largs | No | 265 | No | Yes | Electrified 1985 |
| Stranraer-Ayr | Yes | 213 | 1985/87 | Yes | Declining shipping demand |
| Markinch-Cowdenbeath | No | 98[11] | No | Yes | Half-hourly service, Fife Circle |
| Fort William-Mallaig | No | 176 | 1987 | Yes | Scheduled steam services |
| Dingwall-Kyle of Lochalsh | Yes | 177 | 1985/87 | Yes | Tourist link to Skye |
| Crianlarich-Oban | Yes | 275[12] | No | Yes | Six trains daily, 2014 |
| North Berwick-Drem | No | 55[13] | No | Yes | Electrified hourly service |
| Machynlleth-Pwllheli | No | 232 | 1987 | Yes | Essential rural route |
| Milford Haven-Clarbeston Road | No | 295[14] | No | Yes | Hourly to Cardiff and Manchester |
| Pembroke Dock-Whitland | No | 72 | 1987 | Yes | Two-hourly service |
| Shrewsbury-Llanelli | Yes | 110[15] | 1987 | Yes | Promoted as 'Heart of Wales' line |
| Barrow-Whitehaven | Yes | 185 | 1987/89 | Yes | Promoted by Cumbria |

**Notes**

[1] Wrexham-New Brighton part-time grant  [2] Rock Ferry-Helsby/Chester  [3] £518,000 for whole route to Marylebone  [4] Part-year grant
[5] Huddersfield-Clayton West  [6] Manchester Victoria-Oldham-Rochdale  [7] Part-year grant  [8] East Lincolnshire, part year
[9] Boston-Skegness, part year  [10] Retford-Cleethorpes  [11] Edinburgh-Abroath via Dunfermline  [12] Glasgow-Oban
[13] Edinburgh-North Berwick, part year  [14] Swansea-Carmarthen-Milford Haven  [15] Part-year grant

Source: *Holding the Line*, Richard Faulkner and Chris Austin

## F8: Rural line utilisation Mon-Fri, 2014

Including ex-secondary main lines

| Route | Length (miles) | Average passenger trains per day (each way) |
|---|---|---|
| **England** | | |
| Peterborough–Doncaster Joint Line | 89 | |
|    Werrington Jn–Sleaford | 33 | 13* |
|    Sleaford–Lincoln | 21 | 14 |
|    Lincoln–Gainsborough Trent Jn | 16 | 19 |
|    Gainsborough Trent Jn to ECML | 19 | 5 |
| Hellifield–Carlisle | 87 | 7-8 |
| Barrow in Furness–Carlisle | 85 | 7-9 |
| Hull–Scarborough | 54 | 9** |
| Ipswich–Lowestoft | 49 | 17 |
| Grantham–Skegness | 55 | 15-16 |
| Exeter–Barnstaple | 38 | 14-15 |
| Middlesbrough (Nunthorpe)–Whitby | 35 | 4 |
| Castle Cary–Dorchester West | 32 | 8 |
| Norwich–Sheringham | 30 | 17 |
| Carnforth–Hellifield | 28 | 5 |
| Par–Newquay | 21 | 6 |
| Norwich–Lowestoft | 23 | 18 |
| Norwich–Great Yarmouth | 18 | 23 |
| Truro–Falmouth Docks | 12 | 24 |
| St Budeaux Jn (Plym)–Gunnislake | 11 | 9 |
| Barton on Humber–Habrough | 12 | 9 |
| Oxenholme–Windermere | 10 | 17 |
| Liskeard–Looe | 9 | 12 |
| St Erth–St Ives | 4 | 28 |
| **Total English Mileage** | **710** | - |
| **Wales** | | |
| Llanelli–Fishguard Main line | 104 | - |
|    Llanelli–Whitland | 35 | 25 |
|    Whitland–Pembroke Dock | 27 | 9 |
|    Whitland–Clarbeston Road | 12 | 15 |
|    Clarbeston Road–Milford Haven | 14 | 10 |
|    Clarbeston Road–Fishguard Hbr | 16 | 7 |
| Craven Arms–Llanelli | 90 | 4-5 |
| Shrewsbury–Aberystwyth | 82 | 12 |
| Dovey Jn–Pwllheli | 58 | 8-9 |
| Llandudno–Blaenau Ffestiniog | 31 | 6 |
| **Total Welsh Route Miles** | **365** | - |
| **Scotland** | | |
| Dingwall–Wick/Thurso | 150 | 4 |
| Dingwall–Kyle of Lochalsh | 61 | 4 |
| Helensburgh–Fort William/Mallaig | 139 | 4 |
| Crianlarich–Oban | 42 | 6 |
| Kilmarnock–Gretna Green Jn | 81 | 8 |
| Ayr–Stranraer | 77 | 6 |
| **Total Scottish Mileage** | **532** | - |

**Rural total:** 1,599 route miles with insufficient income from the fare box to cover the costs of infrastructure.

*5 Peterborough-Spalding only
**28 Hull-Bridlington

# Factfile G: Stations

### G1: Summary Provincial/Regional Railways stations 1982-2015

| Year (1 Jan) | Total | Opened Total | Opened Rural | Opened Urban | Closed | Transfered from BR/National Rail | Total |
|---|---|---|---|---|---|---|---|
| 1982 | 1364 | 6 | 2 | - | 4 | - | - |
| 1983 | 1370 | 4 | - | - | 4 | - | - |
| 1984 | 1374 | 12 | 4 | - | 8 | - | - |
| 1985 | 1386 | 15 | 5 | 1 | 9 | 2 | - |
| 1986 | 1399 | 19 | 7 | 3 | 9 | 4 | - |
| 1987 | 1414 | 21 | 3 | - | 18 | 1 | - |
| 1988 | 1434 | 18 | 1 | - | 17 | 2 | - |
| 1989 | 1450 | 14 | 2 | - | 12 | 1 | 8 |
| 1990 | 1455 | 17 | - | - | 17 | 2 | - |
| 1991 | 1470 | 3 | - | - | 3 | 4 | 14 |
| 1992 | 1455 | 15 | - | - | 15 | | - |
| 1993 | 1470 | 15 | 1 | - | 14 | 2 | - |
| 1994 | 1483 | 17 | - | 1 | 16 | 2 | - |
| 1995 | 1498 | 9 | - | - | 9 | 5 | - |
| 1996 | 1502 | 4 | - | 1 | 3 | 1 | - |
| 1997 | 1504 | 3 | - | 1 | 2 | 1 | - |
| 1998 | 1507 | 8 | - | - | 8 | 2 | - |
| 1999 | 1513 | 1 | - | - | 1 | - | - |
| 2000 | 1514 | 4 | - | - | 4 | - | - |
| 2001 | 1518 | 1 | - | - | 1 | - | - |
| 2002 | 1519 | 3 | - | 1 | 2 | - | 3 |
| 2003 | 1519 | 1 | - | - | 1 | - | - |
| 2004 | 1520 | 1 | - | - | 1 | - | - |
| 2005 | 1521 | 8 | - | - | 8 | 1 | - |
| 2006 | 1528 | 1 | - | - | 1 | - | - |
| 2007 | 1529 | 2 | - | - | 2 | - | - |
| 2008 | 1531 | 7 | - | - | 7 | - | - |
| 2009 | 1538 | 2 | - | 1 | 1 | - | 9 |
| 2010 | 1531 | 1 | - | - | 1 | - | - |
| 2011 | 1532 | 2 | - | - | 2 | - | - |
| 2012 | 1534 | 2 | 1 | - | 1 | - | - |
| 2013 | 1536 | 1 | 1 | - | - | - | - |
| 2014 | 1537 | 3 | 1 | - | 2 | - | - |
| 2015 | 1540 | | | | | | |
| **TOTAL** | | **240** | **28** | **9** | **203** | **30** | **34** |

*Three stations are out of use not officially closed – see G3

## G2: New stations opened or reopened 1982-2014

Passengers per annum joining/alighting from ORR 2013/14 survey

| Station | BR Region (1982) | PTE/County | Opened | Passengers '000s |
| --- | --- | --- | --- | --- |
| Fitzwilliam | Eastern | WYPTE | 01.03.1982 | 256 |
| Valley | London Midland | Anglesey | 15.03.1982 | 18 |
| Blaenau Ffestiniog | London Midland | Gwynedd | 22.03.1982 | 45 |
| Deighton | Eastern | WYPTE | 26.04.1982 | 95 |
| Crossflatts | Eastern | WYPTE | 17.05.1982 | 464 |
| Slaithwaite | Eastern | WYPTE | 13.12.1982 | 208 |
| Bramley | Eastern | WYPTE | 12.09.1983 | 317 |
| Cathays | Western | Cardiff | 03.10.1983 | 806 |
| Runcorn East | London Midland | Cheshire | 03.10.1983 | 155 |
| Moss Side | London Midland | Lancashire | 21.11.1983 | 2 |
| Saltaire | Eastern | WMPTE | 10.04.1984 | 807 |
| Auchinleck | Scottish | East Ayrshire/SPTE | 12.05.1984 | 56 |
| Kilmaurs | Scottish | East Ayrshire/SPTE | 12.05.1984 | 107 |
| Lostock Hall | London Midland | Lancashire | 14.05.1984 | 41 |
| South Bank | Eastern | Cleveland | 01.07.1984 | 13 |
| Sherburn in Elmet | Eastern | North Yorkshire | 09.07.1984 | 43 |
| Melton | Eastern | Suffolk | 03.09.1984 | 69 |
| Dyce | Scottish | Aberdeen | 15.09.1984 | 811 |
| Dunston | Eastern | Tyne & Wear PTE | 01.10.1994 | 2 |
| Livingston South | Scottish | West Lothian | 06.10.1984 | 296 |
| Humphrey Park | London Midland | GMPTE | 15.10.1984 | 25 |
| Silkstone Common | Eastern | SYPTE | 26.11.1984 | 30 |
| Mills Hill | London Midland | GMPTE | 25.03.1985 | 303 |
| Loch Awe | Scottish | Argyll & Bute | 01.05.1985 | 3 |
| South Gyle | Scottish | Edinburgh | 01.05.1985 | 575 |
| Loch Eil Outward Bound | Scottish | Highland | 06.05.1985 | 1 |
| Bridge of Allan | Scottish | Stirling | 13.05.1985 | 259 |
| Flowery Field | London Midland | GMPTE | 13.05.1985 | 198 |
| Longbeck | Eastern | Cleveland | 13.05.1985 | 40 |
| Melksham | Western | Wiltshire | 13.05.1985 | 24 |
| Portlethen | Scottish | Aberdeenshire | 17.05.1985 | 48 |
| Roughton Road | Eastern | Norfolk | 20.05.1985 | 12 |
| Dunrobin Castle | Scottish | Sutherland | 30.06.1985 | 1 |
| Smithy Bridge | London Midland | GMPTE | 18.08.1985 | 167 |
| Bromborough Rake | London Midland | Merseyside PTE | 30.09.1985 | 297 |
| Lisvane and Thornhill | Western | Cardiff | 04.11.1985 | 170 |
| Ryder Brow | London Midland | GMPTE | 04.11.1985 | 30 |
| Bathgate | Scottish | West Lothian | 24.03.1986 | 1,061 |
| Livingston North | Scottish | West Lothian | 24.03.1986 | 1,031 |
| Uphall | Scottish | West Lothian | 24.03.1986 | 511 |

**G2: New stations opened or reopened 1982-2014 (continued)**

| Station | BR Region (1982) | PTE/County | Opened | Passengers '000s |
|---|---|---|---|---|
| South Wigston | London Midland | Leicestershire | 10.05.1986 | 67 |
| Cwmbran | Western | Torfaen | 12.05.1986 | 348 |
| Langley Mill | London Midland | Derbyshire | 12.05.1986 | 94 |
| Telford Central | London Midland | Telford | 12.05.1986 | 1071 |
| Armathwaite | London Midland | Cumbria | 14.07.1986 | 8 |
| Dent | London Midland | Cumbria | 14.07.1986 | 10 |
| Garsdale | London Midland | Cumbria | 14.07.1986 | 16 |
| Horton-in-Ribblesdale | London Midland | North Yorkshire | 14.07.1986 | 16 |
| Kirkby Stephen | London Midland | Cumbria | 14.07.1986 | 30 |
| Langwathby | London Midland | Cumbria | 14.07.1986 | 24 |
| Lazonby & Kirkoswald | London Midland | Cumbria | 13.07.1986 | 16 |
| Burnley Manchester Road | London Midland | Lancashire | 29.09.1986 | 245 |
| Hall i' th' Wood | London Midland | GMPTE | 29.09.1986 | 128 |
| Ynyswen | Western | Rhondda | 29.09.1986 | 10 |
| Ystrad Rhondda | Western | Rhondda | 29.09.1986 | 52 |
| Eastbrook | Western | Vale of Glamorgan | 24.11.1986 | 169 |
| Ardrossan Town | Scottish | SPTE | 19.01.1987 | 22 |
| Clitheroe | London Midland | Lancashire | 08.04.1987 | 319 |
| Blackpool Pleasure Beach | London Midland | Blackpool | 13.04.1987 | 96 |
| Ty Glas | Western | Cardiff | 29.04.1987 | 117 |
| East Garforth | Eastern | WYPTE | 01.05.1987 | 223 |
| Hag Fold | London Midland | GMPTE | 11.05.1987 | 57 |
| Heysham Port | London Midland | Lancashire | 11.05.1987 | 9 |
| Rotherham Central | Eastern | SYPTE | 11.05.1987 | 667 |
| Salford Crescent | London Midland | GMPTE | 11.05.1987 | 1142 |
| Wester Hailes | Scottish | Lothian/Edinburgh | 11.05.1987 | 36 |
| Sugar Loaf | Western | Powys | 21.06.1987 | 1 |
| Conwy | London Midland | Conwy | 27.06.1987 | 38 |
| Metrocentre | Eastern | Tyne & Wear PTE | 03.08.1987 | 375 |
| Frizinghall | Eastern | WYPTE | 07.09.1987 | 378 |
| Danescourt | Western | Cardiff | 04.10.1987 | 86 |
| Fairwater | Western | Cardiff | 04.10.1987 | 51 |
| Ninian Park | Western | Cardiff | 04.10.1987 | 100 |
| Birmingham Snow Hill | London Midland | WMPTE | 05.10.1987 | 4402 |
| Curriehall | Scottish | Lothian/Edinburgh | 05.10.1987 | 64 |
| Waun-Gron Park | Western | Cardiff | 02.11.1987 | 55 |
| Sandal & Agbrigg | Eastern | WYPTE | 30.11.1987 | 260 |
| Cononley | Eastern | North Yorkshire | 21.04.1988 | 170 |
| Cottingley | Eastern | WYPTE | 25.04.1988 | 102 |
| Bedworth | London Midland | Warwickshire | 14.05.1988 | 70 |
| Goldthorpe | Eastern | SYPTE | 16.05.1988 | 59 |
| Halewood | London Midland | Merseyside PTE | 16.05.1988 | 97 |

**G2: New stations opened or reopened 1982-2014 (continued)**

| Station | BR Region (1982) | PTE/County | Opened | Passengers '000s |
|---|---|---|---|---|
| Lostock Parkway | London Midland | GMPTE | 16.05.1988 | 269 |
| Thurnscoe | Eastern | SYPTE | 16.05.1988 | 69 |
| Falls of Cruachen | Scottish | Argyll & Bute | 20.06.1988 | 1 |
| Outwood | Eastern | WYPTE | 12.07.1988 | 349 |
| Overpool | London Midland | Cheshire | 16.08.1988 | 143 |
| Abercynon | Western | Rhondda | 03.10.1988 | 251 |
| Aberdare | Western | Rhondda | 03.10.1988 | 558 |
| Cwmbach | Western | Rhondda | 03.10.1988 | 21 |
| Fernhill | Western | Rhondda | 03.10.1988 | 25 |
| Mountain Ash | Western | Rhondda | 03.10.1988 | 92 |
| Musselburgh | Scottish | East Lothian | 03.10.1988 | 439 |
| Penrhiwceiber | Western | Rhondda | 03.10.1988 | 49 |
| Burley Park | Eastern | WYPTE | 29.11.1988 | 588 |
| Tutbury & Hatton | London Midland | Derbyshire | 03.04.1989 | 58 |
| Cannock | London Midland | Staffordshire | 08.04.1989 | 248 |
| Hednesford | London Midland | Staffordshire | 08.04.1989 | 181 |
| Landywood | London Midland | Staffordshire | 08.04.1989 | 110 |
| Bloxwich | London Midland | WMPTE | 17.04.1989 | 44 |
| Airbles | Scottish | SPTE | 15.05.1989 | 113 |
| Drumgelloch | Scottish | SPTE | 15.05.1989 | 345 |
| Greenfaulds | Scottish | SPTE | 15.05.1989 | 131 |
| Milliken Park | Scottish | SPTE | 15.05.1989 | 190 |
| Stepps | Scottish | SPTE | 15.05.1989 | 277 |
| Yate | Western | Gloucestershire | 15.05.1989 | 329 |
| Dodworth | Eastern | SYPTE | 16.05.1989 | 37 |
| Llanwrwst | London Midland | Conwy | 29.07.1989 | 19 |
| Berry Brow | Eastern | WYPTE | 09.10.1989 | 26 |
| Priesthill & Darnley | Scottish | SPTE | 23.04.1990 | 126 |
| Shieldmuir | Scottish | SPTE | 14.05.1990 | 81 |
| Steeton & Silsden | Eastern | WYPTE | 14.05.1990 | 797 |
| Swinton | Eastern | SYPTE | 14.05.1990 | 356 |
| Whinhill | Scottish | SPTE | 14.05.1990 | 26 |
| Tame Bridge Parkway | London Midland | WMPTE | 04.06.1990 | 521 |
| Corkerhill | Scottish | SPTE | 30.07.1990 | 205 |
| Crookston | Scottish | SPTE | 30.07.1990 | 133 |
| Drumbreck | Scottish | SPTE | 30.07.1990 | 131 |
| Mosspark | Scottish | SPTE | 30.07.1990 | 111 |
| Paisley Canal | Scottish | SPTE | 30.07.1990 | 341 |
| Meadowhall | Eastern | SYPTE | 05.09.1990 | 2063 |
| Walsden | Eastern | WYPTE | 10.09.1990 | 94 |
| Worle | Western | Devon | 24.09.1990 | 276 |
| Whiston | London Midland | Merseyside PTE | 01.10.1990 | 371 |

## G2: New stations opened or reopened 1982-2014 (continued)

| Station | BR Region (1982) | PTE/County | Opened | Passengers '000s |
|---|---|---|---|---|
| Woodsmoor | London Midland | GMPTE | 01.10.1990 | 187 |
| Bloxwich North | London Midland | WMPTE | 02.10.1990 | 44 |
| Hawkhead | Scottish | SPTE | 12.04.1991 | 84 |
| Kirk Sandall | Eastern | SYPTE | 13.05.1991 | 95 |
| New Cumnock | Scottish | East Ayrshire | 27.05.1991 | 27 |
| Bentley | Eastern | SYPTE | 27.04.1992 | 119 |
| Featherstone | Eastern | WYPTE | 11.05.1992 | 73 |
| Glenrothes with Thornton | Scottish | Fife | 11.05.1992 | 63 |
| Pencoed | Western | Bridgend | 11.05.1992 | 297 |
| Pontefract Tanshelf | Eastern | WYPTE | 11.05.1992 | 39 |
| Streethouse | Eastern | WYPTE | 11.05.1992 | 28 |
| Hornbeam Park | Eastern | North Yorkshire | 24.08.1992 | 303 |
| Garth | Western | Bridgend | 28.09.1992 | 26 |
| Maesteg | Western | Bridgend | 28.09.1992 | 219 |
| Pontyclun | Western | Rhondda | 28.09.1992 | 281 |
| Sarn | Western | Bridgend | 28.09.1992 | 78 |
| Tondu | Western | Bridgend | 28.09.1992 | 51 |
| Maesteg Ewenny Road | Western | Bridgend | 26.10.1992 | 4 |
| Wildmill | Western | Bridgend | 12.12.1992 | 18 |
| Whifflet | Scottish | SPTE | 21.12.1992 | 233 |
| Hucknall | London Midland | Nottinghamshire | 08.05.1993 | 133 |
| Newstead | London Midland | Nottinghamshire | 08.05.1993 | 29 |
| Manchester Airport | London Midland | GMPTE | 17.05.1993 | 3137 |
| Gretna Green | Scottish | Dumfries & Galloway | 20.09.1993 | 38 |
| Baillieston | Scottish | SPTE | 04.10.1993 | 112 |
| Bargeddie | Scottish | SPTE | 04.10.1993 | 88 |
| Carmyle | Scottish | SPTE | 04.10.1993 | 132 |
| Kirkwood | Scottish | SPTE | 04.10.1993 | 153 |
| Mount Vernon | Scottish | SPTE | 04.10.1993 | 57 |
| Adwick | Eastern | SYPTE | 11.10.1993 | 180 |
| Ashfield | Scottish | SPTE | 03.12.1993 | 74 |
| Gilshochill | Scottish | SPTE | 03.12.1993 | 95 |
| Maryhill | Scottish | SPTE | 03.12.1993 | 77 |
| Possilpark & Parkhouse | Scottish | SPTE | 03.12.1993 | 99 |
| Summerston | Scottish | SPTE | 03.12.1993 | 154 |
| Barrow upon Soar | London Midland | Leicestershire | 27.05.1994 | 89 |
| Bulwell | London Midland | Nottinghamshire | 27.05.1994 | 50 |
| Sileby | London Midland | Leicestershire | 27.05.1994 | 111 |
| Syston | London Midland | Leicestershire | 27.05.1994 | 176 |
| Cam & Dursley | Western | Gloucestershire | 29.05.1994 | 177 |
| Langho | London Midland | Lancashire | 29.05.1994 | 48 |
| Ramsgreave & Wilpshire | London Midland | Lancashire | 29.05.1994 | 114 |

**G2: New stations opened or reopened 1982-2014 (continued)**

| Station | BR Region (1982) | PTE/County | Opened | Passengers '000s |
| --- | --- | --- | --- | --- |
| Whalley | London Midland | Lancashire | 29.05.1994 | 84 |
| Briton Ferry | Western | Neath Port Talbot | 01.06.1994 | 35 |
| Wallyford | Scottish | East Lothian | 13.06.1994 | 268 |
| Llansamlet | Western | Swansea | 27.06.1994 | 33 |
| Pyle | Western | Bridgend | 27.06.1994 | 156 |
| Sanquhar | Scottish | Dumfries & Galloway | 27.06.1994 | 27 |
| Skewen | Western | Neath Port Talbot | 27.06.1994 | 37 |
| Ivybridge | Western | Devon | 14.07.1994 | 67 |
| Prestwick Intl Airport | Scottish | SPTE | 05.09.1994 | 454 |
| Camelon | Scottish | Falkirk | 27.09.1994 | 116 |
| The Hawthorns | London Midland | WMPTE | 02.04.1995 | 406 |
| Eastham Rake | London Midland | Merseyside PTE | 03.04.1995 | 320 |
| Digby & Sowton | Western | Devon | 23.05.1995 | 773 |
| Willington | London Midland | Derbyshire | 26.05.1995 | 21 |
| Jewellery Quarter | London Midland | WMPTE | 24.09.1995 | 386 |
| Smethwick Galton Bridge | London Midland | WMPTE | 24.09.1995 | 562 |
| Mansfield | London Midland | Nottinghamshire | 20.11.1995 | 314 |
| Mansfield Woodhouse | London Midland | Nottinghamshire | 20.11.1995 | 140 |
| Sutton Parkway | London Midland | Nottinghamshire | 20.11.1995 | 135 |
| Yarm | Eastern | Stockton upon Tees | 20.02.1996 | 122 |
| Filton Abbey Wood | Western | South Gloucester | 11.03.1996 | 986 |
| Baglan | Western | Neath Port Talbot | 02.06.1996 | 23 |
| Kirkby in Ashfield | London Midland | Nottinghamshire | 17.11.1996 | 147 |
| Ashchurch for Tewkesbury | Western | Gloucestershire | 01.06.1997 | 84 |
| Rugeley Town | London Midland | Staffordshire | 01.06.1997 | 145 |
| Euxton Balshaw Lane | London Midland | Lancashire | 15.12.1997 | 59 |
| Brunswick | London Midland | Merseyside PTE | 09.03.1998 | 829 |
| Dalgety Bay | Scottish | Fife | 28.03.1998 | 269 |
| Creswell | London Midland | Derbyshire | 24.05.1998 | 42 |
| Drumfrochar | Scottish | SPTE | 24.05.1998 | 69 |
| Langwith Whaley Thorns | London Midland | Derbyshire | 24.05.1998 | 21 |
| Shirebrook | Eastern | Derbyshire | 24.05.1998 | 72 |
| Whitwell | Eastern | Derbyshire | 24.05.1998 | 18 |
| Conway Park | London Midland | Merseyside PTE | 22.06.1998 | 1061 |
| Horwich Parkway | London Midland | GMPTE | 30.06.1999 | 654 |
| Dunfermline Q Margaret | Scottish | Fife | 26.01.2000 | 209 |
| Brighouse | Eastern | West Yorkshire | 28.05.2000 | 372 |
| Wavertree Technical Park | London Midland | Merseyside PTE | 13.08.2000 | 468 |
| Lea Green | London Midland | Merseyside PTE | 17.09.2000 | 382 |
| Howwood | Scottish | SPTE | 12.03.2001 | 51 |
| Beauly | Scottish | Invernesshire | 15.04.2002 | 59 |
| Brunstane | Scottish | Lothian/Edinburgh | 03.06.2002 | 160 |

## G2: New stations opened or reopened 1982-2014 (continued)

| Station | BR Region (1982) | PTE/County | Opened | Passengers '000s |
|---|---|---|---|---|
| Newcraighall | Scottish | Lothian/Edinburgh | 03.06.2002 | 222 |
| Edinburgh Park | Scottish | Lothian/Edinburgh | 04.12.2003 | 960 |
| Sampford Courtenay | Western | Devon | 21.05.2004 | 146 |
| Glasshoughton | Eastern | WYPTE | 21.02.2005 | 178 |
| Gartcosh | Scottish | SPTE/Nth Lanark | 09.05.2005 | 153 |
| Llantwit Major | Western | Vale of Glamorgan | 12.06.2005 | 304 |
| Rhoose Cardiff Intl Airport | Western | Vale of Glamorgan | 12.06.2005 | 185 |
| Kelvindale | Scottish | SPTE | 29.09.2005 | 96 |
| Chatelherault | Scottish | SPTE | 12.12.2005 | 67 |
| Larkhall | Scottish | SPTE | 12.12.2005 | 406 |
| Merryton | Scottish | SPTE | 12.12.2005 | 111 |
| Liverpool South Parkway | London Midland | Merseyside PTE | 11.06.2006 | 1785 |
| Coleshill Parkway | London Midland | Warwickshire | 19.08.2007 | 216 |
| Llanharan | Western | Rhondda | 10.12.2007 | 163 |
| Ebbw Vale Parkway | Western | Gwent | 06.02.2008 | 264 |
| Newbridge | Western | Caerphilly | 06.02.2008 | 134 |
| Risca & Pontymister | Western | Caerphilly | 06.02.2008 | 109 |
| Rogerstone | Western | Caerphilly | 06.02.2008 | 101 |
| Llanhilleth | Western | Gwent | 27.04.2008 | 78 |
| Alloa | Scottish | Clackmannanshire | 19.05.2008 | 384 |
| Crosskeys | Western | Caerphilly | 07.06.2008 | 119 |
| East Midlands Parkway | London Midland | Nottinghamshire | 26.01.2009 | 328 |
| Laurencekirk | Scottish | Aberdeenshire | 18.05.2009 | 103 |
| Blackridge | Scottish | West Lothian | 01.12.2010 | 47 |
| Caldercruix | Scottish | West Lothian | 03.02.2011 | 102 |
| Armadale | Scottish | West Lothian | 04.03.2011 | 164 |
| Fishguard & Goodwick | Western | Pembrokeshire | 14.05.2012 | 19 |
| Conon Bridge | Scottish | Invernesshire | 08.02.2013 | 18 |
| Energlyn & Churchill Pky | Western | Caerphilly | 08.12.2013 | 16 |
| Stratford-on-Avon Pky | London Midland | Warwickshire | 19.05.2014 | n/a |
| John Cook Hospital | Eastern | Middlesbrough | 19.05.2014 | n/a |
| Pye Corner | Western | Newport | 14.12.2014 | n/a |

**G3: Planned station openings and reopenings from 2015**

| Station | BR Region (1982) | PTE/County | Operator | Opening |
|---|---|---|---|---|
| Newcourt | Western | Devon | Gter Western | 2015 |
| Shawfair | Scottish | Midlothian | ScotRail | 2015 |
| Eskbank | Scottish | Midlothian | ScotRail | 2015 |
| Newtongrange | Scottish | Midlothian | ScotRail | 2015 |
| Gorebridge | Scottish | Midlothian | ScotRail | 2015 |
| Stow | Scottish | Borders | ScotRail | 2015 |
| Galashiels | Scottish | Borders | ScotRail | 2015 |
| Tweedbank | Scottish | Borders | ScotRail | 2015 |
| Cranbrook | Southern/Western | Devon | SWT | 2015 |
| Low Moor | Eastern | WYPTE | Northern | 2015 |
| Apperley Bridge | Eastern | WYPTE | Northern | 2015 |
| Kirkstall Forge | Eastern | WYPTE | Northern | 2015 |
| Ebbw Vale Town | Western | Welsh Assembly | Wales & B | 2015 |
| Oxford Parkway | Western | Oxfordshire | Chiltern | 2015 |
| Bermuda Park | London Midland | Warwickshire | London Midland | 2015 |
| Ricoh Arena Coventry | London Midland | Centro | London Midland | 2015 |
| Bromsgrove* | London Midland | Centro/Worcestershire | London Midland | 2015 |
| Ilkeston | London Midland | Derbyshire | East Midland | 2016 |
| Cambridge Science Park | Eastern | Cambridgeshire | Gter Anglia/Thameslink | 2016 |
| Edinburgh Gateway | Scottish | Edinburgh | ScotRail | 2016 |
| Winslow | London Midland | Buckinghamshire | Chiltern | 2019 |
| Kenilworth | London Midland | Warwickshire | Cross Country/London Midland | 2016 |

*Replacement for existing station

**G4: Stations with fewer than 20 passengers a week**

(entries and exits combined, 2013/14)

| Station | BR Region (1982) | Operator | PTE/County/LA | Passengers per year | Av passengers per week |
|---|---|---|---|---|---|
| Achnashellach | Scottish | ScotRail | Highland | 976 | 20 |
| Duirinish | Scottish | ScotRail | Highland | 970 | 19 |
| Ince & Elton | London Midland | Northern | Cheshire W | 944 | 19 |
| Brigg | Eastern | Northern | Lincolnshire | 922 | 18 |
| Dunrobin Castle | Scottish | ScotRail | Highland | 916 | 18 |
| Llandecwyn | London Midland | Wales/Borders | Gwynedd | 880 | 18 |
| Portsmouth Arms | Western | Greater Western | Devon | 844 | 17 |
| Dolgarrog | London Midland | Wales/Borders | Conwy | 822 | 16 |
| Llangynllo | Western | Wales/Borders | Powys | 806 | 16 |
| Roman Bridge | London Midland | Wales/Borders | Conwy | 764 | 15 |
| Polesworth | London Midland | London Midland | Warwickshire | 702 | 14 |
| Springfield | Scottish | ScotRail | Fife | 680 | 14 |

**G4: Stations with fewer than 20 passengers a week (continued)**

| Station | BR Region (1982) | Operator | PTE/County/LA | Passengers per year | Av passengers per week |
|---|---|---|---|---|---|
| Culrain | Scottish | ScotRail | Highland | 628 | 13 |
| Braystones | London Midland | Northern | Cumbria | 620 | 12 |
| Lochluichart | Scottish | ScotRail | Highland | 612 | 12 |
| Locheilside | Scottish | ScotRail | Highland | 588 | 12 |
| Ardwick | London Midland | Northern | GMPTE | 568 | 11 |
| Duncraig | Scottish | ScotRail | Highland | 534 | 11 |
| Loch Eil Outward Bnd | Scottish | ScotRail | Highland | 522 | 10 |
| Beasdale | Scottish | ScotRail | Highland | 506 | 10 |
| Falls of Cruachan | Scottish | ScotRail | Argyll & Bute | 498 | 10 |
| Spooner Row | Eastern | Gter Anglia | Norfolk | 388 | 8 |
| Lakenheath | Eastern | Gter Anglia | Suffolk | 378 | 8 |
| Scotscalder | Scottish | ScotRail | Highland | 376 | 8 |
| New Clee | Eastern | Northern | NE Lincs | 348 | 7 |
| Hubberts Bridge | Eastern | East Midland | Boston | 334 | 7 |
| Rawcliffe | Eastern | Northern | East Riding | 314 | 6 |
| Stanlow & Thornton | London Midland | Northern | Cheshire W | 314 | 6 |
| Clifton | London Midland | Northern | GMPTE | 298 | 6 |
| Havenhouse | Eastern | East Midland | East Lindsey | 278 | 6 |
| Hensall | Eastern | Northern | Selby | 276 | 6 |
| Sugar Loaf | Western | Wales/Borders | Powys | 240 | 5 |
| Chapelton | Western | Gter Western | Devon | 232 | 5 |
| Achanalt | Scottish | ScotRail | Highland | 228 | 5 |
| Acklington | Eastern | Northern | Northumberland | 176 | 4 |
| Elton & Orston | Eastern | East Midlands | Nottinghamshire | 166 | 3 |
| Sampford Courtenay | Western | Gter Western | Devon | 146 | 3 |
| Kildonan | Scottish | ScotRail | Highland | 144 | 3 |
| Altnabreac | Scottish | ScotRail | Highland | 138 | 3 |
| Kirton Lindsey | Eastern | Northern | North Lincs | 120 | 2 |
| Denton | London Midland | Northern | GMPTE | 110 | 2 |
| Golf Street | Scottish | ScotRail | Angus | 90 | 2 |
| Pilning | Western | Gter Western | South Gloucs | 88 | 2 |
| Breich | Scottish | ScotRail | West Lothian | 64 | 1 |
| Coombe | Western | Gter Western | Cornwall | 42 | 1 |
| Barry Links | Scottish | ScotRail | Angus | 40 | 1 |
| Reddish South | London Midland | Northern | GMPTE | 26 | 1 |
| Shippea Hill | Eastern | Gter Anglia | Cambridgeshire | 12 | - |
| Teesside Airport | Eastern | Northern | Darlington | 8 | - |

Source ORR
*Based on a year of 50 weeks incl Bank Holidays
**Heritage service

**G5: Stations closed 1982-2014**

| Stations | Reason closed | Year |
|---|---|---|
| New Hadley | To save expensive repairs – GW wooden halt | 13.05.85 |
| Errol | To accelerate Glasgow – Dundee services | 30.09.85 |
| Gogarth Halt | To save expensive repairs – GW wooden halt | 14.05.86 |
| Abertafol Halt | To save expensive repairs – GW wooden halt | 14.05.86 |
| Cefn Onn | Replaced by Lisvane & Thornhill | 27.09.86 |
| Balloch Pier | *Maid of Loch* withdrawn by SPTE | 28.09.86 |
| Royton | Replaced by Derker on Rochdale trains | 08.05.87 |
| Rowntree Halt (York) | Works shuttle service withdrawn | 08.07.88 |
| Rotherham Masborough | Rotherham Central opened | 03.10.88 |
| Melton Halt (Brough) | Low usage | 08.07.89 |
| Cargo Fleet | Low usage | 21.01.90 |
| Altofts | Trains diverted via Castleford | 12.05.90 |
| Woodlands Road | Low usage | 12.07.91 |
| Llangelynin | Unlit halt – low usage couldn't justify electric supply | 25.10.91 |
| Greatham | Low usage | 24.11.91 |
| Grangetown | Low usage | 24.12.91 |
| Elsham | Low usage | 03.10.93 |
| Brocklesby | Low usage | 03.10.93 |
| Ditton | Liverpool South Parkway replaced | 27.05.94 |
| Pendleton | Fire damage – Salford Crescent adjacent | 17.07.94 |
| Attercliffe Road | Low usage | 28.01.95 |
| Brightside | Low usage – superseded by Meadowhall | 28.01.95 |
| Godley East | Low usage | 27.05.95 |
| Miles Platting | Low usage | 27.05.95 |
| Park | Low usage | 27.05.95 |
| Smethwick West | New station Smethwick Galton Bridge | 15.08.96 |
| Filton | New station Filton Abbey Wood | 14.02.97 |
| Sinfin North | Line closed – taxi some years previously | 27.08.98 |
| Sinfin Central | Line closed – taxi some years previously | 27.08.98 |
| Etruria | Low usage | 21.07.05 |
| Norton Bridge | Low usage (out of use but not officially closed) | 30.09.04 |
| Barlaston | Low usage (out of use but not officially closed) | 30.09.04 |
| Wedgwood | Low usage (out of use but not officially closed) | 30.09.04 |
| **TOTAL: 33** | | |

Source: Theo Steel

## G6: Regional stations transferred from national railway ownership

| Station | BR Region | PTE/County | Date | Reason |
| --- | --- | --- | --- | --- |
| Llanbadarn | London Midland | Ceredigion | 31.03.1989 | Sale of Vale of Rheidol Rlwy |
| Glanrafon | London Midland | Ceredigion | 31.03.1989 | ditto |
| Capel Bangor | London Midland | Ceredigion | 31.03.1989 | ditto |
| Nantyronen | London Midland | Ceredigion | 31.03.1989 | ditto |
| Aberffrwd | London Midland | Ceredigion | 31.03.1989 | ditto |
| Rheidol Falls | London Midland | Ceredigion | 31.03.1989 | ditto |
| Rhiwfron | London Midland | Ceredigion | 31.03.1989 | ditto |
| Devil's Bridge | London Midland | Ceredigion | 31.03.1989 | ditto |
| Crumpsall | London Midland | GMPTE | 16.08.1991 | Converted to tramway |
| Bowker Vale | London Midland | GMPTE | 16.08.1991 | ditto |
| Heaton Park | London Midland | GMPTE | 16.08.1991 | ditto |
| Prestwick | London Midland | GMPTE | 16.08.1991 | ditto |
| Besses o'the Barn | London Midland | GMPTE | 16.08.1991 | ditto |
| Whitefield | London Midland | GMPTE | 16.08.1991 | ditto |
| Radcliffe | London Midland | GMPTE | 16.08.1991 | ditto |
| Bury | London Midland | GMPTE | 16.08.1991 | ditto |
| Old Trafford | London Midland | GMPTE | 24.12.1991 | Converted to tramway |
| Warwick Road | London Midland | GMPTE | 24.12.1991 | ditto |
| Dane Road | London Midland | GMPTE | 24.12.1991 | ditto |
| Sale | London Midland | GMPTE | 24.12.1991 | ditto |
| Brooklands | London Midland | GMPTE | 24.12.1991 | ditto |
| Timperley | London Midland | GMPTE | 24.12.1991 | ditto |
| Brockley Whins | Eastern | T&WPTE | 31.03.2002 | Transferred to Metro |
| East Boldon | Eastern | T&WPTE | 31.03.2002 | ditto |
| Seaburn | Eastern | T&WPTE | 31.03.2002 | ditto |
| Dean Lane | London Midland | GMPTE | 03.10.2009 | Converted to Tramway |
| Failsworth | London Midland | GMPTE | 03.10.2009 | ditto |
| Hollinwood | London Midland | GMPTE | 03.10.2009 | ditto |
| Oldham Werneth | London Midland | GMPTE | 03.10.2009 | ditto |
| Oldham Mumps | London Midland | GMPTE | 03.10.2009 | ditto |
| Derker | London Midland | GMPTE | 03.10.2009 | ditto |
| Shaw | London Midland | GMPTE | 03.10.2009 | ditto |
| New Radcliffe | London Midland | GMPTE | 03.10.2009 | ditto |
| Milnrow | London Midland | GMPTE | 03.10.2009 | ditto |

## G7: Regional Railways stations with listed building status

### England and Wales

| Station | BR Region | Engineer/Architect | Date built | Date listed |
|---|---|---|---|---|
| **Grade I** | | | | |
| Huddersfield | London Midland | J. Piggot Pritchett | 1847-50 | 1952 |
| **Grade II*** | | | | |
| Bridgwater | Western | I.K.Brunel | 1841 | 1971 |
| Chester | London Midland | Francis Thompson | 1848 | 1972 |
| Edge Hill | London Midland | Francis/Haig | 1836 | 1974 |
| Filey | Eastern | G.T.Andrews | 1846 | 1995 |
| Hull Paragon | Eastern | G.T.Andrews | 1847-50 | 1952 |
| Wylam | Eastern | n/a | 1835 | 1972 |
| **Grade II** | | | | |
| Abergavenny | Western | Charles Liddell | 1854 | 1977 |
| Abergele & Pensarn | London Midland | n/a | 1902 | 1997 |
| Aberystwyth | London Midland | n/a | 1864/1924 | 1961 |
| Albrighton | London Midland | Edward Banks | 1849 | 1987 |
| Appleby | London Midland | J.S.Crossley | 1873 | 1990 |
| Appley Bridge | London Midland | Sir J. Hawshaw | 1855 | 1988 |
| Askarn | London Midland | Paley & Austin | 1877 | 1989 |
| Bangor | London Midland | F.Thompson | 1927 | 1988 |
| Beeston | London Midland | n/a | 1847 | 1987 |
| Beverley | Eastern | T.T.Andrews | 1846 | 1986 |
| Blackburn | London Midland | H. Shadmadine | 1888 | 1995 |
| Bodorgan | London Midland | F.Thompson | 1849 | 1990 |
| Borth | London Midland | n/a | 1863 | 1997 |
| Bradford on Avon | Western | I.K.Brunel | 1857 | 1992 |
| Bridlington | Eastern | G.T.Andrews | 1912 | 2003 |
| Brinscough Junc | London Midland | Sir J.Hawshaw | 1855 | 1993 |
| Bury St Edmunds | Eastern | Sancton Wood | 1847 | 1972 |
| Buxton | London Midland | J.W.Smith | 1863 | 1970 |
| Caersws | London Midland | TM & RK Pearson | 1864 | 1996 |
| Chapel en le Frith | London Midland | E.Walters | 1867 | 1984 |
| Charlbury | Western | I.K.Brunel | 1853 | 1975 |
| Chepstow | Western | W.Lancaster Owen | 1850 | 1975 |
| Cleethorpes | Eastern | n/a | 1863 | 1990 |
| Clifton Down | Western | n/a | 1874 | 1995 |
| Codsall | London Midland | E.Banks | 1849 | 1985 |
| Corbridge | London Midland | n/a | 1847 | 1972 |
| Cottingham | Eastern | G.T.Andrews | 1846 | 1988 |
| Crediton | Southern | W.R.Neale | 1854 | 1972 |
| Cressington | London Midland | n/a | 1873 | 1976 |
| Cromford | London Midland | G.M.Stokes | 1860 | 1971 |
| Dawlish | Western | n/a | 1873 | 1951 |

**G7: Regional Railways stations with listed building status (continued)**

| England and Wales | | | | |
|---|---|---|---|---|
| Station | BR Region | Engineer/Architect | Date built | Date listed |
| **Grade II** | | | | |
| Dent | London Midland | J.H.Sanders | 1875 | 1999 |
| Dewsbury | London Midland | n/a | 1889 | 1991 |
| Earlestown | London Midland | n/a | 1835-40 | 1966 |
| Ellesmere Port | London Midland | n/a | 1863 | 1985 |
| Exeter St Thomas | Western | I.K.Brunel | 1846 | 1990 |
| Frodsham | London Midland | n/a | 1850 | 1985 |
| Frome | Western | J.R.,Hannaford | 1850 | 1973 |
| Glossop | London Midland | n/a | 1847 | 1958 |
| Gobowen | London Midland | T.M.Pesor | 1846 | 1994 |
| Goxhill | Eastern | Weightman & Hadfield | 1844 | 1985 |
| Grange-over-Sands | London Midland | E.G.Paley | 1864-72 | 1975 |
| Great Malvern | London Midland | E.W.Elmslie | 1862 | 1969 |
| Hale | London Midland | n/a | 1880 | 1978 |
| Halifax | London Midland | T.Butterworth | 1885 | 1990 |
| Haltwhistle | Eastern | n/a | 1835-38 | 1973 |
| Hamilton Square | London Midland | G.E.Grayson | 1886 | 1990 |
| Headingley | Eastern | n/a | 1847 | 1999 |
| Hebden Bridge | Eastern | n/a | 1906 | 1978 |
| Hellifield | Eastern | C.Trubshaw | 1880 | 1977 |
| Helsby | London Midland | n/a | 1863 | 1985 |
| Hereford | Western | T.M.Penson | 1855 | 1973 |
| Hexham | London Midland | n/a | 1838-81 | 1988 |
| Holyhead | London Midland | n/a | 1860 | 1994 |
| Hough Green | London Midland | n/a | 1874 | 1985 |
| Howden | Eastern | J.Walker | 1840 | 1987 |
| Hoylake | London Midland | n/a | 1938 | 1988 |
| Hunts Cross | London Midland | n/a | 1873 | 1977 |
| Hutton Cranswick | Eastern | G.T.Andrews | 1846 | 1987 |
| Ilkley | Eastern | J.H.Sanders | 1865 | 1976 |
| Keighley | Eastern | C.Trubshaw | 1883 | 1986 |
| Kemble | Western | W.Lancaster Owen | 1872 | 1986 |
| Knaresborough | Eastern | T.Prosser | 1866 | 1988 |
| Leamington | London Midland | n/a | 1938 | 2003 |
| Lincoln Central | Eastern | J.H.Taylor | 1848 | 1973 |
| Little Sutton | London Midland | n/a | 1863 | 1985 |
| Llandovey | Western | n/a | n/a | 2004 |
| Llanrwst | Western | n/a | 1868 | 1993 |
| Llanwrtyd | Western | n/a | 1867 | 2001 |
| Longport | London Midland | M.Hunt | 1848 | 1972 |
| Lowdham | London Midland | T.C.Mine | n/a | 1986 |

**G7: Regional Railways stations with listed building status (continued)**

| England and Wales | | | | |
|---|---|---|---|---|
| Station | BR Region | Engineer/Architect | Date built | Date listed |
| **Grade II** | | | | |
| Maiden Newton | Western | R.P.Bexton | 1875 | 1999 |
| Mansfield | London Midland | n/a | 1872 | 1978 |
| Market Rasen | Eastern | n/a | 1848 | 1984 |
| Matlock | London Midland | Sir J.Paxton | 1850 | 1996 |
| Matlock Bath | London Midland | n/a | 1849 | 1971 |
| Mexborough | Eastern | n/a | 1871 | 1987 |
| Middlesbrough | Eastern | W.Peachey | 1877 | 1968 |
| Morpeth | Eastern | n/a | 1847 | 1996 |
| Mytholmroyd | Eastern | n/a | 1847 | 1984 |
| Nafferton | Eastern | G.T.Andrews | 1846 | 1989 |
| Needham Market | Eastern | F.Barnes | 1847 | 1986 |
| Newark Castle | Eastern | n/a | 1846 | 1971 |
| Newton le Willows | London Midland | n/a | 1848 | 1986 |
| Newtown Powys | Western | J.Locke/AS Jee | 1841 | 1988 |
| Oakham | London Midland | Wood/Ruragwe | 1848 | 1990 |
| Ormskirk | London Midland | n/a | 1849-80 | 1972 |
| Pantyffnnon | Western | n/a | 1857 | 1994 |
| Pembroke Dock | Western | n/a | 1864 | 1986 |
| Penmaenmawr | Western | Francis Thompson | 1865 | 1995 |
| Pontypridd | Western | n/a | 1907 | 1990 |
| Prestatyn | London Midland | Francis Thompson | 1848 | 1997 |
| Pwllheli | London Midland | n/a | 1907 | 1989 |
| Rainhill | London Midland | n/a | 1868 | 2007 |
| Ravensthorpe | Eastern | n/a | 1891 | 1988 |
| Redcar Central | Eastern | J. Pritchett | 1861 | 1988 |
| Redruth | Western | n/a | 1900-38 | 1987 |
| Rhyl | London Midland | n/a | 1901 | 1993 |
| Ruabon | London Midland | n/a | n/a | 1994 |
| Ruswarp | Eastern | G.T.Andrews | 1847 | 1990 |
| Saltburn | Eastern | W.Peachey | 1862 | 1973 |
| Sankey | London Midland | n/a | 1870 | 1984 |
| Saxilby | Eastern | Weightman & Hadfield | 1849 | 1985 |
| Scarborough | Eastern | G.T. Andrews | 1845 | 1973 |
| Selby | Eastern | T.Prosser | 1870 | 1980 |
| Settle | London Midland | n/a | 1875 | 1984 |
| Shrewsbury | London Midland | T.M.Penson | 1849 | 1969 |
| Skipton | London Midland | C.T.Trubshaw | 1886 | 1991 |
| Sleaford | Eastern | W.M. Brydone | 1857 | 1986 |
| Spalding | Eastern | J.Taylor | 1848 | 1990 |
| St Austell | Western | n/a | 1900 | 1996 |

## G7: Regional Railways stations with listed building status (continued)

| England and Wales |||||
| --- | --- | --- | --- | --- |
| Station | BR Region | Engineer/Architect | Date built | Date listed |
| **Grade II** |||||
| St Erth | Western | n/a | 1852 | 1988 |
| Stamford | Eastern | Sancton Wood | 1848 | 1974 |
| Stroud | Western | I.K.Brunel | 1845 | 1989 |
| Swinderby | Eastern | I.A.Davies | 1847 | 1983 |
| Tenby | Western | J.Mathias | 1866 | 2002 |
| Thetford | Eastern | n/a | 1845-89 | 1971 |
| Thurgarton | Eastern | n/a | 1847 | 1974 |
| Thurston | Eastern | F.Barnes | 1846 | 1987 |
| Torquay | Western | J.E.Parks | 1878 | 1986 |
| Torre | Western | I.K.Brunel | 1848 | 1975 |
| Ty Croes | London Midland | F.Thompson | 1872 | 1986 |
| Ulverston | London Midland | Paley & Austin | 1878 | 1975 |
| Valley | London Midland | F.Thompson | 1849 | 1998 |
| Wakefield Kirkgate | London Midland | T.Butterworth | 1857 | 1979 |
| Welshpool | Western | n/a | 1860 | 1974 |
| Whitby | Eastern | G.T.Andrews | 1847 | 1972 |
| Widnes | London Midland | n/a | 1872 | 1983 |
| Wigan Wallgate | London Midland | Henry Sheilmandre | 1866 | 1999 |
| Worcester Shrub Hill | Western | E. Wilson | 1865 | 1972 |
| Worksop | Eastern | J.Drabble | 1849-1900 | 1975 |
| Wrexham General | London Midland | n/a | 1912 | 1987 |
| Wymondham | Eastern | D.A.Ashley Trevor | 1848 | 1972 |
| Yatton | Western | I.K.Brunel | 1841 | n/a |

| Scotland |||||
| --- | --- | --- | --- | --- |
| Station | BR Region | Engineer/Architect | Date built | Date listed |
| **Grade A** |||||
| Aberdeen | Scottish | J.A. Parker | 1916 | 1990 |
| Aviemore | Scottish | n/a | 1892 | 1986 |
| Dumbarton Central | Scottish | n/a | 1856 | 1971 |
| Dunkeld | Scottish | Andrew Heiton | 1856 | 1971 |
| Edinburgh | Scottish | James Bell | 1900 | 1991 |
| Glasgow Central | Scottish | Anderson Miller | 1874-1905 | 1991 |
| Glasgow Queen St | Scottish | James Caswell | 1878 | 1971 |
| Ladybank | Scottish | David Bell | 1847 | 1978 |
| Stirling | Scottish | James Miller | 1912 | 1997 |
| Wemyss Bay | Scottish | James Miller | 1903 | 1971 |
| Broughty Ferry | Scottish | n/a | 1838 | 1985 |

## G7: Regional Railways stations with listed building status (continued)

### Scotland

| Station | BR Region | Engineer/Architect | Date built | Date listed |
| --- | --- | --- | --- | --- |
| **Grade B** | | | | |
| Aberdour | Scottish | n/a | 1890 | 1985 |
| Annan | Scottish | n/a | 1848 | 1986 |
| Ardgay | Scottish | J.Mitchell | 1865 | 1988 |
| Ardlui | Scottish | J.Miller | 1894 | 1996 |
| Arisais | Scottish | n/a | 1900 | 1985 |
| Ayr | Scottish | A. Galloway | 1886 | 1981 |
| Brora | Scottish | W.Roberts | 1895 | 1987 |
| Burntisland | Scottish | D.Bell | 1847 | 1975 |
| Cardross | Scottish | n/a | 1858 | 1996 |
| Coatbridge Sunnyside | Scottish | Symington | 1888 | 1985 |
| Cupar | Scottish | D.Bell | 1847 | 1972 |
| Dalmally | Scottish | n/a | 1877 | 1993 |
| Dalmeny | Scottish | n/a | 1890 | 1990 |
| Drem | Scottish | n/a | 1846 | 1977 |
| Dumfries | Scottish | n/a | 1859 | 1981 |
| Dunblane | Scottish | Sir W.Tite | 1848 | 2002 |
| Fearn | Scottish | M.Paterson | 1864 | 1978 |
| Fort Matilda | Scottish | J.Miller | 1889 | 1979 |
| Garelochead | Scottish | n/a | 1894-01 | 1989 |
| Girvan | Scottish | n/a | 1946 | 2004 |
| Gleneagles | Scottish | J.Miller | 1919 | 1983 |
| Glenfinnan | Scottish | n/a | 1894-1901 | 1987 |
| Golspie | Scottish | W.Fowler | 1868 | 1984 |
| Hamilton Central | Scottish | n/a | 1876-1906 | 1993 |
| Haymarket | Scottish | John Miller | 1842 | 1966 |
| Helensburgh Central | Scottish | n/a | 1890 | 2002 |
| Helensdale | Scottish | W. Fowler | 1871 | 1988 |
| Inverkeithing | Scottish | n/a | 1867 | 2004 |
| Inverurie | Scottish | n/a | 1902 | 1999 |
| Irvine | Scottish | Granger & Miles | 1839 | 1997 |
| Kingussie | Scottish | W. Roberts | 1891 | 1971 |
| Kirknewton | Scottish | Sir W.Tite | 1848 | 1994 |
| Kyle of Lochalsh | Scottish | M.Paterson | 1897 | 1988 |
| Lanark | Scottish | n/a | 1867 | 1995 |
| Laurencekirk | Scottish | n/a | 1849 | 2001 |
| Linlithgow | Scottish | n/a | 1842 | 1992 |
| Lockerbie | Scottish | Sir W.Tite | 1847 | 1988 |
| Mallaig | Scottish | n/a | 1894-1901 | 1996 |
| Markinch | Scottish | D.Bell | 1847 | 1979 |
| Maxwell Park | Scottish | n/a | 1894 | 1990 |

**G7: Regional Railways stations with listed building status (continued)**

| Scotland | | | | |
|---|---|---|---|---|
| Station | BR Region | Engineer/Architect | Date built | Date listed |
| **Grade B** | | | | |
| Milngavie | Scottish | n/a | 1863 | 1975 |
| Monifieth | Scottish | n/a | 1838 | 1985 |
| Nairn | Scottish | W.Roberts | 1885 | 1981 |
| Newtonmore | Scottish | W.Roberts | 1893 | 1979 |
| North Queensferry | Scottish | n/a | 1890 | 1988 |
| Paisley Gilmore St | Scottish | Sir W. Tite | 1840-90 | 1987 |
| Perth | Scottish | n/a | 1848 | 1979 |
| Pitlochry | Scottish | W.Roberts | 1890 | 1994 |
| Plockton | Scottish | M.Paterson | 1897 | 1988 |
| Pollockshaws West | Scottish | n/a | 1848 | 1990 |
| Prestwick | Scottish | n/a | n/a | 2004 |
| Queens Park | Scottish | n/a | 1886 | 1990 |
| Rannoch | Scottish | J.Miles | 1894 | 1988 |
| Saltcoats | Scottish | n/a | 1894 | 1982 |
| Stonehaven | Scottish | n/a | 1849 | 1972 |
| Tain | Scottish | J.Mitchell | 1864 | 1980 |
| Thurso | Scottish | n/a | 1874 | 1984 |
| Troon | Scottish | J.Miller | 1892 | 1986 |
| Tyndrum Upper | Scottish | J.Miller | 1894 | 1986 |
| West Calder | Scottish | n/a | 1869 | 1988 |
| West Kilbride | Scottish | J.Miller | 1900 | 1989 |
| Wick | Scottish | n/a | 1874 | 1984 |

Source: Network Rail

**G7a: Total listed stations: Regional Railways**

| England & Wales | Grade 1 | 1 |
|---|---|---|
| | Grade 2* | 6 |
| | Grade 2 | 134 |
| Scotland | Grade A | 11 |
| | Grade B | 62 |
| **Total** | | **214** |

# Factfile H: People

H1: Eastern and Scotland Regional Railways managers 1982-2014

| Year | Eastern | Anglia | TransPennine | ScotRail |
|---|---|---|---|---|
| | **Provincial Manager** | | | **Passenger Services Manager** |
| 1983 | David Wharton Street | | | Chris Leah |
| 1984 | David Wharton Street | | | Chris Leah |
| 1985 | David Wharton Street | | | Chris Leah |
| 1986 | David Wharton Street | | | Chris Leah |
| 1987 | David Wharton Street | | | Chris Leah[1] |
| 1988 | David Wharton Street | | | Chris Leah |
| 1989 | David Wharton Street | | | Cyril Bleasdale |
| | **Director, North East** | | | **Director ScotRail** |
| 1990 | Aidan Nelson | | | Cyril Bleasdale |
| 1991 | Aidan Nelson | | | Cyril Bleasdale |
| 1992 | Aidan Nelson | | | Cyril Bleasdale |
| | **Director NE (BR)** | **Director, Anglia (BR)** | | **Director ScotRail (BR)** |
| 1993 | Bob Urie | Andy Cooper | | Cyril Bleasdale |
| 1994 | Bob Urie | Andy Cooper | | Chris Green |
| 1995 | Bob Urie | Andy Cooper | | John Ellis |
| 1996 | Bob Urie | Andy Cooper | | John Ellis |
| | **Northern Spirit, MTL** | **Anglia Railways** | | **ScotRail (National Express)** |
| 1997 | Peter Davison | Andy Cooper | | Alastair McPherson |
| 1998 | Peter Davison | Tim Clarke | | Alastair McPherson |
| 1999 | Peter Davison | Tim Clarke | | Alastair McPherson |
| | **Arriva North East** | | | |
| 2000 | Nigel Paterson | Tim Clarke | | Alastair McPherson |
| 2001 | Nigel Paterson | Tim Clarke | | Peter Cotton |
| 2002 | Ray Price | Tim Clarke | | Peter Cotton |
| 2003 | Ray Price | Tim Clarke | | Peter Cotton |
| | | **Nat Express One** | **First TransPennine** | **ScotRail (First Group)** |
| 2004 | Dyan Crowther | Tim Clarke | Vernon Barker | Mary Grant |
| 2005 | Dyan Crowther | Tim Clarke | Vernon Barker | Mary Grant |
| | **Northern (Abellio)** | **National Express East Anglia** | | |
| 2006 | Heidi Mottram | Dominic Booth | Vernon Barker | Mary Grant |
| 2007 | Heidi Mottram | Andrew Chivers | Vernon Barker | Steve Montgomery |
| 2008 | Heidi Mottram | Andrew Chivers | Vernon Barker | Steve Montgomery |
| 2009 | Heidi Mottram | Andrew Chivers | Vernon Barker | Steve Montgomery |
| 2010 | Ian Bevan | Andrew Chivers | Nick Donovan | Steve Montgomery |
| | | **Abellio East Anglia** | | |
| 2011 | Ian Bevan | Ruud Hakket | Nick Donovan | Steve Montgomery |
| 2012 | Ian Bevan | Ruud Hakket | Nick Donovan | Steve Montgomery |
| 2013 | Alex Hynes | Ruud Hakket | Nick Donovan | Steve Montgomery |
| 2014 | Alex Hynes | Jamie Burles | Nick Donovan | Steve Montgomery |

[1] Provincial Manager, ScotRail, from 1987

## H2: London Midland Regional Railways managers 1982-2014

| Year | BR | Central | Merseyrail | East Midlands |
|---|---|---|---|---|
|  | **Passenger Services Manager** |  |  |  |
| 1983 | Chris Stokes |  |  |  |
|  | **Provincial Manager** |  |  |  |
| 1984 | Chris Stokes |  |  |  |
| 1985 | Chris Stokes |  |  |  |
| 1986 | Bob Goundry |  |  |  |
| 1987 | Bob Goundry |  |  |  |
| 1988 | Bob Goundry |  |  |  |
| 1989 | Chris Leah |  |  |  |
|  | **Director North West (RR)** | **Director Central (BR)** |  |  |
| 1990 | Chris Leah |  |  |  |
| 1991 | Chris Leah | Mark Causebrook |  |  |
| 1992 | Chris Leah | Mark Causebrook |  |  |
| 1993 | Bob Goundry | Mark Causebrook |  |  |
| 1994 | Bob Goundry | Mark Causebrook |  |  |
|  | **RR NW (BR)** | **Central Trains (BR)** | **Merseyrail (BR)** |  |
| 1995 | Bob Goundry | Mark Causebrook | Richard Parkins |  |
| 1996 | Bob Goundry | Mark Causebrook | Richard Parkins |  |
|  | **North Western (GW Holdings)** | **Central Trains (National Express)** | **Merseyrail (MTL)** |  |
| 1997 | Peter Strachan | Mark Causebrook | Richard Parkins |  |
|  | **First North Western** |  |  |  |
| 1998 | Mike Mitchell | Mark Causebrook | Richard Parkins |  |
| 1999 | David Franks | Nick Brown | Roger Cobbe |  |
|  |  |  | **Merseyrail (Arriva)** |  |
| 2000 | David Franks | Andy Cooper | Roger Cobbe |  |
| 2001 | Dave Kaye | Andy Cooper | Roger Cobbe |  |
| 2002 | Dave Kaye | Andy Cooper | Bob Hind |  |
| 2003 | Vernon Barker | Andy Cooper | Patrick Verwer |  |
| 2004 | Richard Peck | Andy Cooper | Patrick Verwer |  |
|  | **Combined with Northern** |  | **2nd Concession** |  |
| 2005 |  | Steve Banaghan | Patrick Verwer |  |
| 2006 |  | Steve Banaghan | Patrick Verwer |  |
| 2007 |  | Steve Banaghan | Patrick Verwer |  |
|  |  | **London Midland (Govia)** |  | **EMT (Stagecoach)** |
| 2008 |  | Steve Banaghan | Bart Schmeink | Tim Shoveller |
| 2009 |  | Mike Hodson | Bart Schmeink | Tim Shoveller |
| 2010 |  | Mike Hodson | Bart Schmeink | Tim Shoveller |
| 2011 |  | Mike Hodson | Bart Schmeink | David Horne |
| 2012 |  | Patrick Verwer | Maarten Spaargaren | David Horne |
| 2013 |  | Patrick Verwer | Maarten Spaargaren | David Horne |
| 2014 |  | Patrick Verwer | Alain Chaplain | David Horne |

## H3: Western Regional Railways managers 1982-2014

| Year | BR | Valley lines | Wessex Trains | First Great Western |
|---|---|---|---|---|
| | **Provincial Manager** | | | |
| 1983 | John Pearse | | | |
| 1984 | John Pearse | | | |
| 1985 | John Pearse | | | |
| 1986 | John Pearse | | | |
| 1987 | John Pearse | | | |
| 1988 | John Pearse | | | |
| 1989 | John Pearse | | | |
| | **South Wales & West** | | | |
| 1990 | Theo Steel | | | |
| 1991 | Theo Steel | | | |
| 1992 | Theo Steel | | | |
| | **South Wales & West (BR)** | **Valley Lines (BR)** | | |
| 1993 | Theo Steel | John Buxton | | |
| 1994 | Theo Steel | John Buxton | | |
| 1995 | John Mummery | John Buxton | | |
| 1996 | John Mummery | John Buxton | | |
| | **Wales & West (Prism)** | | | |
| 1997 | David Weir | Tom Clift | | |
| 1998 | David Weir | Tom Clift | | |
| 1999 | Dominic Booth | Tom Clift | | |
| 2000 | Chris Gibb | Tom Clift | | |
| | **Wales & Borders (National Express)** | | **Wessex Trains (National Express)** | |
| 2001 | Chris Gibb | | Charles Belcher | |
| 2002 | Chris Gibb | | Charles Belcher | |
| | **Arriva Wales** | | | |
| 2003 | Peter Strachan | | Charles Belcher | |
| 2004 | Peter Strachan | | Alan Wilson | |
| 2005 | Graham Bunker | | Alan Wilson | |
| | | | | **First Great Western** |
| 2006 | Tim Bell | | | Andrew Haines |
| 2007 | Tim Bell | | | Alison Forster |
| 2008 | Tim Bell | | | Mark Hopwood |
| 2009 | Tim Bell | | | Mark Hopwood |
| 2010 | Tim Bell | | | Mark Hopwood |
| 2011 | Tim Bell | | | Mark Hopwood |
| 2012 | Tim Bell | | | Mark Hopwood |
| 2013 | Tim Bell | | | Mark Hopwood |
| 2014 | Ian Bullock | | | Mark Hopwood |

## H4: Prime Ministers and Secretaries of State for Transport

| Prime Minister | Transport | Date | Party |
|---|---|---|---|
| **Margaret Thatcher** | | **May 1979-Nov 1990** | **Conservative** |
| Norman Fowler[1] | Minister/SofS for Transport | May 1979-Sep 1981 | Conservative |
| David Howell | SofS for Transport | Sep 1981-Jun 1983 | Conservative |
| Tom King | SofS for Transport | Jun 1983-Oct 1983 | Conservative |
| Nicholas Ridley | SofS for Transport | Oct 1983-May 1986 | Conservative |
| John Moore | SofS for Transport | May 1986-Jun 1987 | Conservative |
| Paul Channon | SofS for Transport | Jun 1987-Jul 1989 | Conservative |
| Cecil Parkinson | SofS for Transport | Jul 1989-Nov 1990 | Conservative |
| **John Major** | | **Nov 1990-May 1997** | **Conservative** |
| Malcolm Rifkind | SofS for Transport | Nov 1990-Apr 1992 | Conservative |
| John MacGregor | SofS for Transport | Apr 1992-Jul 1994 | Conservative |
| Dr Brian Mawhinney | SofS for Transport | Jul 1994-Jul 1995 | Conservative |
| Sir George Young | SofS for Transport | Jul 1995-May 1997 | Conservative |
| **Tony Blair** | | **May 1997-June 2007** | **Labour** |
| John Prescott[2] | SofS for Transport | May 1997-Jun 2001 | Labour |
| Stephen Byers | SofS for Transport | Jun 2001-May 2002 | Labour |
| Alistair Darling | SofS for Transport | May 2002-May 2006 | Labour |
| Douglas Alexander | SofS for Transport | May 2006-Jun 2007 | Labour |
| **Gordon Brown** | | **June 2007-May 2010** | **Labour** |
| Ruth Kelly | SofS for Transport | Jun 2007-Oct 2008 | Labour |
| Geoff Hoon | SofS for Transport | Oct 2008-Jun 2009 | Labour |
| Lord Adonis | SofS for Transport | Jun 2009-May 2010 | Labour |
| **David Cameron**** | | **May 2010-** | **Conservative**** |
| Phillip Hammond | SofS for Transport | May 2010-Oct 2011 | Conservative |
| Justine Greening | SofS for Transport | Oct 2011-Sep 2012 | Conservative |
| Patrick McLoughlin | SofS for Transport | Sep 2012- | Conservative |

[1] In cabinet from Jan 1981

[2] Secretary of State for Environment, Transport and Regions

** Coalition with Liberal Democrats until May 2015

# Factfile J: Train franchises and operators

J1: Evolution of train companies post-1994

| BR 1994 | Privatisation 1996 | History post-1997 |
|---|---|---|
| Anglia | **Anglia Railways**<br>GB Railways 05.1.97 | 14.08.03 acquired by First Group<br>01.04.04 absorbed in **Greater Anglia** (National Express)<br>01.02.11 acquired by Abellio |
| Central | **Central Trains**<br>National Express 02.03.97 | 01.12.04 Stratford/Kidderminster to Chiltern<br>01.03.05 Cotswold line transferred to Greater Western<br>01.11.07 split between **London Midland** (Govia), **CrossCountry** (Arriva/DB) and **East Midland Trains** (Stagecoach): some services to Wales & Borders and Chiltern<br>LM franchise runs to 03.16; negs to extend it to 06.17. East Midland franchise runs to 14.10.17 |
| South Wales & West | **Valley Lines**<br>Prism 13.10.96 | 14.10.01 absorbed into Wales & Borders |
| | **Wales & West**<br>Prism 13.10.96 | 31.03.01 acquired by National Express<br>13.10.01 split between Wales & Borders and Wessex |
| | | 14.10.01 **Wales & Border** (National Express)<br>07.12.03 won by Arriva Trains Wales<br>W&B franchise runs to 06.12.18 |
| | | 14.10.01 **Wessex Trains** (National Express)<br>01.04.06 absorbed into Greater GW (First Group); Waterloo-Bristol to SWT<br>Greater Western franchise runs to 03.19 |
| North East | **Northern Spirit**<br>MTL 02.03.97 | 18.02.00 acquired by Arriva Trains North<br>12.12.04 split into Northern & TPE |
| | | 12.04.04 **Northern** (Abellio). Created from Northern Spirit & North Western. Runs to 02.4.16 – now being relet<br>12.12.04 **TransPennine Express** (First Group)<br>Runs to 02.4.16 – now being relet |
| North Western | **North Western**<br>Great Western Holdings 02.03.97 | 30.03.98 acquired by First Group<br>28.09.03 North Wales lines to Wales & Borders<br>12.12.04 split into Northern, TPE, Wales & Borders |
| | **MerseyRail**<br>MTL 19.01.97 | 18.02.00 acquired by Arriva<br>20.07.03 won by NED/Serco<br>Runs to 07.28 |
| ScotRail | **ScotRail**<br>National Express 31.03.97 | 16.10.04 First Group<br>01.04.15 Abellio, runs to 03.22 |

# Factfile K: McNulty Report Recommendations, 2011

### 'The Lower Cost Regional Railway'

| | The Study recommends that the principles outlined in the report should be further developed and piloted in a number of locations so that they can be refined before wider roll-out. An initial pilot would provide early evidence of the disadvantages and advantages of the proposed approach, while a subsequent roll-out to further pilots will test differing local circumstances |
|---|---|
| 1 | Develop criteria to assess which routes are suitable for the lower-cost approach. The criteria would include: |
| 1.1 | Route or routes that would have a degree of segregation from the core network – the greater the segregation, the greater the potential to reduce costs. |
| 1.2. | Using a franchise re-letting point to restructure. |
| 1.3. | The appetite amongst PTEs and other local bodies to play a greater role and adopt the principles outlined by the Study. |
| 2. | Develop a specification for the routes while recognizing that the specific service philosophy would be a matter for the local operator. |
| 3. | Assess the likely cost reductions that a local operator might expect by adoption of the principles outlined by the Study. |
| 4. | Identify the standards that need to be changed – and those that would remain – as part of the process for standards reform described in the Study's review of standards. |
| 5. | Develop minimum national standards for lower-cost regional railways. |
| 6. | In addition the Study recommends that: |
| 6.1 | The rail freight industry should identify routes where there is no prospect of freight activity or where freight operating characteristics can be changed – these routes can be added to the other regional routes as candidates for low-cost operation. |
| 6.2 | A senior industry figure should be appointed, possibly responding to the Rail Delivery Group, to lead the following work streams: |
| 6.2.1 | Develop an implementation plan, linked into the franchising re-letting programme and integrated with the Study's implementation plan. |
| 6.2.2. | Lead the work on reviewing the standards that should apply to the lower-cost regional railway, drawing on best-practice from other railways and in consultation with operators and infrastructure managers. |
| 6.2.3 | Identify suitable pilot routes, covering a range of market and operating scenarios. |
| 6.2.4 | Develop a franchising or concession model that will deliver the benefits. |
| 6.2.5 | A small team should support the leader, who would draw advice from a stakeholder Group represented by the passenger and freight operators, the infrastructure manager and relevant PTEs and local authorities. |

Source: DfT: 'Realising the Potential of GB Rail May 2011'

# Bibliography

McNulty Report Recommendations, 2011 'The Lower Cost Regional Railway'

British Railways Board: Provincial. Cm 584, Monopolies and Mergers Commission, Feb 1989.

Clinker, C. R. *Register of Closed Passenger Stations and Goods Depots in England, Scotland and Wales* (Avon-Anglia Publications, 1979)

Faulkner, Richard and Austin, Chris *Holding the Line* (Oxford Publishing Company, 2013)

Fiennes, Gerard *I Tried to Run A Railway* (Ian Allan, 1967)

Freeman, Roger and Shaw, Jon *All Change: British Railway Privatisation* (McGraw Hill, 2000)

Gourvish, Terry *Britain's Railways, 1997-2005: Labour's Strategic Experiment* (Oxford University Press, 2008)
*British Rail, 1974-97* (Oxford University Press, 2002)
*Light Rail '87* (Light Rail Transit Association, 1987)
*LRT Handbook* (Regional Railways, 1992) (internal)

Maidment, David *The Toss of a Coin* (PublishNation, 2014)

OPRAF Passenger Rail Industry Overview, 1995

Provincial Organisation Simplification Headquarters Team report, 1990 (internal)

'Settle-Carlisle Railway: Opportunities for Development' (Standing Conference for the Settle-Carlisle Railway, 1990)

The Franchising of Passenger Rail Services: A Consultation Document (Department of Transport, 1992)

'The Renaissance of Regional Railways' (Supplement to *RAIL*, 1992)

Thompson, 'D. E. Provincial Resource Usage, 1983-90', 1991 (internal)

TransPennine Express and Northern rail franchise: stakeholder consultation (Department for Transport, 2014)

Welsby, John and Nichols, Alan *The Privatisation of Britain's Railways: An Inside View* (Journal of Transport Economics and Policy, Vol 33, 1998)

Wolmar, Christian *Broken Rails: How Privatisation Wrecked Britain's Railways* (Aurum, 2001)

Issues of *Regional Railways Focus*, ScotRail *Staff Bulletin*, *RAIL*, *Modern Railways*, *Railway Magazine*, *Railway World*, *Today's Railways UK*

# Index

Abellio 67, 106, 129, 130, 166, 172, 180
Aberdare 30, 99, 192
Aberdeen 21, 31, 35, 90, 92, 128-9, 130, 167, 180
Aberystwyth 27, 131, 157, 181
Access charges 59, 61, 62, 70, 76, 194
Accidents 54
  Bellgrove 25
  Clapham 31, 41, 54, 192
  Glanrhyd 33, 192
  Hatfield 69, 74, 75, 193
  Ladbroke Grove 73, 144
  Newton 25
  Polmont 128
  Potters Bar 76
ACoRP (see Community Rail Partnerships)
Adonis, Lord 82-3, 96, 117, 124, 154, 194
Alstom 167, 169, 172, 193
Alloa 55, 81, 82, 194
'Alphaline' 47, 132, 13
Altrincham 92, 93, 103-4, 122, 170
Anglia Railways/franchise 66, 69, 70, 75, 78-9, 120, 156
Appleby 186, 187, 189, 191
APTIS 31, 187
Arriva 31, 64, 74, 79, 122
  Arriva Trains Wales 79, 80, 85, 133, 144, 167
ASLEF 13, 20, 48, 77, 136, 165, 192
ATOC (Association of Train Operating Companies) 59, 70, 82, 83, 111, 194
Austin, Chris 146, 155-6, 235
Ayr/shire 21, 28, 109, 140, 150, 152, 157, 171, 192
Barker, Vernon 72, 123, 124, 125
Barmouth 41, 49, 75, 84
Barnsley 97, 106, 107, 155
Barnstaple 70, 138, 154, 181
Barrow 122, 123, 125, 137
Barton-on-Humber 84, 142-3
Bath 100, 101, 148, 181
Bathgate 29, 30, 77, 98, 129, 192
Bedford 83, 109, 119, 159, 171, 183
Beeching Report/closures 12, 29, 45, 87, 98, 99, 103, 115, 135, 148, 153, 154, 159
Belcher, Charles 74, 77, 154, 156
Bimode trains (AT300) 173, 180, 181-2
Birmingham 24, 25, 26, 27, 32, 36, 39, 49, 53, 59, 60, 80, 81, 89, 112-5, 119, 130-1, 132, 150, 164, 165, 168, 176, 177, 179, 181
  Cross-City line 37, 53, 112-3, 115, 171, 193
  Curzon Street 114-5, 181
  International 112, 131, 181
  Moor Street 18, 86, 112, 113, 131

New Street 33, 48, 61, 87, 95, 112, 113, 114, 120, 130-1
Snow Hill 32, 94, 112, 113, 114, 115, 131, 192
Bishop Auckland 137, 149, 151
Blackburn 13, 87, 97, 125, 149, 157, 182, 186, 191
Blackpool 83, 84, 91, 95, 97, 103, 120, 122, 123, 124, 125, 148, 190
Blair, Tony 11, 67, 73, 77, 82, 95, 193
Bleasdale, Cyril 17, 18, 23, 57, 186, 187
Bletchley 70, 73, 114, 119, 183
Bolton 72, 83, 97, 103, 104, 124
Bombardier 83, 167
Bonham Carter, Richard 44, 45, 54, 189
Booth, Dominic 65, 67, 106
Borders railway 13, 98, 174, 180
Bowker, Richard 76, 156, 194
Bradford 25, 87, 88, 115, 116, 117, 120, 125, 148, 178, 179
Bridgend 52, 55, 100
Brighton 49, 132, 133
Bristol 47, 73, 80, 84, 87, 89, 92, 100-1, 119, 120, 132, 133, 139, 150, 151, 153, 173, 181
  Light rail 92, 94
  'Metro' 101, 181
  Parkway 92, 181
  Temple Meads 101, 181
British Rail(ways) 7, 9, 14-5, 29, 39, 42, 44, 51, 52, 53, 54, 57, 58, 60, 61, 62, 66, 67, 69, 70, 72, 73, 74, 78, 80, 81, 87, 88, 93, 94, 96, 99, 103, 104, 105, 109, 110, 113, 114, 116, 119, 120, 131, 137, 138, 139, 142, 147, 148, 150, 152, 153, 154, 159, 160, 166, 167, 171, 186-8, 192-3
  And PTEs 89, 91-2, 96, 162
  Board 15, 17, 18, 20, 29, 35, 36, 39, 45, 46, 51, 92, 93, 119, 136-7, 147, 159, 175, 186, 187, 193, 210
  British Rail Engineering Ltd (BREL) 34, 37, 57, 162, 163-5, 166, 167, 168, 169, 171, 172
  Policy unit 17, 45, 92, 186
  Research 135, 159, 163
  Sectors 9, 17, 18, 139, 143, 192-3
  Workshops 22, 25, 161, 171
Brown, Gordon 11, 82-3, 95, 194
Burnley 125, 126, 157
Burton-on-Trent 30, 55, 150
Bury 88, 92, 103, 104, 170
Buses/coaches: 94, 128, 135, 136, 142
  'Bus bandits' 70, 138
  Bus-rail interchanges 97, 107, 112, 116
  Busways 95, 149

Deregulation 31, 90, 92, 97, 106, 110-1, 112
  Municipal 87, 90, 110
  National Bus Company 31, 65
  Operators 65, 70, 90, 139
  'Quality buses' 95, 108
  Rail Replacement 76
  Substitution 13, 78, 109, 137-9, 186
Buxton 76, 123, 126
Calder Valley line 83, 104, 121, 125-6, 178
Cambrian (coast) line 28, 43, 84, 131, 152, 185, 194
Cambridge 25, 27, 28, 49, 119, 120, 127, 131, 149, 182, 183
Cameron, David 11, 83, 194
Campaign for Better Transport (Transport 2000) 147, 186
Car ownership 12, 45, 87, 108, 135
Cardiff 24, 30. 33, 34, 40, 47, 49, 52, 53, 65, 66, 70, 74, 77, 87, 97, 99, 100, 120, 122, 131-3, 139, 152, 173, 181, 192
  Bay 96, 99-100, 166, 181
  Railway/Valleys 59, 65, 66, 74, 83, 96, 97, 99, 100, 149, 181, 193, 194
Carlisle 111, 120, 126, 135, 140, 155, 162, 163, 185, 186, 188, 190, 191
Carriages 61, 203
  Mk 1 21, 119, 159
  Mk II 9, 21, 42, 121, 128, 159
  Mk III 21, 48, 128, 159, 163
  20/23/26-metre 164, 165-6, 167, 169, 172, 173
Castle, Barbara 12, 87, 88, 149, 155
Causebrook, Mark 10, 22, 23, 24, 25, 35, 39, 41, 48, 63, 112, 114, 116, 121, 187
Central Trains/franchise 10, 59, 66, 67, 68, 75, 80, 114, 126, 127, 131, 133, 185, 193
Central Wales Line 33, 64, 80, 136, 138, 144, 157, 160, 181
Channon, Paul 31, 36, 57, 104, 139, 188, 192
Chester 27, 44, 84, 93, 97, 105, 121, 122, 131, 133, 137, 152, 167, 171, 181
Chester-le-Street 31, 111-2
Chiltern Railways/franchise 59, 66, 73, 80, 113, 131, 163, 168, 179, 193
Cleaning 34, 45, 51, 65, 91, 144
Cleethorpes 31, 123, 126, 127, 144
Closures 82, 91, 153, 159
  Lines 13, 22, 101, 106, 108, 110, 119, 132, 135, 136-9, 142, 147, 148, 149, 186-91, 206
  Recommended for closure 1979 210
  Stations 31, 55, 70, 109, 112, 115, 135, 142, 143, 153
Coal traffic 23, 81, 94, 99, 139, 140, 189

# INDEX

Community Rail (Partnerships) 13, 141, 142, 145, 146, 147, 153, 155-7, 194
   ACoRP 155-6, 157
'Congestion-busting' 45-6, 87, 91
Control Periods 79
   CP 1 (1994-99) 61, 193
   CP2 (1999-2004) 73, 76, 194
   CP3 (2004-09) 79, 194
   CP4 (2009-14) 82, 194
   CP5 (2014-19) 84, 101, 194
   CP6 (2019-24) 96
Copy Pit line 83, 125
Cornwall 32, 33, 54, 74, 84, 141, 149, 150, 151, 152, 161, 173, 181-2
Cornell, Jim 10, 17, 19, 24, 28-9, 53-4, 61, 76, 193
Cotswold Line 153, 154
Cotton, Ron 186, 190
Coventry 13, 30, 48, 83, 89, 112, 113
Crewe 20, 24, 27, 28, 34, 44, 49, 50, 53, 75, 120, 131, 132, 133, 154, 167, 177, 178, 181
CrossCountry (TOC/franchise) 59, 62, 70, 77, 80, 106, 114, 127, 130, 131, 132, 185
'Crosslink' 69, 120
Cumbernauld 55, 108, 109
Cummins engines 162, 164, 165
Customer satisfaction 51-2, 198
Cycling 73, 130, 157, 180
Darling, Alistair 77-82, 95, 106, 194
Darlington 28, 64, 119, 122, 137, 150, 152
Davies, John 32-3, 99
Dawlish 84, 182, 193
Department of/for Transport 11, 14-5, 17, 20, 25, 29, 31, 36, 44, 46, 54, 58, 59, 64, 69, 72, 77, 78, 79, 82, 83, 85, 93, 94, 95, 96, 97, 103, 108, 110, 114, 116, 117, 118, 122, 124, 127, 128, 137, 142-3, 144, 147, 149, 153, 155, 156, 171, 175-7, 178, 182, 186, 188, 193, 194, 235
   Ministers/Secretaries of State 232
Depots 33, 70, 122
   Canton 28, 33, 53, 68
   Closures 25, 48, 105
   Corkerhill 27
   Crown Point 28
   Eastcroft 70
   Fratton 33, 53
   Gateshead 121
   Haymarket 28, 128
   Heaton 28, 33
   Longsight 169
   Neville Hill 28, 34, 192
   Newton Heath 23, 28
   Shields Road 171
   Soho 70, 114
   Swansea (new) 180
   Toton 120
   Tyseley 28, 32, 112

   York Clifton 25, 121
Derby 24, 27, 34, 38, 52, 53, 82, 83, 101, 114, 150, 158, 160, 162, 166, 167, 192, 201
Derbyshire 30, 101, 106, 150
Devolution 58, 81, 87, 97, 145, 149, 152, 175-6, 178, 180
   Within BR 10, 40, 48
Devon 70, 141, 149, 161, 181-2
   & Cornwall Rail Partnership 141, 154, 193
Diesel Multiple Units (DMUs) 18, 20, 21, 23, 33, 48, 49, 70, 80, 85, 89, 91, 96, 97, 100, 104, 112, 113, 120, 122, 125, 128, 138, 142, 149, 153, 159-68, 170, 173, 178, 202
   'Heritage' 49, 103, 143, 159, 163, 166
   'LEV' prototypes 159-60
   'Pacers' (Classes 140-144) 19, 22, 25, 27, 29, 33, 36, 37, 49, 70, 81, 83, 89, 92, 96, 97, 100, 103, 116-7, 119, 125, 152, 159-63, 166, 176-7, 182, 186, 192
   'Sprinters' (Classes 150-155) 4, 20, 27, 28, 29, 33, 36, 53, 70, 74, 83, 92, 100, 113, 119, 121, 122, 125, 130, 132, 143, 144, 150, 154, 162, 163-4, 166, 168, 182, 186, 192
   Class 101 37, 72, 159, 166
   Class 108 166, 186
   Class 116-118 166
   Class 117 18
   Class 121 100, 166
   Class 124 120
   Class 139 93
   Class 140 160-1
   Class 141 19, 49, 108, 116, 125, 161-2
   Class 142 'Skippers' 27, 32, 41, 68, 103, 125, 148, 151, 154, 161
   Class 143 162
   Class 144 116, 161
   Class 150 26, 27, 34, 41, 58, 72, 121, 137, 141, 155, 158, 163-4, 165, 192
   Class 151 163-4
   Class 153 33, 49, 54, 55, 70, 133, 134, 138, 142, 143, 164-5, 191, 192
   Class 154 165
   Class 155 28, 33, 40, 116, 138, 164-5, 192
   Class 156 'Super Sprinter' 27, 28, 71, 121, 125, 142, 164-5, 186, 192
   Class 157 169
   Class 158/159 27, 33, 34-5, 37, 38, 44, 47, 48, 49, 50, 53, 54, 57, 59, 66, 74, 77, 116, 119, 120, 121, 122, 123, 125, 126, 127, 128, 131, 132, 133, 138, 144, 151, 165, 166, 167, 168, 182, 189, 191, 192, 193, 200, 201
   Class 165/166 'Networker Turbo 113, 168, 181
   Class 168/170/172 'Turbostars' 27, 79, 113, 120, 124, 127, 129, 131, 163, 164, 167, 168, 185, 193
   Class 175 'Coradia' 4, 123, 167, 193
   Class 185 118, 123, 124, 125, 167, 168, 194

Class 210 159, 160, 163
Class 220 'Voyager' 84, 168
Class 222 'Meridian' 81, 126, 127
Dilton Marsh Halt 82, 153-4
Diversionary routes 61, 84, 139, 140-1, 186, 189
Doncaster 19, 31, 42, 78, 84, 96, 106, 107, 108, 117, 126, 127, 138, 142, 170
Driver-only operation (DOO) 77, 83, 109, 157, 170, 176
East Coast Main Line (ECML) 23, 28, 50, 75, 81, 84, 98, 111, 126, 130, 139, 140, 142, 147, 183, 187
East Midlands Trains 71, 77, 80, 126, 127, 143, 194
East Suffolk Line 25, 135, 138, 143, 153
East-West Rail 73, 148, 182-3
Eastern Region 9, 25, 29, 187
Edinburgh 20, 23, 27, 29, 35, 51, 52-3, 60, 67, 77, 87, 98-9, 128-9, 170, 176, 192, 193, 200
   Airport and rail link 77, 98, 99
   Trams 98, 99, 194
Edmonds, John 10, 22-33, 39, 61, 73, 113, 119, 121, 125, 137, 143, 164, 165, 169, 187, 192
Electric Multiple Units (EMUs) 19, 70, 76, 85, 91, 106, 159, 168-73, 202-3
   AT200 173
   'Blue Trains' (Classes 303, 311) 108, 109, 171, 172
   'Heritage' 159
   'Networkers' (Classes 316, 365, 457, 465, 466) 37, 169
   Class 303 108-9, 171
   Class 304 159, 169
   Class 305 48, 169, 170
   Class 307 117, 170
   Class 308 113, 115, 117, 171, 193
   Class 309 42, 43, 120
   Class 310 113, 168, 169
   Class 311 171
   Class 314 90
   Class 317 159, 171
   Class 318 171
   Class 319 83, 97, 170
   Class 320 172, 193
   Class 321 116, 117, 170, 171, 172-3
   Class 322 120
   Class 323 37, 49, 53, 54, 70, 89, 102, 103, 112, 113, 114, 117, 169, 171, 192, 193
   Class 333 116, 117, 171, 172, 193
   Class 334 'Juniper' 82, 172, 193
   Class 350 83, 127, 128, 170, 194
   Class 380 85, 172, 180, 194
   Class 381 109
   Class 395 'Javelin' 173
   Class 504 103, 170

### INDEX

Class 506  170
Class 507/508  79, 105, 171
Electrification  35, 48, 52, 73, 81, 82-4, 91, 93, 96, 97-8, 100, 103, 104, 105, 106, 108, 109, 112, 114, 115, 117, 119, 127, 130, 151, 152, 162, 173, 178, 183, 185, 194
  Birmingham Cross-City  97, 113-4, 169, 193
  Edinburgh-Glasgow (EGIP)  128, 172, 173, 180
  Great Western/Valleys  168, 173, 180-1
  Leeds North West  97, 115, 116, 117, 169, 170, 193
  Merseyrail  97, 104-6, 152, 171
  North West Triangle/Manchester-WCML  83, 104, 128, 170, 175, 176, 194
  Northern Electrification Task Force  83-4, 126, 194
  Regional lines electrified  206
  Scheduled/reviewed for electrification  207-8
  Trans-Pennine  53, 61, 97, 117, 122, 125, 178, 181
  Scotland  109, 128, 130, 171, 192
Ely  52, 126, 127
ERTMS signalling  185
European Regional Development Fund  55, 152, 153
European Union  58, 108, 141, 152
Euston  24, 40, 60, 67, 120, 131, 179
Exeter  28, 48, 74, 76, 84, 100, 119, 148, 181, 182
Falkirk  31, 67, 128, 129, 159, 162
Falmouth  141, 152-3, 155, 182
Far North line  21, 28, 77, 135-6, 143, 152, 166
Fares  21, 31, 35-6, 43, 45, 50-1, 52, 78, 79, 84, 89, 97, 106, 109, 116, 138, 156, 157, 176, 184, 187, 192, 196
Fearn, Dick  10, 31, 35, 88, 116, 119, 150, 162
Fiennes, Gerald  10, 153, 235
Fife  99, 147, 149
Filton Abbey Wood  54, 100, 101, 149
Fishguard  66, 144, 145
First Group  31, 70, 72, 77, 78-9, 80, 83, 85, 90, 123, 124, 129
  First Great Western  80, 100, 133, 134, 141, 151, 164, 173, 181-2
  First North Western  72, 75-6, 123, 166
  First TransPennine Express - see TransPennine
Flexible rostering  13-4, 15, 20, 192
Fort William  21, 60, 136, 145
Forth Bridge  43, 81, 192
Fowler, Norman  13, 57, 137, 139, 192
Franchises  7, 46, 58, 59, 65-7, 69, 73, 96, 119, 152, 156, 182, 193, 235
  And operators  233
  Micro  59, 181, 183

Regional  61, 67, 69, 73
Renewal/redrawing  73, 78, 80, 83, 125, 131, 175-7, 180, 194
'Shadow'  59, 62, 131, 193
Franchising Director  59, 73, 193
Freeman, Roger  46, 59, 171, 192, 235
Freight  9, 23, 36, 52, 53, 61, 72, 73, 84, 94, 96, 101, 103, 104, 107, 108, 110, 121, 125, 127, 136, 139, 140, 150, 157, 182, 186, 189
Gibb, Chris  10, 24, 40, 44, 52, 53, 60, 64-5, 66, 70, 74, 77, 132, 133, 138, 147, 154
Glasgow  21, 29, 35, 52, 60, 77, 84, 87, 99, 108-10, 120, 126, 128, 129, 136, 140, 148, 152, 165, 168, 170, 171, 176, 177, 185, 186, 191, 192, 193, 200
  Argyle Line  89, 108, 109
  Cross-city link (City Union line)  61, 110
  Central  11, 31, 51, 61, 67, 71, 108, 110
  Queen Street  21, 31, 51, 67, 108, 109, 128, 129, 181
  Subway  97, 108
Gloucester  52, 53, 69, 148, 150
Go Ahead  31, 64
Goldstein, Alfred  15, 139
Goundry, Bob  24, 27, 39, 63, 66, 72
Gourvish, Terry  17, 23, 75, 77-8, 79, 166, 235
Grand Central  117, 120, 125
Great Malvern  30, 31, 49, 168
Great(er) Western (franchise)  62, 66, 72, 73, 76, 80, 120, 180, 194
Great Western Holdings  63, 66, 193
Great Western main line (GWML)  83, 84, 139, 140, 181, 183
Greatorex, Gill  39, 42
Green, Alex  42, 50, 56, 63, 186
Green, Chris  11, 20-2, 23, 24, 27, 29, 31, 62, 83, 108, 123, 136, 151
Grimsby  84, 92, 142
Growth, passenger  9, 15, 24, 33, 35, 36, 44, 45, 70, 75, 78, 81, 84-5, 89, 96, 105, 108, 115, 117, 119, 122, 123, 127, 130, 138, 142, 143, 144, 145, 152, 153, 155, 156, 166, 168, 171, 173, 175, 182, 198
Halifax  25, 117, 120, 125
Harrogate  25, 88, 95, 116, 120
Hazel Grove/chord  103, 126
Health & Safety Executive  75, 79, 154, 194
Hednesford  13, 14, 15, 113
Hellifield  186, 188, 190
Hereford  26, 32, 34, 52, 179
Heritage railways  117, 137, 142, 153, 157, 161, 189
Higgins, Sir David  83, 177, 178
High Level Output Specification (HLOS)  79, 194
High Speed 1 (HS1)  73, 76, 173
High Speed Train (HST)  18, 20, 21, 27, 28, 73,

74, 81, 119, 121, 122, 127, 130, 140, 159, 173, 180, 182
High Speed 2 (HS2)  50, 82, 83, 104, 107, 114, 115, 177, 178, 179, 181, 194
'High Speed 3'  125, 177, 179
Highland line  128, 129-30, 152
Hitachi  83, 167, 172, 173, 180, 181-2
Hodson, Mike  10, 63-4, 92, 107, 111, 114, 116-7, 122, 126
Holyhead  25, 27, 49, 65, 132, 133, 181
Hope Valley  107, 157, 178
Huddersfield  77, 106, 115, 117, 121, 124, 125, 155,
Hull  31, 78, 84, 121, 122, 123, 124, 127, 141, 142, 151, 164, 177, 178, 179
Hull Trains  75, 120
Hunslet (-Barclay)  37, 54, 165, 169
Ilkley  88, 115, 116
Infrastructure  22, 24, 28, 31, 36, 39, 40, 43-4, 54, 61, 69, 78, 85, 96, 110, 144, 150, 152, 175, 176, 183, 193
  Capacity enhancements  208-9
Integrated Electronic Control Centres (IECCs)
  Duddeston  113
  Sandhills  52, 53
  Tyneside  94
  Yoker  28, 53, 109
Integrated Transport Authorities  87, 97, 151, 194
InterCity  9, 10, 17, 18, 19, 23, 27, 31, 36, 41, 45, 49, 51, 53, 59, 60, 62, 66, 67, 89, 119, 130, 131, 136, 159, 186
Inter-City Express programme (IEP)  83, 173, 181
Interurban services  7, 33, 36, 44, 46, 58, 59, 69, 80, 97, 103, 106, 115, 117, 118-133, 139, 144, 145, 157, 164, 173, 175, 177, 182, 183, 191, 199
Inverness  21, 33, 100, 128, 129, 130, 136, 143, 180, 187
Ipswich  120, 126, 127, 182-3
Ivanhoe Line  30, 55, 150
'Joint' line  84, 138, 140
Kidderminster  113, 114, 131
Kilmarnock  140, 165, 185
King, Dr Paul  10, 39, 45-7, 54-5, 58, 59, 60, 61, 62, 63, 66, 67, 68, 70, 77, 122, 144, 145, 192
King's Cross  117, 125, 142
Kyle of Lochalsh  21, 145, 180
Lancashire  30, 33, 87, 97, 103, 149, 151, 157, 176
Lancaster  84, 122, 137, 141, 154
Largs  109, 152, 171
Larkhall  81, 82, 194
Leah, Chris  10, 24, 41, 45, 52, 57, 86, 91-2, 103, 105
Leamington Spa  48, 112, 113, 131

# INDEX

Leeds 19, 25, 27, 33, 35, 53, 61, 78, 87, 88, 89, 95, 97, 98, 106, 115-7, 119, 120, 121-2, 124, 125, 126, 144, 151, 168, 169, 170, 177, 178, 179, 186, 190, 191
  Leeds First 96
  Supertram 94-5, 193
Leicester 27, 28, 30, 55, 101, 131, 150, 166, 192
Level crossings 28, 45, 84, 93, 119, 136, 138, 143, 185
(British) Leyland 31, 159-60, 162, 164
Lichfield 54, 112-3, 169
Light rail 87, 92-6, 97, 99, 104, 110, 141, 178
  LRT Handbook 93, 235
  Very Light Rail 93-4, 182
Lincoln 27, 82, 83, 84, 101, 120
Liverpool 27, 33, 59, 64, 81, 83, 84, 87, 88, 96, 97, 104-6, 120, 121, 122, 124, 125, 126, 127, 128, 132, 166, 168, 177, 178, 179
  Light rail 106
  Loop & Link 89, 105
  South Parkway 97, 105, 106
Liverpool Street 49, 147, 153
Local Transport Act, 2008 87, 97, 194
Loco-hauled trains 19, 25, 27, 119, 121, 130, 153, 159, 163, 164, 186, 203
Locomotives, diesel
  Class 20 119
  Class 27 128, 157
  Class 31 9, 25, 42, 43, 91
  Class 33 132
  Class 37 21, 42, 60
  Class 45 120, 121
  Class 47 66, 83, 121, 127, 130, 200
  Class 50 19
  Class 66 152, 190
Locomotives, electric
  Class 90 48
London 39, 53, 59, 60, 97, 119, 120, 139, 176, 177, 180, 182
London Midland (franchise/operator) 77, 80, 114, 134, 168, 179, 194
London Midland Region(LMR) 9, 20, 22, 24, 25, 34, 35, 36, 41, 44, 52, 112, 121, 186-7
Looe 64, 70, 134, 141, 142, 144, 182
'Lower-cost regional railway' 83, 138, 183
Long, Jeremy 66, 120, 156
Lyons, Mick 89, 94, 116, 117
MacGregor, John 53, 54, 61, 193
Maintenance
  Rolling stock 24, 27-8, 61, 70, 91, 117, 164, 169, 182
  Track 28, 61, 62, 73, 75, 79, 140, 168, 184, 186, 193, 194
Major, John 11, 37, 49, 51, 53, 57, 58, 62, 192, 193
Management buyouts 62, 63-4, 65, 66, 72, 166, 167

Manchester 24, 27, 31, 33, 34, 35, 40, 41, 52, 53, 63, 64, 72, 77, 83, 84, 87, 92, 97, 98, 103-4, 108, 119, 120, 121-2, 123, 124, 125, 127, 131, 132, 148, 155, 157, 164, 167, 168, 169, 176, 177, 178, 179, 181, 189
  Airport 35, 43, 50, 53, 95, 104, 120, 121, 122, 123, 124, 125, 147, 169, 178, 193
  Oxford Road 124, 125
  Piccadilly 37, 41, 50, 54, 61, 70, 76, 92, 93, 103, 121, 124, 125, 126, 157, 169, 170
  Victoria 27, 50, 58, 91, 92, 93, 102, 103, 121, 124, 125, 126, 170
Marylebone 33, 73, 113, 120, 131, 139
Mather, David 53, 64, 100
Mawhinney, Dr Brian 61, 62, 67, 94, 193
McLoughlin, Patrick 83, 85, 176-7, 180, 194
McNulty Report 10, 45, 83, 138, 139, 183, 184, 194, 234, 235
McTavish, Alec 22, 23, 29, 39
Meadowhall 35, 96, 107, 111, 155, 173
Melksham 52, 149, 150
Merseyrail 41, 52, 59, 64, 66, 70, 74, 75, 79, 96, 97, 116, 171, 193, 194
Metro (Tyne & Wear) 89, 90, 91, 92, 94, 96, 110-1, 192
Metro-Cammell 163, 164, 167
MetroCentre 35, 111, 112
Metrolink (Manchester) 50, 92, 93, 94, 95, 103, 104, 124, 170, 192, 193
Metropolitan counties 89, 106, 116, 155, 192
Mid Glamorgan 55, 99, 152
Middlesbrough 64, 119, 120, 122, 123, 124, 136, 142, 178
Midland Metro 92, 94, 95, 113,114, 115, 193
Midland Mainline (franchise) 62, 74, 80, 151, 193
Midline 32, 113
Milford Haven 49, 53, 70, 132, 133
Mitchell, Dr Mike 72, 79, 96
*Modern Railways* 77, 79, 142, 169
Monopolies & Mergers Commission (MMC) 16, 29, 35-6, 51, 87, 138, 192, 235
Moore, John 31, 137, 192
Morecambe 78, 84, 144, 148, 188
Morton, Sir Alastair 73, 75, 76, 77, 193-4
Mottram, Heidi 78, 96, 151, 190
MTL 64, 65, 66, 70, 74, 105, 117, 122, 193
National Express 31, 35, 65, 66, 67, 70, 74, 79, 128, 129, 138, 167, 193
National Parks 31, 157
National Union of Railwaymen (NUR); see also RMT 23, 62, 108, 147, 192
NedRail (see also Abellio) 78, 79, 104, 105-6
Nelson, Aidan 10, 122
Nelson, John 32, 62
Ness bridge 33, 192
Network Rail 10, 52, 69, 76, 79, 81, 82, 83, 84,

85, 97, 100, 103, 105, 111, 125, 143, 145, 152, 156, 157, 175, 180, 181, 183, 185, 189, 194
Network SouthEast (London & South East sector) 9, 10, 17, 18, 19, 33, 35, 37, 45, 48, 89, 91, 113, 115, 117, 131, 133, 151, 160, 166, 169, 170, 171, 172, 192
Network NorthWest 33, 36, 49
Newcastle 28, 64, 87, 94, 110-2, 119, 120, 121, 122, 123, 124, 126, 135, 139, 140, 155, 161, 177, 178, 179
Newey, Sidney 17, 28, 32, 33-6, 93, 119, 122, 138, 152, 162, 186, 192
Newport 24, 25, 52, 100, 131, 133, 181
Newquay 53, 80, 142, 149, 182
Norfolk 149, 150, 182
'North & West' line 44, 131-3
North Berwick 48-9, 85, 98, 146
North East (franchise) 66, 67, 70, 74, 117, 122, 123, 193
North West(ern) (franchise) 66, 70, 73, 78, 120, 123, 127, 193
'Northern Hub' 84, 103, 104, 107, 117, 124, 125, 173, 177, 194
'Northern Power House' 97, 177, 178, 179
Northern Rail/franchise 69, 77, 78, 96, 97, 104, 111, 115, 117, 124, 125, 126, 142, 150, 156, 157, 169, 170, 175-7, 178, 190, 194, 235
Northern Spirit 37, 74, 75, 78, 122
Norwich 25, 59, 81, 120, 126-7, 130, 137, 141, 156, 166, 182
Nottingham 27, 81, 88, 89, 97, 101, 126, 127, 131, 147, 151, 156, 186, 191
Nottingham Express Transit (NET) 92, 94, 101
Nottinghamshire 30, 101, 150
NSKT (No Signalman Key Token) 136
Nuneaton 13, 30, 80, 113, 130, 179
O'Brien John 66, 67, 73, 193
Office of Rail Regulation (ORR, now Office of Rail and Road) 79, 132, 153, 194
Okehampton 84, 148, 149, 182
Oldham 72, 95, 104
'One North' 125, 177-8
OPRAF 59, 61, 64, 65, 70, 72, 73, 85, 193, 235
ORCATS/'raiding' 31, 47, 59, 70
Ordsall curve 103, 124, 125
Organisation Simplification 33, 41, 119, 235
Organising for Quality (OfQ) 36, 39, 40, 52, 53, 54, 57, 58, 61, 193
Osborne, George 125, 177, 182
Oxford 73, 83, 119, 120, 153, 183
'Pacers' - see DMUs
Paddington 49, 66, 113, 173, 181, 182
Paisley 71, 109, 110, 171, 192
Palmer, John 8, 14-5, 22, 137, 139
Park-and-ride 113, 117, 141, 150, 182
Parker, Sir Peter 17, 22, 51, 102, 137, 147, 155, 192

# INDEX

Parkgate  96, 108, 173
Parkinson, Cecil  26, 36, 57, 113, 143, 192
'Parry People Mover  93
Passenger Focus  147, 152
Passenger Service Requirement (PSR)  60, 64-5, 70, 144, 150
Passenger Transport Executives (PTEs)  12, 18, 22, 23, 24, 30, 31, 35, 36, 37, 41, 42, 44, 58, 59, 60, 62, 64, 67, 78, 83, 86-98, 102-17, 119, 122, 144, 149, 150, 151, 152, 160, 162
    Further  87, 89, 97
    (Transport for) Greater Manchester  41, 58, 59, 73, 89, 91-2, 96, 103-4, 125, 157, 169, 170, 179, 192
    Merseyside (Merseytravel)  41, 79, 89, 91, 97, 104-6, 194
    Passenger Transport Executive Group (PTEG)  89
    South Yorkshire  89, 90, 91, 106-8, 126, 155, 162, 170
    Strathclyde  22, 54, 59, 62, 89, 90, 108-10, 152, 169, 172
    Tyne & Wear (Nexus)  88, 90, 91, 97, 107, 110-2, 149
    West Midlands (Centro)  32, 59, 73, 84, 89, 90, 91, 97, 112-5, 131, 149
    West Yorkshire (Metro)  28, 84, 88, 90, 91, 94-5, 96, 107, 115-7, 125, 151, 155, 162, 164, 170, 171, 188, 193
Passenger's Charter  51-2, 193
Passenger Focus  147
Paytrains  135, 143
Peck, Richard  72, 75-6, 117
Penistone line  96, 107, 155
Penryn  141, 149, 152-3
Penzance  32, 49, 53, 132, 141, 182
Perth  20, 21, 52, 85, 128, 129
Peterborough  81, 119, 126, 127, 131, 182
Pettitt, Gordon  10, 14, 33, 35, 36-53, 54, 55, 57, 58, 59, 64, 70, 78, 91, 93, 96, 103, 106, 117, 122, 138-9, 143-4, 147, 151, 153, 162, 165, 166, 171, 192- 193
Picc-Vic project  89, 103
Pitt, Andy  10, 24, 48, 133
Plymouth  32, 53, 70, 84, 141, 154, 173, 182
Pontefract  116, 117, 144
Pontypridd  99, 100, 152
PORTIS  31, 143
Portillo, Michael  188, 190-1, 192
Portishead  101, 151, 181
Portsmouth  25, 33, 40, 53, 89, 94, 131, 132, 133, 192
Prescott, David  31, 35, 121, 124, 187
Prescott, John  68, 72-6, 94, 147, 193
Preston  23, 50, 97, 106, 124, 125, 128, 157
Prism Rail  31, 65-6, 70, 74, 100, 193
Privatisation, rail  7, 46, 48, 53, 54, 56-85, 96, 97, 105, 114, 119, 120, 126, 128, 132, 138, 144-5, 150, 166, 167, 168, 169, 171, 185, 189, 193
'Prospectus for Quality"  40-1, 51, 193
Provincial sector  7, 9, 12, 15, 17-37, 39, 49, 50, 53, 57, 86, 87, 89, 90, 92, 99, 100, 101, 103, 106, 109, 111, 113, 116, 119, 121, 124, 132, 134, 136, 137, 138, 142, 143, 149, 150, 151, 159-66, 168, 169, 170, 171, 173, 186, 188, 192
    Finances  195
Public Performance Measure (PPM)  73
Public Service Obligation (PSO)  10, 13, 17, 18, 24, 25, 31, 35, 36, 39, 40, 44, 54, 119, 136, 152
Rail Delivery Group  83, 194
'Rail North'  127, 151-2, 175-7, 179-80, 194
Rail Partnership funding/schemes  73, 77, 156
Rail Regulator  59, 61, 73, 79, 193
RailFuture (Railway Invigoration/Development Society)  148, 186
Railtrack  10, 55, 59, 60, 61, 62, 64, 66, 69, 70, 73, 74, 75-6, 82, 93, 96, 97, 100, 115, 120, 143, 175, 189, 193-
    Administration  76, 194
    Privatisation  61, 62
Railway Heritage Trust  117, 188-9
Railways Act, 1974  136
Railways Act, 2005  79, 153, 194
Railways & Transport Safety Act 2003  194
Railways Bill/Act, 1993  58-9, 193
Redditch  54, 113, 115, 169
Regional Development Agencies (RDAs)  151
Regional Railways  7, 10, 12, 32, 36, 37, 38-67, 69, 70, 86, 90-6, 99, 100, 103, 113, 114, 116, 118, 119, 120, 122, 124, 127, 130, 131, 142, 143-4, 147, 149, 151, 153, 158, 164, 166, 167, 169, 170, 182, 188, 192-3, 235
    Central  41-2, 45, 48, 49, 52, 66, 126, 131
    Corporate identity  39, 42
    Executive board  42, 193
    Finances  195-6
    Headquarters ( Meridian)  39, 53, 166, 192
    Managers  229-31
    North East (RRNE)  51, 63-4, 66. 74, 92, 107, 116, 122, 126, 155
    North West  41, 42, 50, 63, 66, 86, 91
    South Wales & West (SW&W)  10, 42, 47, 48, 49, 53, 55, 64, 99, 132, 133, 153, 154, 193
Reid, Sir Robert (I)  9, 17, 18, 19, 20, 22, 31, 36, 39, 57, 90, 137, 186, 187, 192
Reid, Sir Robert (II)  36, 38, 39, 53, 67, 90, 192, 193
Reopenings
    Lines  30, 73, 83, 98, 114, 116, 149, 151, 204-5
    Stations  30, 73, 98, 109, 111, 112, 122, 125, 143, 149, 152, 186
RETB (Radio Electronic Token Block)  28, 135-6, 143
Ribblehead/Viaduct  25, 186-90
Ridley, Nicholas  22, 31, 57, 137, 186, 192
Rifkind, Malcolm  49, 51, 58, 193
Ritchie, Alex  64, 89, 90, 91, 94, 102, 106-7, 162
RMT  62, 77, 97, 147
Robin Hood Line  30, 54, 55, 70, 94, 101, 150, 193
Rochdale  95, 104, 120, 125
Rolling stock  18, 58, 61, 69, 80, 103, 116, 120, 121, 132, 139, 143, 158, 167, 177, 181, 192
    Freeze on orders, 1993-96  96, 169, 171, 193
ROSCOs  61, 62, 70, 72, 91, 167, 193
Rotherham  31, 96, 106, 107, 108
Rugeley  113, 114, 115, 179
Rural services  7, 12, 13, 21, 22, 44, 45, 96, 134-145, 155, 159, 164, 182, 183, 211
Rutherford, David  10, 39, 42, 45, 61
St Ives  56, 141, 182
St Pancras  109, 126, 159, 166, 171, 192, 201
Salmon, Roger  59, 60, 61, 62, 67, 193
Scarborough  25, 27, 28, 120, 121, 122, 123, 125, 141, 142, 164, 178
Scotland  20-2, 24, 28, 30, 33, 39, 40, 55, 60, 63, 81, 83, 84, 87, 89, 97, 127-30, 137, 141, 145, 152, 156, 157, 167, 175, 194
Scottish Government  79, 99, 129, 130, 180, 194
Scottish Office  22, 29, 87, 152
Scottish Region  9, 20-1, 23, 135, 152, 192
ScotRail  21-2, 27, 29, 31, 32, 33, 42, 48, 50, 52, 57, 59, 62, 66, 67, 70, 74, 77, 79, 81, 119, 121, 122, 127, 128-30, 136, 143, 145, 151, 157, 159, 173, 180, 192, 193, 194
    'ScotRail Express'  128-30, 166
Section 20 agreements/grants  37, 59, 88, 89, 91, 106, 109
Sector Directors  9, 18, 19, 36
Selby  28, 125, 142, 151
Serco  78, 79, 104, 105-6
Serpell Report  10, 14-5, 20, 134, 137, 139, 186, 192
Settle & Carlisle line  20, 25, 31, 57, 139, 140, 143, 150, 153, 186-91, 192, 235
Sheffield  27, 84, 88, 90, 92, 94, 96, 97, 98, 106-8, 119, 123, 126, 127, 142, 144, 147, 151, 155, 157, 170, 177, 178, 179, 186
Sheringham  137, 156, 157
Shire counties  89, 122, 149
Shooter, Adrian  82, 97, 131, 154, 163
Shrewsbury  25, 27, 32, 52, 120, 131, 133, 137, 154, 179, 181
Shrubsole, Martin  93
Siemens  70, 83, 117, 124, 167, 170, 171
Signalling (S&T)  20, 28, 34, 39, 41, 52, 53, 61, 62, 70, 73, 82, 83, 91, 94, 99, 100, 109, 113,

116, 117, 119, 121, 127, 135-6, 138, 142, 143, 151, 152, 181, 183, 184, 186, 189, 192, 193
   Signal boxes 44, 52, 53, 76, 109, 117, 130, 135, 136, 185, 189
Skegness 31, 81, 119, 127, 184
'Skippers' - see DMUs
Skipton 84, 88, 115, 116, 117, 148, 186, 191
Sleepers (trains) 31, 67, 80, 182
'Social railway' 12-3, 136, 182
Sole/Prime User 22, 35, 186
South Glamorgan 55, 91, 99
South West Trains (SWT) 47, 48, 66, 80, 85, 124
Southampton 83, 89, 119, 133
Southern Region 9, 25, 36, 147, 154
Southport 88, 89, 91, 104, 105, 106, 122, 123, 148
Speller Act 13, 113, 186
'Sprinters' - see DMUs
Staff numbers 24, 48, 52, 53
Stagecoach 31, 80, 104, 108, 138
Stansted Airport 35, 49, 131, 147, 182, 192, 193
Statement of Funds Available (SOFA) 79, 194
Stations
   Adoption 154/5, 156, 186
   Busiest 97-8
   Closed 221
   Least used 142, 219-20
   Listed 43-4, 91, 115, 150, 223-8
   Most dilapidated 83, 88, 117, 124, 151
   New 13, 15, 55, 70, 73, 81, 98, 99, 100, 107, 112, 116, 117, 130, 131, 138, 141, 142, 143, 144, 145, 149, 150, 151, 170, 213-8
   'Open' 13, 109, 151
   Planned 219
   Total by year 212
   Unstaffed 135, 143, 156
Steam trains 57, 145, 157, 186
Steel, Theo 10, 40, 67, 71, 99, 144, 149, 152, 153
Stockport 76, 92, 93, 103, 122
Stokes, Chris 20, 24, 59, 60, 61, 73, 78, 119, 155
Stourbridge 93, 112, 113
Stranraer 21, 89, 140, 157
Strategic Rail Authority (SRA) 69, 72-9, 80, 81, 97, 114, 123, 124, 131, 143, 149, 155-6, 191, 193-4
Strathclyde Region/Strathclyde Partnership for Transport - see Passenger Transport Executives
Strikes 9, 23-4, 62, 109, 136
Sub-sectors (Provincial) 10, 90, 192
   Eastern 24-5, 31, 35, 121

   Managers 229-31
   Midland 24-5, 35, 41
   Western 24-5, 35
Sugar Loaf Halt 64, 65
Summers, Jim 20-1, 52, 108, 147
Sunday working 36, 77, 80, 101, 145, 149, 157
Sunderland 64, 74, 84, 89, 94, 96. 110, 111, 112, 122
'Swanline' 54, 70, 71, 99, 152
Swansea 47, 54, 97, 180-1,
Swift, John QC 59, 73, 193
Swindon 24, 35, 40, 119
Temporary Speed Restrictions (TSRs) 54, 75, 189, 193
Thames Trains/Valley 66, 73, 76, 80, 168
Thameslink 10, 61, 73, 83, 170, 179
Thatcher, Margaret 11, 22, 23, 37, 57, 90, 139, 188, 192, 193
Timetabling 20-21, 40, 49, 52, 97, 113, 121, 122, 131, 141, 175, 183
TPWS (Train Protection & Warning System) 77, 111, 144
Train Operating Units/Companies (TOUs/TOCs) 55, 59, 61, 62, 63, 69, 70, 73, 74, 75, 76, 77, 79, 80, 82, 83, 84, 93, 124, 147, 149, 153, 154, 162, 167, 193
   Managers 229-31
Train performance 197
Tram-train 84, 93, 96, 100, 104, 155, 173, 178, 181
Trans-Pennine routes/services 24, 27, 29, 33, 35, 50, 59, 77, 84, 104, 120-4, 161, 166, 167, 179, 192, 193
   North 123-5
   North West 123
   South 123, 126-7, 178
TransPennine Express (franchise/network) (TPE) 10, 69, 70, 78, 80, 83, 85, 104, 111, 115, 118, 119, 121, 123-6, 127-8, 170, 175-7, 178, 194, 197, 235
Transport Act, 1947 153
Transport Act, 1968 12, 87, 88, 110
Transport Act, 1985 87, 90, 149, 192
Transport Scotland 79, 85, 108, 109, 128, 130, 145, 194
Transport Users' Consultative Committees (TUCCs) (later Rail Users' Committees) 138, 147, 153, 155, 186
Treasury, HM 12, 44, 49, 57, 58, 59, 61, 70, 73, 82, 85, 94, 138, 144, 152, 180
Truro 32, 53, 154
Tweedbank 13, 98, 180
Urban services 7, 12, 30, 31, 33, 35, 36, 44, 45, 46, 47, 58, 78, 80, 82, 86-117, 122, 141, 142, 143, 144, 145, 155, 157, 175, 177

User groups 153, 157
Vale of Rheidol 57, 187
Valleys - see Cardiff
Vertically integrated railway 39, 52, 61, 62, 193
Virgin 70, 75, 76, 81, 83, 114, 120, 132
Voith transmissions 162, 164, 165
Wales 32-3, 74, 119, 131, 145, 152, 153, 175
   North 24, 29, 78, 120, 121, 122, 132, 133, 181
   Mid- 181
   South 30, 70, 90, 99-100, 133, 141, 180
   West 33
Wales & Borders (franchise) 74, 75, 78, 194
Wales & West (W&W)(franchise) 64, 66, 70, 74, 138, 154, 194
Walsall 13, 112, 113, 114, 115
Waterloo 36, 47, 48, 66, 74, 76, 77, 80, 119, 132, 154, 171
Waugh, Malcolm 89, 109
Welsby, John 10, 17, 18-22, 25, 27, 29, 36, 40, 54, 57, 58, 62, 67, 72, 73, 93, 137, 139, 143, 160, 163-4, 187-8, 192, 193, 235
Welsh Assembly/Government 74, 79, 99, 133, 144, 152, 157, 181, 194
Welsh Office 55, 87, 99, 100
Wessex (franchise) 74, 75, 76, 80, 154, 194
West Coast Main Line (WCML) 41, 70, 80, 81, 83, 104, 106, 112, 113, 114, 115, 120, 139, 140, 183, 186, 187
West Coast Route Modernisation 61, 73, 75-6, 79, 120, 189
West Cumbrian/Cumbrian Coast line 43, 184, 186
West Glamorgan 99, 152
West Highland line 21, 109, 136, 145, 166, 180
West Midlands Rail 32, 152, 179-80
Westbury 28, 133, 149, 153
Western Region 9, 24, 25, 32, 33
Wharton-Street, David 24, 28, 29, 32, 33, 35, 111, 138, 143, 147, 163, 186-8
Whitby 136, 141, 142, 149, 157, 184
Wick 20, 143, 144, 187
Wiltshire 149, 150, 154
Windermere 35, 48, 123, 184
Winsor, Tom 73, 76, 79, 132, 193
Wolverhampton 48, 89, 112, 114, 120
Woodhead line 126, 155, 170
Workington 82, 83, 164, 183
Worksop 30, 71, 101, 106
Wrexham 65, 74, 84, 97, 106, 132, 181
   Wrexham Shropshire & Marylebone 120
Yarmouth 41, 49, 66, 119, 126
York 19, 23, 24, 25, 27, 28, 31, 121-2, 124, 125, 142, 144, 163-4, 167, 171, 172

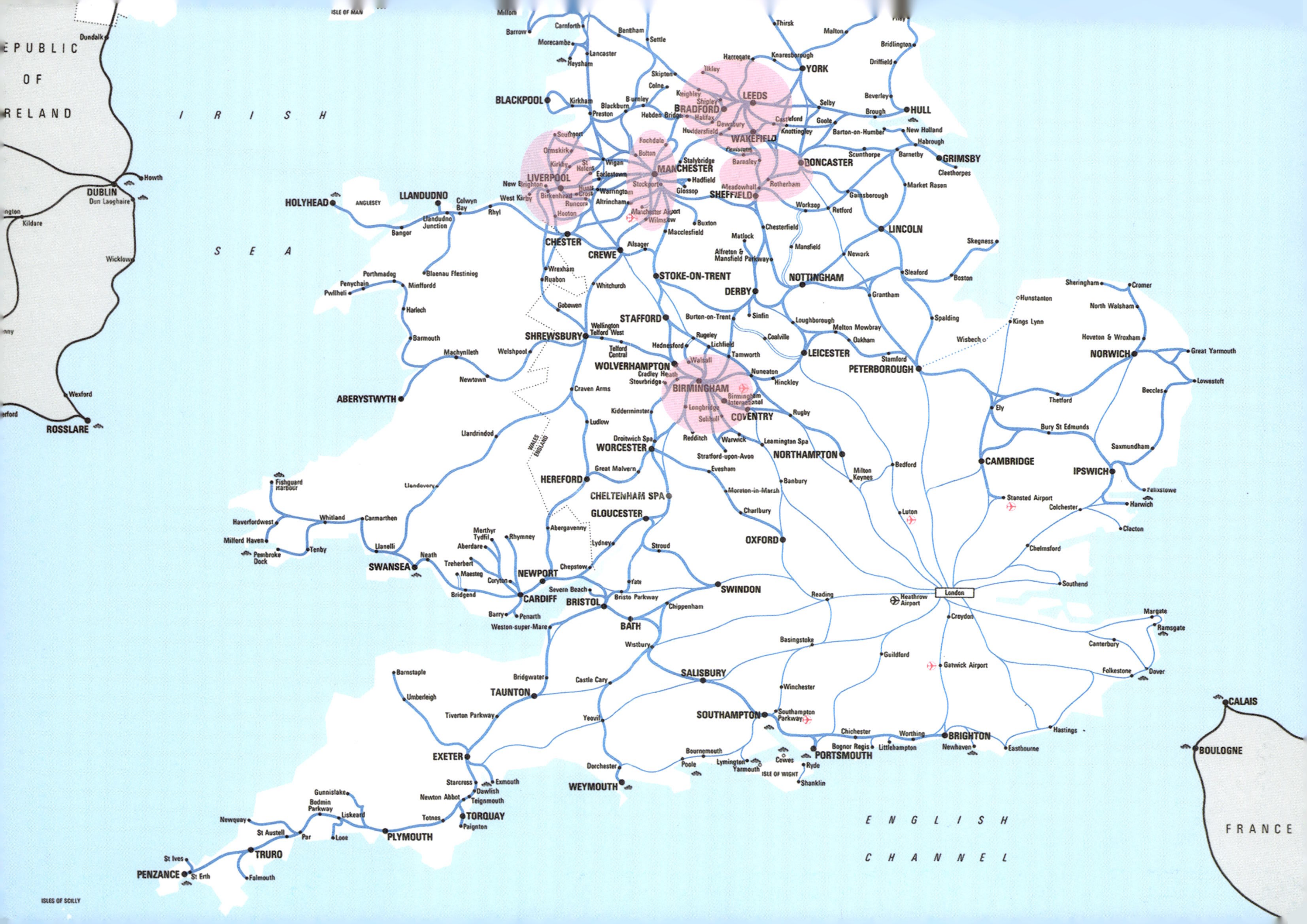
REPUBLIC OF IRELAND
IRISH SEA
ENGLISH CHANNEL
FRANCE
ISLES OF SCILLY
ISLE OF MAN
ISLE OF WIGHT
ANGLESEY
WALES
ENGLAND
PENZANCE
TRURO
PLYMOUTH
TORQUAY
EXETER
TAUNTON
WEYMOUTH
SALISBURY
SOUTHAMPTON
PORTSMOUTH
BRIGHTON
BATH
BRISTOL
CARDIFF
NEWPORT
SWANSEA
SWINDON
GLOUCESTER
CHELTENHAM SPA
HEREFORD
WORCESTER
OXFORD
ABERYSTWYTH
SHREWSBURY
WOLVERHAMPTON
BIRMINGHAM
COVENTRY
NORTHAMPTON
LEICESTER
STAFFORD
STOKE-ON-TRENT
DERBY
NOTTINGHAM
CREWE
CHESTER
HOLYHEAD
LLANDUDNO
LIVERPOOL
MANCHESTER
SHEFFIELD
DONCASTER
WAKEFIELD
LEEDS
BRADFORD
BLACKPOOL
YORK
HULL
GRIMSBY
LINCOLN
PETERBOROUGH
CAMBRIDGE
IPSWICH
NORWICH
London
ROSSLARE
DUBLIN
BOULOGNE
CALAIS